AF607888

THE QUEST FOR CERTAINTY IN EARLY MODERN EUROPE: FROM INQUISITION TO INQUIRY, 1550–1700

THE UCLA CLARK MEMORIAL LIBRARY SERIES

THE QUEST FOR CERTAINTY IN EARLY MODERN EUROPE

FROM INQUISITION TO INQUIRY, 1550–1700

Edited by Barbara Fuchs and Mercedes García-Arenal

Published by the University of Toronto Press in association with the UCLA Center for Seventeenth- and Eighteenth-Century Studies and the William Andrews Clark Memorial Library utorontopress.com

ISBN 978-1-4875-0706-0 (cloth)
ISBN 978-1-4875-3549-0 (EPUB)
ISBN 978-1-4875-3550-6 (PDF)

Library and Archives Canada Cataloguing in Publication

Title: The quest for certainty in early modern Europe: From inquisition to inquiry, 1550–1700 / edited by Barbara Fuchs and Mercedes García-Arenal.
Names: Fuchs, Barbara, 1970– editor. | García-Arenal, Mercedes, editor.
Series: UCLA Clark Memorial Library series ; 28.
Description: Series statement: UCLA Clark Memorial Library series ; 28 | Includes bibliographical references and index.
Identifiers: Canadiana (print) 20190207914 | Canadiana (ebook) 20190207949 | ISBN 9781487507060 (cloth) | ISBN 9781487535490 (EPUB) | ISBN 9781487535506 (PDF)
Subjects: LCSH: Religion and civilization – History – 17th century. | LCSH: Religion and science – Europe – History – 17th century. | LCSH: Certainty – History – 17th century. | LCSH: Europe – Civilization – 17th century.
Classification: LCC CB401.Q47 2020 | DDC 940.2/52–dc23

This book has been published with the help of a grant from the UCLA Center for Seventeenth- and Eighteenth-Century Studies.

The research leading to this study has received funding from the European Research Council under the European Union's Seventh Framework Programme (FP7/2007–2013)/ERC Grant Agreement no. 323316, project CORPI "Conversion, Overlapping Religiosities, Polemics and Interaction: Early Modern Iberia and Beyond."

University of Toronto Press acknowledges the financial assistance to its publishing program of the Canada Council for the Arts and the Ontario Arts Council, an agency of the Government of Ontario.

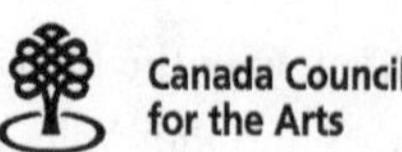

Funded by the Government of Canada | Financé par le gouvernement du Canada | Canadä

Contents

Acknowledgments

This book originated in a conference of the same name that took place at UCLA on 21–2 October 2016, organized by Barbara Fuchs, Mercedes García-Arenal, and Carlos Cañete. The conference was a joint venture of UCLA's Center for Seventeenth- and Eighteenth-Century Studies and the European Research Council Advanced Grant project "Conversion, Overlapping Religiosities, Polemics and Interaction: Early Modern Iberia and Beyond."[*] We wish to acknowledge the work done by Carlos Cañete in organizing the conference and his contribution to making this book possible. We would also like to acknowledge Nicholas Callaway as translator and language editor of several chapters of this volume. At UCLA, Allison Collins and Rhonda Sharrah provided invaluable editorial assistance, and in CSIC Madrid, Teresa Madrid Álvarez-Piñer and Mario Frade Blas (who compiled the Index) for which we are truly thankful. We also are grateful to the two anonymous reviewers who read the manuscript for University of Toronto Press, and to Mark Thompson for seeing the project through.

Not all the papers presented in Los Angeles are included in this book, and others have been added, two of which were first presented as seminars at the Consejo Superior de Investigaciones Científicas in Madrid (spring and fall 2018).

* European Research Council under the European Union's Seventh Framework Programme (FP7/2007–2013)/ERC Grant Agreement number 323316, project CORPI "Conversion, Overlapping Religiosities, Polemics and Interaction: Early Modern Iberia and Beyond."

THE QUEST FOR CERTAINTY IN EARLY MODERN EUROPE: FROM INQUISITION TO INQUIRY, 1550–1700

Introduction: Facing Uncertainty in Early Modern Iberia

MERCEDES GARCÍA-ARENAL

During the sixteenth century, the inhabitants of Iberia had to live through some of the most daunting experiences that a culture can undergo: the loss of the limits of space and time, and the end of their confidence in their own vision of the world. The encounter with the new territories on the other side of the Atlantic featured the "discovery" of a whole new branch of humanity, a whole new natural world. This encounter was to coincide with the crisis created in Europe by Luther's preaching and his excommunication by the Roman Church. The fracture of Christianity in the West and the ensuing wars of religion contributed both to the loss of certainty and to an urgent desire for it. Luther had blazed a trail in his criticism of the church's authority. Once that authority had been challenged, the need arose to seek out a criterion for truth. Doubt and scepticism were inseparable from this search.[1]

These two powerful experiences, the encounter with the Americas and with the Reformation, impinged in Iberia on the tensions created by its singular social and religious development, in particular the far-reaching effects of the forced mass conversions of Jews and Muslims that had taken place since the end of the fourteenth century (with violent attacks on Jewish communities since 1391) and had culminated at the end of the fifteenth and beginning of the sixteenth with forced conversion and expulsion of Jews (1492) and of Muslims (1502). The anti-Jewish trend initiated in 1391 was followed by riots in 1449 in Toledo and again in 1473 in Andalusia. In 1449 Pedro Sarmiento's *Sentencia-Estatuto* made it mandatory to demonstrate one's "blood purity" (i.e., that one did not descend from Muslims or Jews) in order to hold positions in Toledo's municipal government or cathedral. This statute – which was quickly imitated by universities, military orders, and other prestigious bodies – made explicit the association between genealogy and the physical body of Christian society.

Over roughly a century, Iberia was transformed from the religiously plural society that it had been during the Middle Ages into a mono-confessional one. This change from religious pluralism to enforced homogeneity was sustained by the establishment of the Inquisition in Castile in 1481. With its power to bar those convicted of heresy, as well as their descendants down to the fourth generation, from public office, the Inquisition converged with the purity laws to extend the status of *converso* (i.e., of being a "convert") to subsequent generations, suggesting a religious category of lasting dishonour, a stain that could not be removed by baptism. The idea of conversion as a transmutation that occurred instantaneously at the moment of baptism was replaced by a period of assimilation extending even beyond a person's lifetime to future generations. Ultimately, the concept of blood purity undermined genuine conversion by treating social, cultural, and religious differences as heritable categories.

As a consequence of both the forced conversions and the Inquisition, the Iberian Peninsula, which had always included multiple religious beliefs, faced the possible discrepancy between religious adherence and inner belief, between the external practice of religious ritual and internal religiosity. Nominal religious conformity produced many different tools to respond to accusations of heterodoxy and of apostasy. Dissimulation became to an unprecedented extent the all-pervading ingredient in the cultural and religious life of early modern Spain. The relation between dissimulation and scepticism, as we explore in this book, requires a reconsideration of the whole cultural history of the Hispanic world.

One of the outcomes of forced mass conversions was paradoxically the exposure of the population to an array of different religions, by airing the tenets of religious faiths that during the Middle Ages had been encapsulated within their own communities. Public indoctrination, evangelization, and religious polemics all became part of everyday life for the inhabitants of Iberia. The Inquisition also played an important pedagogical role as its officers publicly decried the heretical beliefs and rituals through which religious dissidence or heterodoxy were to be detected by neighbours and witnesses. As I have argued elsewhere, the Christian polemical tradition's confrontational method of comparison effectively placed the idea of truth within a context that invited vacillation, doubt, and unbelief.[2] In the framework of our ERC Project[3] on the consequences of forced conversion, we began by exploring religious polemics[4] and more specifically doubt, scepticism, and unbelief – the subject of a previous book edited by Stefania Pastore and myself.[5] In that volume we delved into the question of how, in an Iberian world apparently far removed from the battlegrounds of modernity and secularization, doubt and unbelief found fertile soil. The crisis of identity produced by forced mass conversion touched off inner crises about the nature of truth. The insistent and widespread efforts by both religious and civil authorities to regulate religious practices and beliefs inadvertently gave rise to anxiety, doubt, and indeterminacy over the essence of these beliefs and practices, and even over the very essence of religion itself. There was also a key change in the allegiance that religion (or rather these same religious authorities) demanded from the believer: the comfortable faith in the ancestral traditions of one's family or group would no longer suffice. Knowledge was necessary for belief, and belief was equated with obedience.[6] In that previous book we concluded, among other things, that it is necessary to attend to the question of belief as much as to the fraught and complex voicing of epistemological and sceptical doubt.[7] In the confessional tumult of Counter-Reformation Spain, the need for assurance permeated all areas of science, knowledge, and religion, as part of the difficulty of transiting between belief and knowledge, and between knowledge and conviction. *The Quest for Certainty* deals with theologians, jurists, and science practitioners wrestling with what to do when faced with the inevitability of imperfect knowledge.

The encounter with the New World and the desire to understand its nature posed an unprecedented conceptual and methodological challenge in the history of Europe. Royal cosmographers at the Casa de Contratación in Seville searched fruitlessly for a way of determining longitude at sea or finding the *punto fijo*, problems that would not be solved until well into the eighteenth century.[8] Cosmographers and a wide spectrum of scientific practitioners tried to unravel the natural world's most complicated enigmas. The inability of Aristotelian natural philosophy to give satisfactory explanations about this new natural world was a leading factor in the early modern "crisis of knowledge."[9] Spanish natural philosophers and scientific practitioners realized that existing natural philosophical systems were no longer suitable tools for producing new knowledge. Take the case of Francisco Hernández (1514–1587), physician of Philip II, translator of Pliny, to whom the king entrusted the first scientific expedition to New Spain. He was there from 1570 to 1577 and gathered an enormous amount of information about plants, minerals, and animals that he tried to classify and organize according to his classical parameters and with the aid of Nahuatl-speaking local physicians and healers. In the many volumes that he wrote for the king of Spain, his *Historia natural de la Nueva España*, he had to wrestle with natural philosophical explanations based on Galenic or Aristotelian principles and the taxonomic system of Dioscorides that could not encompass the richness of the vegetation found in Mexico. He was trying to emulate Pliny in his writings while performing experiments that revealed the inability of existing systems to account for the nature he was encountering first hand. Hernández is also a good example of the utility of science for consolidating an empire.[10] His medical expertise was of immediate necessity to stop the demographic catastrophe that epidemics were causing in the New World. It was fundamental for pursuing the colonial and evangelizing enterprise. Spanish bureaucratic and economic structures demanded utilitarian results from these scientific practitioners that resulted in adjustments to the methodologies and epistemic criteria used to ascertain facts.[11]

Empiricism, direct experience, and utility were the criteria of the new Spanish scientist. Elsewhere in Europe the existence of different criteria also created the impulse to discover and test the truths of nature through empiricism and direct experience, triangulating between nature, revelation, and history.[12] As the natural sciences expanded enormously, the imperative for the empirical and critical demonstration of truth was to affect every field of knowledge, as has been demonstrated by scholars focusing mainly on the Protestant North. Much of the historiography has linked these ways of critically searching for truth to modernity and to modern secularism, understood as a product of the Reformation.[13] Historiography has tended to dismiss the alternative ways in which Spanish scientific enterprise addressed the crisis of knowledge that had overtaken European natural philosophical thought.[14] However, more recent scholarship has shown how in the seventeenth-century Catholic world the natural sciences and its methods were also all-pervasive, and even impacted areas that had previously been the exclusive domain of faith: biblical exegesis, the authorization of relics and miracles, and canonization procedures, all of which began to require empirical observation, and even forensics,[15] aspects addressed by A. Katie Stirling-Harris's and María Luz López Terrada's essays in this volume. Stefania Tutino has proposed that the affirmation of certainties in post-Reformation culture was not a reaction against uncertainty but instead went hand in hand with the exploration and recognition of the enigmatic and the uncertain.[16]

History was also assessed with these new scientific tools.[17] If at first the history of a new Spanish people united in a single faith, and of the encounters of Spaniards with the Americas, was written using the usual antiquarian humanist tools – epigraphic inscriptions, tombs, documents – the interaction with new populations soon required the redefinition of notions such as idolatry and superstition, but also "civilization," "barbarians," and "true religion."[18] On what terms would a new wave of conversion to Catholicism be implemented? The famous Junta de Valladolid of 1550–1 and the debate between Bartolomé de las Casas and Juan Ginés de Sepúlveda on the rights of the "naturales" of New Spain and the legitimacy of the Spanish conquest was more than a theological controversy, and aired deep anxieties about doubt and certainty.[19] Similarly, the Junta de Valencia of 1608–9 on the Moriscos (converted Muslims), convened by Philip III at the requirement of Archbishop Juan de Ribera,[20] centred on whether the Moriscos should be deemed "flagrant heretics and apostates" (*notorios herejes y apóstatas*). The jurists did not agree in general with the theologians: the legal concept of *notoriedad de hecho* (factual flagrancy) differs from the ideas of *evidencia* (obviousness) or *fama* (reputation) employed by moralists, insofar as it requires evidence-based certainty beyond a shadow of a doubt. However, for Ribera, the conviction that every last Morisco was a heretic and an apostate ultimately outweighed all other considerations. The expulsion of the Moriscos from Spain was decreed in 1609. Beyond the larger questions of theology and jurisprudence, one of the major topics addressed in this collection is how questions about certainty intersected with the function of the state, as discussed in the essays by Ruth MacKay and Carlos Cañete.

As Iberian explorers expanded the limits of the known world and scholars engaged the classical past in new ways, established truths were increasingly questioned.[21] The encounter with the Americas and the resulting emergence of comparative ethnography and religion created a complex set of new ventures of knowledge, which touch on the questions addressed in this book.[22] Those who travelled to the new worlds built their authority on "witnessing," both seeing what they related and giving testimony as an "I," thereby incorporating a valuable new critical tool – empirical experience – as a necessary ingredient in *historias verdaderas* (true histories), as in the title of Bernal Díaz del Castillo's groundbreaking work *Historia verdadera de la conquista de la Nueva España* (1568) or that of Francisco Hernández's successor in New Spain, the physician Juan de Barrios's *Verdadera medicina, cirugía y astrología en tres libros dividida* (1607). But was "seeing" enough in order to bear witness to truth? How could "true" and "false" knowledge be distinguished from one another? Authority, for an empiricist, did not lie in the natural philosophical system that interpreted the observation of experience, but rather in the credibility of the observation and the quality of the witness. For the witness to become a fundamental source of evidence, as in Bernal Díaz del Castillo's self-representation, credibility – a reputation for reliability that inspires trust – was essential. The need to trust the witness in order to arrive at the truth is a recurring issue throughout the contributions to this volume.

When describing new worlds, chronicles and travel books transmitted the first news of phenomena so unheard of that readers often believed true accounts to be false or, conversely, mistook works of sheer hyperbolic fantasy for truth.[23] Common sense and the collective imagination had to adjust to the new facts at hand. Under the new precepts of empiricism and realism, the witness became the privileged author. At the same time, although there were attempts to establish a correlation between validation and worth, or legitimacy and authenticity, believable falsehoods continued to add to the author's worth, as in the story of the giants called "Patagones," which lent Patagonia its name. The Patagones were sighted (*avistados*) in 1520 during Magellan's expedition around the globe, and were described first by Antonio Pigafetta, who participated in the voyage, and later by Francisco López de Gómara.[24] The "sighting" of the Patagones was clearly influenced by the character Patagon in the famous *libro de caballerías* (chivalric romance), *Primaleón* (1512). The information received in Spain from the new lands was never totally reliable. In a case like this, the paradox of believability was resolved in light of the degree of acceptance the witness enjoyed among his or her readership, but this acceptance depended in turn on what the readership already knew or was familiar with. This communal recognition became crucial in other areas as well, such as medicine (as discussed by María Luz López Terrada and Ruth MacKay, in this volume). The sort of knowledge that was grounded in the words and authority of others required belief as much as knowledge. Trust and belief, *fides humana,* were particularly useful in the study of human history. Facts no longer spoke for themselves. José de

Acosta in his treatise *De temporibus novissimis* (1590) wrote about his first contact with the realities of the New Word:

> In my case the things of the Indies seemed after I had had personal experience of them to be both the same as I had heard and not the same. Indeed I found them the same in that those who told me about them had not actually lied to me about them; but nevertheless I judged them to be different and very unlike what I had first thought. For this reason I found that my way of thinking about them was different.[25]

The appellative *verdadero*, so frequent in the titles of history books, is likewise used in theatre – *actuar de veras* (see Paul Johnson`s contribution) – or in paintings – *retratos verdaderos*. The need for truth and the criteria for reaching it also affected literature and the arts. Felipe Pereda has shown how the concept of "evidence" in science, religion, and art in the early modern world impacted the field of Christology, as sacred texts, their testimonies, and material vestiges (such as the Shroud of Turin) became objects of historical criticism and empirical observation. The body of Christ, in Spanish sculpture and paintings, incorporated new observations of medical science on blood, sweat, and water, to arrive at the truth of Christ in a realistic image, *una imagen verdadera*. Images, according to Pereda, not only describe but also confer authority and authenticity on what is shown, which is why the new sciences were put to use in this field.[26]

In their search for truth, the Iberians had recourse to the rhetoric of law and to legal procedures. Legal language was intertwined with medicine and diagnosis (see the contributions of López Terrada, MacKay, and Tutino in this volume),[27] as well as with the procedures used by civil and inquisitorial trials to decide whether a defendant was insane (and therefore not responsible for his or her acts) or engaging in witchcraft.[28] The practice of magic is one example of the limits of the witness, as one often sees what one believes. The complex sensory, emotional, and epistemological process through which inquisitors and legal experts evaluated suspects pleading insanity is addressed here by López Terrada and Johnson.

The Inquisition also searched for evidence and guidance on how to interpret external signs in order to learn about defendants' internal dispositions. The Holy Office's obsession with discovering the hidden truths in multilayered appearances led to an outsize reliance on the defendants' lineage. Because lineage and genealogy were in principle verifiable, they became one of the basic means to establish a person's true faith, so that religion became increasingly associated with ethnicity. To be reputed as a good Christian required that your ancestors were what was now called "Old Christians." Genealogy became an obsession.

There was also in early modern Iberia an intellectual, epistemological scepticism, or "Pyrrhonism." Interest in Pyrrhonian scepticism arose in Spain in the second half of the sixteenth century, following Juan Páez de Castro's translation of Sextus Empiricus.[29] Although Páez de Castro's interest was based not only on epistemology, but also on Sextus Empiricus's importance "for our religion," the spread of Pyrrhonian scepticism altered the tone of the debates around knowledge, infusing them with a profound sense of epistemological and moral pessimism.[30] Other sceptical works also had an impact in Spain: Francisco Sanches's 1576 *Quod nihil scitur*, or Huarte de San Juan's 1575 *Examen de ingenios para las ciencias* (discussed in this volume by Patiño Loira), published just one year apart, were also important. Whereas Jeremy Robbins and Stefania Pastore attribute the pragmatic attitude towards knowledge in early modern Spain to an interest in rediscovered Pyrrhonism and neo-Stoicism, María M. Portuondo and Javier Patiño Loira suggest that the readers of *Quod nihil scitur* were guided by their frustration with scholastic Aristotelianism and the confusion caused by the many alternative natural philosophical systems circulating at the time. Beyond Pyrrhonism, other intellectual trends became influential, such as Tacitism, the sceptical and secular political and historical thought inspired by the Roman historian Cornelius Tacitus,[31] neo-Stoicism, and anti-Machiavellianism. These are the intellectual currents that traverse and connect the different chapters of this book.

In Inquisition trial documents from the late fifteenth century onwards, defendants make many of the same points that the European sceptics were subsequently to raise: the relativity of opinion, the lack of criteria for certain judgment, the inaccessibility of truth, or the inability of reason to prove that any of the religions is the true one. The inquisitors themselves were far from univocal. They also doubted, as their correspondence with the Suprema (supreme court of the Inquisition) on a multitude of aspects demonstrates. The line between assuredness and incredulity was fragile and produced what might be called "popular scepticism."

The sceptics of the early modern period acknowledged the inaccessibility of knowledge about the reality of nature, and therefore focused their reflections on truths that were probable or convincing based on appearances. The problem was then to discern between the mere appearance of truth, that is, verisimilitude, and truth itself.[32] Attempts to attain the truth had to take into account the distance between what is said and what is meant (as is taken up by Fernando Rodríguez Mediano). The rift between verisimilitude and truth shows up again in debates about word and meaning, or content and form, that impacted the translation of sacred texts, in particular the Bible, and their censorship, as well as the debate over literalism and allegory.[33] The debate over the relationship between form and content reflected the lack of certainty engendered by misleading appearances, as discussed by Jeremy Robbins.[34] Doubt and hypocrisy were often connected, as the rift between interiority and external performance, between private heresy kept in the heart and ritual orthodoxy maintained in public, came to haunt religious belief. This debate, then, became yet another front in the assimilation of new converts and the struggle over orthodoxy. Many, including new converts, sought out and took refuge in interiority and practices of self-scrutiny fostered by an explosion of disciplines known as *ejercicios espirituales* (spiritual exercises). As Moshe Sluhovsky has shown, practices of religious interiority are conducive to a form of knowledge based on "knowing oneself" or one's "true self," or simply attaining "truth" (see Patiño Loira in this volume). Practitioners of interior religiosity and self-knowledge achieved transformations of the self by acquiring skills of imagination and enacting ways of scrutinizing their thoughts, emotions, and sensory experiences.[35] All this contributed to the appearance of a new, modern subject,[36] to the importance of the "I" and the multiplication of first-person narratives in the larger process of examining what it means to construct or achieve certainty (see Barbara Fuchs and Paul Johnson in this volume). The need for dissimulation and its connection with scepticism fostered an interior search for a true self. However, this concern for self-examination coincided with increasing doubts about the transparency of the subject to oneself, that is, the ability to actually know oneself (as discussed by Patiño Loira).

The rise of interest in scepticism in late sixteenth-century Spain compelled Spaniards to confront the moral and political consequences of human ignorance and a worldview premised on the omnipresence of dissimulation and the treacherous relationship between appearance and reality. Jeremy Robbins has vividly described the main features of a mentality steeped in epistemological (and thence moral) pessimism, largely fostered by the sustained creative interaction of the scepticism and Stoicism that were so characteristic of seventeenth-century Spain. This interaction forged a distinctive view of the nature and extent of human knowledge and had a decisive influence on questions of agency, morality, reason of state, trust, and honour.[37] In Spain, the implications of sceptical doubt were mainly formulated in terms of moral doubt, especially through probabilism, a strain of casuistic reasoning advanced by the theologians of the School of Salamanca in the mid-sixteenth century that remained extremely influential up to the 1640s. Probabilism (addressed in this volume by A. Katie Stirling-Harris and Stefania Tutino) represented a significant and controversial novelty in Catholic moral theology. Against a deep-seated theological tradition that defended the rigid application of moral rules, early modern probabilists (usually Jesuits) maintained that one could legitimately follow a course of action if, in the absence of absolutely certain norms governing the matter, it was supported by a probable opinion, however tenuous and disputable. The doctrine of probabilism played an important role in allowing early modern Catholic theologians to grapple with and manage both moral and epistemological doubt. Probabilists sought certainty – at least moral certainty – by accommodating doubt and uncertainty in moral choices and decisions.[38] They held that, in the face of doubt or difficult moral choices, it is enough to choose the most probable option, but it is also legitimate to choose the less probable option, since according to them, no opinion was totally false or totally true. Although probability did not provide certainty, it did at least eliminate the danger of acting while in a state of doubt. It was a doctrine that was condemned by many, and eventually even by Rome, for leading to moral laxity.

In the face of doubt, as with hypocrisy, discernment proves crucial.[39] The risk of appearances not being truthful leads to the question of whether seeing ensures certainty. Doubt produces scepticism and unbelief but is also a critical tool for arriving at the truth. It is part of a hermeneutical process, an intrinsic element for cognition, yet also has the potential to serve as a definitive obstacle to certainty. Does doubt negate the very idea of finding firm, unshakeable truths in the beliefs, particularly religious beliefs, that regulate peoples' lives? These two faces of doubt are epitomized by the well-known passage in the Gospel of John where the apostle Thomas doubts news of Jesus's resurrection. He tells the other disciples, who claim to have seen him, that he will not believe it until he has touched the wounds for himself; when Jesus finally does appear again, he invites Thomas to do just this.[40] Thomas was seeking certainty. The story of Thomas also ties my discussion back to empiricism and to "seeing": Thomas needs to put his fingers inside Jesus's wound. Seeing Jesus was not enough for him, seeing did not produce conviction. Maybe we can remember Sor Juana Inés de la Cruz's famous dictum: "I only see what I touch."[41]

The story of Thomas, as we know, was discussed and painted often in early modern Spain and assigned a range of meanings. I will borrow from Felipe Pereda an example from a 1582 Inquisition trial in which two men are talking in a tavern.[42] One, Andrés, is a Catholic Castilian and the other, Anton (the accused), is from France, and is on the verge of being charged with harbouring Lutheran tendencies. In the course of their conversation the case of St Thomas comes up. Andrés espouses the maxim "ver y creer como Santo Tomás" (seeing and believing as St Thomas did), but Anton counters with an apparently minor exegetical difference, "el que no lo ve no lo cree" (he who sees not, believes not). For the Catholic man, seeing is believing, but what he sees only confirms what he already believes. Meanwhile, the Frenchman Anton will not believe what he cannot empirically verify. This is very much in the same vein as many a Jewish *converso* voicing their rejection of Eucharistic transubstantiation, as when Marina de Ávila in Granada in 1592 said during mass: "I see a piece of bread; I believe in the Lord instead" or when Gonzalo Vaz said in 1543: "I see old bread and wine, and I believe in the Law of Moses" or "I see water and wine; I worship Adonai divine."[43] What they saw did not support the tenets of the Catholic sacrament: for Catholics it was indeed bread and wine, but most importantly it was also the flesh and blood of Christ. Marina and Gonzalo negate the Catholic sacrament by keeping to strict empiricism, much as does the Lutheran Anton.

These stories deal as much with conviction as with certainty. And they bring us back to the all-pervading issue of religious conversion, both in the Peninsula and in the New World. The Inquisition insisted in the "obstinacy" and "blindness" of Jews and Muslims who denied the Christian truth even when it was taught to them. But the ease with which indigenous populations in the Americas converted was also deeply unsettling: Manuel da Nóbrega (1517–70), first provincial of the Society of Jesus in Brazil, explains in his *Diálogo sobre a Conversão do Gentio* (Dialogue on the conversion of the heathen): "Do you know what is the greatest difficulty I find in them? Being so easy to say 'yes' to everything.... They approve of everything right away, and with the same ease with which they say 'yes,' they say 'no.'"[44] To believe was to obey,[45] as Nóbrega very clearly states:

> If they had a king it would be possible to convert them or if they worshipped something. But as they do not even know what it is to believe or to worship, they cannot understand the preaching of the Gospel; for preaching is based on being made to believe in and adore God and to serve him. And as these people worship nothing, nor believe in anything, nothing that is said to them means anything.[46]

The questions of doubt and certainty, two faces of the same coin, constitute a vast subject that is impossible to fully encompass, much less to condense into the space of this introduction. I have tried to trace the trajectory we have been following in conceiving of this book and to frame the subjects addressed by the contributors. The essays gathered here approach certainty – and the lack thereof – from a variety of disciplines that include social history, literature, history of religion, and history of emotions, and constitute a rich and innovative whole that will add to discussions currently taking place mainly in history of science and focused for the most part on Reformation Europe.

The first part of the book is titled "Staging Inquisitions: Nature, Culture, Religion." The first three chapters focus on questions of voice, representation, and impersonation, paying particular attention to first-person accounts. Barbara Fuchs begins by dealing with first-person narratives in genres such as accounts of captivity or geographical descriptions, which offer the authority of the witness as guarantor via experience, followed by an analysis of the picaresque genre. In the picaresque novel as portrayed by Fuchs, the narrator closest to the action is in fact the least reliable witness, thereby turning on its head the force of the "I" as guarantor of truth. As such, Fuchs shows how the picaresque novel acts as a locus for scepticism. Her reading of Mateo Alemán's *Vida del pícaro Guzmán de Alfarache* demonstrates how fictionality permeates society in deceptions large and small. Certainty remains elusive while fiction appears both as endemic and necessary. As David Gitlitz has said in his work on another picaresque narrative, *Lazarillo de Tormes,* truth is identical to what seems true; verity and verisimilitude are one and the same.[47] Paul Johnson also works with first-person narratives and in particular with the autobiographical texts – *Discurso de su vida* – that the Inquisition required of individuals accused of heresy. The defendants testified in front of an audience of inquisitors and therefore the narrative strategies of self-representation were accompanied by body language, vocal modulation, gestural expressions, and other displays of emotion. It was a performance that, Johnson argues, had as much in common with theatre as with autobiography. The parallel between theatre and the Inquisition that he proposes revolves around the themes of truth and certainty, and around the question of sincerity, a core inquisitorial concern and an important device for actors who were said to perform *de veras*. The play that he analyses, Lope de Vega's *Lo fingido verdadero*, reflects on the nature of reality and illusion, and is a radical affirmation of sceptical thought.

The third chapter also shows the emotional aspect of the search for certainty, and considers the *muestras* or *señales* (signs) of repentance performed by defendants before the Inquisition, and so connects with Johnson's contribution on the paradox of using emotions as a device for achieving certainty. As part of the omnipresent debate on the correspondence between outward expression and inward feelings, María Luz López Terrada explores the testimony of healers, patients, and physicians in Inquisition trials and the recurring question of truthfulness, as well as their conflicting approaches to health practices. The Inquisition is confronted with conflicting certainties: the certainty presented by the empiricism of healers, the inquisitors' certainty that magic and covenants with the devil are at play, the certainty of the patients who have been healed, and the communal recognition of the healer's ability to cure. The fact that the accused were deftly able to avoid implicating themselves in crimes suggests that there was a great deal of certainty among all the defendants regarding what was socially acceptable and what was prohibited. In fact, some of the *procesos* brought to light by López Terrada take on the characteristics of the picaresque novels analysed by Fuchs. Indeed, like in these novels, what the trial documents narrate is an individual's evolution through time and space, and the influence of the surrounding social environment throughout this life journey. There is, then, a character who emerges out of a social context with which he or she maintains a conflictive and dialectical relationship, embodied by the other characters mentioned in the trial documents, but also by others who may have crossed paths with the defendant. We come away from these three essays with a vision of the Inquisition's connection not only with staging and therefore theatre, but also with autobiography and the

"I" as a voice authorized by empirical experience and, ultimately, with picaresque narrative and its essentially sceptical perspective. This is an "I" at once in search of the truth and perpetually working to obscure it.

These two essays dealing with Inquisition materials bring us face to face with the critical issue of the first-hand witness and witnesses' credibility. Not only is the reliability of witnesses of capital importance, but also their number. In other words, the more witnesses who attest to a fact, the more credible it is. Ruth MacKay shows in her essay how for both the medical and legal professions, it was repetition and accumulation that mattered most. She analyses the reports and inquests made by notaries and physicians during the great Castilian plague of 1596–1601. These medical and legal professionals were engaged in efforts to discern the truth (if a town or city had been hit by the plague) through observable facts and testimony. City councils dissimulated: they did not want to admit the existence of the plague because that meant putting their town in quarantine, to the great detriment of the life of the city. The common good relied upon a generally accepted truth, but everybody knew that truth was relative. Since, faced with quarantine, only lies could save the integrity of a community in the short term, everybody lied about their state of health, and inspectors knew they were lying. The system of enquiry, then, was to obtain written and notarized testimony from witnesses who could back up what they said with verifiable facts so that "truth can be determined."

In an essay focused on the Society of Jesus, Javier Patiño Loira turns from the health of actual bodies to the spiritual body of the community. Namely, he focuses on how superiors assessed and classified Society students according to their physical and spiritual qualities. This classification system constituted a fundamental tool for forging a systematic hierarchy from among the natural diversity of the students, guiding their development and careers in accordance with their capabilities. Patiño Loira argues that this assessment was not only justified in terms of its supposed practical effectiveness, but furthermore offered, for the Jesuits, a greater form of legitimization related to the problem of truth. Indeed, properly assessing and guiding students towards the disciplines most suited to their nature was a key weapon in the intellectual struggle against heresy and scepticism. It allowed the most capable and astute of the Society's leaders to craft an intellectual community whose members would be committed to the idea of certainty within their respective fields of knowledge. In the Society's view, to engage in a discipline for which one was not naturally disposed ran the risk of destroying one's ability to distinguish between appearances and truth. The Jesuits argued that heretics were often students who might have excelled in the arts or sciences for which they had talent, but did not know themselves well enough to choose properly and so were misguided. As such, the Jesuits considered the freedom to choose one's area of study to be an error that would lead students astray and frustrate them – disastrous outcomes in an intellectual field where the risk of falling into scepticism was already high. The practice of hand-picking students was therefore essential in order to ensure the common good of the republic, thus situating the Jesuits within the intellectual tradition of the *examen de ingenios* (examination of wits), which included such important figures as Huarte de San Juan. Self-knowledge and specialization were considered basic tools in this selection process, combatting the arrogance of those who considered themselves to be outstanding and capable of excelling in all fields of knowledge, on and beyond their natural abilities. Patiño Loira analyses the moral implications of this practice of *selección de ingenios* (selection of wits). On the one hand, it seems to run contrary to the principle of free will; on the other, it stands at odds with the insatiable desire for learning, and therefore with the cultural model of the Renaissance and its emphasis on encyclopedic, universal knowledge.

The second part of the book deals with negotiating history and theology. A. Katie Stirling-Harris addresses moral certainty as different from metaphysical certainty and even physical certainty through a seventeenth-century case of relic theft and relic identification and authentication. She starts from a pious crime, a *furta sacra* or theft of relics, which for Catholics did not imperil the authenticity of the remains, to explore how Catholic authorities met the challenge of the uncertainty of relics. Certitude required defining the degree of certainty necessary to distinguish false relics from authentic ones. To do so, authorities applied the category of moral certainty, accommodating doubt by defining relics as acceptably contingent and probable, subject to the limits of human testimony and human knowledge. Stirling-Harris shows how moral theologians and casuists alike incorporated doubt and an acknowledgment of the limits – but not the impossibility – of human knowledge. Probabilist theologians elaborated a hierarchy of certainty that took into account these constraints. By the second half of the seventeenth century, natural philosophers used the concept of moral certainty as a means of discussing scientific facts based on empirical experimentation and human testimony. In law, moral certainty came to occupy an important place in categories of proof and in criteria for judicial decisions.

Moral theology is also the subject of Stefania Tutino's contribution. Her essay explores the role that the doctrine of probabilism played in allowing early modern Catholic theologians to manage both moral and epistemological uncertainty. She argues that probabilism was not simply a tool to justify morally lax behaviour but a means to articulate a veritable epistemology of uncertainty. She supports her argument by focusing on the much-debated issue of establishing when human life begins and the legitimacy of baptizing premature fetuses, a debate that affects both science and medicine. Catholic theologians, physicians, and natural philosophers could not reach a consensus and were prone to confusion and uncertainty: probabilism was a controversial but influential and powerful attempt to take advantage of the epistemological potential of these grey areas in which no consensus could be reached.

The last two chapters of the book address the construction and use of history. Fernando Rodríguez Mediano's chapter deals with aspects also addressed in Stirling-Harris's contribution, namely the tension between sacred and profane history in sixteenth-century Spain. To tackle this problem, one of the most important European theologians of the period, Melchor Cano, in his *De locis theologicis* argued that human history was itself a "theological place," that is, a place or vantage point from which to build the case for theology's truth. Cano's argument contradicted the traditional vision that theology was the source of historical truth, and opened the door to writing profane history from within the Catholic world. Rodríguez Mediano analyses Cano's arguments from various points of view: first, from the perspective of Cano's participation in the trial against Archbishop Bartolomé de Carranza, which debated how truth might reside somewhere between words and thoughts. The problem of conceding a form of certainty to external expression factors into Cano's critique of non-sacred historians, but also of scripture itself, where proper interpretation depends on the ability to distinguish between allegorical and literal meaning. Lastly, Cano's move has a political dimension as well, since it identifies trust as an essential element in the establishment of human communities. To clarify the scope of Cano's arguments, Rodríguez Mediano contrasts them with the work of another intellectual, Pedro Malón de Chaide, who had a very strict conception of the value of the sacred arts over the profane. The juxtaposition of these two figures offers a vision of an intellectual field wherein the truth of history and scripture was subject to debate, as was the proper way to compose a "true history."

True history, or rather secular history as opposed to biblical history, is the subject of Carlos Cañete's essay, which approaches the problem of certainty through the figure of Isaac La Peyrère and his groundbreaking *Prae-Adamitae* (1655), in which he upheld the existence of human beings prior to Adam. Published at a key moment in the seventeenth century, La Peyrère's work has been considered a milestone in the intellectual history of European modernity, in dialogue with major authors like Hobbes or Spinoza. Cañete proposes this work be studied through the lens of the ambivalent character of European modernity itself. In this view, modernity was not a linear process whereby a new model of rational and universal truth unseated the traditional models. Rather, the general reconsideration of the concept of truth itself gave rise to ambivalent outcomes in which, alongside the affirmation of reason and humanity's universality, local projects such as the nation or the modern state gained legitimacy. From this premise, Cañete analyses the work and figure of La Peyrère in broad terms, integrating his Calvinism with his work as a jurist interested in the problem of the law as a way of understanding the tension between nature and city (polis) in the constitution of political communities. In this analysis, La Peyrère was not a sceptic who set out to undermine the authority of scripture, but rather a millenarian whose vision of a non-Adamite humanity led him to a progressive conception of history whereby human societies transform by virtue of the law, in an evolution culminating in the establishment of the French monarchy as the final instrument of salvation, capable of joining together various religious communities under its sole authority. Cañete establishes a relationship between these ideas and those of Hobbes, and points out the existence of a general historical framework in which (as was the case for the Hispanic monarchy) a universalist political and intellectual project paradoxically involved the affirmation of cultural differences and local identities.

By the end of the volume, we are presented as much with the quest for certainty as with the lack of certainty. We are also confronted with the various ways in which Catholics in Iberia and beyond tried to grapple with the difficulties of reaching true knowledge in the face of pervasive scepticism. The collection foregrounds, by turns, the silence of the prudent Tacitist, the alleged "laxism" of the probabilists, and the sceptics' claim that no certain knowledge was possible in any area of human activity, from broad intellectual disciplines all the way down to the simplest acts of perception. The difficulty in arriving at forms of truth hidden by layers of appearance was to become the central focus of discussion and the key moral dilemma for many in Spain and in Catholic Europe in the seventeenth century.

This volume coheres around its attention to moral, theological, and legal questions, and their translation in social and cultural history. Not every aspect of the problem is represented here. Fittingly, we believe that in response to our own quest for certainty the volume raises at least as many questions as it answers, and we would not have it any other way.

NOTES

1 Richard Popkin, *The History of Scepticism from Erasmus to Spinoza* (Berkeley: University of California Press, 1983), 41; and Popkin, *The History of Scepticism: From Savonarola to Bayle* (Oxford: Oxford University Press, 2003).

2 Mercedes García-Arenal, "'Mi padre moro, yo moro': The Inheritance of Belief in Early Modern Iberia," in *After Conversion: Iberia and the Emergence of Modernity*, ed. Mercedes García-Arenal (Leiden: Brill, 2016), 304–35.

3 European Research Council under the European Union's Seventh Framework Programme (FP7/2007–2013)/ERC Grant Agreement number 323316, project CORPI "Conversion, Overlapping Religiosities, Polemics and Interaction: Early Modern Iberia and Beyond."

4 Mercedes García-Arenal and Gerard Wiegers, eds, *Polemical Encounters: Christians, Muslims and Jews in Iberia and Beyond* (University Park: Pennsylvania State University Press, 2019).

5 Mercedes García-Arenal and Stefania Pastore, eds, *From Doubt to Unbelief: Forms of Scepticism in the Iberian World* (Oxford: Legenda, 2019).

6 Jean Wirth, "La naissance du concept de croyance (XII–XVII siècles)" (1983), reprinted in Wirth, *Sainte Anne est une sorcière* (Geneva: Droz, 2003), 113–76; John H. Arnold, *Belief and Unbelief in Medieval Europe* (London: Hodder, 2005).

7 Jeremy Robbins, "All Things to All People: Baltasar Gracián, Dissimulation and the Question of Interpretation," in *From Doubt to Unbelief*, ed. García-Arenal and Pastore, 137–54.

8 Antonio Lafuente y Antonio Mazuecos, *Los caballeros del punto fijo: ciencia, política y aventura en la expedición geodésica hispanofrancesa al virreinato del Perú en el siglo XVIII* (Barcelona, Madrid: Serbal, CSIC, 1987). María M.

Portuondo, "On Early Modern Science in Spain," in *The Early Modern Hispanic World: Transnational and Interdisciplinary Approaches*, ed. Kimberly Lynn and Erin Rowe (Cambridge: Cambridge University Press, 2017), 193–219, at 194.

9 Portuondo, "On Early Modern Science," 194–7.

10 Maria Eugenia Cadeddu and Marco Guardo, eds, *Il Tesoro Messicano. Libri e saperi tra Europa e nuovo mondo* (Florence: Leo S. Olschki, 2013), especially Jesús Bustamante, "Un libro, tres modelos y el Atlántico. La obra naturalista de Francisco Hernández y sus concreciones escritas," 25–37, and José Pardo Tomás, "¿Viajes de ida o de vuelta? La circulación de la obra de Francisco Hernández en México," 39–66.

11 Portuondo, "On Early Modern Science," 200.

12 Sarah Mortimer and John Robertson, "Nature, Revelation, History: Intellectual Consequences of Religious Heterodoxy c. 1600–1750," in *The Intellectual Consequences of Religious Heterodoxy*, ed. Sarah Mortimer and John Robertson (Leiden: Brill, 2012), 1–46.

13 Brad S. Gregory, *The Unintended Reformation: How a Religious Revolution Secularized Society* (Cambridge, MA: Harvard University Press, 2012); Webb Keane, *Christian Moderns: Freedom and Fetish in the Mission Encounters* (Los Angeles: University of California Press, 2007).

14 With the brilliant exception of Jorge Cañizares-Esguerra, *How to Write the History of the New World: Histories, Epistemologies and Identities in the Eighteenth-Century Atlantic World* (Stanford: Stanford University Press, 2001); and Cañizares-Esguerra, *Nature, Empire and Nation: Explorations of the History of Science in the Iberian World* (Stanford: Stanford University Press, 2006).

15 Anthony Grafton, *Defenders of the Text: The Traditions of Scholarship in an Age of Science, 1450–1800* (Cambridge, MA: Harvard University Press, 1991). For medieval precedents, see Katharine Park, "The Criminal and the Saintly Body: Autopsy and Dissection in Renaissance Italy," *Renaissance Quarterly* 47, no. 1 (1994): 1–33; Joseph Ziegler, "Practitioners and Saints: Medical Men in Canonization Processes in the Thirteenth to Fifteenth Centuries," *Social History of Medicine* 12, no. 2 (1999): 191–225.

16 Stefania Tutino, *Shadows of Doubt: Language and Truth in Post-Reformation Catholic Culture* (Oxford: Oxford University Press, 2014).

17 Katrina Olds, *Forging the Past: Invented Histories in Counter-Reformation Spain* (New Haven: Yale University Press, 2015).

18 Joan-Pau Rubiés, "The Concept of Cultural Dialogue and the Jesuit Method of Accommodation: Between Idolatry and Civilization," *Archivium Historicum Societatis Iesu* 74 (2005): 237–80. Cañizares-Esguerra, *How to Write the History of the New World.*

19 Anthony Pagden, *The Fall of Natural Man: The American Indian and the Origins of Comparative Ethnology* (Cambridge: Cambridge University Press, 1982), chapter 5.

20 Rafael Benítez Sánchez-Blanco, *Heroicas decisiones. La Monarquía Católica y los Moriscos valencianos* (Valencia: Institucio Alfons el Magnànim, 2001), 369ff.

21 Pagden, *The Fall of Natural Man.*

22 See, for example, Stuart B. Schwartz, ed., *Implicit Understandings: Observing, Reporting and Reflecting on the Encounters between Europeans and Other Peoples in the Early Modern Era* (Cambridge: Cambridge University Press, 1994); Joan-Pau Rubiés, *Travellers and Cosmographers: Studies in the History of Early Modern Travel and Ethnology* (Aldershot: Ashgate, 2007). Also, Elvira Vilches, *New World Gold: Cultural Anxiety and Monetary Disorder in Early Modern Spain* (Chicago: University of Chicago Press, 2010).

23 Jean Paul Duviols, *L'Amérique espagnole vue et revue. Les libres de voyages de Christophe Colomb à Bougainville* (Paris: Promodis, 1985).

24 Antonio Pigafetta, *Primer viaje alrededor del globo* (Primo viaggio in torno al Globo Terracqueo), ed. Benito Caetano (Seville: Fundación Civiliter, 2012), 21.

25 Acosta, *De temporibus novissimis* (Rome, 1590), 154, quoted in Pagden, *The Fall of Natural Man*, 155.

26 Felipe Pereda, *Crimen e ilusión. El arte de la verdad en el Siglo de Oro* (Madrid: Marcial Pons Historia, 2017); English ed., *Crime and Illusion: The Art of Truth in the Spanish Golden Age* (New York: Barnes and Noble, 2019).

27 Andrew Keitt, "The Miraculous Body of Evidence: Visionary Experience, Medical Discourse, and the Inquisition in Seventeenth-Century Spain," *The Sixteenth Century Journal* 36, no. 1 (2005): 77–96; Adriana María Alzate Echeverri, "Reconocedores: médicos, empíricos y profanos en las decisiones judiciales. Nuevo Reino de Granada, siglo XVIII," *Anuario Colombiano de Historia Social y de la Cultura* 45, no. 1 (2018): 47–78.

28 María Tausiet, *Abracadabra Omnipotens. Magia urbana en Zaragoza en la Edad Moderna* (Madrid: Siglo XXI, 2007); Dale Shuger, "Madness on Trial," *Journal of Spanish Cultural Studies* 10, no. 3 (2009): 277–97, and Shuger, "Beyond Allegory: The Meanings of Madness in Early Modern Spain," in *Diseases of the Imagination and Imaginary Disease in the Early Modern Period*, ed. Yasmin Haskell (Turnhout: Brepols, 2011), 181–200.

29 Marcelino Menéndez y Pelayo, *De los orígenes del criticismo y del escepticismo y especialmente de los precursores españoles de Kant*, Discurso de recepción en la Real Academia de Ciencias morales y políticas (Madrid: Tipografía de Ricardo Fe, 1891).

30 In 1549 Juan Páez de Castro wrote to his friend Jerónimo Zurita: "Agora entiendo en hazer latino a Sexto Empyrico Cheroneo que son dos libros

de filosofía de los Pyrrhonios [...]. Haré una prefación, en que pondré grandes cosas de lo que toca a esta disciplina y del útil para nuestra religión"; Arantxa Domingo Malvadi, *Bibliofilia Humanista en tiempos de Felipe II. La biblioteca de Juan Páez de Castro* (Salamanca: Universidad de Salamanca, 2011), 386. Luciano Floridi, "The Diffusion of Sextus Empiricus's Works in the Renaissance," *Journal of the History of Ideas* 56 (1995): 63–85. Also, Floridi, *Sextus Empiricus: The Transmission and Recovery of Pyrrhonism* (Oxford: Oxford University Press, 2002), 70–2.

31 Ronald W. Truman, *Spanish Treatises on Government, Society and Religion in the Time of Philip II* (Leiden: Brill, 1999). See especially chapter 6.

32 Fernando Rodríguez de la Flor, *Pasiones frías. Secreto y disimulación en el Barroco Hispano* (Madrid: Marcial Pons, 2005).

33 Fernando Rodríguez Mediano, "Biblical Translations and Literalness in Early Modern Spain," in *After Conversion*, ed. García-Arenal, 66–94.

34 Jeremy Robbins, *Arts of Perception: The Epistemological Mentality of the Spanish Baroque, 1580–1720* (New York: Routledge, 2007). See also María Tausiet, ed., *Alegorías: Imagen y discurso en la España Moderna* (Madrid: CSIC, 2014).

35 Moshe Sluhovsky, *Becoming a New Self: Practices of Belief in Early Modern Catholicism* (Chicago: University of Chicago Press, 2017), 1.

36 Carlos Cañete and Fernando Rodríguez Mediano, "Interiority, Subject, Authority: Conversions and Counter-Reformation in the Construction of the Modern Subject (16th–17th centuries)," *Culture & History Digital Journal* 6, no. 2 (2017), https://doi.org/10.3989/chdj.2017.v6.i2.

37 This is the general argument of Robbins, *Arts of Perception*, especially chapters 1 and 2.

38 Stefania Tutino, *Shadows of Doubt*, 34–9.

39 Moshe Sluhovsky, *Believe Not in Every Spirit: Possession, Mysticism and Discernment in Early Modern Catholicism* (Chicago: University of Chicago Press, 2007), 22, 180.

40 Glenn W. Most, *Doubting Thomas* (Cambridge, MA: Harvard University Press, 2005).

41 Simon Ditchfield "From Absence to 'Condensed Presence,'" in Roland Clark, Luke Clossey, Simon Ditchfield, David M. Gordon, Arlen Wiesenthal, and Taymiya R. Zaman, "The Unbelieved and Historians, Part III: Responses and Elaborations," *History Compass* 15, no. 12 (2017), 6, https://doi.org/10.1111/hic3.12430; William B. Taylor, *Theater of a Thousand Wonders: A History of Miraculous Shrines and Images in New Spain* (Cambridge: Cambridge University Press, 2016), 200.

42 As told by Pereda in the second chapter of *Crimen e ilusión*.

43 David M. Gitlitz, *Secrecy and Deceit: The Religion of the Crypto-Jews*

(Albuquerque: University of New Mexico Press, 2002), 151–2. "Pan y vino veo y en la ley de Moysén creo" (175); "Pan a vinho vejo e creio na lei de Moysés" (176); "agua y bino beo en Adonay adoro e creo" (176).

44 Manuel da Nóbrega, *Diálogo sobre a conversão do gentio* (1559), in Serafim Leite, ed., *Cartas dos primeiros Jesuitas do Brasil,* vol. 2: *1553–58* (São Paulo: Serviço de comemorações culturais; Coimbra: Impr. da Atlântida, 1954), 317–45. Quoted by Simon Ditchfield in Clark et al., "The Unbelieved and Historians," 6.

45 Pierre Veyne, *Did the Greeks Believe in Their Myths? An Essay on the Constitutive Imagination* (Chicago: Chicago University Press, 1988), 32.

46 Nóbrega, *Diálogo sobre a conversão do gentio,* 53, in Pagden, *The Fall of Natural Man,* 157.

47 David Gitlitz, "Inquisition Confessions and *Lazarillo de Tormes,*" *Hispanic Review* 68, no. 1 (2000): 53–74, at 54–6.

PART 1

STAGING INQUISITIONS

NATURE, CULTURE, RELIGION

chapter one

Trusting the "I": The Uncertainty of Picaresque Confession in *Guzmán de Alfarache*

BARBARA FUCHS

Ya todo es mohatra.
Mateo Alemán, *Guzmán de Alfarache*

The quest for certainty in the early modern period appears, *prima facie*, a problem for the disciplines of history, history of science, or history of religion, all of which are cogently represented in this volume. Yet any account of the larger cultural implications of the phenomenon must necessarily consider also the literary sphere. With the tremendous explosion in prose narrative and, particularly, in first-person accounts in the sixteenth and seventeenth centuries, literature participates in the larger process of examining what it means to construct or achieve certainty. As it ironizes the authority of the witness and rehearses scepticism in the context of fictionality, literature adumbrates the quest for certainty that animates other spheres.

If the larger critical project upon which so much current scholarship on the early modern Hispanic world across the disciplines is embarked involves tracing the relations between dissimulation and scepticism, then literary texts, with their keen interest in questions of voice, representation, and impersonation, must surely be part of the story. As Mercedes García-Arenal notes in her introduction to this volume, over the course of the sixteenth century, the narrating "I" plays an important role in the quest for certainty. In a context that combines expanding imperial geographies and minute scrutiny of individual belief, relating what the narrator has witnessed or experienced lends authority, and serves to warrant the narration.[1] In genres from the *relación* to the confession to the captivity narrative, first-person authority ostensibly signals reliability.

Picaresque narration emerges into this heightened epistemological context with ironic force, demonstrating that the narrator closest to the action may in fact be the least reliable. The unreliable voice of the picaresque narrator thus challenges the authority of the witness, destabilizing the possibility of trustworthy representation precisely because s/he is so intimately involved with his or her material. As *Lazarillo de Tormes* (1554) makes clear with its famous prefatory apologia to "Vuestra Merced," an account provided by a fundamentally interested party requires a different mode of reading, with attention to the various forces shaping and distorting the narration. As it interrogates the very forms of telling and knowing, the picaresque troubles certainty to produce a less credulous, more sceptical reader. In what follows, I propose an instrumental reading of the picaresque that foregrounds the literary as a locus for this particular version of scepticism in early modern Spain.

I focus here on Mateo Alemán's two-part *Vida del pícaro Guzmán de Alfarache* (1599, 1604), often considered the echt-picaresque,[2] in order to illuminate some of these larger claims. Hugely popular in Spain and soon translated across Europe, the *Guzmán* foregrounds how the picaresque ironizes the force of the narrative "I" as guarantor of truth. Fully implicated in the story he tells, the protagonist alternates between moralizing retrospectively in the voice of a reformed *pícaro* and minutely relating the adventures that eventually necessitated his reformation. The text thus serves as an examination, by a consummately unreliable narrator, of the kinds of narrative that might stand in for an unavailable or even indeterminable truth. Unlike *La lozana andaluza* or even *Don Quijote*, in which the contest for narrative authority becomes an explicit part of the text and its form, the *Guzmán* internalizes the struggle, giving us a single narrator and his imperfect attempts to convince the reader whom he repeatedly addresses.

Critics have long debated how convincing Guzmán proves, noting how late his reformation comes within an extensive diegesis of picaresque mayhem. Much of the renewed interest in the text from the 1980s onward has been the product of this critical scepticism.[3] At the same time, the most recent generation of critics to take the text at its word, arguing for the moral force of Guzmán's narrative voice, underscore its commitment to reform, and to the social nature of morality.[4] My interest is less in the intentionality of *Guzmán de Alfarache* than in how it complicates the supposed referentiality and reliability of the first-person voice. Although I ground my reading in the historical conditions of the text's production, I want to underscore how that "real" is itself discursively produced, in constant negotiation with often contradictory versions.[5] Although *Guzmán* ironizes a broad range of texts and institutions, from the class structure of early modern Spain to the Catholic Church in Italy, my focus here is on how the *pícaro*'s perverse negotiation of credit – as both ethical reliability and economic trust – upends the mechanisms of interpersonal and commercial exchange on which early modern mercantile circuits relied.

Throughout the two parts of the *Guzmán de Alfarache*, the eponymous *pícaro* plays a multitude of tricks on his victims, subjecting them to ridicule and swindling them of their property. So many schemes are described that the *Guzmán* at times feels closer to the contemporary coney-catching pamphlets of the English tradition, which purport to expose rogues and warn their victims even as they entertain readers, than to the compromised innocence of *Lazarillo de Tormes* (1554), traditionally considered the chef-d'oeuvre for the Spanish picaresque tradition. The crucial difference between *Lazarillo* or *Guzmán de Alfarache* and the coney-catching pamphlets, however, is surely the narrative voice: how to trust a first-person narrator who evinces his rhetorical slipperiness even as he purports to confess?

Among Guzmán's plethora of strategies, many stemming from a long folkloric tradition, are a number of episodes that invoke and pervert mercantile procedures. These feature our narrator as a canny manipulator of credit, leveraging his reputation and his carefully calculated actions to dupe his unwitting partners. Hence the broader threat of the *pícaro*: his untrustworthy, implicated "I" is not merely a literary puzzle, but a challenge to the emerging economic institutions that are based on the gradual development of credit. Certainly, the *pícaro* is unproductive and focused on aping his (aristocratic) betters, as Guzmán, like Lázaro before him, does when he buys a sword and cloak with his money rather than investing or saving the capital. Or perhaps, we might suggest, this is an alternative form of investing, to secure a different kind of capital. Guzmán's relation to the world of money is complex: as nominally the son of a Genoese *levantisco*,[6] he understands the mechanisms of commercial exchange and manipulates them to his advantage, disrupting the structures of credit, broadly understood, on which mercantile activity depends. If, as Laurence Fontaine has argued, credit is a complex structure, linking together various social milieus in a negotiation of power, the *pícaro*'s impostures and his corrupt schemes expose the dangers of such exchanges.[7] Guzmán moves between the worlds of aristocrats and merchants, easily upending any distinctions between them with his ploys.

Sebastián de Covarrubias's definition of *crédito* in his 1611 *Tesoro de la lengua* succinctly gathers the overlapping meanings of the term in the period: "la credulidad que damos a lo que se nos dize. Crédito, buena opinión y reputación. Crédito, entre mercaderes, abono de caudal y correspondencia con los demás. Acreditar a uno, abonarle. Acreditarse, cobrar crédito" (Credit: the belief we grant what is said to us. Credit, good standing and repute. Credit, among merchants, payment of funds and correspondence with others. To credit someone, to pay him. To credit oneself, to gain credit).[8] Already in the first chapter of Part 1 Guzmán considers the possibility of a narrator who manipulates the story in order to "acreditar su discreción" (credit his intelligence; 1.127). Yet his own adventures with credit go well beyond rhetoric, so that the problematization of narrative authority expands onto those broader realms of representation supposedly warranted by an "I" who claims probity. Before considering Guzmán's financial exploits, therefore, I examine how Alemán's text negotiates the problem of personal credit – the "buena opinión y reputación" in Covarrubias's definition above. Interestingly, this problem connects the author, the text, and the protagonist, as the reputation of one affects those of the others.

An Inquisition into Origins

Although Guzmán relates many different kinds of deception, he is particularly fixated on questions of origins, genealogy, and class. From Américo Castro on, critics have read this sort of textual preoccupation as evidence for authors' *converso* origins.[9] Beyond the uncertain evidence for Alemán himself, I am much less concerned with the autobiographical register than with the broader intersection of literary fiction and social anxiety as expressed in the particular epistemological crisis that the first-person narrator insistently recalls. Alemán's narrator shares his character's preoccupation with origins in a series of paratexts addressed to very different classes of readers. Yet whereas the dedications attempt to fix hierarchies, much like the text itself they ultimately reflect the fragility and opacity of social categories. As Guzmán's own first-person narrative demonstrates, perceptions of identity and lineage are highly susceptible to inflation, despite the careful mechanisms set in place to verify origins. The *pícaro*'s account provides alternative versions of the self, underscoring the partiality and interestedness of any such narrative.

A number of legal and bureaucratic procedures, of which *probanzas* are the best known, examined early modern Spanish subjects and their associates for their legitimacy and *limpieza de sangre*, or absence of Semitic origins, and more generally for the status and lineage of their families. In his account of the procedures for granting university positions, for example, Baltasar Cuart Moner reconstructs the fascinating complexities attendant upon the investigations *de vita et moribus*.[10] Everyone knew how much was at stake in such processes, and how likely it was that witnesses would be swayed by their own sympathies or antipathies, or by the influence of those investigated.[11] As Cuart Moner argues, all involved recognized that memory itself, as well as the process of relating what they remembered to investigators, was fully manipulable.[12] The investigations *de vita et moribus* were only one genre of inquiry into origins and identity; a whole range of bureaucratic and judicial structures existed to try to place subjects within a social hierarchy, and an increasingly racialized religious landscape: *averiguaciones de limpieza, relaciones de méritos y servicios*, and so forth. All were similarly susceptible to the manipulations that Cuart Moner records.[13]

The *pícaro*'s amoral, interested narrative picks up on this profoundly flawed system of identitarian certification, flouting legalities and social constraints to offer a different version of how identity is constructed. Guzmán's pointed satire of prestige for sale or identities easily fabricated on the move is fictional, to be sure, yet it slyly signals the extent to which every identity was also susceptible to fictionalization. The restlessness of the *pícaro* and the resulting episodic narrative increasingly removes him from his origins, making them more difficult to trace. As the 1551 testimony cited by Cuart Moner states, "siempre los advenedizos traen sospecha con su benida" (those who have just arrived are always suspect for their coming here).[14] Thus even the episodic form of the picaresque refracts the suspicion attendant upon those who move between geographic or social spaces.

Alemán's prefatory paratexts, which occupy the liminal zone between the text and the world, return obsessively to the problem of status and reputation. The narrator appears exquisitely sensitive to how writing the picaresque exposes him to calumny. His address to Francisco de Rojas, marquess of Poza, imagines the act of dedication, rather than anything in the book itself, as the greatest transgression, from which only the nobleman's ample clemency will shelter him. Beyond the conventionality of the form, Alemán imagines the marquess's favour trumping all social distinctions: it will transform the protagonist, making "de un desechado pícaro un admitido cortesano" (of a shunned *pícaro* an admitted courtier; 1.107).

Conversely, Alemán's pugnacious prefatory letter to the uneducated ("Al vulgo") condemns not only the ignorance of that potential audience, but their predilection for calumny and dishonour: "qué presto en disfamar, qué tardo en honrar" (how quick to defame, how slow to honour; 1.108). A long list of rhetorical questions charts the malice of this vulgar reader (or listener), who is not only ready to find fault where there is none, but unwilling to dissimulate faults where they do exist: "¿Cuáles defetos cubre tu capa? ¿Cuál atriaca miran tus ojos, que como basilisco no emponzoñes? ¿Cuál flor tan cordial entró por tus oídos, que en el enjambre de tu corazón dejases de convertir en veneno? ¿Qué santidad no calumnias? ¿Qué inocencia no persigues?" (What defects does your cape cover? What antidote do you look upon without poisoning it like a basilisk? What cordial flower enters your ears without becoming venom in the hive that is your heart? What sanctity do you not calumny? What innocence do you not persecute?; 1.108). Alemán plays a game of dare with his reader that is reminiscent of Cervantes's *Retablo de las maravillas* – if s/he participates in the calumny, s/he belongs in the category of the uneducated.

Alemán then turns to the wise reader ("Al discreto lector") for refuge and consolation, yet he also admits that he has misrepresented his book: "Empeñeme con la promesa deste libro; hame sido forzoso seguir el envite que hice de falso" (I pledged myself with the promise of this book; now I've been forced to follow through on my bluff; 1.110). The doubleness of *empeñar* – to pursue something, and to pawn or leave as security – further complicates the claim here: Alemán's determination to go forward involves borrowed credit as well as the card-sharp's trickery. As I argue in the last section of this essay, "credit" itself becomes a loaded term within the *Guzmán*, setting trust into mercantile circulation and mobilizing it for chicanery.

Unlike the dedication to the marquess, which imagined the *pícaro* ennobled by the nobleman's favour, the preface to the *discreto* imagines a very different kind of transformation. Whatever the learned reader might find in the text that is neither "grave ni compuesto" (serious or composed; 1.112), Alemán warns, is simply due to "el ser de un pícaro el sujeto de este libro" (this book having a *pícaro* as its subject; 1.112). But then the narrator imagines a reader slumming as s/he reads or, in effect, becoming a *pícaro*: "Las tales cosas, aunque sean muy pocas, picardea con ellas" (with those things, although they be very few, make like a *pícaro*; 1.112). Although the entire text is ostensibly offered for its moral value as a counterexample ("no te rías de la conseja y se te pase el consejo," do not laugh at the tale and miss the moral; 1.111), here Alemán imagines readers whose best response to picaresque episodes is effectively to treat them as exempla.

Alemán's paratexts work within the conventions of the dedication – self-deprecation, *captatio benevolentiae*, praise for the patron and the educated reader. Yet they also enact a hierarchy of readers (noble/low/educated) only to recall its fragility. Moreover, as the invitation to *picardear* suggests, the transformations of identity within the *Guzmán* extend beyond class to morals. The key question that Alemán must address in this respect, especially for his first part, is how to reconcile the *pícaro* whose adventures we trace in the text's pages with the first-person narrator who claims repentance as he relates them. His moralizing offers the illusion of access to a reformed self, but only foregrounds the question of that self's opacity.[15] If what the narrative reveals is a series of tricks, what is to say that the revelations themselves are any more reliable?

In the prefatory "Declaración para el entendimiento de este libro" (Declaration for the understanding of this book), Alemán takes on the problems caused by the publication of only half the *pícaro's* story. (This moment anticipates the unrepentant, cocky galley slave Ginés de Pasamonte of *Don Quijote* 1.22, who indignantly explains that the story of his life cannot possibly be finished yet, since he is still alive.) Only the entirety of Guzmán's story, which Alemán had not written by the time he published the first volume in 1599, but which he claims as done, will reveal the moral arc that leads to the narrator's reformation. Much depends on the claim that Alemán uses to justify the first-person narrator's moralizing tone:

> Él mismo escribe su vida desde las galeras, donde queda forzado al remo por delitos que cometió, habiendo sido ladrón famosísimo, como largamente lo verás en la segunda parte. Y no es impropiedad ni fuera de propósito si en esta primera escribiere alguna dotrina; que antes parece muy llegado a razón darla un hombre de claro entendimiento, ayudado de letras y castigado del tiempo, aprovechándose del ocioso de la galera.
>
> (He himself writes his life from the galleys, where he is forced to row for the crimes he committed, having been a most famous thief, as you shall see at length in the second part. And it is not an impropriety or impertinent if in this first one he should write some doctrine; rather it seems most reasonable for a man of clear understanding to offer it, aided by learning and chastised by time, making good use of idle moments on the galley; 1.113)

The uncertainty about origins that haunts the *Guzmán* is thus matched by an uncertainty about ends: how exactly does the *pícaro* get from immorality to morality, and what kind of trust in the narrator can sustain the reader in the temporal gap before the second part? What does it mean to publish an entire text that does not include the rationale for its narrative voice, except in the extraneous paratext designed for that purpose, and which can only claim a retrospective logic? In a sense, Alemán's insistence that the end of *Guzmán* is the key to believing or understanding the eponymous narrator may be read as a corrective to the overdetermined inquisition into origins in early modern Spain. However much Guzmán ponders his own genealogy, however problematic his many adventures, all that this extensive narration achieves is to postpone the supposed reformation that both authorizes him and makes him an author.

Guzmán's opening salvo to his readers invokes the context of scholastic inquiry, such as the *de vita et moribus* investigations, which could quickly shade into very personal inquisitions. In a first chapter significantly entitled, "En que cuenta quién fue su padre" (In which he relates who was his father; 1.125) Guzmán claims to have been in such a hurry to tell his story that he neglected his origins: "me olvidaba de cerrar un portillo por donde me pudiera entrar acusando cualquier terminista de mal latín, redarguyéndome de pecado, porque no procedí de la difinición a lo difinido, y antes de contarla no dejé dicho quiénes y cuáles fueron mis padres" (I forgot to close the loophole through which any scholastic with bad Latin could get in [to me], accusing me, arguing that I had sinned because I did not proceed from the definition to the thing defined, and did not establish who and which my parents were before telling it; 1.125–6). Beyond the striking sexualization of the imagined accusation by a second-rate scholastic, Guzmán's defensiveness highlights precisely that which he would avoid. Although he admits that there is no way to bypass his lineage, his extensive preamble sets up a supremely self-conscious and deliberate version of the story. Guzmán demurs – he wants neither to be like the hyena, who digs up dead bodies, nor to go against the commandment to honour his parents. Ultimately, he decides to proceed only because by relating the "puro y verdadero texto" (pure and true text; 1.127) of their story he might undo the glosses that have adorned it. His detailed account of how susceptible the story is to perspective and interest stands as a warning to the reader:

> Pues cada vez que alguno algo dello cuenta, lo multiplica con los ceros de su antojo, una vez más y nunca menos, como acude la vena y se le pone en

capricho; que hay hombre [que], si se le ofrece propósito para cuadrar su cuento, deshará las pirámidas de Egipto, haciendo de la pulga gigante, de la presunción evidencia, de lo oído visto y ciencia de la opinión, sólo por florear su elocuencia y acreditar su discreción.

(For any time that someone tells of it, he multiplies it with as many zeroes as he pleases, making more of it but never less, as the whim takes him. For there are those who, in order to square their story, will tear down the pyramids of Egypt, making a giant of a flea, evidence of surmises, something seen of what was merely heard, and science of opinion, only to show off their eloquence and credit their intelligence; 1.127)

Caveat lector. The mercantile overtones of the proliferating zeroes anticipate the problem of Guzmán's merchant and Semitic origins, while the reference to the pyramids places him even further beyond a Spanish context. Perspective is everything as the story is squared and a flea becomes a giant. The central concern becomes how truth is constructed: once presumption becomes evidence, hearsay witnessing, or opinion science, all to bring credit to the teller, it becomes very difficult to rely on any particular version of the story.

When Guzmán finally moves to the story of his parents, it becomes clear why it required such extensive prefacing. As Anne Cruz notes, "His is ... an overdetermined status, one that encompasses all the dubious circumstances of the 'other.'"[16] Famously, the narrator identifies a certain *levantisco* (man of the Levant/man from the east; 1.130) merchant as his father, while his mother, mistress to a "caballero viejo de hábito militar" (old gentleman in military garb; 1.144), could not really have said whose son he was. The boy's name will reflect the uncertainty: once all possible fathers are dead, Guzmán abandons his mother, his house, and his name, taking his mother's fanciful, aggrandizing last name as his first, and a place name – Alfarache – as his last.[17]

Guzmán notes the possibilities of deception about rank and lineage as part of his general moralizing, but also experiences them first-hand. By describing the problem, the moralizing commentary (which will become far more pronounced in Part 2) offers reassurance that deception will not succeed:

El mal nacido y por tal conocido quiere con hinchazón y soberbia ganar nombre de poderoso, porque bien mal tiene cuatro maravedís, dando con su mal proceder causa que hagan burla dellos, diciendo quién son, qué principio tuvo su linaje, de dónde comenzó su caballería, cuánto le costó la nobleza y el oficio en que trataron sus padres y quiénes fueron sus madres. Piensan estos engañar y engáñanse …

Otros engañan con fieros, para hacerse valientes, como si no supiésemos que sólo aquellos lo son que callan. Otros con el mucho hablar y mucha librería quieren ser estimados por sabios y no consideran cuánta mayor la tienen los libreros y no por eso lo son.

(One who is of low birth and known as such wishes with haughtiness and arrogance to be known as a powerful man, while he scarcely has four cents to his name, and his ill behaviour gives others occasion to mock him, asking who he is, of what origin was his lineage, where his nobility came from, and how much the title cost him, what was his father's trade and who was his mother. These set out to deceive and deceive themselves …

Others deceive with their fierce looks, trying to appear brave, as though we did not know that the truly brave keep quiet about it. Others with their talking too much and their many books want to be taken for learned men, and they do not consider how many more books the booksellers have, and they are no wiser for it; 2.75)

Unlike the accusatory dedication to the *vulgo* in Part 1, Guzmán's satiric account here involves the reader ("como si no supiésemos") in a general ability to see through deceptions, even as the narrator obliquely pokes fun at his own bookish authority. Guzmán also underscores the central role of testimony in the construction of identity: false witnesses are a dime a dozen, and they can be persuaded to claim "ochenta años de conocimiento" (eighty years' knowledge) of a family's history or, alternatively, to destroy "seiscientas mil honras" (the honour of six hundred thousand; 2.265).[18] At the same time, the *pícaro* notes the power of wealth to undo all obstacles, making truth relative: "¿Qué alturas no allanó? ¿Cuáles dificultades no venció? ¿Qué imposibles no facilitó?" (What great heights did it not bring low? What difficulties did it not conquer? What impossibles did it not ease?; 2.334) In a perfect circuit, riches undo their own negative effects: "siendo como es un tan ponzoñoso veneno … es justamente con esto atriaca de sus mismos daños: en ella está su contraveneno" (although it is a most poisonous venom … it is the antidote to its own harm: in it lies the counter-venom; 2.334). As Guzmán's experiences in Italy will confirm, riches can effectively construct an identity no longer bound by the inconvenient facts of one's origins, especially in conjunction with physical distance from the circumstances of birth. Thus however clear-eyed the moralizing Guzmán might be on the construction of identity, his own experiences confirm how difficult it is to ascertain the truth behind a convincing narrative.

Credit and *Cambio*

Michel Cavillac's influential account of the *Guzmán* finds in the text a sustained bourgeois critique of the financial credit industry, dominated by the Genoese, which threatened to annihilate the commercial bourgeoisie of Castile.[19] Cavillac's reading, based on the pioneering research of economic historian Felipe Ruiz Martín, locates the text precisely in relation to a number of pressing economic debates in the period, as a series of reformers attempted to alert the Spanish monarchs to the true costs of Genoese credit. While Italo-Hispanic credit circuits may well be Alemán's immediate target, however, the *Guzmán* offers a much broader reflection on the rhetorical dimensions of credit. Crucially, rhetoric serves to mask the tortuous development of alternatives to moneylending, nominally forbidden to Christians, as complex word games cover for a necessary yet despised economic activity. Thus the *mohatra* (from the Arabic *muḫāṭarah*, to take a risk), a term that recurs frequently in the *Guzmán*. In lieu of lending money at interest, the *mohatra* involved selling something at an inflated price to a person who actually wanted to borrow money, to then buy it back at a much lower price once the period of the loan was over. Covarrubias notes, "Los que se veen en necessidad para cumplir alguna deuda, hazen estas mohatras" (those who are in need to pay back a loan, make these *mohatras*).[20] Although technically they involved no loan and no interest, *mohatras*, which existed across the continent, were forbidden in the *Nueva instrucción* of 1543 and condemned by the Vatican.

Cervantes's use of the term in the second *Quijote* charts how the meaning of *mohatra* gradually came to exceed the purely financial to designate any impersonation or subterfuge: Don Quijote worries that if Sancho behaves boorishly the Dukes will think he is a "*caballero de mohatra.*"[21] Already in the *Guzmán* there is a sense that the financial *mohatra* contaminates other spheres, posing a significant threat to social interactions and probity more generally. As the novel explores the intersections between financial, rhetorical, and moral misrepresentation, the *pícaro*'s malfeasance not only participates in but reveals the broader disorder of the credit economy.

One of Guzmán's signal strategies is precisely to *acreditarse*, or gain the trust of his future victims, by first investing his own resources in the schemes that will serve to fleece them. His key alliance with the captain who will spirit him away from Genoa after he exacts his revenge on his father's family, for example, comes about when Guzmán, perceiving the other's need, gives him part of his winnings at cards, observing: "Tiempos hay que un real vale ciento y hace provecho de mil" (There are times when one *real* is worth a hundred and does as much good as a thousand; 2.273). The move becomes, in proverbial terms, "aguja de que había de sacar una reja" (2.273) – literally, the needle from which one gets a wrought-iron gate, or, apparently in the equivalent English proverb, the sprat thrown out to catch a mackerel. Beyond ensuring the captain's loyalty, Guzmán's handouts buy him credit all around: "viéndome afable, franco y dadivoso, me acredité de manera que les compré los corazones, ganándoles los ánimos" (upon their seeing that I was affable, generous and open-handed, I gained credit with them so that I bought their hearts and gained their goodwill; 2.273). He even invokes the biblical parable to shore up his point: his largesse is as the seed that falls on good earth and leads to a good harvest (2.273). This is perhaps the greatest irony of Guzmán's strategies: they reliably produce increase even though they are based on deception.

In order to take revenge on those Genoese relatives who had once denied him but embrace him when he appears rich, Guzmán plans carefully, mobilizing the lessons he has learned during his time in Italy, and deciding on a lasting financial wound over any physical vengeance. First, he convinces the captain whom he has carefully cultivated with money that he had only come to Italy to seek revenge, and needs his assistance to escape back to Spain. Then he systematically inflames the greed of the newfound Genoese relatives by displaying his wealth, entertaining them, and gambling conspicuously. As his plan matures, he asks his uncle to hold his heavy chests, supposedly full of plate and jewelry, for safekeeping. In an elaborate plot that again evokes the parable from Matthew, he claims to have promised to provide the jewels for the wedding of two Spanish nobles, and announces that he will pawn his own great chain in order to secure them. The seed falls on fertile ground: Guzmán's uncle, convinced that his rich long-lost nephew merely has a short-term cash-flow problem, assures him that there will be jewels enough from his many family members to fulfill his obligations. And so the jewels pour in, while Guzmán pawns a fake chain for extra cash. Having taken the utmost advantage of his relations far and wide, Guzmán skips town with the loot and sails for Spain.

Where does the money that Guzmán so liberally distributes in Genoa come from? It is itself the result of an elaborate earlier scheme, much more complex and explicit in the text, by which different *pícaros* invest in deception, effectively manipulating commercial norms. In Milan, Guzmán notices his associate Sayavedra deep in conversation with Aguilera, a "fino español" (fine Spaniard; 2.233) and a "gran escribano y contador" (a great notary and accountant; 2.234), who has invested a year of his time in working as a cashier for a merchant in the city, himself in the business of *logros* (loans for profit) and *mohatras*.[22] Sayavedra informs Guzmán that Aguilera now needs accomplices, and then slyly allows Guzmán to insist on participating. Guzmán carefully considers risk and investment in this "negocio de consideración" (significant business; 2.236), as a good businessman might: "Que meter costa en lo que ha de hacer poco provecho es locura. Los empleos han de hacerse conforme a las ganancias" (For to sink resources in what will be of little advantage is madness. One must employ oneself according to the profits to be made; 2.236). Ironically, Aguilera's "tan buena relación" (such a good narrative; 2.239) convinces Guzmán to trust him, although he is aware of Aguilera's duplicity towards his master. The *pícaro* is as susceptible to rhetoric as his eventual victims.

Guzmán comes up with an elaborate plan to ask the merchant to hold his supposed cash and then demand it back, without ever having deposited it – the ultimate *mohatra*. Guzmán's purported need is that of any actor in a primitive credit system: the supposed cash that he needs to pay for wedding jewels leaves him vulnerable to theft, and the merchant is the closest thing to a bank. The swindle replicates the forms of credit negotiation in the period, mobilizing the rich resonances between mercantile accounting (*cuentas*) and Guzmán's account (*cuento*).[23] Aguilera extracts the merchant's *borrador*, which serves as his *libro de memoria* (2.245), and Guzmán adds a fake entry, which acknowledges the cash received from Guzmán, in the exact currency that Aguilera knows the merchant keeps locked up from him, and then, in a different hand, a statement that it has been returned. Thus this everyday, most informal of account books both preserves information for memory and offers the possibility of erasure and rewriting. It contrasts with the *libro manual* and the *libro mayor* in which all important transactions would eventually be recorded, and echoes the selective rewriting in the *pícaro*'s own tale, the book that we are reading.[24] The better to pull off the swindle, and as part of his investment in it, Guzmán has Aguilera *add* money to the merchant's stash, planting specific denominations as evidence.

Guzmán then goes back to the merchant and asks him to return the money when his servant comes for it. The merchant agrees, assuming Guzmán speaks of a future conditional, or at least a future perfect: once Guzmán has actually left the money with the merchant, he will send his servant to retrieve it from him. But Guzmán changes the notional terms of deposit, requesting his money then and there. Now the merchant must explain to witnesses why he has just said he would return Guzmán's money, when he claims he has none of it. To add drama to his performance, Guzmán first calls for the *libro mayor*, then the *libro manual*, before finally insisting on the *borrador*, which reveals the false transaction planted there (2.249). The cancelled entry in the *borrador* that serves as *libro de memoria*, the exact denominations planted earlier, even the location of the cash within the merchant's office all match Guzmán's claims perfectly, and convince the law that the merchant owes the money: "Eran en mi favor la voz común, las evidencias y experiencias vistas y su mala fama" (All spoke with one voice in my favour, as did the evidence and the events seen, and the merchant's ill repute; 2.253). Guzmán's successful swindle thus depends on mirroring mercantile practices, even as he mobilizes a personalized form of credit beyond any institutional structure.

Perhaps the most elaborate scheme in the novel features Guzmán back in Spain and in cahoots with his *mohatrero* father-in-law, who advises him, "También habéis de hacer como con vuestro buen crédito paséis adelante. Y, si habéis de ser mercader, seáis mercader, poniendo aparte todo aquello que no fuere llaneza, pues no se negocia ya sino con ella y con dinero: cambiar y recambiar" (You must also use your good credit to get ahead. And if you are to be a merchant, be one, setting aside anything that is not plain dealing, for none trades in anything but that and money: changes and exchanges; 2.369). Echoing Guzmán's earlier account of his own Genoese relatives, his father-in-law urges him to join him as a *mohatrero*. Setting Guzmán up in business involves creating capital where there is none by manipulating the institutions of credit, from written documents to personal testimony. As the father-in-law explains, in what is a baroque account of a baroque operation:

> Otorgaránse luego dos escrituras y dos contraescrituras. La una sea *confesando* que me debéis cuatro mil ducados, que os presté, de la cual os daré luego carta de pago como la quisierdes pintar. Y ambas las guardaremos para si fueren menester, aunque mucho mejor sería que tal tiempo nunca llegase ... La otra será: yo haré que os venda mi hermano quinientos

> ducados que tiene de *juro* en cada un año y haráse desta manera. No faltará un amigo cajero, que por amistad haga muestra del dinero, para que pueda el escribano *dar fe* de la paga, o ahí lo tomaremos y nos lo prestarán en el banco a trueco de cincuenta reales. Y cuando se haya otorgado la escritura de venta, vos le volveréis a dar a él poder en causa propia, *confesando* que aquello fue fingido; mas que real y verdaderamente siempre los quinientos ducados fueron y son suyos.
>
> (Then there shall be issued two deeds and two counter-deeds. One will *confess* that you owe me four thousand ducats, which I have loaned you, and to cancel this I shall then give you a receipt in any form you like. And we'll save them both in case we ever need them, though it would be best if such a time never came ... The other will be that I shall have my brother sell you five hundred ducats that he has per year *in a bond*, and it shall be done in this way: we'll find a cashier willing to make a show of the money for friendship's sake, so that a notary may *avow* that it was paid, or else we'll take it there and they'll lend it to us in a bank for fifty *reales*, and once this bond is made over to you with a deed of sale, you will return it to him, *confessing* that it was all feigned, and that really and truly the five hundred ducats were and still are his; 2.372, my italics)

Confieso, juro, doy fe: all these supposed attestations of truth underlie debased financial transactions, as *reales* disguise what *is real y verdaderamente* the case. The (in)famous *juros* – performative guarantees transformed into credit mechanisms – make the irony patent: once discounted, instruments of credit undo the force of testimony more broadly.[25] Moreover, part of the discomfort of Guzmán's strategies is how they evoke or mirror the financial manoeuvres to which even the crown turned when necessary. As historian I.A.A. Thompson reminds us, the systematic defalcation of unsuspecting creditors was not simply practiced by *pícaros* and *mohatreros* in the period: "The ability of the Spanish Crown to replace creditors worn out by its own defalcations with a succession of fresh opportunistic lenders, and thus to draw on the capital generated and then released by the progressive stages through which the world economy was passing in the sixteenth and seventeenth centuries, was the benefit it derived from heading a world empire and the secret of its survival."[26] Thus the problem of credit complicates the larger question of the narrator's reliability, and the broader implications of the *Guzmán*: even as the *pícaro* reveals to us the mechanisms of his transgressions, he reminds us that his doings are not specific to him or to picaresque spaces, but permeate the economic system. Moreover, the text's constant reflection on credit and trustworthiness reminds the reader that she, too, participates in the dynamic that Guzmán delineates if she places any credit in his confession.

Beyond the specifics of any particular swindle, Guzmán treats his own reputation – his good credit – as an investment, giving alms in order to be considered virtuous and exacting his enhanced reputation as payment: "todos aquellos pasos eran enderezados a cobrar buena fama" (all of my steps were aimed at acquiring a good reputation; 2.476). His credit with the public is an essential part of the business model:

> ¡Oh cuántas veces, tratando de mis negocios, concertando mis mercaderías, dando mis logros, fabricando mis marañas por subir los precios, vendiendo con exceso, más al fiado que al contado, el rosario en la mano, el rostro igual y con un "en mi verdad" en la boca – por donde nunca salía –, robaba públicamente de vieja costumbre! Y descubriólo el tiempo. Quién y cuántas veces me oyeron y dije: "Prometo a Vuestra Merced que me tiene más de costo y no gano un real en toda la partida y, si la doy barato, es porque tengo de dar unos dineros para ..." Y daba otras causas, no habiéndolas para ello más de querer ganar a ciento por ciento de su mano a la mía. ¡Cuántas veces también, cuando tuve prosperidad y trataba de mi acrecentamiento – por solo acreditarme, por sola vanagloria, no por Dios, que no me acordaba ni en otra cosa pensaba que solamente parecer bien al mundo y llevarlo tras de mí ...!

> (How many times, when dealing with my business, arranging for my merchandise, charging my interest, fabricating my ruses to raise prices, selling overmuch, more on credit than on the spot, with a rosary in my hand and an expression on my face to match and an "Upon my word!" in my mouth – which never spoke true – I stole openly as was my old custom. And time told all. How many times and how many heard me say, "I promise your lordship that it costs me more and I will not make a penny in the whole business, and if I charge so little, it's because I need to raise some monies for ..." And I would give other causes, when the only real one was the desire to make one hundred percent on what came from his hand to mine. How many times, too, when I was well off and intent upon my climbing, simply to credit myself, and for vainglory, rather than for God, did I forget everything but looking good to the world so that I could bring it along with me ...! 2.475)

Guzmán's narration itself participates in this economy, for what is the extended confessional text, if not an attempt to display the narrator's newfound virtue and secure credit from the reader? It is impossible to escape the unease that comes from the repeated account of how those who have placed their credit in Guzmán in the past have been fleeced.

One might also read the text as an extended meditation on the double sense of *cambio,* as ongoing mercantile exchange, which had been the business of Guzmán's father (1.131), or reformation, which animates the narrative of his son. Covarrubias is again helpful here, with a double definition: "cambiar vale solamente trocar y permutar una cosa por otra … Cambio, en sinificación más ceñida, vale la persona pública, que con autoridad del príncipe o de la república, pone el dinero de un lugar a otro con sus interesses" (to change is to transform and permutate one thing for another … Change, in a more narrow sense, is the public person, charged by the prince or the republic, who moves money from one place to the other with its interest).[27] Strikingly, the second, economic definition stresses movement across places, which, as Guzmán's peripatetic Mediterranean relation repeatedly shows, opens up the space for deception. *Cambios* attempt to stabilize the relationship of distance to credit, enabling international financial transactions and, more generally, mercantile activity, as in Cervantes's fantastically detailed account of how the queen of England manages a payment to her Spanish protégée during the Anglo-Spanish war, in "La española inglesa."[28] Yet, in the hands of the *pícaro,* distance destabilizes truth, so that *cambio* becomes instead the duplicitous exchange of one thing for another. Whether in legitimate or illegitimate exchange, moreover, the economic meanings of *cambio* function very differently from the moral economy of reformation. The final conversion at the end, which ostensibly warrants the *pícaro*'s account and takes him out of circulation as a corrupt economic actor, replaces his own circulation with that of the more reliable text – or at least so Guzmán would have us believe.

Guzmán's transformation aboard the galleys also explores the limits and possibilities of change, in both moral and identitarian terms. Convicted and condemned to forced labour, he seems to be undergoing a gradual process of reform, only to find that he has no more credit. Paradoxically, now that Guzmán finally serves loyally, he is effectively framed as a thief by his enemy, Soto. Tale and teller find themselves at a rhetorical impasse: paradoxically, the proof of Guzmán's sincerity, at long last, is the generalized lack of belief in him. Yet unless he can convince anyone of his reformation, he will not live to tell the tale. In a narrative departure that effectively externalizes what has been throughout the *pícaro*'s intimate conflict, Guzmán is saved by Soto's attempted mutiny and plot to flee to North Africa. The other's perfidy, and the supposed starkness of the divide between Christianity and Islam, Europe and Africa, Spain and its historical enemies, provide the perfect occasion for Guzmán to prove his good intentions:[29]

> Soto, mi camarada, no vino a las galeras porque daba limosnas ni porque predicaba la fe de Cristo a los infieles; trujéronlo a ellas sus culpas y haber sido el mayor ladrón que se había hallado en su tiempo en toda Italia ni España. Una temporada fue soldado. Sabía toda la tierra, como quien había paseádola muchas veces. Viendo que las galeras navegaban por el mar Mediterráneo y se encostaban otras veces a la costa de Berbería buscando presas, imaginó de tratar, con algunos moros y forzados de su bando, de alzarse con la galera.

> (My friend Soto did not end up on the galleys for giving alms or for preaching the faith of Christ to the infidels; he was brought there by his faults and by having been the greatest thief of his time in all of Italy and Spain. He was for some time a soldier. He knew the land well, as one who had traversed it many times. When he saw that the galleys sailed on the Mediterranean and that at times they drew close to the coast of Barbary in search of prizes, he decided to attempt to take the galley with some Moors and convicts of his band; 2.520)

The cutting irony here with regard to Soto's presence on the galleys reminds the reader that Guzmán, too, has been sentenced for a reason. With its geographic and cultural range, the passage addresses the impasse of Guzmán's fate by expanding the diegetic universe. Infidels to be converted, thieves and soldiers operating in Italy and Spain, Mediterranean itineraries that bring North Africa into the picture – all of these telescope out from the intimate problem of Guzmán's inner conviction to a series of stages on which loyalty to Spain and to Catholicism might be proved. In this sense, the final test of Guzmán's allegiance echoes the problematic conversion of Ozmín and Daraxa in the interpolated Maurophile novella in Part 1 of Alemán's novel, in which intimate conviction must negotiate *realpolitik*.[30]

Although Guzmán never specifies Soto's willingness to renege, claiming only that the proximity of North Africa encourages him to mutiny, the spectre of that irredeemable change haunts Guzmán's own supposed conversion and the reversal of his fate. Ever wily, Guzmán pretends to join the conspiracy, but instead reveals it to the captain, who "casi no me daba crédito" (could barely credit me; 2.521). Thus the *pícaro* must return to his lying ways if only to unmask the conspiracy. Yet his fate hinges on whether the captain can lend him the necessary credence, which, in his eyes at least, Guzmán has not earned. Ultimately, it is the enormity of Soto's proposed treason, which would deliver the galley to North Africa and to Spain's enemies, that underwrites Guzmán's legitimacy, despite his duplicity until the end. Credit and *cambio* remain intricately intertwined, and it is by no means clear that the final change in the *pícaro* merits our crediting the moralizing portions of his narrative. The ambivalence is underscored by the narrative's lack of resolution: Guzmán narrates his life during that infinitely postponed wait for the king to resolve whether or not he will be pardoned, and although the narrative eventually brings us to his present moment, his future is never decided.[31]

Yet Guzmán's extended narrative is devastating whether or not we believe in the sincerity of his conversion. Over and over again, whether in the theory of his moralizing or in the practice of his own adventures, he demonstrates how fictionality, hardly ensconced within the literary, permeates society in deceptions large and small, many of them arguably inescapable if that society is to function. From the shared genealogical constructs on which Spanish hierarchies depend, to the successful impersonation of wealth, to the fragility of mercantile credit, Guzmán presents a world permeated by doubt despite constant inquisitions. Certainty remains elusive, while fictions, dangerously vulnerable to manipulation, appear both endemic and necessary.

NOTES

1 On the relationship between the picaresque and inquisitorial investigations, see David Gitlitz, "Inquisition Confessions and *Lazarillo de Tormes*," *Hispanic Review* 68, no. 1 (2000): 53–74. On the picaresque and the *relación*, see Roberto González Echevarría, "The Law of the Letter: Garcilaso's *Commentaries* and the Origins of the Latin American Narrative," *Yale Journal of Criticism* 1 (Fall 1987): 107–31. On the negotiation of certainty in fictional narration, see my "Suspended Judgments: Scepticism and the Pact of Fictionality in Cervantes's Picaresque Novellas," *MLQ* 76, no. 4 (December 2015): 447–63.

2 Michel Cavillac, one of the foremost critics of the *Guzmán*, demurs. In his view, categorizing Alemán's text as a picaresque diminishes it: it should

be considered simply a novel, with no reductive qualifier. Although I fully concur with Cavillac's account of the complexity of the text, my own study proposes a richer understanding of the picaresque, so that including *Guzmán* in this category no longer implies a simplistic reading. See Cavillac, Guzmán de Alfarache *y la novela moderna* (Madrid: Casa de Velázquez, 2010), especially 197–215. The *Guzmán* was first translated into English by James Mabbe as *The Rogue, or the Life of Guzman de Alfarache* (London: Edward Blount, 1623).

3 For influential readings that question Alemán's reformation, see Joan Arias, *Guzmán de Alfarache: The Unrepentant Narrator* (London: Tamesis, 1977); Benito Brancaforte, *Guzmán de Alfarache: ¿Conversión o proceso de degradación?* (Madison: Hispanic Seminary of Medieval Studies, 1980); Judith Whitenack, *The Impenitent Confession of Guzmán de Alfarache* (Madison: Hispanic Seminary of Medieval Studies, 1985); and Carlos Antonio Rodríguez Matos, *El narrador pícaro: Guzmán de Alfarache* (Madison: Hispanic Seminary of Medieval Studies, 1985).

4 See Katharina Niemeyer, "'… El ser de un pícaro el sujeto de este libro': La *Primera parte de Guzmán de Alfarache*," in *La novela picaresca: Concepto genérico y evolución del género (siglos XVI y XVII)*, ed. Klaus Meyer-Minnemann and Sabine Schlickers (Madrid: Iberoamericana Editorial, 2008), 98. See also Cavillac, *Pícaros y mercaderes en el* Guzmán de Alfarache*: Reformismo burgués y mentalidad aristocrática en la España del Siglo de Oro*, trans. Juan M. Azpitarte Almagro (Granada: Universidad de Granada, 1994).

5 See the important theoretical intervention by Paul Julian Smith, "The Rhetoric of Representation in Writers and Critics of Picaresque Narrative: *Lazarillo de Tormes, Guzmán de Alfarache, El Buscón*," *Modern Language Review* 82, no. 1 (January 1987): 88–108.

6 Mateo Alemán, *Guzmán de Alfarache*, ed. José María Micó (Madrid: Cátedra, 1994), 1.130. Subsequent citations appear in the text by volume and page number.

7 See Laurence Fontaine, *The Moral Economy: Poverty, Credit, and Trust in Early Modern Europe* (Cambridge: Cambridge University Press, 2014). On the negotiation of trust in cross-cultural trade, see Francesca Trivellato, *The Familiarity of Strangers: The Sephardic Diaspora, Livorno, and Cross-Cultural Trade in the Early Modern Period* (New Haven: Yale University Press, 2009).

8 Sebastián de Covarrubias, *Tesoro de la lengua castellana o española*, ed. Martín de Riquer (Barcelona: Alta Fulla, 1998), s.v. *crédito*, 368b. All translations are mine unless otherwise noted. Cf. the three linked definitions of *crédit* in Antoine Furetière's *Dictionnaire universel* (The Hague and Rotterdam, 1690): "Crédit: croyance, estime qu'on s'acquiert dans le public par sa vertu, sa probité, sa bonne foy & son mérite … Crédit, se dit aussi de la puissance, de

l'autorité, des richesses qu'on s'acquiert par le moyen de cette réputation qu'on a acquise … Crédit, se dit plus ordinnairement dans le commerce de ce prest mutuel qui se fait d'argent et de marchandises, sur la réputation de la probité & solvabilité d'un négociant" (Vvv3).

9 Américo Castro, *Cervantes y los casticismos españoles* (Madrid: Alfaguara, 1966). The evidence on Alemán is inconclusive. More importantly, the epistemological uncertainty of his text does not depend on, or even reflect, the author's identitarian condition. See Cavillac, Guzmán de Alfarache *y la novela moderna*, 30–5.

10 Baltasar Cuart Moner, "El juego de la memoria: Manipulaciones, reconstrucciones y reinvenciones de linajes en los Colegio Mayores salmantinos durante el siglo XVI," in *Cultura, política y práctica del derecho: Juristas de Salamanca, siglos XV–XX*, ed. S. de Dios and E. Torijano (Salamanca: Universidad de Salamanca, 2012), 71–142.

11 Cuart Moner, "El juego de la memoria," 74.

12 Ibid., 78.

13 See also the classic study of *limpieza* and its blind spots: Albert Sicroff, *Les controverses des statuts de "pureté de sang" en Espagne du XVe au XVIIe siècle* (Paris: Didier, 1960).

14 Cuart Moner, "El juego de la memoria," 80.

15 Although Niemeyer unproblematically aligns the moralizing narrator with the "implied author" against the *pícaro*, I concur with Whitenack in finding this identification far less stable; that is, the reliability of the reformed narrator is consistently undercut by his own narrative. Cf. Niemeyer, "' … El ser de un pícaro,'" and Whitenack, *The Impenitent Confession*.

16 Anne Cruz, *Discourses of Poverty: Social Reform and the Picaresque Novel in Early Modern Spain* (Toronto: University of Toronto Press, 1999), 100.

17 As Micó reminds us in his edition, the name "Guzmán" was perhaps the one most often selected by those who wanted to invent an ancient and distinguished lineage for themselves (1.161n90).

18 Guzmán invokes his own direct witnessing as he describes the abuses that occur in "ventas y posadas" (inns and hostels; 1.272). Yet direct observation leads only to *occupatio*, and whatever effect it might have immediately pales before the mediating force of habit: "Soy testigo de haber visto cosas que en mucho tiempo no podría decir de aquestas insolencias, que si las oyéramos pasar entre bárbaros, como a tales los culpáramos y, tratándolas a los ojos, no hacemos caso dellas" (I have witnessed such things as I could not relate their insolence in a long while, and if we heard of their occurring among barbarians, we would condemn them as such, yet when we see them with our very eyes we pay them no heed; 1.272).

19 Cavillac, *Pícaros y mercaderes*, especially 193–251, and "La figura bifronte del mercader en el *Guzmán de Alfarache*," in Guzmán de Alfarache *y la novela moderna*.

20 Covarrubias, *Tesoro*, s.v. *mohatra*, 809b.

21 Miguel de Cervantes Saavedra, *Don Quijote de la Mancha*, ed. Martín de Riquer (Barcelona: Planeta: 1997), 790.

22 This merchant, described as "hombre del más mal nombre que tiene toda la ciudad, y el peor quisto de toda ella" (the most infamous man in the city, and the most reviled, 2.239), anticipates Guzmán's own exploits back in Madrid (Rodríguez Matos, *El narrador pícaro*, 37).

23 Rodríguez Matos, *El narrador pícaro*, 37–9.

24 On early modern account-books, see Fernando Ramos González, "Libros de contabilidad" (Alicante: Biblioteca Virtual Miguel de Cervantes, 2014), www.cervantesvirtual.com/obra-visor/libros-de-contabilidad/html/db70e24c-51e9-4cab-8180-66c44e91b2ae_2.html#I_0_. On the suggestive relation between the *libro de memoria* and Guzmán's story, see Rodríguez Matos, *El narrador pícaro*, 37–8.

25 On the long-term interest-bearing bonds known as *juros*, see I.A.A. Thompson, "Castile: Polity, Fiscality, and Fiscal Crisis," in *Fiscal Crises, Liberty, and Representative Government: 1450–1789*, ed. Philip T. Hoffman and Kathryn Nohrberg (Stanford: Stanford University Press, 2002), 140–80.

26 Thompson, "Castile," 159. The echoes of the global financial crisis of 2008, precipitated by obscure instruments of credit, are striking. See Michael Lewis, *The Big Short: Inside the Doomsday Machine* (New York: Norton, 2010).

27 Covarrubias, *Tesoro*, s.v. *cambio*, 276a.

28 Miguel de Cervantes, "La española inglesa," in *Novelas ejemplares*, ed. Harry Sieber (Madrid: Cátedra, 1997), 2.272. The transaction requires three separate merchants, based in London, Paris, and Seville.

29 The episode anticipates the remarkable scene in "La española inglesa" in which the recusant Englishman Ricaredo, riven by national, religious, and romantic obligations, must decide whether to attack Spanish ships. He is saved by the appearance of a Turkish ship, which provides an uncomplicated prey (Cervantes, 2.252–4).

30 On the relation between the novella and the broader text, see Hortensia Morell, "La deformación picaresca del mundo ideal en *Ozmín y Daraja* del *Guzmán de Alfarache*," *La Torre* 13, no. 87–8 (1975): 101–25, and Whitenack, "The *alma diferente* of Mateo Alemán's 'Ozmín y Daraja,'" *Romance Quarterly* 38, no. 1 (1991): 59–71.

31 Manuel Montalvo, "La crisis del siglo XVII desde la atalaya de Mateo Alemán," *Revista de Occidente* 112 (1990): 116–35, at 135. Cavillac, *Guzmán de Alfarache*

y la novela moderna, 112–13. This open-endedness anticipates the unresolved condition of the detained *moriscos* Ricote and Ana Félix in the second part of *Don Quijote,* whose fate remains similarly undecided by the authorities, and whose story similarly turns on crediting a highly suspect narrator, in this case a transvestite and possibly renegade *morisca* corsair captain (Cervantes, *Don Quijote,* part 2, chaps 63–5).

chapter two

Feeling Certainty, Performing Sincerity: The Emotional Hermeneutics of Truth in Inquisitorial and Theatrical Practice

PAUL MICHAEL JOHNSON

> In the absence of actual certainty in the midst of a precarious and hazardous world, men cultivated all sorts of things that would give them the *feeling* of certainty.
>
> John Dewey, *The Quest for Certainty*

The diverse autobiographical texts that flourished in early modern Spain have much in common with the inquisitorial testimony that was required of those everyday individuals who were unfortunate enough to be accused of heresy. In recent years, these parallels between "voluntary" and "involuntary autobiography" have greatly interested scholars, and some have cogently argued that the existence of the Holy Office itself jump-started the development of first-person writing.[1] Truth, however, was not necessarily a constitutive motive of these early forms of autobiography, as James S. Amelang has perceptively observed.[2] Even in the written confessions and saints' lives that precede the genre as such, the aim was not to give an unbiased account of oneself for the sake of historical record as much as to "[craft] an exemplary life" and "smooth out the autobiographer's road to sainthood."[3] David Gitlitz describes a plethora of rhetorical tools the speaking subject deployed in both Inquisition trials and autobiographical texts, including "techniques of disclosure and evasion, strategies of self-promotion and vindication," and, in the case of a confession, ways to make it "be true-seeming; that is, internally consistent, psychologically convincing, and seemingly anchored in verifiable events."[4] Most importantly, whether in confessions or the testimony of witnesses, Gitlitz concludes that "truth is identical to what seems true: verity and verisimilitude are one and the same."[5] Stated another way, the certainty of the observer or reader in such cases hinges not on an external standard of truth but, to a notable extent, on the rhetorical prowess of those under oath to mould their version of events to their own advantage. Guilt or innocence is at least partly determined by good storytelling, the skill to weave a compelling narrative. But we must remember that those accused by the Inquisition deposed the details of their lives not in the written form that is most closely associated with autobiography – such as the case of *Lazarillo de Tormes* and the picaresque, saints' lives, captivity narratives, and other forms of first-person writing. They testified, rather, before a live audience of inquisitors.[6] This suggests we must attend not only to narrative and linguistic strategies of self-presentation, but also to the non-verbal cues, however ephemeral or minute, that emerge in trial records and transcripts. If the survival of intellectuals and *conversos* required "habits of thought which prepared one to give autobiographical account on demand,"[7] then it surely also demanded some measure of attention to other, more improvisational aspects of self-presentation such as modulating the voice, deploying bodily and gestural expressions, and managing the emotions. In short, inquisitorial testimony was a kind of performance, and thus it may have as much in common with theatre as with autobiography as such.

In early modern Spain, the orbital paths of the Inquisition and the theatre also found occasion to intersect in ways both cooperative and contentious. Critics have typically approached these affiliations from two focal points: the Holy Office's role in censoring discrete dramatic works or the *comedia* in general, and the theatrical qualities of spectacles like the *auto de fe*. In these ambits, by and large, the question of certainty is already settled or foretold: censorship is predicated on the suppression of ideas that could undermine a hegemonic version of truth, while the *auto de fe* was an unequivocal display of the Inquisition's efficacy in uncovering facts, proving guilt, and assuring spectators that they, too, were subject to the pervasive reach of the institution. On the question of truth, the casual observer might conclude that the cultural spheres of the Inquisition and the theatre were diametrically opposed. The Holy Office defined itself in direct relation to the concept, in terms of both the legal process of obtaining testimony and pronouncing verdicts and the more specific charge to defend the "truth" of Christian dogma before the threat of Judaism, Islam, Lutheranism, witchcraft, and other illicit, unorthodox systems of belief. Accordingly, "verdad" and its variants are some of the most recurrent words in trial proceedings. Though the juridico-religious institution's purview expanded and evolved over the course of its more than three-hundred-year history, it was the original problem of false converts that, with pressure from the Catholic monarchs, prompted Sixtus IV to issue the papal bull *Exigit sincerae devotionis affectus* authorizing its founding in 1478. Thus the question of sincerity was a principal inquisitorial concern from the outset. How to certify that religious conversions, and especially confessions, were truly genuine became for inquisitors a fundamental site of uncertainty, leading them to scrutinize ever-more-subtle gestural and affective cues while interrogating prisoners, weighing their confessions, and pronouncing sentences.

Dramatic arts, *prima facie*, had rather different concerns. Expanding the frontiers of fiction, early modern theatre enthralled spectators as the prime venue for popular entertainment. Of course, as scholars have noted at length, it also challenged the threshold between simulacrum and truth, representation and the real.[8] That such distinctions appeared more conspicuous in early modern Europe was due, in a sense, to anxieties about precisely the narrowing gap between "true" and "false": while moralists worried about the corrupting influence of the theatre on playgoers, they also cried foul at actors who deigned to lead dissolute lifestyles at odds with the upstanding and even saintly characters they portrayed in the *corrales.* Opponents of the theatre thus conflated dramatic performance with real life in a way that ironically reflected the trope of the *theatrum mundi* that was a hallmark of the baroque. In Spain, they also openly fretted that, while the Inquisition could and did censor printed texts, the dynamic, improvisational nature of the stage made it impossible to control what emerged at any given performance.[9] Complicating matters further, with the gradual professionalization of actors came not only a renewed interest in perfecting the art of performance, but a new theatrical vocabulary that equated this mastery with truth. Actors who were said to perform "de veras" were those who had transcended both the mere imitation of nature and the stiff histrionics of old to portray emotions with a high degree of realism.[10]

It is this affective content of performance that will be the focus of this chapter, offering a hitherto unexplored parallel between the theatre and the Inquisition that coalesces around the themes of truth and certainty. Indeed, we might locate the very distinction between these two concepts in the subjective realm of emotion: while truth is, at least in theory, dependent on a collective evaluation and divorced from psychological bias, certainty is contingent on a host of phenomenological conditions of personal experience. Unlike the absolute quality of truth, certainty is frequently expressed in relative terms. It takes its place on a spectrum of doubt whose threshold between assuredness and incredulity is porous and therefore delineated necessarily at the level of the individual. Since it implies desire, the quest for certainty is a highly affective act. As John Dewey would describe it in the early twentieth century, and as noted in the epigraph above, certitude itself can be considered a "*feeling*."[11] It may well be that in the confessional tumult and precarity of Counter-Reformation Spain the "felt need for assurance" was a "dominant emotion."[12] What I will seek to demonstrate in what follows is that the feeling of certainty was itself mediated, reinforced, or undermined by other feelings, both as actors took to the stage and as the accused took the stand.

Emotional expression played a vital role in convincing inquisitors of the apparent veracity of a confession, as well as convincing spectators of the apparent veracity of a theatrical performance. The juxtaposition of these cultural contexts, along with their shared use of figurative, gestural, and affective language, reveals mutual implications and broader stakes for the concept of certainty, as well as for what we might call theatrical truth and legal fiction.[13] One of the most enduring commonplaces of early modern European cultural and social history is that theatricality could be found in all corners of everyday life. Particularly with the rise of court society and the baroque spectacle, everyone is said to be an actor performing a role, projecting an ideal image while masking the true self.[14] John Martin has recently offered a more nuanced view of these familiar tropes. Innovatively approaching inquisitorial practices as a touchstone for understanding the nature of the Renaissance individual has allowed him to catalogue the existence of various "selves." What he deems the "prudential self" is one who is keen to dissimulate his or her thoughts and convictions and is therefore more likely to be a heretic. The "performative self" is similarly self-conscious but more given to the theatrics that might buttress the appearance of innocence in a courtroom setting. In contrast, Martin defines the "sincere self" as an individual for whom the revealing of internal beliefs is "a matter of great urgency, even an ethical imperative," noting furthermore that "sincerity was ... an important new ideal in the sixteenth century."[15] Though his focus is predominantly on Renaissance Italy, Martin's distinctions are important because they deconstruct reductionist views that either held that everyone was a performer or deprived early moderns of individual interiority altogether. While this paints a more lucid picture of the period for contemporary critics, the reality of contending with multiple "selves" could not but have rendered the charge of inquisitors even more uncertain.

One way they approached this landscape of unstable links between the internal self and outward self-representation was to devote ever-greater scrutiny to the non-verbal, affective cues that accompanied confessions of guilt. To a great extent, this is what the judge or juror in a modern courtroom does: observe the finer details of testimony to intuit the credibility of a witness or defendant, attempting to discern which ones are sincere and which are performed. Since Aristotle, in effect, the importance of emotion for rhetorical persuasion had been firmly established. In Book 2 of the *Rhetoric*, he discusses at length the various emotions at play in oratory and their role in moving an audience to accept the truth of an argument, even defining emotions themselves as "all those feelings that so change men as to affect their judgements, and that are also attended by pain or pleasure."[16] "Particularly in deliberative oratory, but also in lawsuits," the Stagirite notes, "it adds much to an orator's influence that his own character should look right and that he should be thought to entertain the right feelings towards his hearers."[17] Cicero will extend Aristotle's line of thinking by associating oratory with acting in his legal defence of the actor Roscius. The Roman orator asserts that it is impossible that the judge should feel emotions for the defendant, "or that he should be moved to compassion and tears, unless all those sensations which the orator would awaken in the judge shall appear to be deeply felt and experienced by the orator himself." Though he claims that "simulation or deceit" are impossible because the force of these emotions cannot but genuinely affect the defendant who enacts them,[18] Cicero advises that the judge will not "be moved to pity, unless you give him plain indications of your own acute feeling, by your expressions, sentiments, tone of voice, look, and finally by sympathetic tears."[19] A little more than a century later, Quintilian will further strengthen the links between the courtroom and the stage, describing "how the orator establishes his sway over the emotions of his audience, forces his way into their very hearts and brings the feelings of the jury into perfect sympathy with all his words."[20]

And yet to study emotional rhetoric and performativity in the Inquisition is consequential for two reasons: first, because the popular associations of the institution and its archival legacy do not readily lend themselves to this sort of affective analysis. Justifiably, the emotion we most immediately ascribe to the Holy Office is terror. We imagine its abettors as, at best, cold, detached functionaries immune to the more sympathetic feelings, for example, that might be roused by emotional acuity and exchange with its victims.[21] I hasten to note that it is not my intention to humanize the work of an institution guilty of heinously persecuting racial and religious minorities for centuries but, rather, to contest the assumptions we have inherited about emotions in general, as well as their place in the archives. Second, my close reading of the affective dimensions of inquisitorial confessions is possible only because of the dual nature of the institution as both juridical and religious. Though it is not my purpose to do so here, it could even be argued that the subjective attention to the sincerity of these confessions is itself a by-product of the robust emphasis the post-Tridentine Church placed on the purely liturgical sacrament of penance.[22] My principal interest will be to interrogate the means by which inquisitors, in their quest for certainty as to the sincerity of confessions, turned to the affective realm at roughly the same time that many of the same gestures they sought to scrutinize were being codified and mastered by actors in the burgeoning art of theatrical performance. In fact, if in the theatre emotions took centre stage as the pinnacle of what was paradoxically called "true" acting, then in inquisitorial proceedings they were largely viewed as the opposite: a signifier of natural sincerity. Ironically, this suggests that an institution constituted by its defence of truth found itself relying on the mere *feeling* of certainty.

Though scholars have acknowledged how suspected heretics might negotiate the purely narrative or linguistic challenges of testimony, to date little to no attention has been paid to the affective dimensions of performativity in inquisitorial proceedings. Doing so here allows me to posit a sphere of influence tacitly shared between the Inquisition and the theatre akin, if only marginally, to the impact of the Holy Office on the genre of autobiography that critics have recently identified.[23] To fully reconstruct the details of what we might call involuntary performances would be impossible, since all that survives are the transcripts that scribes produced according to relatively standardized, economic protocols, which prioritized ostensibly objective facts while tending to elide elements like tone, emphasis, and gesture. And yet a close reading of these texts does reveal the presence, however fleeting, of emotional subjectivity. A broader yet secondary purpose of this essay will therefore be to signal new critical avenues for the history of emotions, a growing interdisciplinary field that scholars of early modern Iberia, on the whole, have been curiously slow to take up. My analysis here, if anything, certifies the Spanish Inquisition and theatrical tradition as areas ripe for further studies that attend to the affective dimensions of interiority.[24]

Throughout the seventeenth century, philosophers, sceptics, painters, authors, and dramaturges would all engage with a baroque "problem of thought" that William Egginton has recently called "the theater of truth."[25] One of the most representative examples of how Spanish drama played with its own fictional frame as a vehicle for reflecting on the nature of reality and illusion is Lope de Vega's *Lo fingido verdadero.*[26] Likely written around the year 1608, it reimagines the classical legend of the pagan actor Genesius of Rome for theatregoers of Counter-Reformation Spain.[27] In brief, the work dramatizes the meteoric rise of the emperor Diocleciano, an aficionado of the theatre and of the sublime acting talents of Ginés, who performs two plays before the imperial court. In the first, the actor portrays a man in love and, in the second, a Christian. In both cases, however, Ginés's performance is informed by his real life: his true love for Marcella allows him to more convincingly enact that which in the play he shows for her character, Fabia, while his embodiment of a Christian character is aided by the miraculous revelation of an angel and the actor's conversion on stage, which leads to his death as a Christian martyr. There can be little doubt that Lope, himself an ordained priest, regarded the play as an affirmation of the power of religious conviction and the truth of Catholic doctrine. But more recently critics have taken a renewed interest in its metatheatrical engagement with the *teatro del mundo* or "all the world's a stage" trope and the broader ways in which Lope not only lays bare the baroque fascination with the slippages between fiction and reality but betrays, *malgré lui*, a subtle challenge to early modern Spanish piety. Barbara Simerka, for example, conceives of the "meta-artistry" of *Lo fingido verdadero* "as a radical affirmation of the skeptical mode of thought" and an indication "that epistemological certainty is an elusive goal."[28]

Though I concur with these analyses as crucial correctives to prior interpretations that had endorsed the potency of the play's religious overtones, the vital work of emotion in the play, and its role in destabilizing certainty therein, has been largely ignored. Let us begin by considering Ginés's description of how actors are to convincingly portray emotions on stage:

> El imitar es ser representante;
> pero como el poeta no es posible
> que escriba con afecto y con blandura
> sentimientos de amor, si no le tiene
> ...

así el representante, si no siente
las pasiones de amor, es imposible
que pueda, gran señor, representarlas;
una ausencia, unos celos, un agravio,
un desdén riguroso y otras cosas
que son de amor tiernísimos efectos,
harálos, si los siente, tiernamente;
mas no los sabrá hacer si no los siente.

(To imitate is to be an actor; but just as it is not possible for the poet to write with tenderness and feeling about love unless he himself is in love, ... so it is impossible that the actor, if he does not feel the passions of love, should be able, good sir, to portray them; an absence, some jealousy, an insult, severe disdain, and other things that are the most tender effects of love, the actor will re-enact tenderly if he feels them; but he will not know how to do so if he feels them not.)[29]

Though critics have frequently cited these lines as proof of the play's more general engagement with baroque tropes of reality versus fiction, Ginés's words actually reflect a much more classical concept. As early as Plato's *Ion*, performers have been said to adopt as their own the emotions called for in the script they wish to enact. Socrates ascribes to divine inspiration Ion's success in reciting Homer and captivating his audience, while the prize-winning rhapsode chalks his abilities up to *feeling* the poetry, unmediated by critical or professional distance: "Listen, when *I* tell a sad story, my eyes are full of tears; and when I tell a story that's frightening or awful, my hair stands on end with fear and my heart jumps."[30] Horace will express a similar idea in the *Ars poetica* that an actor's real, personal feelings bolster the ability to portray artificial ones on stage.[31] Ginés's insistence that it is "impossible" to represent passions of love without feeling them first, however, does harbour significant implications when considered alongside his performance later in play. His most acclaimed part has been that of a farcical Christian, and this is why Diocleciano, after seeing his convincing performance as a jealous lover, requests that he reprise his more famous role in the final act of *Lo fingido verdadero.* Though his performance overshoots the mark when he is miraculously inspired by the angel, the point to recognize is that his dramatic reputation as a "good Christian" had already been well established. Unlike his performance of love, in other words, Ginés's flair for religious affects does not depend on experiencing the real sort or espousing Catholic doctrine in advance. While Ginés's prior fame in portraying a Christian is key to the doubts engendered among the audience and his fellow players as to the sincerity of his conversion, it also undermines the certainty of religious conviction more broadly.

So, too, does Lope's character remind us that the turn of the seventeenth century represented a critical crossroads in the professionalization of actors. It would still be a couple of centuries before comprehensive acting manuals began to circulate widely, and so performers learned their craft in one of two ways: by being born into a *farándula* or family of show business or, more generally, by following what doubled as a classical mimetic precept and practical advice to imitate nature. Mimicking the gestures of different emotions in everyday life was a common vehicle for reproducing them on stage. Even if the albatross of a reputation for moral corruption and libertine lifestyles lingered, the establishment of semi-professional acting troupes paved the way for the burgeoning popularity of the *comedia* and allowed the dramatic arts to aspire to an elevated status alongside poetry and painting. Key to this enterprise was the gradual development of a *techne* that superseded the strictures of *imitatio* by vindicating the merits of a more embellished performance on stage. Though the classical mimetic precepts of *actio naturalis* still held sway, the bold idea that actors might transcend the model of nature began to take root, particularly with the rise of the baroque theatre. Alonso López Pinciano, author of the most extensive aesthetic treatise on theatre in early modern Spain, recommends that "el actor mire la persona que va a imitar y de tal manera se transforme en ella, que a todos parezca no imitación, sino propiedad" (the actor look at the person he is going to imitate and thus be transformed into that person, so that it appears to everyone that he no longer imitates, but makes it his own).[32] This transformation into the character required what in *Pedro de Urdemalas* Cervantes calls a "cuidadoso descuido" (careful carelessness): a technique that, like that of courtly *sprezzatura*, is fastidiously honed to appear effortlessly natural.[33]

Emotions are at the forefront of such techniques, as Evangelina Rodríguez Cuadros – the scholar to have dedicated by far the most attention to early modern Spanish acting – has recognized.[34] Some of the most famous playwrights of the seventeenth century reflected on the performance of emotion in their dramas. Pedro Calderón de la Barca's character Isabel, for instance, enumerates in *El alcalde de Zalamea* myriad emotional states and their corresponding declamation:

pues (calle aquí la voz mía),
soberbio (enmudezca el llanto),
atrevido (el pecho gima),
descortés (lloren los ojos),

fiero (ensordezca la envidia),
tirano (falte el aliento),
osado (luto me vista) …,
y si lo que la voz yerra,
tal vez el acción explica.
De vergüenza cubro el rostro,
de empacho lloro ofendida,
de rabia tuerzo las manos,
el pecho rompo de ira.
Entiende tú las acciones;
pues no hay voces que lo digan.

[So (stifle here my voice), arrogant (quiet my weeping), daring (my chest moans), discourteous (my eyes cry), fierce (deafen my envy), tyrannical (lose my breath), audacious (I dress for mourning) … and when the voice falters, perhaps the gesture explains it. In shame I cover my face, my qualms make me cry, offended, from anger I wring my hands, from rage my breast heaves. You must understand the gestures, since there are no voices to declare them.][35]

Here bodily movements and affects stand in for words, reflecting the idea among Renaissance thinkers that, at least in the theatre, the latter paled in comparison to the expressiveness of the former.[36] The *gracioso* Bato in *Las fortunas de Andrómeda y Perseo* similarly underscores the importance of gesture in expressing emotions on stage:

… No se engañen;
facción por facción me miren,
vean, que soy como un ángel;
Miren qué rostro, si lloro;
si río, miren qué semblante;
al mesurarme, qué tez;
y qué ceño al enojarme.

(… Don't be deceived; look at me feature by feature, see that I am like an angel. Look at what a face, if I cry; if I laugh, look at what a demeanour; when restraining myself, what a complexion; and what a frown when I get angry.)[37]

As these examples demonstrate, even in the absence of a comprehensive acting manual, performers of the late sixteenth and early seventeenth centuries called upon an increasingly codified corpus of gestures to express the emotions of their characters with a degree of excellence or *propiedad* made possible only by the ability to surpass the limitations of simple imitation.

Perhaps it was inevitable, then, that theatrical performance would become intertwined with the concept of truth and further blur the boundaries between reality and fiction. Remarking on a case akin to Lope's Ginés, in which the spectators struggle to distinguish between a comic actor's performance and his behaviour in real life, El Pinciano stresses "lo mucho que importa que el actor haga su officio con mucho primor y muy de veras; que, pues nos lleuan nuestros dineros de veras, y nos hazen esperar aquí dos horas, razón es que hagan sus acciones con muchas veras" (how important it is that the actor do his job with much skill and very truly; since they take our money truly and make us wait here two hours, it is only fair that they should do their acting with lots of truth).[38] Notwithstanding his touch of irreverent humour, El Pinciano's repeated emphasis on truth ("veras"), descriptive as much as it is prescriptive, offers a telling window onto early modern performance. Leone de' Sommi, the Jewish-Italian author of the most complete treatise on theatre in the Renaissance, echoes El Pinciano's insight when stressing that the player must perform his or her part in a "lively" and "very vivacious way" ("vivezza"; "vivacissima maniera").[39] Such techniques go beyond the more general watchword of verisimilitude, an Aristotelian precept that guided much Renaissance poetics, as Rodríguez Cuadros underscores: "*truth* and *veracity* are progressively understood in their capacity for persuasion, in the case of the actor, by way of a corporal and vocal stylistics that makes interior emotions especially accessible."[40] Once again, it is emotions that become the key to unlocking the performative enterprise of staging persuasive or "true" portrayals.

In the process, the roles of character and actor become conflated, as attested by several theatrical anecdotes about spectators as well as the preoccupations of moralists opposed to the theatre. Lope recounts a couple of cautionary tales of actors who embodied their roles to such a degree as to be mistaken for their characters outside the proscenium.[41] These fusions of player and character help to explain the anxieties of the many writers who disparaged and condemned the *comedia* for its morally deleterious effects, denunciations that often converged upon the performers themselves. A central theme that emerges from these writings is the impropriety of actors whose debauched lifestyles were dissonant with the saintly characters they represented on stage. For example, in

1689 the preacher Ignacio Camargo excoriated actresses who played the Virgin Mary and mouthed the gospel in plays while leading a life of scandal offstage.[42] Nearly a century earlier, Lupercio Leonardo de Argensola had lamented that, backstage, performers "were drinking, swearing, blaspheming, and gambling in their costumes of saints, angels, the Virgin Mary, and even God" while, onstage, "feigning tears and making light of what always should have been truthful and treated by upstanding people."[43] Such complaints bespeak the increasing ability of actors to realistically simulate emotions on stage – including the capability of producing false tears – and are symptomatic of broader anxieties about the need to reassert the ebbing distinction between truth and fiction.

As with early autobiography and theatre, the Inquisition's own relationship with truth was more complex and ambivalent than it might first appear. Francisco Peña's heavily glossed edition of Nicolau Eimeric's *Directorium Inquisitorum*, which enjoyed seven printing runs between 1578 and 1607, essentially authorizes the same kind of rhetorical trickery employed by the accused in order that inquisitors might counter equivocal or dissembling testimony. In the section "Cautelæ Inquisitorum contra hereticorum cauillationes & fraudes" (Ten tricks of the inquisitor to spoil those of heretics), the verb "fingere" performs a leading role. The text suggests, for example, that inquisitors feign the need to leave town for an extended period of time in order to pressure suspects into confessing.[44] Tellingly, the manual's attention to details like what sort of tone is most persuasive means that much of this advice reads rather like theatrical stage directions, urging officials to deliver "verba bona, semper sine turbatione" (seemingly benign words, without becoming irritated).[45] It even suggests some lines of vernacular dialogue to use in this case: "videas, ego compatiebar tibi ... habeo recedere à te, & ire vbi sum valde necessarius, & nescio quando reuertar: Nunc autem postquam non vis fateri veritatem, cum displicentia ego habeo te in carcere dimittere compeditum vsque ad regressum meum, & displicet mihi, quia nescio quando regrediar" (Look, I have pity on you ... I have to report to where duty calls me and I don't know when I'll be able to return. You don't want to admit the truth, and so you make me leave you locked up until I come back. I feel sorry for you, because I don't know when I'll return).[46] With these informal and unabashedly manipulative lines, the manual promises its inquisitor-readers a greater likelihood of success in eroding the prisoner's resolve and obtaining a confession. To assuage any moral objections to such flagrant artifice, Peña hastens to explain the need to distinguish lies and deceit according to their purpose, concluding that the Inquisition's worthy ends justify the use of such means.[47]

These brief examples betray the fact that the principal aim of an Inquisition trial was not to uncover wrongdoing for its own sake, but rather to obtain a confession and, as Eimeric and Peña concede, to instil fear in the populace at large.[48] Nor was it overly concerned to absolve the innocent: the *Directorium* remarks that the truly inculpable souls who were steadfast enough to endure the entire process without succumbing to the relief of a false confession would go on to die as martyrs.[49] In short, inquisitors were reassured that, eventually, a higher form of justice would be served. Thus it bears asserting, once again, that the Holy Office was invested not so much in the truth of a particular verdict, but in the ultimate goal of collecting confessions, which were regarded as the most conclusive proof of guilt.[50] Henry Charles Lea noted long ago the "curious assumption" among inquisitors that confessions should be both "judicial and sacramental."[51] To be fully valid, they had to exhaustively acknowledge each transgression, lest they be nullified as *ficta* or *diminuta* and thereby incur the grave consequences of impenitence. Inquisitors were therefore justified in leveraging not only rhetorical persuasion and trickery, but multiple coercive means to secure complete confessions, including threats, prolonged incarceration, and torture. The duress suffered throughout these processes frequently led to declarations of questionable veracity, offered not because of a bona fide desire for atonement but because victims quickly realized they were simply the most expedient avenue for escaping further torment. It soon became clear that heretics could go relatively scot-free by simply confessing their sins at the outset, with little real incentive to reform.

Uncertainty was thus a prominent feature of inquisitorial trials from early on, not just in the more obvious sense of whether or not the accused were guilty of heresy, but whether a primary mechanism for certifying that guilt – confession – was a sufficient bulwark for the dominant Catholic orthodoxy. Sentences of reconciliation were by far the most common, and the reliance on confession as the paramount objective of inquisitorial trials proved rather quickly to be an intractable problem of the institution's own making. On the one hand, the Inquisition sought to counterbalance its reputation for terror by promoting an image of mercy that was consistent with Catholic teachings on the forgiveness of sin. The inauguration of a new regional tribunal was always accompanied by a grace period (*época de gracia*), during which locals could enjoy immunity from the crimes they voluntarily registered. By reserving capital punishment largely for what the Holy Office considered impenitents and relapsed heretics (and even then, always under the formality of "relaxing" to the secular arm of justice), it aimed to capture the goodwill of those who might confess more freely. On the other hand, extorting more confessions led, almost inevitably, to diminishing returns of their sincerity, particularly once word had escaped that an early confession equalled greater leniency. The widespread conceit that a confession could redeem a trial otherwise plagued by irregularities only spurred inquisitors to pursue that finality more doggedly.[52] As a yardstick of success, it could be argued that confession actually hamstrung the institution from realizing its loftier goal of rooting out "true" heretics. These competing pressures required inquisitors to devote ever greater scrutiny to *ad eruendam veritatem*, the question of whether or not a given expression of repentance was genuine.

Inquisition manuals were accordingly swift to sound the alarm on the possibility of false confessions, beginning with the *Instrucciones* of the first inquisitor general, Tomás de Torquemada, who advises "que los Inquisidores miren mucho como reciben a reconciliacion, y carcel perpetua a los que agora despues de presos confiessan" (that inquisitors should look closely at how they offer reconciliation and perpetual prison to those that confess now after being arrested).[53] His warning contains two pivotal insights. The first is that a correspondence exists between the timing of a given confession and its sincerity. Early stipulations held that in order to garner clemency a confession had to be recorded before the pronouncement of sentencing. But confessors were on hand for impenitents throughout the *autos de fe*, right up until the execution of punishment, should they feel compelled to recant when faced with the imminent, material prospect of burning at the stake. As their procedures evolved, officials appear to become increasingly concerned with the authenticity of last-minute confessions. They are advised in 1498 to be particularly sceptical of those proffered after an arrest and that the suspect should only be granted reconciliation "[depending] upon the inquisitor's belief in his sincerity."[54] One concrete method for appraising confessional sincerity that eventually took hold was a chronological one: whether a heretic admitted guilt before the filing of a formal accusation, before the presentation of evidence, before torture, or before the *auto de fe* corresponded to gradually more severe punishment, from short imprisonment, the *sambenito*, and various forms of spiritual penance for early confessions, to longer prison sentences and five years of service in the galleys for those pronounced at the eleventh hour.[55]

Still, to determine the finer gradations of this scale required that inquisitors attend to less objective and more qualitative circumstances of a given confession. This is the second, more subtle insight that emerges from Torquemada's injunction. Confessions obtained after the publication of charges and deposition of witnesses could still procure a lesser sentence, but with one important caveat, which the inquisitor general notes parenthetically: "(saluo, si atenta la forma de su confession, y consideradas algunas otras conjeturas, segun su aluedrio, les pareciere, q[ue] la conuersion, y reconciliaciõ del tal herege es fingida, y simulada, y no verdadera ...)" (unless, having paid attention to the form of his confession and considered other circumstances as inquisitors see fit, the conversion and rehabilitation of a given heretic seems to be feigned, fabricated, and not true ...).[56] In such cases of "feigned" confessions, he concludes, the prisoners can be legitimately characterized as impenitents and relaxed to the secular arm in order to be put to death. The instructions compiled by Fernando de Valdés in 1561 take a similar stance, exhorting inquisitors that "deuen siempre estar sospechosos de que puedan recebir engaño, assi en la testificacion, como en las confessiones: y con este cuidado, y rezelo miraràn, y determinaràn la causa conforme a verdad, y justicia" (they should always be suspicious of deception, during testimony as much as confessions: and with this care and distrust they will look at and determine the verdict in line with truth and justice).[57] Beyond more general appeals to inquisitors' conscience or intuition, the key commonality of these instructions is the subtle attention to non-verbal aspects of confession ("atenta la forma de su confession") and, above all, their emphasis on the visual, couched in the verb "mirar" ("que miren mucho"; "mirarán, y determinarán"). Pablo García's *Orden de Procesar,* printed in 1591 yet likely in circulation earlier, reinforces these directives while standardizing the language that would be used for sentences of rehabilitation: the inquisitor should be "atento que el dicho fulano, en las confesiones que ante nos hizo, mostró señales de contrición y arrepentimiento ... de puro corazón y fe no fingida y que ha confesado enteramente la verdad" (attentive to whether so-and-so prisoner showed signs of contrition and repentance ... purely from the heart and with unfeigned faith, and whether he has wholly confessed the truth).[58]

Concerning the details on scrutinizing words and speech, Inquisition manuals supply little explicit guidance on how to carry out these visual inspections of sincerity. For instance, the section "De signis & indiciis exterioribus, quibus diuersarum sectarum hæreteci cognosci possint" (External signs and indicators by which various kinds of heretics are recognized) of Eimeric and Peña's *Directorium Inquisitorum* addresses, almost exclusively, religious practices, forms of dress, and outward physical appearance.[59] The external markers of false penitents, or what exactly the inquisitor should look for to identify them, are apparently left to the imagination.[60] Other *Instrucciones* and the *cartas acordadas* or administrative orders that were intended to supplement them are, as far as I have been able to ascertain, similarly muted on these questions. Of course, such guidelines were not always followed strictly or universally among the different tribunals, nor were they the only procedural models at the disposal of inquisitors. Particularly in the early years of the institution, officials turned to canon law or other legal doctrines to conduct their proceedings. Confessors' manuals are another source with which inquisitors were likely to have been familiar, especially given the wide popularity and extensive print runs they enjoyed in the sixteenth and seventeenth centuries. But though these texts offer advice to both confessor and penitent, like the *Instrucciones* they largely pass over methodological details in favour of general pronouncements on the importance of attending to non-verbal, affective cues. This is not entirely surprising, as the stakes were obviously lower in a purely confessional, non-juridical setting. Though to be fully absolved before God one was expected to feel pain for having sinned – therefore the "dolor" of the penitent is often referenced in such manuals – this was an affective state the confessor was intended to promote rather than one whose sincerity he was to judge.[61]

Where we do encounter more concrete, if similarly economical, details with respect to appraising sincerity is in the transcripts of Inquisition trials themselves. In essence, to evaluate the credibility of repentance inquisitors decided it was necessary to study the more nuanced physiological and emotional cues that emerged in the midst of formal testimony. One can perceive in trial records, particularly the *sentencia*, an attention to such markers, often codified generically, as García recommended, as "muestras" or "señales de arrepentimiento" ("signs" or "signals of repentance").[62] Their appearance not only denotes the justification of what is typically a lighter sentence but, more importantly, evinces material attempts to penetrate the domain of individual interiority. That an observer might thus discern innocence, guilt, or sincerity of remorse recalls the classical fascination with physiognomy, *chironomia*, and similar pseudo-sciences that experienced a resurgence in the late Renaissance.[63] Perhaps it is Cervantes's Don Quixote who most effectively summarizes the competing views as to the legitimacy of such practices. When dispatching his squire Sancho on an embassy to his imaginary maiden, Dulcinea, he professes his ability to decipher the "certísimos correos que traen las nuevas de lo que allá en lo interior del alma pasa" (the very true dispatches that carry the news of what happens there on the inside of the soul). He therefore instructs Sancho to take careful note of Dulcinea's "acciones y movimientos exteriores" (exterior movements and affects), from which Don Quixote plans to infer her feelings for him: "sacaré yo lo que ella tiene escondido en lo secreto de su corazón acerca de lo que al fecho de mis amores toca" (I will capture what she has hidden in the secret parts of her heart about that which concerns the fact of my love for her).[64] The superlative truth the mad knight grants the art of physiognomy ("certísimos correos"), along with the parodic outcome of the embassy later in the novel, underscores the popularity of such practices while ironizing their dubious reliability. A slew of early modern Spanish treatises promised discerning readers similarly quixotic abilities to interpret the character and temperament of others through all manner of physiognomic features. Due to their association with chiromancy and witchcraft, however, many ran afoul of the Inquisition itself. Incidentally, though the "signals" that inquisitors sought to decipher among those they interrogated are far less exaggerated, their reliance on facial and bodily legibility does align them, if only marginally, to the practices they more often found themselves prosecuting.

Two case studies from Inquisition trials will aid in clarifying how inquisitors scrutinized and evaluated external gestures in practice. Though representative of procedures that took place elsewhere as well, I have elected these examples from Valencia in part because this particular tribunal has been qualified as "a cautious Inquisition" comprised of "sceptical inquisitors."[65] We might therefore expect them to have been more dubious of and alert to theatricality in their courtroom, a possibility I will explore below. Charges of wanton heresy brought Pedro Lázaro, a local Valencian merchant, before the city's Inquisition in 1566. The suspect confessed to having performed various rituals to bewitch women in order to elicit their romantic affection. These included writing certain words on a heart painted with saffron, or casting spells with such objects as a black cat, five swallows, a raven's quill, holy oil, or a peach seed that one of his female clients had tossed into the street. But in spite of Lázaro's persistence in pursuing these "conjuros e invocaciones de demonios" and "delitos manifiestamente sospechosos de heregía" ("spells and incantations of demons" and "manifestly suspicious crimes of heresy"), the inquisitors opted for an abjuration *de levi*, sentencing him to perform the penitential rites of visiting the poor in hospitals, giving alms, fasting on Fridays, and publicly confessing his sins in an *auto de fe*, along with other forms of penitence and pecuniary penalties.[66] Similar clemency was granted to Maria Gomez, a woman from Lisbon who had faced the Valencia Inquisition a few years earlier for Judaizing rituals. While noting that her crimes of "aver passado a los rytos y cerymonias de los judíos y tenido y creydo nefandos y abominables herrores" (having turned to the rites and ceremonies of the Jews and held and believed vile and abominable errors) would have justified the death penalty, the inquisitors demonstrated lenience in their judgment by condemning her to perpetual imprisonment.[67] The common denominator in these cases was that, in addition to willingly confessing, each had shown outward signs of remorse ("señales de arrepentimiento"): Lázaro "con lágrimas diversas vezes nos a pedido penitencia con misericordia" (with tears on diverse occasions he has asked us for penitence with mercy) and Gomez "por muchas y diversas vezes hyncada de rodillas con muchos sospiros y lagrimas" (kneeling on many and diverse occasions with many sighs and tears).[68] It is the external cues of tears, sighs, and similar emotional signifiers of grief, affliction, and remorse that spare the accused a worse fate.

Such pronouncements are far from unique in the annals of inquisitorial practice, and this is likely one of the reasons why they have been overlooked or taken as rote or mechanical formalities. But they are significant insofar as they disclose, once again, the scrutiny paid by inquisitors to seemingly minute and subjective emotional details. If what the trial records refer to as "muestras" and "señales" became indispensable for reconciliation by somehow signifying repentance itself, then their absence often connoted a lack of remorse and, therefore, the impossibility of reconciliation. And yet it is imperative to recognize that, as is the case with the vast majority of emotions in general, the discrete elements of these "signals" were culturally mediated by early modern Spanish social customs, rituals, and religiosity. In the words of Pierre Bourdieu, they constituted a distinct emotional *habitus*. For example, the act of falling to one's knees is, even today, widely recognized as a sign of pleading mercy and demonstrating reverence, worship, or vulnerability before a more powerful entity. But in the sixteenth and seventeenth centuries, genuflection was a ubiquitous physical gesture one could expect to encounter in liturgical settings and on various penitential occasions. Even Jews and Muslims, whose own rituals for kneeling and prostration differed from the dominant Christian practice, would have been capable of falling to their knees and reproducing the iconographic gesture that Maria Gomez adopts, on multiple and seemingly spontaneous occasions, before her inquisitors. Though they might appear even more universal or "natural," sighs are similarly informed by cultural and historical factors. Luis F. Avilés has studied, for instance, how in the *Abencerraje* the sigh functions as a proto-linguistic signifier that prompts intercultural exchanges on the Moorish frontier. There it is the characters' careful attention to others' "suspiros" that invites them to release an affective burden.[69] The sigh was thus understood not exclusively as a sign of exasperation – as it is perhaps most commonly deployed today – but one of psychological anguish capable of engendering sympathy by way of access to individual interiority.

The same can be said for tears, which performed remarkably complex yet culturally specific social functions. Often regarded as emblematic of Counter-Reformation religiosity, weeping acquired a particularly strong association with repentance. While Protestantism would accept only two sacraments – baptism and communion – since the Fourth Lateran Council of 1215 the Roman Catholic Church had promoted that of penance as well. To stress the importance of confession in the liturgy, the church championed the apostle Peter, who according to the four Gospels cried in atonement after having betrayed Christ. Graphic and textual representations of the lachrymose saint proliferated in late sixteenth- and early seventeenth-century Spain, reinforcing the popular association of weeping with repentance.[70] Tears shed in remorse for a prior transgression served for the believer as a purifying balm that, like St Peter's, purged sinfulness and assured redemption before God.[71] According to María Tausiet, however, the intimate, almost mystical communion implied by such divine tears made the church fret that it could give way to unorthodox or even heretical forms of spirituality, and so it soon channelled the power of tears into collective rites of devotion.[72] Occasions for communal crying abounded in early modern Spain, from processions and public spectacles to funerals and all manner of *ars moriendi.* The ability to shed copious tears became almost de rigueur, and so there emerged not only concerted efforts to summon them at will, but professional mourners who were already skilled in spontaneous sobbing.[73] The church itself frequently promoted these ritualized outpourings of emotion. St Ignatius of Loyola, whose own facility with weeping was the stuff of legend, instructed his spiritual followers to cry on command, while in the following century Francisco Santos would complain openly of the "brutos o tarascas," or the rented penitents whose hypocritical tears wetted the streets of Madrid during Holy Week processions.[74] In a word, tears had become theatrical.

Around the same time, a plethora of treatises on the bodily fluid emerged in print, such as Roberto Bellarmino's *The Book of the Cry of the*

Dove, which described a typology of good and bad tears. While benevolent tears proceeded from a host of natural inclinations and situations, whether spiritual or quotidian, the malevolent variety reflected the ancient notion of "crocodile tears": those produced wilfully to feign sympathy, sorrow, or some other instrumental, emotional end. In Counter-Reformation Spain, this latter sort became understood as a manifestation of the devil himself, whose power could be expunged most effectively by pious, virtuous tears or what Juan de Marieta, in his 1615 biography of Fray Luis de Granada, called the "water of angels" ("agua de ángeles").[75] It was this divine grace of the *donum lacrymarum* or "gift of tears" that in turn gave rise to the commonplace that witches were incapable of crying. Thus, just as the display of tears before the Inquisition could denote the sincerity of a confession, their lack could also indicate guilt. At a secular trial in Huesca in 1534, the judges scrutinized the countenance of Dominga Ferrer to determine "si salian lagrimas de los ojos de la dicha Domenica al tiempo que hazia como que lloraba, o no" (if tears issued from the eyes of the aforementioned Domenica at the time she pretended to cry, or not). That they eventually certified that "ningunas lagrimas parescieron que le saliessen de sus ojos" (no tears appeared to leave her eyes) reinforced her presumed guilt of engaging in witchcraft.[76] It was for similar reasons that, while applying various forms of torture on suspects who were reticent to confess, inquisitors took careful note not only of the words they uttered, but of the visual and aural cues that emerged in response to harm. The exclamatory *ayes* or shrieks of agony that characteristically punctuate the transcripts of *tormentos* were scrupulously recorded to demonstrate a prisoner's tolerance for pain as much as to probe, once again, his or her sincerity of emotional expression, for the ability to endure high levels of pain without breaking automatically aroused suspicions of demonic possession.

In sum, in early modern Spain tears encoded an ambiguous and sometimes contradictory array of cultural associations, superstitions, fetishes, and prohibitions. Their abundance or absence could alternately raise suspicions of heterodoxy or endorse compliance with orthodoxy. They were at once envied as an uncommon individual gift and emblematic of a spectacular culture of the masses. They flowed involuntarily but could be summoned intentionally. What is most noteworthy about the case of tears, however, is how for inquisitors they continued to underwrite the sincerity of confession long after the church had identified, and perhaps nearly exhausted, them as a performative feature of public devotion. This is not to imply that the Inquisition was naive or self-deluded. Even if Valencia's tribunal was, as has been suggested, notably more sceptical, inquisitors on the whole were accustomed to and adept at recognizing all manner of deceptions. The intriguing case of Bartolomé Sánchez, a wool carder tried by the Inquisition of Cuenca for heresy between 1553 and 1560, offers singular evidence of the fact that not even abundant tears could sway the conviction of the most perceptive judges. Having already supplied varying types of testimony on multiple occasions, one day Sánchez requested an audience with the inquisitor Pedro Cortes only to appear before him silently weeping and wiping the tears from his eyes with a handkerchief. Asked to explain why he was crying, Sánchez proffered an apparently feeble attempt at admitting his wrongs and claiming insanity. Cortes remained unconvinced and proceeded to expound on the differences between contrition – an authentic desire for atonement – and attrition, a confession tendered for self-serving reasons. He concluded by telling Sánchez to dry his tears and aspire to the former: "Separate yourself from that [crying] and throw it away. Serving God with work, He will give you the reward and consolation that you desire."[77] Inquisitors did not rely on "muestras" and "señales" as a simple checklist for noting the presence or absence of particular cues but, as Sánchez's case bears out, on even more intangible and intuitive aspects of a prisoner's demeanour for certifying the authenticity of remorse. Salient, then, in inquisitorial procedures of dealing with penitential confessions is not that they were readily accepted as true or rejected as false but, rather, predisposed to a degree of doubt that necessitated the development of an emotional hermeneutics.

And yet because the subjective signifiers of reform and contrition become increasingly minute, this was an unstable hermeneutics that in their quest for certainty could ultimately grant inquisitors but the feeling thereof. The convergence of the inquisitorial reliance on emotional expression and the codification of highly verisimilar affective gestures in the fictitious setting of the theatre subjected innocence, repentance, and tears all to the possibility of being feigned. Thus like the intradiegetic playgoers in Lope's *Lo fingido verdadero* who struggle to differentiate between Ginés's character and his true self, one cannot say for certain whether the feelings expressed by inquisitorial penitents were genuine, whether their newfound religious convictions would be robust enough to weather the test of time. If for spectators of the play-within-the-play the greatest proof of the actor's conversion to Christianity is his willingness to die as a martyr, such finality was in no way certain for inquisitors, since those who died at the stake were deprived of absolution, their ultimate beliefs remaining inscrutable to all but divine eyes. The most credible proof that a given confession had been sincere was essentially the long-term absence of evidence to the contrary: that a rehabilitated individual carried out his or her punishment and was never seen or heard by the Holy Office again. Yet even the reappearance before inquisitors of a penitent who had previously passed through their chambers, despite the presumption of relapsing into heresy, could not objectively warrant the invalidation of his or her prior confession as necessarily false. As with Lope's play, the difficulty lies in stepping definitively outside a continuously expanding frame of potential performativity. The trials of Lázaro and Gomez, as well as numerous others that attend to the "muestras" or "señales" of the repentant, become a point of convergence for perennial debates on the correspondence between outward expression and inward feelings, troubling the boundaries between not only genuine and artificial emotions, but those that governed the historic spaces of the witness stand and the theatrical stage, courtroom and *corral.* Their cases disclose the ironic stakes of using emotions as a device for certainty by an institution that considered itself the supreme arbiter of religious truth.

ACKNOWLEDGMENTS

I acknowledge the support this project received from the interdisciplinary research group History and Philosophy of Experience (HIST-EX), sponsored by Spain's Ministerio de Economía y Competitividad (FFI2016-78285-R). I am also grateful to Ignacio Panizo of the Archivo Histórico Nacional and my research assistant Melinda Franke for their help in the archives, as well as to James Amelang and William Christian, who read an earlier version of this chapter.

NOTES

1 Among the most prominent examples are James S. Amelang, *The Flight of Icarus: Artisan Autobiography in Early Modern Europe* (Stanford: Stanford University Press, 1998); Amelang, "Tracing Lives: The Spanish Inquisition and the Act of Autobiography," in *Controlling Time and Shaping the Self: Developments in Autobiographical Writing since the Sixteenth Century*, ed. Arianne Baggerman, Rudolf Dekker, and Michael Mascuch (Leiden: Brill, 2011), 33–48; Richard L. Kagan and Abigail Dyer, eds, *Inquisitorial Inquiries: Brief*

Lives of Secret Jews and Other Heretics (Baltimore: Johns Hopkins University Press, 2004); and David Gitlitz, "Inquisition Confessions and *Lazarillo de Tormes*," *Hispanic Review* 68, no. 1 (2000): 53–74.

2 Amelang, *The Flight of Icarus*, 181–95.

3 Kagan and Dyer, *Inquisitorial Inquiries*, 5.

4 Gitlitz, "Inquisition Confessions," 54–6.

5 Ibid., 62.

6 Amelang would call this an "autobiographical speech act"; for other examples, see his "Tracing Lives," 38.

7 Gitlitz, "Inquisition Confessions," 60.

8 See, for instance, the classical treatment by Lionel Abel, *Metatheatre: A New View of Dramatic Form* (New York: Hill and Wang, 1963); and for a critical synthesis of the problems inherent in Abel's study and the concept of the metatheatrical, see Catherine Larson, "Metatheater and the *Comedia*: Past, Present, and Future" in *The Golden Age Comedia: Text, Theory, and Performance*, ed. Charles Ganelin and Howard Mancing (West Lafayette: Purdue University Press, 1994), 204–21.

9 So lamented Juan Ferrer in *Tratado de las Comedias* of 1618, in Emilio Cotarelo y Mori, *Bibliografía de las controversias sobre la licitud del teatro en España*, ed. José Luis Suárez García (Granada: Universidad de Granada, 1997 [1904]), 257b.

10 One of the most notable examples was María Riquelme, who performed in plays by Lope, Quevedo, and Quiñones de Benavente and was renowned for her uncanny ability to embody the emotions of her characters on stage. The poet and preacher Hortensio Félix Paravicino lauded her talent for performative blushing thus: "María, a tal propiedad / vuestra imitación aspira / que a hilos de la mentira / corre sangre a la verdad" (María, your acting aspires to such perfection that on threads of lies blood runs to the truth). Félix de Arteaga, *Obras póstumas, divinas, y humanas* (Alcalá: María Fernández, 1650), fol. 95r. Unless otherwise noted, all translations are my own.

11 John Dewey, *The Quest for Certainty: A Study of the Relation of Knowledge and Action* (New York: Minton, Balch and Company, 1929), 33.

12 Ibid., 9.

13 "Scenic truth" is the term Constantin Stanislavski would use in his influential acting manuals of the twentieth century. See *An Actor Prepares*, trans. Elizabeth Reynolds Hapgood (New York: Routledge, 1989), 128. With "legal fiction," on the other hand, I do not intend to imply an affinity with William Blackstone's founding definition of the term in the eighteenth century.

14 See, for example, Emilio Orozco Díaz, *El teatro y la teatralidad del barroco* (Barcelona: Planeta, 1969), 87–118.
15 John Martin, *Myths of Renaissance Individualism* (New York: Palgrave Macmillan, 2004), 32–8.
16 Aristotle, *Rhetoric*, in *The Complete Works of Aristotle: The Revised Oxford Translation*, vol. 2, ed. Jonathan Barnes (Princeton: Princeton University Press, 1984), 1378a21–2 (2195).
17 Ibid., 2, 1377b25–28 (2194).
18 "Let me assure you, in those thoughts and sentiments which you apply, handle, and discuss in speaking, that there is no occasion for simulation or deceit; for the very nature of the language which is adopted to move the passions of others, moves the orator himself in a greater degree than any one of those who listen to him ... But ... that this may not appear surprising in us, what can be more fictitious than poetry, than theatrical representations, than the argument of a play? Yet on the stage I myself have often observed the eyes of the actor through his mask appear inflamed with fury, while he was repeating these verses." Cicero, in Toby Cole and Helen Krich Chinoy, eds, *Actors on Acting: The Theories, Techniques, and Practices of the Great Actors of All Times as Told in Their Own Words* (New York: Crown, 1949), 22. Cicero thus anticipates the modern view of William James that it is language itself that is responsible for our emotions. According to this theory, we are sad because we weep, and not the other way around.
19 In Cole and Chinoy, *Actors on Acting*, 22.
20 Quintilian, *Institutio Oratoria: Books I–III*, trans. H.E. Butler (Cambridge, MA: Harvard University Press, 1996), 249–51.
21 Karen Sullivan attempts to penetrate this façade in *The Inner Lives of Medieval Inquisitors* (Chicago: University of Chicago Press, 2011), albeit with little attention to emotion per se.
22 In a different yet related vein, Martin has studied the emergence of the concept of sincerity in the Renaissance by associating it with the Protestant emphasis on individual conviction vis-à-vis the highly ritualized nature of Catholicism. See John Martin, "Inventing Sincerity, Refashioning Prudence: The Discovery of the Individual in Renaissance Europe," *American Historical Review* 102 (1997): 1309–42.
23 Any such influence has conventionally been taken as detrimental, as Ronald Surtz recognizes: "It is generally agreed that the inquisitorial indexes had a negative effect on the development of the sixteenth-century Castilian theatre." He adds, however, that the institution's record-keeping has been a boon to modern critics of the theatre. See Surtz, "Spain: Catalan and Castilian Drama," in *The Theatre of Medieval Europe: New Research in Early*

Drama, ed. Eckehard Simon (Cambridge: Cambridge University Press, 1991), 200.

24 For an overview of how the history of emotion can engage with early modern Spanish theatre, see Paul Michael Johnson, "Estudio crítico," in *Celos, amor y venganza, o No hay mal que por bien no venga*, by Luis Vélez de Guevara, ed. William R. Manson and C. George Peale (Newark: Juan de la Cuesta, 2018), 15–20. Among the scant studies that juxtapose emotions and the Inquisition are Ascensión Mazuela-Anguita, "'Música para los reconciliados': Music, Emotion, and Inquisitorial 'Autos de Fe' in Early Modern Hispanic Cities," *Music & Letters* 98, no. 2 (2017): 175–203; and Johnson, "'Salido a la vergüenza': Inquisition, Penality, and a Cervantine View of Mediterranean 'Values,'" *Cervantes y el Mediterráneo / Cervantes and the Mediterranean*, spec. issue of *eHumanista / Cervantes* 2 (2013): 340–61. Referencing Barbara Rosenwein's concept of "emotional communities," Mercedes García-Arenal offers a passing yet insightful observation that certain groups like the *alumbrados* are constituted "by emotive, rather than strictly confessional or ideological, ties": "A Catholic Muslim Prophet: Agustín de Ribera, 'the Boy Who Saw Angels,'" *Common Knowledge* 18, no. 2 (2012): 271. Much work remains to understand such communities in medieval and early modern Spain. For a compelling analysis of inquisitional attempts to penetrate interiority more generally, see Dale Shuger, "The Language of Mysticism and the Language of Law in Early Modern Spain," *Renaissance Quarterly* 68, no. 3 (2015): 932–56; and the pathbreaking study, originally published in 1996, by Adriano Prosperi, *Tribunali della coscienza: Inquisitori, confessori, missionari* (Turin: Giulio Einaudi, 2009).

25 William Egginton, *The Theater of Truth: The Ideology of (Neo)Baroque Aesthetics* (Stanford: Stanford University Press, 2010), 2.

26 Translations of the work's title have ranged from *Acting Is Believing* and *The Great Pretenders* to *True Pretense* and *What You Pretend Has Become Real*. More literally, it juxtaposes the feigned ("lo fingido") with the true ("verdadero").

27 Sainz de Robles offers the range of 1604 to 1618 for the genesis of the text in Lope, *Lo fingido verdadero: Obras escogidas, Tomo III: Teatro*, ed. Federico Carlos Sainz de Robles (Madrid: Aguilar, 1967), 165; while McGaha suggests 1607 or 1608 in his "Introduction: Lope de Vega and Acting Is Believing," in *Acting Is Believing*, trans. Michael D. McGaha (San Antonio: Trinity University Press, 1986), 25–6. It was first published in the *Decima sexta Parte de las Comedias de Lope de Vega Carpio* in 1621.

28 Barbara Simerka, "Metatheater and Skepticism in Early Modern Representations of the Saint Genesius Legend," *Comparative Literature Studies* 42, no. 1 (2005): 71, 61. See also Egginton, *How the World Became a Stage*.

Presence, Theatricality, and the Question of Modernity (Albany: SUNY Press, 2003), 113–21; and Seth Kimmel, "'No milagro, milagro': The Early Modern Art of Effective Ritual," *MLN* 128, no. 2 (2013): 438–40.

29 Lope de Vega, *Lo fingido verdadero,* 180.

30 Plato, *Complete Works,* ed. John M. Cooper (Indianapolis: Hackett, 1997), 943.

31 He does so via the dictum *si vis me flere, dolendum est primum ipsi tibi.* Horace, *Satires, Epistles, and Ars Poetica,* trans. H. Rushton Fairclough (Cambridge, MA: Harvard University Press, 2005), 458. Denis Diderot will rather famously rebut this notion by claiming that effective acting is impossible "until the fury of the passions is subdued, until the head is cool and the heart under control." Diderot, *The Paradox of Acting* [*Paradoxe sur le comédien*], trans. Walter Herries Pollock (London: Chatto and Windus, 1883), 28.

32 Alonso López Pinciano, *Philosophia antigua poética,* ed. Alfredo Carballo Picazo (Madrid: CSIC, 1973), 3.282. According to the *Diccionario de autoridades,* "propiedad" means "proporción, naturalidad o perfección" (proportion, naturalness or perfection) of an imitation, but its etymology also connotes the idea of making one's own. *Diccionario de autoridades, Edición facsímil,* ed. Real Academia Española (Madrid: Gredos, 1964 [1726–39]), http://web.frl.es/DA.html.

33 Cervantes, *Comedias y tragedias,* ed. Luis Gómez Canseco (Madrid: Real Academia Española, 2015), 897, v. 2911.

34 "The rational key gives way to emotivity … aspiring to surpass nature, something reachable only insofar as emotion can transfigure the image, moving from considering it merely a mirrored reflection of reality to carrying it beyond its natural possibilities." Rodríguez Cuadros, *La técnica del actor español, en el Barroco: Hipótesis y documentos* (Madrid: Castalia, 1998), 401.

35 Pedro Calderón de la Barca, *El alcalde de Zalamea,* ed. Ángel Valbuena-Briones, 22nd ed. (Madrid: Cátedra, 2009), 163, vv. 1971–85; ellipsis in original; punctuation modified for clarity.

36 "The actor's movements … are of so great importance that perhaps the power of words is not more than the power of gesture" (Leone de' Sommi, in Cole and Chinoy, *Actors on Acting,* 48).

37 Calderón de la Barca, *Las comedias de D. Pedro Calderón de la Barca,* ed. Juan Jorge Keil (Leipzig: Ernesto Fleischer, 1829), 3.240.

38 López Pinciano, *Philosophia antigua poética,* 3.284.

39 Leone de' Sommi, *Quattro dialoghi in materia di rappresentazioni sceniche,* ed. Ferruccio Marotti (Milan: Il Polifilo, 1968), 46.

40 Rodríguez Cuadros, *La técnica del actor español*, 396.

41 In the dedication to *El rústico del cielo*: "Sucedió una cosa rara: que un famoso representante … se transformó en [el personaje], de suerte que, siendo de los más galanes y gentil hombres que habemos conocido, le imitó de manera que a todos parecía el verdadero y no el fingido; no sólo en la habla y en los donaires pero en el mismo rostro" (A strange thing happened: a famous actor transformed himself into [the character] so much that, being one of the most gallant gentlemen that we have known, he imitated him in such a way that to all of us he seemed the real thing and not the feigned one; not only in his speech and the grace of his gestures but in the face itself) (Lope, quoted in José María Ruano de la Haza, *La puesta en escena en los teatros comerciales del Siglo de Oro* [Madrid: Castalia, 2000], 298). And in *Arte nuevo de hacer comedias*: "si acaso un recitante / hace un traidor, es tan odioso a todos, / que lo que va a comprar no se le vende, / y huye el vulgo dél cuando le encuentra" (if by chance an actor plays a traitor, he is so hated by everyone that what he wants to buy is not sold to him, and the common people flee when they encounter him), while one whose character is virtuous will reap the corresponding rewards of public praise: "y si es leal le prestan y convidan / y hasta los principales le honran y aman, / le buscan, le regalan y le aclaman" (and if he is loyal they reach out to him and regale him, and even highborn people honour and love him, seek him out, pamper him, and hail him). Lope de Vega, *Arte nuevo de hacer comedias*, ed. Enrique García Santo-Tomás, 2nd ed. (Madrid: Cátedra, 2009), vv. 331–7.

42 "¿Qué fealdad más indigna que ver hacer el papel de la Virgen Purísima y Reina Soberana de los ángeles (de quien no podemos sufrir el ver una pintura indecente y fea) á una vil mugercilla, conocida por todo el auditorio por liviana y escandalosa, recibir la embajada del ángel y decir las palabras divinas del Evangelio …?" (What more despicable depravity than seeing the role of the Purest Virgin and Sovereign Queen of the angels (of whom we cannot abide seeing a foul and indecent painting) played by a vile, abominable woman, known by the whole audience to be lecherous and scandalous …?) Camargo, *Discurso theológico sobre los theatros y comedias*, in Cotarelo, *Bibliografía*, 127b.

43 "En su vestuario están bebiendo, jurando, blasfemando y jugando con el hábito y forma exterior de Santos, de ángeles, de la Virgen Nuestra Señora y del mismo Dios. Y después salen en público fingiendo lágrimas y haciendo juego de lo que siempre había de ser veras y tratado por gente limpia." Argensola, *Memorial sobre la representación de comedias*, in Cotarelo, *Bibliografía*, 67b.

44 "Si videat fic hæreticum in negatiua perseuerantem, fingat se longius debere ire." Nicolau Eimeric and Francisco Peña, *Directorium Inquisitorum*

(Rome: In aedibus Populi Romani, apud Georgium Ferrarium, 1587), 434. When citing Eimeric and Peña, I have also consulted the modern Spanish edition of the text, *El manual de los inquisidores*, ed. Luis Sala-Molins, trans. Francisco Martín (Barcelona: Muchnik, 1983). On the limitations of Sala-Molins's edition, see Agostino Borromeo, "A proposito del *Directorium Inquisitorum* di Nicolás Eymerich e delle sue edizioni cinquecentesche," *Critica Storica* 20 (1983): 499–547.

45 Eimeric and Peña, *Directorium Inquisitorum*, 433.

46 Ibid., 434.

47 "Has autem vsurpare ad fraudes detegendas, ad vitia præcauenda, & ad peccatores conuertendos valde est laudabile" (ibid., 435).

48 "Neque obstat ratio initio allata, quoniam punitio non refertur primo & per se in correctionem & bonum eius qui punitur, sed in bonum publicum vt alii terreantur, & à malis committendis auocentur" (ibid., 432). The frank admission emerges in the discussion of prisoners who feign insanity.

49 Henry Charles Lea, *A History of the Inquisition of Spain* (New York: Macmillan, 1906), 2.586.

50 "The confession of guilt was considered the maximum proof, as the queen of evidence." Francisco Tomás y Valiente, "El proceso penal," *La Inquisición*, spec. issue of *Historia* 16, Número Extraordinario 1 (1986): 17.

51 Lea, *A History of the Inquisition of Spain*, 2.569–70. According to Prosperi, "the Inquisition, in short, increasingly became one with the confession," because "it found that violence on bodies could not be done without deciphering hearts" (*Tribunali della coscienza*, 548). Similarly, Sullivan notes that the inquisitor "remained an ecclesiastic, who welcomed any confession elicited during the trial as, at least purportedly, the product of a change of heart" (*The Inner Lives of Medieval Inquisitors*, 2).

52 Lea, *A History of the Inquisition* of Spain, 2.570.

53 Gaspar Isidro de Argüello, *Instrucciones del Santo Oficio de la Inquisición, sumariamente, antiguas, y nuevas, puestas en abecedario* (Madrid: Imprenta Real, 1630), fol. 13r. Argüello's edition, whence my citations of *instrucciones* will also proceed below, was first published in Madrid in 1627 and included what are commonly known as the "Antiguas" (those instructions penned by Torquemada, Deza, Cisneros, and Adriano) as well as the "Nuevas" (those by Valdés).

54 Lea, *A History of the Inquisition of Spain*, 2.580.

55 Ibid., 2.581.

56 Argüello, *Instrucciones del Santo Oficio de la Inquisición*, fol. 5v.

57 Ibid., fol. 29v.

58 Pablo García, *Orden de Procesar*, in Miguel Jiménez Monteserín, ed.,

Introducción a la Inquisición española: Documentos básicos para el estudio del Santo Oficio (Madrid: Editora Nacional, 1980), 433.

59 Peña says as much when explaining that, though the external signs of heresy have evolved since Eimeric's time, it can still be detected by attention to words and deeds: "Rursus, omnis hæresis, omnisue hæreticus bisariam deprehenditur, verbis, aut factis: verba enim & facta signa sunt indicantia interiorem mentis conceptum" (Eimeric and Peña, *Directorium Inquisitorum*, 439).

60 The most damning proof of a false confession came only after the fact: the failure to carry out the penance or punishment meted out at sentencing (Lea, *A History of the Inquisition of Spain*, 2.101).

61 To cite merely one example from a prodigious corpus, the confessor is instructed to move the penitent to the pain of repentance by himself showing emotions and, if God wills it, contagious tears: "Y en esta industria de mover a dolor, no fuese tanto de palabras, como de sentimiento y afecto pedido a Dios, que salga de corazón: y mas aprovecharia si Dios le diesse al confessor lagrimas para mover a ellas" (And in this craft of moving to pain, it is not so much words as sentiment and emotion that, by appealing to God, come from the heart; and it would be more advantageous if God gave the confessor tears to move the penitent to tears as well). Antonio Fernández de Córdoba, *Instrucción de confessores* (Granada: Martín Fernández Zambrano, 1623), fol. 48r–v.

62 For more on inquisitorial sentences, see María del Camino Fernández Giménez, *La sentencia inquisitorial* (Madrid: Editorial Complutense, 2000), esp. 112–17.

63 Among the most popular were Della Porta's *De humana physiognomonia* (1586) and, in Spain, Jerónimo Cortés's *Fisonomía y varios secretos de naturaleza* (1597).

64 Cervantes, *Don Quijote de la Mancha*, ed. Francisco Rico et al. (Barcelona: Galaxia Gutenberg / Círculo de Lectores / Centro para la Edición de los Clásicos Españoles, 2004), 764.

65 Gunnar W. Knutsen, *Servants of Satan and Masters of Demons: The Spanish Inquisition's Trials for Superstition, Valencia and Barcelona, 1478–1700* (Turnhout: Brepols, 2009), 139, 147. Knutsen makes this claim about the Valencia Inquisition with respect to its handling of witchcraft and superstition, which he supports with statistics (51–81). For additional information on the Valencia Inquisition, see Stephen Haliczer, *Inquisition and Society in the Kingdom of Valencia, 1478–1834* (Berkeley: University of California Press, 1990). Further work might illuminate how or whether the phenomena I examine here varied geographically or historically among Inquisition tribunals.

66 Archivo Histórico Nacional, Inquisición, legajo 934, caja 1.

67 Ibid. "Cárcel perpetua" did not usually equate to a life sentence as it is known today, but was frequently commuted to a term of three to eight years. According to Haliczer, during the sixteenth century it was in fact rare that a prisoner serve more than one year (*Inquisition and Society in the Kingdom of Valencia*, 83).

68 Archivo Histórico Nacional, Inquisición, legajo 934, caja 1.

69 Luis F. Avilés, "Los suspiros del *Abencerraje*," *Hispanic Review* 71, no. 4 (2003): 453–72.

70 Pictorial works included those by El Greco and José de Ribera, and poetic renditions, those by Damián Álvarez, Rodrigo Fernández de Ribera, Luis Gálvez de Montalvo, and Cervantes, which were based on Luigi Tansillo's Italian *Le lagrime di San Pietro* of 1585.

71 El Tostado, quoted in William A. Christian, "Provoked Religious Weeping in Early Modern Spain," in *Religion and Emotion: Approaches and Interpretations*, ed. John Corrigan (Oxford: Oxford University Press, 2004), 43.

72 María Tausiet, "Agua en los ojos: El 'don de lágrimas' en la España moderna," in *Accidentes del alma: Las emociones en la Edad Moderna*, ed. María Tausiet and James S. Amelang (Madrid: Abada, 2009), 169–70.

73 On these *lloronas*, see James S. Amelang, "La viuda alegre: Miedo y luto en el llanto ritual," in Tausiet and Amelang, *Accidentes del alma* 203–26.

74 "And here begin," instructed Ignatius of Loyola, "with much effort to force [yourself] to sorrow, mourn, and weep, and continue doing so while considering the following points" (quoted in Christian, "Provoked Religious Weeping," 44); Francisco Santos, *Las tarascas de Madrid, y tribunal espantoso* (Valencia: Francisco Antonio de Burgos, 1694).

75 Fray Juan de Marieta, *Historia y vida del padre y célebre maestro, Fray Luis de Granada, de la Orden de Predicadores* (Barcelona: Hieronymo Margarit, 1615), 189.

76 Archivo Histórico Provincial de Zaragoza, quoted in Tausiet, "Agua en los ojos," 182.

77 Quoted in Sara Tilghman Nalle, *Mad for God: Bartolomé Sánchez, the Secret Messiah of Cardenete* (Charlottesville: University Press of Virginia, 2001), 106–7. The case is engagingly treated by the author in its entirety.

chapter three

Conflicting Certainties or Different Truths? Healers and Inquisition in Baroque Spain

MARÍA LUZ LÓPEZ-TERRADA

In 1653, Isabel Gómez, a midwife from Portugal who lived in Madrid, was accused of being a Jew. The inquisitors asked her whether she could read and write and whether or not she had any forbidden books. The documents of the Inquisition contain her answer: "She said that she cannot read or write, nor does she have any forbidden books, although she has books relating her work."[1]

Isabel Gómez and her response to the inquisitors' question perfectly represent the uncertain world of inquisitorial processes. Uncertainties and different truths about forms and modes of healing appear when religious authorities face and try to control the complex world of popular healers in baroque Spain. In this essay, I will examine certainty and truth in a very specific context: the Tribunal of the Inquisition, and the healers that were brought before the Inquisition. My focus will be on conflicting certainties, or different truths, that often surfaced in an inquisitorial trial.

This is part of a work in progress, a cultural approach to the history of medicine in baroque Spain that analyses three groups normally studied separately: physicians, healers, and patients. This history identifies interactions and exchanges among all three groups. As Michael Stolberg has pointed out, "Learned physicians and lay persons lived in a common medical cosmos, shared the same medical ideas, and trusted the same diagnosis and therapeutic practices."[2] Thus, in order to understand the complexities of recovering from diseases, it is necessary to consider broadly the medical cultures of the population – their *Weltanschauung*, or beliefs about health and disease – especially when one considers that belief (in this case how someone becomes ill and how one is healed) "is one of the bases of the consistent integration of society," as López

Austin demonstrates in *Los mitos del tlacuache*.[3] Moreover, understanding the mechanisms for recovery from disease allows us to consider the roles of the spiritual and magic in everyday culture and the systems of belief about the body. To understand this complexity, it is necessary to keep in mind the theoretical framework of what historians of medicine call medical pluralism or the coexistence of different forms of medical treatment, from the most academic to the most superstitious,[4] and to focus on how common people fought diseases.[5] After all, the healer does not exist without patients.

My focus on the search for certainty, for the truth of what was narrated and experienced, in order to understand properly and holistically the processes of health and disease, will centre on three different perspectives. First I consider healers' perspective on their identity, as evidenced by how they provide their autobiography and their descriptions of how they learned to heal. As Bolufer and Morant note, the healer's identity is a "lived, tested, and intimately felt identification."[6] The second is the perspective of community witnesses regarding the healers, and the final perspective is that of the accusers.

Through case studies that bring out this complexity, I illuminate how in the Holy Office's trials there are three different stories, representing competing certainties about how medical knowledge or healing ability is acquired, as well what type of practice the healers engage in. The court appears as a space for coping strategies and creative improvisation, including endless debates about how to properly distinguish natural not only from the supernatural but also from "the notoriously slippery category, the preternatural, which comprised the machinations of spiritual beings such angels and demons."[7]

The Sources

In this study I examine trials against healers between 1590 and 1720 in the tribunals of the Spanish Inquisition. There are many inquisitorial processes in which healers are mentioned, and while some of them have been studied, stories of healing have long been considered as "sorcery and superstition," so that only recently have scholars begun to recognize the value of inquisitorial archives for the history of health-care networks and beliefs about health and illness in the baroque.[8] For this history, the Inquisition records are a privileged source: not only do they provide a way to recapture the unwritten, oral transmission of medical knowledge, but in the detailed annotations of the inquisitors we can hear the voice of the healer. Two parts of the proceedings furnish all the necessary details to reconstruct the multiple identities of the healers and the ways in which they learned to heal in a largely illiterate society. First, the so-called *Discurso de su vida* was a mandatory story that the accused had to present in his or her defence in every inquisitorial process, and in which he or she answered a series of standard questions on family origins and his or her life to that point. Here the prisoners tried to construct an image of themselves that would grant them some degree of legality or demonstrate that they were not guilty in principle. The voices of the accused also appear in the first person when they answer the prosecutor's accusations, based on the statements of those who had testified against them.

In the proceedings there are rich biographical materials of very different types. However, information varies according to who provides it: that of healers is of an autobiographical nature, whereas that provided by the complainant, witnesses, relatives, clients, and authorities is biographical, of varying degrees of objectivity and subjectivity. Just as autobiography in a court context is conditioned by the situational demands of the court, biographical information offered by witnesses also varied according to the speaker's relationship with the accused. As J.S. Amelang has pointed out, these situational demands suggest the challenge of using autobiographies as historical sources.[9] In fact, before the tribunal, the accused narrated their autobiography and recounted the methods of healing they employed in various, sometimes contradicting, versions. Additionally, the healer's narratives often contrasted with the accounts that the witnesses and the accusers offered. These competing versions, instead of attenuating the problem of veracity, always present in an inquisitorial process, accentuate it.

The Healers

In what follows, I will examine examples of people brought before the Holy Office – those accused not of witchcraft and causing disease but of healing by supernatural means. In early modern Spain, medical pluralism involved the coexistence of academic medicine – the Galenism taught in universities to surgeons and apothecaries – and other forms of medical practice. Recent studies demonstrate that alternatives to traditional Galenic therapies were present in all of the territories of the Spanish monarchy.[10] Moreover, there was a multitude of healers, so that their existence and function cannot be attributed to the scarcity of doctors. As current medical anthropology suggests, the abundant examples of extra-official and official practitioners working at the same time and in the same localities can only be made sense of through cultural explanations.[11] Although traditional historiography has tended to attribute the ubiquity of healers to a lack of physicians, surgeons, and educated pharmacists, and to the nescience of the sick people, it is now clear that this was not the case. Even in urban areas where there was no shortage of physicians, folk healers regularly saw patients, and those patients included the rich and educated as well as the poor and uneducated. Rich and poor alike turned to folk healers.[12]

In order to avoid a simplistic explanation of the behaviour and mentality of healers in the early modern age, and to explore their complexity and individuality, I will analyse the construction of the self as a product of the tension between the individual and the social self,[13] the establishment of social selves within the community, and the construction of an individual self that makes healers different. As Giovanni Levi said, we "explain individual behaviours as a result of a compromise between subjectively desired behaviour and socially required behaviour."[14]

Each of the healers put on trial by the Inquisition had a very different life and belonged to a very different world. The majority of medical practitioners in the early modern world were women, and the most frequent sites of "medical education" (broadly understood) were families, households, and neighbourhoods.[15] Some of the accused women, such as midwives, were associated with "official" medicine. But many healers were marginal and had no official training or study. Although some worked as "illicit" practitioners, with a self-conscious separation from learned physicians and surgeons, many others practiced medicine as accepted and integrated members of their community.[16] *Curanderos* included men and women, people living in small towns and people who lived in court, teachers of Latin and illiterate people, people attending to farmers and people who treated courtiers and high nobility, persons of intermediate social strata, and slaves.

There were also vastly different ways in which healers learned their methods and in which those healing processes were exposed in the court of law. When in front of inquisitors, healers could adopt several individual identities, representing themselves as academic, empiric, or magical healers. The represented identity varied according to the context and the expectations of the person or group before which they performed.[17] The problem of certainties and uncertainties about the identities of healers before the Inquisition thus requires examining the lives of ordinary people and their seemingly insignificant stories. This essay aims to construct a history of ordinary people from their fragmentary and seemingly impossible biographies, thereby providing a history of figures who were an essential part of baroque medical culture.

This study does not focus on beliefs about witchcraft in baroque Spain, because the problem of veracity in inquisitorial trials against healers in seventeenth-century Spain is in fact more complex than whether or not people believed in witches. There were those who healed, and those who caused sickness, but also those who healed at some times and caused sickness at other times. This essay focuses on people who healed as represented through three narratives of evidence: the healer's story, the community members' stories, and the accuser's story.

The Healer's Story

Defendants accused of superstition by the Inquisition tried to construct an image of themselves during a part of the trial known as the *Discurso de su vida*. This was both autobiographical and mandatory, and the prisoner constructed a chronological narrative. The *Discurso de su vida* was a story that defendants presented in their defence during the inquisitorial process; it provided the accused the opportunity to demonstrate legally that they were not guilty, at least in principle, of a charge not yet known. Because the *discurso* is induced by the logic of a coercive inquisitorial system, it is reasonable to assume that these stories are conditioned by the fear felt by the accused. Prisoners introduce elements that they hope will lead to their exculpation; in other words, they "constructed narratives of their actions that they hoped would buy back their lives."[18] In the process of declaring themselves before the Inquisition, each healer achieves three things: they construct their own individual identity, they assert their identity as healers and ask the community to recognize them as such, and they assert their innocence of the accusations made to the tribunal.[19]

The strategies of the prisoners in these first-person stories are varied and are adapted in each case to the personal circumstances of the defendant before knowledge of what crime he or she will be charged with. For example, *ferrata* Berber Isabel de la Cruz, captured in Algiers, said she was a descendant on her mother's side from captive Old Christians.[20] José Rodríguez, a grammar teacher and herbalist, arrested in a small village near Madrid in 1669, insisted that he belonged to a prominent family in Valencia, that his brother – chair of medicine at the Studi General in Valencia – was a familiar of the Inquisition, and finally that he had others brothers who were priests.[21] Isabel Bautista, a woman of Seville who ended up in Toledo, was accused of amatory witchcraft, but claimed instead that she was a healer, was literate, and belonged to a wealthy family in Seville.[22] María Francisca Espinosa de los Monteros, a former slave, defined herself as a healer when accused in 1649 of casting spells using human hair in order to get a man.[23]

Before the inquisitors, healers represented themselves as individuals belonging to the established social order, which sometimes differed from their representations when dealing with the sick. For example, during the *Discurso de su vida,* the defendant never refers to supernatural practices. Thus, the representation of the healer's subjectivity accords with the context and the purposes the *discurso* is intended to achieve. Obviously sensitive heretical practices are not revealed by the defendants. In this way, represented subjectivity is intimately related to the expectations of a group: I do what you want me to do, and I perform cures that respond to the beliefs and convictions we as a group share and accept. But there is another identity, another truth created by the defendant, constructed from the answers to the accusations. Here the obvious contradictions about the life of a person judged by the Inquisition – the self he makes before his patients, the self-image offered by the inmate during the *discurso,* and the self he constructs in response to the accusation – are clearly manifested and differentiated. We see here the incoherence of subjectivity, and how various strategies are fundamental to the construction of the self. Just as, for example, St Teresa has been seen as a model of a writer who used strategies to avoid prosecution by the Inquisition, illiterate healers also had strategies to avoid condemnation after they were accused of witchcraft.

When considering female healers in particular, we must keep in mind that the public persona of women was restricted in many ways: "The women healer and midwife became emblematic for the official male view of the empiric as the ignorant intruder into the medical domain."[24] *Sanadoras* (female healers) thus construct a narrative self that has many parts, including, crucially, the source of their ability to cure. Before the accusation of healing through practices of witchcraft by pact with the devil, baroque healers self-defined as possessing knowledge acquired in an empirical way. This story enabled them to act as healers and be recognized as such by a society in which only men could obtain an official licence to be doctors, surgeons or apothecaries.[25]

The strategies of the prisoners in these first-person accounts before the inquisitors were adapted to their personal circumstances. There are some healers whose identity or subjectivity is constant in all contexts, conveying a coherent perception of their unique identity. For example, José Rodríguez always identifies himself as empirical.[26] As such, his identity is constant in different contexts: he maintains that self-image before the inquisitors, before his patients, and before his family. José claims that in Italy he learned how to prepare an ointment with herbs that heals a range of different diseases and that was unknown to Spanish doctors at the time. A very different, but likewise consistent, identity was built by Mariana Alvarez, a woman from Talavera, who had never left her village and was married to a collector of *alcabalas* (sales tax). Mariana was accused of having "cured the evil of fire with superstitious means." She responded by representing herself as a very faithful housewife, who actually performed these cures, but armed herself with a heavy burden of Catholic orthodoxy that ostensibly dated from the very moment she began learning the ritual. Thirty years earlier, being herself ill of *mal de fuego* (fire sickness), she was healed by a religious person of the Dominican Order of the convent of St Agnes of Talavera. This Dominican had cured many people using a particular system. Mariana then told the inquisitors how the Dominican had taught her to heal the *mal de fuego*: she took a knife in her right hand, placed it over the sick and the crippled part, and made three crosses with the knife, praying "in the name of the Father, and of the Son, and of the Holy Spirit ... and three creeds to the Holy Trinity, and the Our Father, and a Hail Mary to St Anthony." She then with oil "smeared the sick part with a little white ointment, and if the patients had scabs, she sprinkled them with a little white wine to soften them."[27] Mariana's strategy was thus to claim religious and empirical practice, such as the application of an ointment, against the accusation of superstitious practices.

There were other healers whose subjectivities were more diverse and flexible. As a result, they adapted, adjusted, and conformed to certain sociocultural environments. This is the case for Isabel de la Cruz, the Berber whom witnesses claimed carried out complex rituals to cure a man who was *atontado* (befuddled). She relates how a slave of the duke of Maqueda taught her the properties of plants and, to prove it before the inquisitors, recounts in detail the virtues of different plants that she bought from herbalists. This is important because herbalists were people who were authorized to sell medicinal plants. With the plants that Cruz had bought, she made a *sahumerio* to produce aromatic smoke. The smoke from the *sahumerio* was an external rather than an internal remedy, so Cruz was not intruding on the privileges of physicians or surgeons. Finally, just like Mariana, Cruz claimed that she learned the prayer from a monk. At the same time, she accused the sick man's wife of magical practices and denounced another Moorish slave for being a Muslim, so that there are many accusations and counter-accusations in her case. Ultimately, Isabel de la Cruz's accusations are not believed by the inquisitors and she is found guilty of superstitious practices.[28]

Mariana Pérez tells a story of her poverty, her itinerant life, her illnesses, and the time she spent as a patient in hospitals and how she learned to cure with plant-based remedies, or *bizmas*, to earn a living. Perez claimed that she learned to use *bizmas* from her uncle. However, when called before the inquisitors to make a second statement, she changes her testimony to match what her community says about her. She says that she told witnesses that she could cure with her saliva and prayers because she was born with grace, an element that she inherited from her father. This is a very different story than she told the first time. Grace is supernatural, a power a healer possesses from birth, yet one perfectly integrated into the Catholic worldview and consequently an accepted and allowed element, and a legitimate strategy to explain the cures she accomplished.[29] Additionally, Pérez claims that the Court of the Inquisition of Logroño considered the use of saliva an acceptable curing practice. The Inquisition of Logroño even gave her a written licence that allowed her to cure people with her saliva. The third part of Perez's testimony involves proof, which is supposed to validate everything else that she says, especially her claim that she cures thanks to grace: Mariana claims to have an image of the cross under her right breast. To check the veracity of this statement, the inquisitors called an "expert" surgeon, named Juan de la Banca, to examine Mariana's body and check the authenticity of this sign. This is clearly a case of an identity full of uncertainties, as she gives different testimonies about the same cures. At one point, she claims she cures with plants, thanks to the knowledge she learned from her uncle. This is an empirical cure and the "real" explanation that she gives the judge. At another point, she claims she cures thanks to the grace that she inherited from her father, just as her patients claim that they are cured thanks to Mariana's grace. At different moments, Mariana manipulates different belief systems, according to the context.[30]

Very different is the long and complex case of María Sánchez de la Rosa and her daughter Elena de Tordesillas in 1699. The lawsuit against María Sánchez began when she was accused of making Ana Sans sick through a spell. Ana was the cousin of Juan de Ochoa, chaplain of the duke of Osuna. María Sánchez de la Rosa belonged to the artisan strata of court, and her daughters were married to a printer and a silversmith. In her *Discurso de su vida*, before she knew what she was accused of, she said that she lived "with a poultry farm and chocolate farming." But when she knew that she was accused of being a famous sorceress, she constructed an identity as a healer. According to the accuser, Juan de Ochoa, María and her daughter had made the whole family sick,

> particularly regarding Ms. Ana Sans, who is bewitched in a way that affects her health. The exorcist who assists her said the spells are rooted deep inside her, causing sleep deprivation. After he gave the inquisitor the documents for the denunciation, Ana's pain and dismay augmented. Moreover, she has completely lost her appetite, and she is therefore being drained of life.[31]

This origin of the disease (the bewitchment) is certified by two experts: a doctor and a priest. That is, family, patients, churchmen, and doctors all attribute the illness to supernatural forces, because the same beliefs are shared about health and illness.

María now represents herself as an expert healer, stating that she was called to cure Ana Sans with "pills that healed the four humours,"[32] which she herself made, and claimed other women had bewitched the sick. Later, at the insistence of Juan de Ochoa that she must cure his sister, María, she demurred:

> She excused herself by saying that she didn't know how to cure that disease, that she only knew remedies that could cure morbo gallico with pills made of sweet mercury, senna leaves, acibar, anise, and bread dough; the mixture had to be aged in order for the pills to be more effective.[33]

That is to say, María defends herself against the accusation of being a famous sorceress by claiming her identity as an empirical healer, with a precise knowledge of the preparation of pills and the simples of which they were composed. Moreover, the pills were used to cure a very specific illness: the French disease. This identity as a healer is shown even more clearly by María Sánchez de la Rosa when she justified the medicinal products in her house, which had been carefully inventoried by an apothecary of the court.

In summary, healers represented themselves, in accordance with the most appropriate strategy, as empirical, academic, or supernatural healers. How they represented their identity at a given time responded to the expectations of the people or groups they faced. Some, such as José Rodríguez, presented a consistent identity or subjectivity in all contexts, while others were more variable and flexible in different contexts, as they adapted to a particular sociocultural environment. We are thus faced with different representations of the paths of the collective imaginary, including not only a reaffirmation of the "empirical" self, but different narratives of the magical-credential that lay between orthodoxy and heterodoxy. The subjectivity represented was intimately related to the expectations of a group and the different roles they performed in different contexts and before different "audiences": I do what you want me to do, and I perform cures that respond to shared and accepted beliefs.

The Community's Story

During the reign of the Hapsburgs, legal and institutional systems were developed to control the health professions in early modern Spain. Doctors, surgeons, and apothecaries were corporative groups, organized into colleges or other entities concerned with the maintenance of control over their respective *corpora* of knowledge in the face of extra-official competitors; as noted above, women were explicitly excluded. Moreover, university-trained physicians of the late sixteenth and early seventeenth centuries attempted to dominate the practice of medicine and differentiate themselves from the competition.[34] Within this context, institutions of the old regime (the Inquisition, the civil and criminal courts) and the structures established to maintain "social order" tended to view *curanderos* with suspicion and derision, and to reject extra-academic *curanderos*. As B.J. Mollmann concludes, in Castile "authorities were far more concerned with quotidian uses of demonic power and the Spanish Inquisition arrested many more people for allegedly demonic healing than they did for witchcraft."[35] At the same time, in the communities in which they healed or acted as healers, *curanderos* were respected and recognized. Despite their lack of regulated qualifications, they were identified as people able to cure diseases, within a complex landscape of medical pluralism.

In order to "sell their cures" to the public, healers build an individuality that entails belief in their power to heal (*curan de muchos males*) and use the superstitious mentality of the baroque cosmology, as well as their ability and the effectiveness of their empirical practices. Healers explain their ability to heal not only by appealing to their neighbours' belief in the supernatural but also by presenting themselves as having the same cultural perception of health and sickness. In other words, healers often allow their communities to believe that the cures are supernatural, even when the *curanderos* themselves believe that the cures are natural.

As has been established in studies on identity and culture in the baroque, culture is never a monolithic or unique system, but is composed of different belief systems of subcultures with interrelated values.[36] People participate individually and collectively in such systems and in their conflicts and contradictions. For example, women, both as healers and as members of domestic and community life, were familiar with many medieval, Renaissance, and Counter-Reformation religious and medical stereotypes that were disseminated in sermons, books, paintings, and treatises that formed part of the popular culture that circulated in the streets. At the same time, women had other experiences that offered a different construction of the feminine through their everyday experiences as healers.[37] This produces two accounts, two stories that *curanderos* tell judges of the Inquisition: one of natural cures related for exculpation and another of what people believe about the supernatural cures. As J.A. Maravall pointed out, people all over Europe were inclined to hope for magical effects, for extra-natural events to bring them hope.[38] Belief in the supernatural held particular importance in popular practices surrounding health and disease: healers and patients were nourished with different medical practices throughout their lives, and the belief in magic and the supernatural was part of their socialization and acculturation.[39] The healer incorporates these assumptions into his or her treatments, to adapt to the expectations of patients. Conversely, expectations and interests defined the healer's identity before the community, as is clear in the testimonies for and against the accused.

For example, according to witnesses, Isabel de la Cruz, the Berber *ferrata* and former slave in mid-seventeenth-century Madrid, healed a man who was suffering from bewitchment through a complicated ritual lasting several days and using turtles and eels. In one part of the cure, Isabel de la Cruz wraps an egg in paper and buries the egg in a field. She then lies down on the egg. While she is lying on the spot where she has buried the egg, she instructs the sick man to step on her. If the egg breaks, he will be cured.[40] Similar marginal procedures, outlined in detail, appear in the stories of witnesses in the trial of Mariana Pérez, the itinerant woman who cured eye diseases with her saliva in Cuenca. In fact, in the case of Mariana Pérez, according to a witness, it was "publicly known that her saliva had the virtue of healing all diseases, and this was very well known to very different people in different parts."[41] Thus the community's story was told by patients as witnesses at the trial, and at the same time the sick people and their families explained the treatments carried out and the social perceptions of the healer.

The case of José Rodríguez is different. The grammar teacher and Valencian herbalist was arrested near Toledo, where he was teaching Latin and Greek and healing his patients with herbs. Rodríguez always claimed that he "only healed with herbs" and people of all ages turned to him for help. He cured men and women, noblemen and humble people unable to give something in return for the assistance. He cured cripples and the hobbled, ailing breasts and injured hands. Patients reported their experience and perception of a wholly empirical treatment; in other words, Rodríguez cured without resorting to the supernatural, a fact through which he achieved great fame.[42]

The testimony of the community could support or contradict accusations of superstition. Before the trial, patients, families and other community members had shared and exchanged experiences with a particular healer. From these shared experiences the healer acquired a good or bad reputation within the community. In the aforementioned process of María de la Rosa, Juan de Ochoa, who had denounced her, related how he found out about this woman from what was said in the community:

> Know, my friend, that this woman is the daughter of Rosa, the greatest witch of these times, who is imprisoned and was punished by the Inquisition. This old man is her servant and abettor of all her evils. He and his family were stunned, and the lady and his servant agreed that it would not be to their credit if these people were to enter her home.[43]

As witnesses to the proceedings, these same patients, relatives, and friends reproduced their experiences and perceptions, sometimes ambiguous and contradictory, before the court. Thus, Dominga Peláez, another patient of María de la Rosa, testified how she had suffered from a rare disease, symptoms of which included very large bumps on her head and chest. Deemed terminally ill by "surgeons and chemists," Dominga, upon the recommendation of other people in the community, sought Maria's help:

> The witness was in good health, but several big lumps grew on her head and chest, without her knowing the cause. She then called different people, from surgeons to chemists, in order to be healed, but all of them stated that there was no cure that could possibly make those lumps disappear. While

> in this state and feeling aggrieved, she learned of how María de la Rosa healed several diseases. Because of their existing friendship, she came to her for help.[44]

In conclusion, when patients, family, and friends accused certain healers of performing supernatural cures, these charges stemmed from complex circumstances and contexts, including the attitude of patients and their families before the practitioner and their therapeutic expectations. Accusations thus originated in the patient's behaviour and social environment as the cure progressed.[45]

The Accusers' Story

Accusers alleged that the healer performed superstitious practices, normally involving a pact with the devil. According to the accusation, this explained the success of the cures, which could not be explained as a result of natural causes. To defend themselves against the accusations, the healers claimed their knowledge was acquired empirically, and appealed to ideas from natural philosophy, as well as explanations from academic medicine. As Guido Ruggiero notes, the Holy Office "became heavily involved in investigating, documenting, and trying to discipline everyday culture in order to bring its spirituality and understanding of the world into the line with the formal teachings of the church."[46] Church teachings classified cures as natural or supernatural. The latter could include demonic or divine causes.

Was a cure natural or supernatural? This uncertainty was central to many of the accusations by inquisitors. It was at this point that a problem of natural philosophy appeared in most of the cases, as expressed in ratifications and in statements by the inquisitors. If the cure was achieved through the virtues of plants only, it pertained to what was "natural." If the cure could not be explained by reference to the natural effects or virtues of plants, inquisitors would consider it supernatural and attribute the cure to a covenant with the devil. Importantly, inquisitors did not always believe healers who said that they cured with herbs, as they claimed that only they could distinguish reliably between natural and supernatural. As Caro Baroja explains, the judges of the Inquisition were part of the same magical world they tried to destroy.[47] Even more important than the beliefs of the healers themselves were the beliefs that others had about them.

Inquisitors shared a baroque belief in magic, which led them to conceive of two categories of healing. On the one hand, there were totally acceptable practices, such as the use of medicinal plants or curing with grace. That is, while there were supernatural medical practices that were clearly religious deviations, and consequently had to be persecuted and punished, others had a supernatural origin very similar to the cures attributed to the saints, like grace. To these, we can add *saludadores* who cured with saliva and were authorized by the Inquisition to practise legally. In fact, many healers, such as Ambrosio Montes in the 1630s or Mariana Pérez, after a meeting with Inquisition theological consultants, received formal permission to practise.[48] On the other hand, there were illicit and illegal practices, or those who practised using falsified credentials.

In order to determine the truth, inquisitors resorted to experts who could ascertain certainty, including doctors and surgeons as well as priests and monks. But medical discourse was also important in assessing the veracity of the healers. As Andrew Keitt has observed, feigned sanctity "could be explained in pure physiological terms. The human body thus became a body of evidence in the Inquisition's attempt to distinguish" the natural from supernatural.[49] Take, for example, the aforementioned trial of two "urban" healers, the mother and daughter named María Sánchez de la Rosa and Elena Tordesillas, respectively, with contacts to the duke of Osuna.[50] Inquisitors ordered the seizure of the women's goods and a thorough inventory of all that was in the house. They then called an apothecary as an expert to examine medicinal products found there. The apothecary made a detailed report of each product and its pharmaceutical use and effects.[51] This process introduced the criterion of truth as determined by a scientific authority. In this trial, the apothecary and his inventory were ecclesiastical tools of control. Moreover, once the inventory was completed, the inquisitors asked María for what purpose she used the products they considered suspicious, and she answered

> that it is true that among the items she had in her house, she had several jars. These jars contained melted ram sebum, which was used for urinary diseases, melon seeds in case she wanted to prepare tiger nut milk with almonds, an ointment brought to her from the Antón Martín Hospital, and she also had items to cure sore shins and for healings in general.[52]

In María's answers about how she used each of the suspect products, her voice appears at the forefront. Furthermore, the problem of certainty here returns in all its complexity, as she claims that all were used either to cure people or for cooking, while according to the accusation they were used for bewitching practices.

In this same process there was also uncertainty about the origin of the disease, for which the inquisitors called another expert, a doctor. The doctor gave his opinion as to whether the illness suffered by Ana Sans had a natural or supernatural cause. In this case, the doctor could find no medicine that would have had any effect on her disorder, so her cousin suspected that his relative's condition was the work of a witch. For this reason, he formally accused María Sánchez de la Rosa and her daughter before the Tribunal of the Inquisition of being "dangerous sorceresses." That is, as in many other inquisitorial trials, medical discourse was employed in the scrutiny of extraordinary spiritual phenomena. Acts of this kind appear in other contexts, as in the case of Mariana Pérez. A surgeon and an apothecary were asked to explain what had happened with a patient who died after being treated by Pérez. The apothecary's response reveals his Galenism: "and while laughing, said apothecary said that everything had been done by orders of a woman, without preparing the patient. Therefore, the deponent … deduced that the patient had had the stroke because bloodletting hadn't taken place."[53] The inquisitors also drew on theological texts to authorize the judicial process. Scholars often tend to focus on the *Malleus maleficarum*, but there were other writings and books that were more commonly used, written in the language of the accusers and published in the same society and culture to which the accusers and denouncing witnesses belonged. The accusations and denunciations of the healers include ideas directly taken from theological texts written in Spanish, which provide textual authority for the accusations and serve to formulate the accusations.

I conclude with the aforementioned case of José Rodríguez. Rodríguez's problems began with an accusation of medical intrusion, that is, that he was improperly intruding into the domain of physicians. In particular, Rodríguez had a conflict with a doctor, Gaspar de Mayorga, that began with the arrival of Rodríguez in a rural Castilian town. As Timothy D. Walker has noted for Portugal and David Gentilcore for Naples, university physicians and surgeons were often very active in the inquisitorial proceedings against popular healers, and were frequently those who accused them.[54] In the case against José Rodríguez there were clear cultural reasons motivating the accusation, since the confrontation took place in the sphere of a system of beliefs and conceptions about health and illness that contained shared values, ideas, and concepts of rural life. At the same time, there was a clear problem of competition.

Rodríguez patently committed a wrong by intruding on the professional domain of physicians. He interfered with ongoing treatments, promising to heal by gentler methods, and also accepted cases rejected by physicians and surgeons. Rodríguez succeeded using unsanctioned methods, and denigrated physicians and surgeons in front of his patients, accusing them of ignorance or bad practice. In the case of the use of a *nómina*, before the healing of the sick, there was a dispute between the town doctor, Mayorga, and Rodríguez about how to heal a patient named María Moreno. The doctor said clearly that Rodríguez should not treat the sick woman, since her case was Mayorga's responsibility. Rodríguez, however, ignored this opinion, and insisted that he was able to heal patients whom traditional medicine had been unable to help. The resolution depended on the decision of the patient: although the intrusion was a crime because it cured by irregular means without respecting the legislation, it was the patient who determined in the end if intrusion had occurred.[55]

The conduct of the herbalist, on one hand, and the demand from patients, on the other hand, led to the direct confrontation between José Rodríguez and Mayorga, and the former was denounced to the Inquisition. The hostility between a man who was a teacher of grammar and herbalist and healthcare professionals of the area was evident from the beginning of the process. Mateo Terán, neighbour and surgeon of Villarejo de Salvanés, testified that Rodríguez's bad relationship with Mayorga was public and notorious, and this was confirmed by several witnesses.

It is not, therefore, strange that Rodriguez knew from the very beginning who had denounced him and why, even without knowing what he was going to be charged with: "He is in prison because of false witnesses that wish him wrong; they are barbers, surgeons, doctors and the like, because this one cures with herbs and he is said to have a pact with the devil." Mayorga is identified as his capital enemy: "He is a doctor, an enemy of his who wants to finish him ..., and wants him dead because he heals."[56]

The first letter of accusation from Mayorga, dated 17 July 1668, presents a whole series of reasons for the denunciation. It concludes that although Rodríguez appeared to heal with herbs, he was really curing by supernatural means and was misleading his desperate patients. Mayorga argues that Rodríguez had gained so much fame in such a short time that he could not have been using herbs to make the cures and insists that only supernatural elements could explain these unnatural cures. In this instance, it was the effectiveness of the cures that caused suspicion that

Rodríguez had used unorthodox remedies, since it was impossible to explain the healings from the perspective of academic medicine. This view is also supported by royal doctors, professors of the University of Alcalá, and classical medical texts. Therefore, Mayorga continues, he befriended Rodríguez in order to figure out what Rodríguez actually did to heal the sick. In other words, the doctor only pretended to befriend Rodríguez in an attempt to learn Rodríguez's secrets. The rest of the letter is full of the horror produced by the facts he is about to narrate. Finally he claims that Rodríguez cured patients thanks to a pact with the devil: "And he implied, with fear in his heart, which Lucifer had come from hell."[57] The main accusation was that the ointment was prepared with herbs, "and this way of healing he used as an instrument and to please people, so he did not want it to be known that it was with an express agreement with the devil"[58] (i.e., he was successfully healing with an ointment that, according to the medicine of the time, was likely to have no effect). Mayorga's inability to explain the cure in natural terms made him highly suspicious, so he accused Rodríguez of having a pact with the devil, the only possible way of explaining the healings he performed.

Another expert called in the case against Rodríguez was a Mercedarian friar, who claimed that the devil must be involved "because [in this case] the forces of nature do not have sufficient vigour to have power as medicine. That is St Thomas's opinion."[59] That is, based on Aquinas's doctrine on the natural law, the friar considered that it was impossible to justify a cure made by José Rodríguez using only plants' natural forces as medicine. Therefore, the only possible explanation was the use of a supernatural force, specifically a pact with the devil. Similarly, the unsystematic use of herbs was a central concern for both inquisitors and accusers. Inquisitors were especially suspicious whenever healers seemed to use herbs inconsistently, because this might be evidence that it was the devil and not the herbs that performed the cure. Inquisitors wanted to see consistent use of herbal remedies, or else they suspected supernatural causes.

Rodríguez was accused of conversations and deeds that had taken place before a series of witnesses, and of possession of a paper with a prayer that he used to cure the sick. It is curious that these charges exactly follow the "propositions from the mind of St Thomas" in the book of Pedro Sánchez de Acre, the Cathedral of Toledo *racionero* (prebendary), entitled *Historia moral y filosófica*, and published in Toledo in 1590.[60] While a more detailed analysis of this similarity is beyond the scope of this essay, this fact, given the place of publication of the work and the continuous use of the authority of St Thomas by one of the main accusers, the Mercedarian Pedro Cortegada, suggests a specific source, and a specific quarrel. Nevertheless, in the Spain of the time, there circulated abundant anti-superstition literature and there was a "profusion of theological theorizing on the subject." For example, Jerónimo Planes in his *Tratado del examen de las revelaciones verdaderas, y falsas, y de los raptos*, used arguments based on humoralism to explain extraordinary events such as raptures and human revelations.[61]

One of the accusers, the priest Francisco Joseph Martínez, relates that during the confrontation between the monk Cortenaga and the healer, Rodríguez said that St Thomas had never written about magic:

> A certain person from the church was arguing with him, mentioning a passage in which St Thomas condemned that way of healing. The convict said in public that St Thomas hadn't written about magic, in order to defend his doctrine and its practice.[62]

Martínez claims this to support the main charge that José Rodríguez was a necromantic expert who possessed, and had offered other people, a ring that contained within it a demon of great power. The demon inside this ring could give him all sorts of things, from treasures to love to, as for Faust, the promise of unlimited knowledge. From here the accusations alleged that he had detailed knowledge of demonology. Moreover, he was accused of having a copy of the *Key of Solomon*, a book of spells or *grimoire* of complicated textual transmission and a synthesis of magical writings attributed to Solomon, that was believed to provide its users with supernatural powers and influence over devils.[63] However, there was no indication that Rodríguez had books beyond those used to teach grammar. Finally, all the priests and friars who testified against Rodríguez accused him of cures that could only have been achieved through magic all based on the discussion that he had with Fray Pedro Cortegada about the authority of St Thomas on magic.

He was also accused of curing with *nóminas*. These *nóminas* were little pieces of paper that were carried in a small bag worn around the neck like a necklace. The *nóminas* contained the images of different saints as well as the text of Catholic prayers and strange characters: "Those lines contained the name of a demon in every one of its syllables; all the major ones, and the princes of hell."[64] This paper could cure diseases and prevented the carrier from being injured from a stab wound. Similarly, the inquisitors claimed that Rodríguez had diagnosed Matías Álvarez's sickness through supernatural means. Rodríguez in his defence said that what he reported next to the bed of the patient was a story of a sorceress of Valencia about a wax pin head; this was simply a story, not the means of treatment.[65]

In conclusion, despite the declared empiricism of Rodríguez, who presented himself as a pious person who performed healings with a universal remedy taught to him by an Italian, he was repeatedly charged with using magical practices. Even though the supernatural plays the most important role in the indictment against him, the majority of patients, with some exceptions, did not incorporate superstitious elements into their stories; they emphasized instead the manufacture and application of the ointment. Moreover, a sick woman eliminated any suspicion of a superstitious practice when she insisted that the cure was performed "without saying any words."[66]

This does not imply that the supernatural was not present in the perceptions of his patients. Popular medical culture has a long historical continuity, and is deeply interconnected with local customs. The supernatural was clearly part of the medical cultures of early modern Spain. But in the particular case of the herbalist Rodríguez, the supernatural did not have the significance for his patients that it had for his accusers: there were three stories, three sources, and three truths.

Conclusion

Why are these three stories different? The defendant and the witnesses do not necessarily have the same perception of crime, nor the same perception of a healer's training and practice. While for the inquisitors a certain practice was heretical, for the accused it might not be heresy. Thus the problem of truthfulness, always present in these trials, becomes even more complex. Moreover, while the medical practices in these cases are possible religious deviations (and as such punishable), they have a supernatural origin very similar to the cures attributed to the saints. Medical practice can thus be considered natural or supernatural, and if supernatural, either demonic or divine. Before the Inquisition there were three truths: the certainty of empiricism held by the healers, the certainty of magic and covenants with the devil held by the inquisitors, and the certainty of the patients about the healer's identity, given a communal recognition of the healer's ability to cure.

ACKNOWLEDGMENTS

This work is an outcome of the research project *Desde los márgenes. Cultura, experiencia y subjetividad en la Modernidad: Género, política y saberes (siglos XVII–XIX).* PGC2018-097445-A-C22, funded by Ministerio de Ciencia, Innovación y Universidades.

NOTES

1 Archivo Histórico Nacional, Madrid (hereafter AHN), Inquisición, 131, Exp. 10. All translations from period sources written originally in Spanish are my own.

2 Michael Stolberg, "Learning from the Common Folks: Academic Physicians and the Medical Lay Culture in the Sixteenth Century," *Social History of Medicine* 27, no. 4 (2014): 649–67; and the essential study by David Gentilcore, *Healers and Healing in Early Modern Italy* (Manchester: Manchester University Press, 1998).

3 Alfredo López Austin, *Los mitos del tlacuache: Caminos de la mitología mesoamericana* (Mexico: UNAM – Instituto de Investigaciones Antropológicas, 2006), 375.

4 About medical pluralism: Robert Jütte, Motzi Eklöf, and Marie C. Nelson, eds, *Historical Aspects of Unconventional Medicine: Approaches, Concepts, Case Studies* (Sheffield: European Association for the History of Medicine and Health, 2001); Robert Jütte, ed., *Medical Pluralism: Past, Present, Future* (Medizin, Gesellschaft und Geschichte 46) (Stuttgart: Franz Steiner Verlag, 2013); Gentilcore, *Healers and Healing* and "Was There a 'Popular Medicine' in Early Modern Europe?" *Folklore* 115, no. 2 (2004): 151–66; Laurence Brockliss and Colin Jones, *The Medical World of Early Modern France* (Cambridge: Cambridge University Press, 1997); and Willem De Blecourt and Cornelie Usborne, "Preface: Situating 'Alternative Medicine' in the Modern Period," *Medical History* 43, no. 3 (July 1999): 283–5.

5 Stolberg, *Experiencing Illness and the Sick Body in Early Modern Europe* (Basingstoke: Palgrave Macmillan, 2011); Philip Rieder, *La figure du patient au XVIII siècle* (Geneva: Droz, 2010); Wendy D. Churchill, *Female Patients in Early Modern Britain: Gender, Diagnosis, and Treatment* (Farnham: Ashgate, 2012); Carolin Schmitz, "Los enfermos en la España barroca (1600–1740) y el pluralismo medico: Espacios, estrategias y actitudes," PhD diss., Universitat de Valencia, 2016.

6 Mónica Bolufer Peruga and Isabel Morant Deusa, "Identidades vividas, identidades atribuidas," in *Entre dos orillas: Las mujeres en la Historia de España*

y América Latina, ed. Pilar Pérez-Fuentes (Barcelona: Icaria, 2012), 318.

7 Andrew Keitt, "The Miraculous Body of Evidence: Visionary Experience, Medical Discourse, and the Inquisition in Seventeenth-Century Spain," *The Sixteenth Century Journal* 36, no. 1 (2005): 83.

8 A seminal work is Luis Garcia Ballester, *Los moriscos y la medicina: Un capítulo de la medicina y la ciencia marginadas en la España del s. XVI* (Barcelona: Ed. Labor, 1984). New historiographical approaches can be found in María Tausiet, "Healing Virtue: *Saludadores* versus Witches in Early Modern Spain," *Medical History* 53, no. S29 (2009): 40–63; Fabián Alejandro Campagne, "El sanador, el párroco y el inquisidor: Los saludadores y las fronteras de lo supernatural en la España del Barroco," *Studia Historica: Historia Moderna* 29 (2007): 307–41 and *Strix hispánica: Demonología cristiana y cultura folklórica en la España moderna* (Buenos Aires: Prometeo Libros, 2009); Timothy D. Walker, *Doctors, Folk Medicine and the Inquisition: The Repression of Magical Healing in Portugal during the Enlightenment* (Leiden: Brill, 2005); Schmitz, "Los enfermos en la España barroca"; and Vincent Parello, "Entre herejía y hechicería: Isabel María de Montoya ante la Inq. de Toledo (1671)," *Les Cahiers de Framespa* 20 (2015), http://journals.openedition.org/framespa/3571 ; DOI: 10.4000/framespa.3571. Although the following refer to Mexico, they are extremely useful in understanding learning and revelation processes, and provide countless examples of inquisitorial trials against healers that are totally applicable to the area under study here: Gonzalo Aguirre Beltrán, *Medicina y magia: el proceso de aculturación en la estructura colonial* (México: Instituto Nacional Indigenista, 1973); Noemí Quezada, *Enfermedad y maleficio: El curandero en el México colonial* (Mexico: Universidad Nacional Autónoma de México, 1989), 35–43; and Mary Elizabeth Perry and Anne J. Cruz, eds, *Cultural Encounters: The Impact of the Inquisition in Spain and the New World* (Berkeley: University of California Press, 1991).

9 James S. Amelang, "Los loros de Parets: Reflexiones sobre una fuente autobiográfica," *Estudis* 30 (2004): 7–20 and *The Flight of Icarus: Artisan Autobiography in Early Modern Europe* (Stanford: Stanford University Press, 1998).

10 A comprehensive account of these studies does not fall within the limits of this analysis; the works in note 8 are worthy of mention and contain more complete bibliographies.

11 Enrique Perdiguero, "El fenómeno del pluralismo asistencial: Una realidad por investigar," *Gaceta Sanitaria* 18, no. 4 (August 2004): 140–5.

12 M.L. López-Terrada, "The Control of Medical Practice under the Spanish Monarchy during the Sixteenth and Seventeenth Centuries," in *Más allá de*

la Leyenda Negra: España y la Revolución Científica / Beyond the Black Legend: Spain and the Scientific Revolution, ed. Victor Navarro Brotons and William Eamon (Valencia: Instituto de Historia de la Ciencia y Documentación López Piñero, 2007), 281–94.

13 Bolufer and Morant, "Identidades vividas, identidades atribuidas," 330.

14 Giovanni Levi, *La herencia inmaterial: La historia de un exorcista piamontés del siglo XVII* (Madrid: Nerea, 1990), 12.

15 Mary Lindemann, *Medicine and Society in Early Modern Europe* (Cambridge: Cambridge University Press, 1999), 121–2, 249.

16 Alison Klairmont Lingo, "Empirics and Charlatans in Early Modern France: The Genesis of the Classification of the 'Other' in Medical Practice," *Journal of Social History* 19, no. 4 (1986): 583–603.

17 Natalie Zemon Davis, *Fiction in the Archives: Pardon Tales and Their Tellers in Sixteenth-Century France* (Stanford: Stanford University Press, 1987), 4.

18 Barbara B. Diefendorf and Carla Hesse, *Culture and Identity in Early Modern Europe (1500–1800): Essays in Honor of Natalie Zemon Davis* (Ann Arbor: University of Michigan Press, 1993), 7, 280.

19 Bolufer and Morant, "Identidades vividas, identidades atribuidas," 317–52.

20 AHN, Inquisición, 84, Exp. 9.

21 AHN, Inquisición, 94, Exp. 13.

22 AHN, Inquisición, 82, Exp. 26 and 27.

23 AHN, Inquisición, 86, Exp. 11.

24 Lingo, "Empirics and Charlatans," 593.

25 Gianna Pomata, "Practicing between Earth and Heaven: Women Healers in Seventeenth-Century Bologna," *Dynamis* 19 (1999): 119–43.

26 AHN, Inquisición, 94, Exp. 13. About his life and his patients, see C. Schmitz and M.L. López-Terrada, "Josep Rodríguez, herbolari valencià, i els seus pacients de la ribera del Tajo: Les cultures mèdiques en el món rural barroc," *Afers: Fulls de recerca i pensament* 30, no. 82 (2015): 523–50.

27 "En el nombre del Padre, del Hijo y del Espíritu Santo ... y tres credos a la Santísima Trinidad, y el Padrenuestro, y un Avemaría a señor San Antoni ... untaba la parte enferma con un poco de ungüento blanco y si tenían costras los enfermos los rociaba con un poco de vino blanco para que se ablandaran." AHN, Inquisición, 82, Exp. 8.

28 AHN, Inquisición, 84, Exp. 9.

29 For the meanings of the Spanish word *gracia* (grace) in early modern Spain and as a general anthropological concept, see Julián Pitt-Rivers, "El lugar de la gracia en la antropología," in *Honor y gracia*, ed. Julián Pitt-Rivers and J.G. Peristiany (Madrid: Alianza, 1993), 280–321.

30 Archivo Diocesano de Cuenca (hereafter ADC), 1655, legajo 496, Exp. 659.

31 "En particular a la dicha doña Ana Sans, que la tiene hechizada en tanta forma que no ha tenido ora de salud. Y el exorcista que la asiste ha dicho que los tiene muy profundos, de forma que no puede dormir. Y después que dio el papel para denunciación al Señor Inquisidor se le aumentaron los dolores y congojas y del todo se le han sacado las ganas de comer, de forma que se va secando." AHN, Inquisición, legajo 96, Exp. 2–3.

32 "Píldoras que curaban de los cuatro humores." AHN, Inquisición, legajo 96, Exp. 2–3.

33 "Se escusó diciendo no savia curar de aquel mal, que solo savia remedios para curar el morbo gálico con unas píldoras que se componen de mercurio dulce, oja de sen, acivar, anis y masa de pan, que estuviese bien añexa la masa de dichas píldoras porque asi obraban mexor." AHN, Inquisición, legajo 96, Exp. 2–3.

34 For this period see Lingo, "Empirics and Charlatans." For Spain: López-Terrada, "Control of Medical Practice."

35 B.J. Mollmann, "Healing with Demons? Preternatural Philosophy and Superstitious Cures in Spanish Inquisitioral Courts," in *Demons and Illness from Antiquity to the Early Modern Period*, ed. Sian Bhayro and Catherine Rider (Leiden: Brill, 2016), 386.

36 Harald E. Braun and J. Pérez-Magallón, *The Transatlantic Hispanic Baroque: Complex Identities in the Atlantic World* (London: Routledge, 2014) and other essays of the Conflicting Identities research group, http://baroque-identities.mcgill.ca/. In medicine: J. Slater, M.L. López-Terrada, and José Pardo-Tomás, eds, *Medical Cultures of the Early Modern Spanish Empire* (Farnham: Routledge, 2014).

37 Diefendorf and Hesse, *Culture and Identity*, 3, 280; James Casey, "Quebrar el espejo: El 'yo' y la contrarreforma," in *El otro, el mismo: Biografía y autobiografía en Europa (siglos XVII–XX)*, ed. J. Colin Davis and Isabel Burdiel (València: Universitat de València, 2005), 125.

38 José Antonio Maravall, *La cultura del Barroco* (Barcelona: Ariel, 1990), 461–2.

39 Stolberg, *Experiencing Illness*; Schmitz, "Los enfermos en la España barroca."

40 AHN, Inquisición, 84, Exp. 9.

41 ADC, 1655, legajo 496, Exp. 6592.

42 AHN, Inquisición, 94, Exp. 13.

43 "Pues sabed amigo que ésta mujer es hija de la Rosa, la mayor bruja que es conozida en estos siglos, la qual está en la galera, y fue castigada por el Santo Tribunal, y este viejo es su criado encubridor en todas sus maldades. Y el referido y su familia se quedaron aturdidos y se dieron por entendidos dama y criado que no convenía a su crédito entrasen en su casa." AHN, Inquisición, legajo 96, Exp. 2–3.

44 "Y estando la testigo buena y sana la salieron unos bultos muy grandes en la cabeza y en el pecho sin saber la causa que podía haver para aquello, y llamó a diferentes personas así zirujanos como químicos para que la curasen, y en efecto todos comunicaron en que no havía cura ni la allaban para quitarla dichos bultos. Y allándose aflixida la dieron noticia como la dicha María de la Rosa curava de diferentes achaques y por la amistad que le tenía con ella la buscó para que la curase." AHN, Inquisición, legajo 96, Exp. 2–3.

45 R.C. Sawyer, "'Strangely Handled in All Her Lyms': Witchcraft and Healing in Jacobean England," *Journal of Social History* 22, no. 3 (1989): 469; Schmitz, "Los enfermos en la España barroca."

46 Guido Ruggiero, "The Strange Death of Margarita Marcellini: Male, Signs, and the Everyday World of Pre-modern Medicine," *American Historical Review* 106, no. 4 (October 2001): 1141–58.

47 J. Caro Baroja, *Vidas mágicas e Inquisición* (Madrid: Taurus, 1967), 136–7.

48 Mollmann, "Healing with Demons?," 396–411; Mariana Pérez: ADC, 1655, legajo 496, Exp. 6592.

49 Keitt, "The Miraculous Body of Evidence," 83.

50 Carolin Schmitz and I are currently working on a monographic work about these two women and their patients.

51 "Dixo que los jeneros referidos son en numero hasta veinteyocho ... Y que los reconocidos son: flor de açufre, piedra imán, çinabiro, antimonio, pepitas de melones, cañamones, papeles de recetas medicinales, y un libro mano escripto que trata de operaciones químicas minerals." AHN, Inquisición, 96, Exp. 2.

52 "Que es cierto que entre los demás trastos que tenia en su casa tenía diferentes vasijas varias cosas, en unas sebo de carnero derretido para untarse para el mal de urina, pepitas de melón por si se ofrecía hazer una orchata almendrada, ungüento de unciones que le llevó de Antón Marín, y le tenía para curar si se ofrecía algún sobregueso y para las sanaciones." AHN, Inquisición, 96, Exp. 2.

53 "Y riyéndose dicho Voticario dixo que todo se avía echo de horden de una mujer, y esto sin prepararle ni disponerle, de donde coligió este declarante ... la aplopesia abía resultado de no aberle sangrado ni purgado." ADC, 1655, legajo 496, Exp. 6592.

54 Walker, *Doctors, Folk Medicine and the Inquisition;* Gentilcore, *Healers and Healing.*

55 Schmitz and López-Terrada, "Josep Rodríguez, herbolari valencià," 523–50.

56 "Es que está preso por testigos falsos que le quieren mal, que son barberos, zirujanos y médicos y otros tales, porque éste cura con yerbas, y que dizen que este tiene pauto"; "es un médico enemigo capital suyo que le tiene

jurado ante Dios, ... y que a éste le quiere mal de muerte porque cura." AHN, Inquisición, legajo 94, Exp. 13, fols 101v and 119v.

57 "Y me dijo el corazón traspasado de miedo, entendiendo abía baxado Lucifer de su infierno." Additionally, Mayorga frequently spoke in his statements about his close relationship with the Protomedicato; thus he was also seeking civil legitimacy through this accusation, and attempted to demonstrate tacitly that, unlike Mayorga, the herbalist was practising medicine without being approved. AHN, Inquisición, legajo 94, Exp. 13, fol. 7r. About the Protomedicato as a Spanish board of physicians responsible for regulating medical practitioners and inspecting apothecary shops see Soledad Campos, *El Real Tribunal del Protomedicato castellano: Siglos XIV–XIX* (Cuenca: Ediciones de la Universidad de Castilla-La Mancha, 1999).

58 "Y modo de curar lo tomaba por instrumento y por cumplir con la jente para que no viniesen en conocimiento de que su obrar era con pacto expreso con el diablo." AHN, Inquisición, legajo 94, Exp. 13, fol. 11r.

59 "Por raçón de que le faltan las fuerças de la naturaleça para poder llevar el vigor de la medicina. Y esta es opinión de Santo Tomás." AHN, Inquisición, legajo 94, Exp. 13, fol. 76r. On Thomas Aquinas and cures considered miracles: Michael E. Goodich, *Miracles and Wonders: The Development of the Concept of Miracle, 1150–1350* (New York: Routledge, 2016), esp. 55–6.

60 Pedro Sánchez de Acre, *Historia moral y filosófica* (Toledo: En casa de la viuda de Juan de la Plaza, 1590), fols 145r–147r.

61 Jerónimo Planes, *Tratado del examen de las revelaciones verdaderas, y falsas, y de los raptos* (Valencia: Por la viuda de J.C. Garriz, 1634), fol. 379ff. About the incorporation of medical discourse into anti-superstitious literature, see Keitt, "The Miraculous Body of Evidence," 83; and Campagne, *Homo Catholicus, Homo Superstitiosus: El discurso antisupersticioso en la España de los siglos XV al XVIII* (Buenos Aires: Miño y Dávila, 2002).

62 "Arguyendo con él cierta persona eclesiástica i citándole una autoridad de santo Thomas que reprovava sus modos de curar, dijo en voz publica el reo: que Santo Tomás, ni santo Thomás, que santo Thomás no escribió sobre lo májico, sustentando su doctrina i práctica de ella." AHN, Inquisición, legajo 94, Exp. 13, fols 44v–45v.

63 Caro Baroja, *Vidas mágicas,* 136–7, 141, 146; Federico Barbierato, *Nella stanza dei circoli: Clavicula Salomonis e libri di magia a Venezia nei secoli XVII e XVIII* (Milan: Edizioni Sylvestre Bonnard, 2002).

64 "Aquellos renglones en cada sílava y razón de ellos, se contenía un nombre de un demonio, i que todos eran de los príncipes i maiores." AHN, Inquisición, legajo 94, Exp. 13, fol. 114v.

65 Ibid., fol. 120v.

66 Ibid., fols 41v–42r.

chapter four

True *Peste* and False Doors: Medical and Legal Discourse during the Great Castilian Plague, 1596–1601

RUTH MacKAY

When Philip III in 1599 asked Dr Luis Mercado to reissue his plague treatise in the vernacular, the monarch wrote: "Given that one understands there is great hardship in my kingdoms of Castile, with the *peste* occurring in such a widespread and pernicious manner, it seems necessary to write a treatise so that all provinces, cities, towns, and villages can understand and know with certainty which disease it is and how they should protect themselves."[1] It was certainty that was needed.

Philip came to the throne shortly after the arrival of the Iberian Peninsula's worst episode of bubonic plague. It landed in November 1596 in Santander, on board a ship from the Low Countries, and departed some five years later after an estimated half-million people had died, possibly 10 per cent of the population of Castile.[2]

In sickness and in health, Castilians never lost sight of the common good, whether genuinely or rhetorically. This was true even during times of terrible hardship, though in sixteenth-century Castilian villages and towns hardship was no stranger, and famine always hovered nearby. Despite the enormous suffering unleashed by the turn-of-the-century plague, there was no chaos and things did not fall apart. Rather, deep-seated practices, ideas, and memories grounded in political and juridical structures were put to use, as always. Just because one's neighbours were dying and one was trapped behind a quarantine was no reason to abandon centuries of law and custom. The plague wrecked hundreds of thousands of lives and large swaths of the economy. But it did not destroy Castilians' reverence for the machinery of justice and politics, for the methods that for centuries had helped them determine what was true, what was fair, what had been done in the past. Those procedures were their way of understanding the world and weighing evidence, regardless of whether to settle a dispute, make a claim, or cure a disease.

Medical treatises, like legal briefs, laid out the observable facts and testimony, offered a narrative, then ventured diagnoses. Though medical and legal professionals were concerned with different things, both engaged in efforts to discern truth. In both cases it was repetition that counted; always, more was better. The quality of a particular statement mattered less than the quantity, though it is important to note that even an argument backed up by piles of papers, testimony, and precedents was still only a starting point for negotiations, whether in a court of law or in the medical arena.[3] Medical and civil authorities during the time of pestilence used evidence-based procedures to determine the identity of the disease, its presence or absence, its impact on local economies, and the reliability and credibility of witnesses providing information. As medical experts and practitioners conducted their research they collected testimony on everything, allowing civic and royal officials to decide how much to bend rules or give in, and what was the most prudent thing to do. Enough precedents might add up to the truth.

As they conducted their inquiries, these authorities were accompanied by notaries, who were ubiquitous and essential in all Castilian civic and legal affairs. One could make decisions only when one was in a position of knowing something, and the presence and seal of a notary was proof or authentication that something had in fact been said or done. Notaries followed doctors around, stood by the town gate as the poor were expelled and given pocket money, recorded oral testimony, noted down requisitioned properties, wrote city council minutes, and tagged along on inspections of pestilent houses. Their names and seals were on safe-conducts stating where travellers were coming from and if they had been anywhere infected.[4]

Almost immediately after word arrived of the plague's likely approach, town officials sent out what amounted to a small army of envoys, messengers, and inspectors who crowded the pestilent roads and paths of Castile attempting to verify and quantify the alarming rumours and, as the king had requested, to "understand the nature of the illness." They were city council members, doctors, police constables (*alguaciles*), notaries, or deputized town citizens whose mission it was to find out what was going on elsewhere. Their efforts, obviously, completely undermined the quarantine. The messengers not only gathered what they hoped was reliable information; they also disseminated it in the form of orders. Envoys travelled holding high the staff of justice, *la vara alta de justicia*, making them the visible and rightful personification of royal authority. Local authorities had to receive and acknowledge these orders, swear to uphold them, and arrange for their own town criers to publicize them. The criers (*pregoneros*) themselves frequently were notaries, hence speakers of truth, or were accompanied by notaries as they informed townspeople of the latest edicts. In small towns *pregoneros* probably would limit themselves to the main square, church steps, and a few other important gathering places, but in larger cities they were everywhere as they walked defined routes; in Madrid on 12 June 1602, *pregones* warning residents about all the towns in the south suffering from plague were cried aloud at as many as thirty-four sites.[5] During plague years, town criers read (and reread) the lists of pestilent towns, warned innkeepers to reject guests without proper identification, ordered people to report their dead and hand over their linens, threatened punishments for tearing down portions of walls, and summoned the poor to gather at specific locations for sorting and expulsion after distribution of alms. Their shadows, the notaries, were there not only to make sure the correct information was being read aloud, but also as witnesses to testify that the act had, indeed, occurred. When several muleteers were prohibited from entering Burgos in January 1597, very few people in the city would have missed the news:

> In the city of Burgos on this day month and year, before me, the public notary, in the plaza of this city, Francisco de la Cruz, the city's public *pregonero*, read in a loud and intelligible voice what had been ordered and agreed upon by the above-noted gentlemen ... and I, the said notary [declare] that there were many people in the plaza of this city ... and it was *pregonado* again ... before many *vecinos* and people in the *arrabal* of San Esteban and in the little plaza of San Esteban and in many other places ... where such *pregones* usually are by custom read aloud, and there were many people present.[6]

The announcements and inspections were undertaken to impart and receive information. But that process faced the immediate challenge of how to determine if that information was any good. Everyone lied about their state of health, cheerfully reassuring all who asked that really, they were just fine. Everyone else knew that this was the case, as they themselves were doing the same, or would do so once the disease arrived, so the trick was for one town to figure out ways of truly knowing what their neighbours' state of health was. In their frantic efforts to find out the truth, town councils instructed their messengers which specific questions to ask and of whom, always draping the exercise in legal ceremony.

One example of improved specificity came when Burgos sent Cristóbal de Morales to visit the important and very troubled town of Melgar de Fernamental and its neighbours in April 1598. He was given a list of questions to ask: when had the disease arrived; what sort of disease was it; how many people got sick and died, what were their names and what sort of people were they; if the houses where they got sick and died had been closed up and if they were now open; if the houses had been reopened, how had they been reopened, and had they been cleaned with perfumed vinegar; had the clothing and linens been burned; and if the town or village was healthy, how long had it been healthy? For every item, Morales was to obtain written and notarized testimony from witnesses who could give reasons for what they said and explain how they knew what they said, and point to people, houses, and linens "so the truth can be determined" (*de suerte que se averigue verdad*). Once the questioning was over, Morales was to summon a variety of officials in every town he visited, put them under oath, and then ask them if the town was healthy and free of contagion and *peste* and for how long it had been that way, "so that without endangering or harming health the said town may conduct business and communication with this city of Burgos and the other cities, towns, and villages in these kingdoms, warning them that if they should declare something other than the truth and if some hardship or harm should occur as a result, they will be severely punished … And in the same manner you should summon the chapter of the clergy in the town and have them testify."[7] Finally, Morales was told to be very careful about his own health, stay in each place as briefly as possible, and charge each town a prorated daily rate of four hundred *maravedies* for his efforts.[8]

Almost by definition, nearly all stories about how the plague reached a given place involved someone coming from elsewhere, whether a visitor, a vendor, a vagabond, or someone expelled from another town. Often it was a woman carrying cloth or a man seeking lodging. Travellers brought news and essential products, yet they also brought disease. By tradition they were to be welcomed; now they were to be feared. We have a small, vivid example from Cogollos, just outside Burgos. City authorities in July 1597 told Philip II how some people from Santander had lodged in Cogollos, and how after they shared food and space with their hosts the deadly disease made its way through the town, and now thirty-six people were dead.[9] But during much of those six months of tenacious infection, Burgos, just a few miles up the road, apparently had been in the dark. Cogollos had been deliberately secretive, the Burgos governor (*corregidor*) told the king, which was why Burgos's attempts at information-gathering had been fruitless until the death toll reached such a point that there was no possibility anymore of hiding the dreadful truth. Churchmen were dispatched to order the town priest to open up his registry, where the dead were listed. The churchmen were followed by a surgeon and, naturally, a notary. Until then, there had been rumours, sightings of houses where no one remained, suggestions not to tie up one's horses in a given spot, but the news was not reliable, nor were the city's orders obeyed.

No one from Santander was supposed to enter Cogollos in the first place – or anywhere else, for that matter. Such a disaster could have happened only if there were no guards at the town gates or if the guards were not doing their job properly. Anyone who wanted to go in or out of a town in theory had to present proof that they were free of disease and had not been anywhere that was infected. Safe-conducts were signed by priests and notaries, the two classes of people with unquestioned access to truth. Vendors might have a collection of these papers by the end of their journey, testifying to their route through allegedly healthy towns and to the cleanliness of all the merchandise they were carrying. The documents also certified where they were from, so that even when they were on the road they still belonged somewhere.

In Segovia, one of the log books kept by guards during the plague has survived.[10] It lists those who entered the city through the Cal de Gascos gate in 1598, though not those who were turned away. Possibly the absence of the latter means no one was refused entry, but that is unlikely. The book opens with instructions from the *corregidor* stipulating that guards (who were deputized citizens of the city) were to work in pairs from 4 a.m. to 10 p.m. and that violations would be punished "rigorously." The book also includes ever-changing lists of infected, off-limits towns that the guards consulted as people appeared at the gate. On 28 June, for example, guards Juan Navarro (an apothecary) and Juan de Montoya recorded around thirty individuals or groups entering the city, including Juan de Piedra, a *vecino* from Pedraza carrying testimony from the Pedraza notary;[11] Juan de Baeza, Francisco López, and Juan García de Andrés, *vecinos* from a village near Pedraza, who were carrying three loads of wool certified by the notary in Collado; two more *vecinos* from the same place with ten cartloads of wool who explained that they had obtained testimony from the Collado notary only because they had passed through there; Alonso Martínez, a *vecino* from Tudela de Duero with notarized testimony from Tudela; Francisco Sastre Capón, a Segovia *vecino* heading home with wine from Tudela de Duero; and María, a priest's servant, who had testimony from the notary of Sotosalbos, Alonso del Cauto. On 6 July two women from Navafría arrived. They were *vecinas* and "said their names were" Juana Álvarez, fifty years old, and María García, twenty, daughter of Juana. They were short, the guard wrote. They swore their testimony was true. A boy around fifteen years old dressed in black also entered, coming from Collado. On 17 July a man named Lucas García came in from Sepúlveda in search of his master. These travellers and many more came from throughout the province of Segovia and the surrounding provinces; they were farmers, vendors, servants, muleteers, clerics. On the busiest day, 23 July, there were seventy-four individuals or groups, though that was unusual.

The traveller's truth, as reflected in his or her papers, might not match the truth of the guard, who in theory abided by the list of infected towns posted at the gate (sometimes hidden to travellers, so they couldn't improvise accounts of their itinerary) and by their own instincts, which naturally were open to persuasion. Guards let in people from suspect places and blocked travellers with clean bills of health, in both cases presumably because they stood to gain, but whatever the outcome, all parties offered defences for their actions that relied upon certificates, royal orders, notaries' seals, and testimony.

If itineraries had to be proven (or alleged) to make a case for sickness or health, a similar exercise took place with staged truth-finding sessions to determine if the debacle of the plague truly merited reducing a town's or city's taxes, a frequent request once the disease had moved on. One after another, *vecinos* (or *vecinos* from neighbouring towns, who were said to be more objective) testified as to the appalling state of affairs in a given town, always contrasting it to a much sunnier recent past. One after another, these witnesses who had seen or experienced the facts in question said one-third or three-quarters of the townspeople had died or left; a local tax collector showed how much he used to collect and how much he collected now; old people with long memories confirmed the dramatic losses. The notarized testimony was sent off to the relevant authority (financial councils, the Cortes, or even the king). If it was rejected, more testimony was collected and sent off again.

At the start of this chapter I referred to deep-seated practices, ideas, and memories that somehow survived the onslaught of disaster. In that regard, there was possibly no more important and resilient structure than the judiciary, both institutionally and discursively. The crisis of the plague would to a large extent be managed through the use of longstanding judicial mechanisms and procedures adapted to the suddenly urgent circumstances. Wherever one was, socially or geographically, to receive justice one had to speak, stating verifiable facts – the truth – again and again, in as many forums as necessary. The proliferation of courts and tribunals offered the possibility for nearly endless appeals or, at the very least, long negotiations. The nature of the system, both in good times and in bad, was always to appeal and tell one's story to make sure one's truth was heard.[12]

Medicine was not much different, following similar steps as legal and civic truth-testing, where a multitude of statements was required. Medical debates were often a collective affair that took place not only in palaces and city halls, as the crown and towns summoned medical experts to rule, as it were, on the disease, but also in public with the public. Doctors and officials relied on the observations of *vecinos* and local medical staff and listened carefully (or carefully read) their responses to the batteries of questions put to them, which were often the same as the questions put to civic leaders: When did the disease first arrive? What were the symptoms? How did the illness move? How many had died? What sort of people were they? Doctors seem to have violently disagreed with one another, which was sometimes taken as evidence (again) that they really didn't know very much. Indeed, some treatises opened with sarcastic references to the author's patently inferior colleagues: Miguel Martínez de Leyva, a former doctor who had worked in a Seville hospital during an epidemic in the 1580s that probably was influenza, not plague, noted that practitioners were "veterinarians and idiots" looking for buboes that did not exist.[13] And the accomplished doctor Valentín de Andosilla griped about "pseudo-doctors with tyrannical interests and vile earnings committing a thousand idiocies and reckless acts with patients, hitting the nail once for every hundred swings of the hammer."[14]

Andosilla was one of the very few medical professionals I could find who wrote a practical account of his experience during the plague epidemic (in La Rioja, in his case). He suggested remedies (including in places where he said there were no doctors, surgeons, or medicines) and described in detail what would appear to have been sensible public health programs to halt what he was convinced was not *peste* at all but rather a new disease. Another writer who relied upon empirical evidence was Antonio Ponce de Santa Cruz, a professor of medicine in Valladolid and the first to spot a plague patient in his city, though the city council disagreed with him and ignored his alert. (The plague was in any case surely impossible to prevent in Valladolid, which lost nearly 20 per cent of its inhabitants, but had his advice been taken perhaps it could have been curtailed.)[15] Ponce de Santa Cruz later wrote a bitter treatise mocking those (including the more famous Luis Mercado) who rejected *peste* as a diagnosis because not enough people had died. His supremely logical argument once again reflects the truth-finding methods of practising physicians:

> There are those who think a disease is not *peste* until it affects many people and kills most of them. It is a sad occasion when a doctor and a republic must wait until most of the population is finished off before they can identify the enemy in their home ... Let me make clear that *peste* exists starting with the first patient, and there is no need to wait for others to be infected ... I ask those who commit this error: when they see a fire from afar but do not feel its heat, is it any less a fire? They are obliged to say no ... they wish that it not be *peste* because it has not killed many ... by which they are confusing Act 1 with Act 2.[16]

Most other accounts were less narrative and far more formulaic than Andosilla's and Santa Cruz's.[17] They listed the various foods that should or should not be consumed and discussed air quality, bleeding techniques, potions, vapours, the moon, the essential trueness or falseness of the disease, and the quality (pernicious or not) of the buboes. It is hard to believe they were of any use; one exception may have been recipes and lists of permitted foods for plague patients, probably consulted overwhelmingly by women.[18] Far more useful was the trial and error described in municipal documents, the sifting of evidence, the formal and informal surveys, the summing up of cases with enough evidence to prove one conclusion or another. As with the negotiations to obtain tax reductions, and the incessant public meetings to discuss security matters such as walls and guard duty, the wide-open space of the public sphere, be it physical gatherings or the exchange of written opinions and featuring as many responsible voices as possible, provided some guarantee to good medical professionals that they might be able to venture an intelligent opinion. The disease, after all, was a public matter, and *vecinos* were in effect participating as health officials; it was they who stopped or allowed traffic, oversaw cleaning campaigns, watched over sick houses, carried the dead, probably spied on their neighbours, and certainly spread rumours. This was what Andrew Mendelsohn has called “knowing in common.”[19]

The determination of truth obviously entailed the rejection of falsity, in an era obsessed with disguise and dissimulation. The municipal and medical battle against bubonic plague involved sniffing out what were called false keys (to evade gate controls), false doors (passageways carved out of walls or simply spaces punched through quarantine barriers), false news, false plague (any disease that pretended to be plague but was not), the ever-present false poor, and disguised travellers, meaning anyone who entered a town bringing disease with them. They were disguised, they were false, they had violated the peacefulness and truth of a town's prior existence. Such was the case in Andosilla's experience: "During this peaceful time it is said that a disguised young woman came from a place where people were sick with this poison, and she died very quickly with burning fever and swelling [*su seca*]." For a while no one else died, but then suddenly they did, "and as the enemy had approached with such slow steps, it could easily deceive us."[20] A man prosecuted in Burgos for having sheltered travellers from the north likewise was accused of dissimulation. The prosecutor pointed out how grave a crime Andrés Alonso had committed by taking in people from Santander, thereby risking "the total ruin and death of the city," and by having "disguised the enemy in clothing very different from what they wore when they went to his house, knowing full well that they were sick and pestilent" and were from a land "devastated by plague." He was a "traitor to the patria," and had shown malice aforethought (*dolo*) in giving refuge to the three pestilent men. In fact, the prosecutor argued, Alonso deserved the death penalty not only for having endangered the city but for having dissimulated.[21]

As the plague advanced, towns set up blockades (whether bureaucratic, physical, or fiscal) impeding products, people, and money. In these conditions survival often depended upon deceit, and not only for people like Andrés Alonso, or someone escaping quarantine to visit family, or a travelling salesman trying to bring cloth into a town. It was also the case for the very officials who were issuing the quarantine orders and writing the latest versions of the surveys aimed at establishing certainty.

Underlying it all was the question of trust. The fact that assurances of good health from one town were generally met with a small invasion of messengers and spies sent by another town whose job it was to determine the true state of affairs indicates that most towns distrusted the claims of others, probably because they knew that, were the situation reversed, they too would lie, saying they were healthy when they were not. At stake was reputation, and there were few more important concepts in Castile. As Mark Harrison wrote, commerce during times of plague is "a game of chess with many players, each of which attempts to second-guess the actions of the others."[22]

Lies, or simply breezy assurances of health, work only if they are credible; if everyone is doing it, then credibility is strained. Liars, in other words, have good reason to distrust others. But, possibly outweighing that drawback, the more good news there is floating around, the less the potential risk of lost reputation. Lies thus reflected a way of doing business within a network of political relations. Officials everywhere who reported early calamities assured the palace that great care had been taken to keep the matter quiet, to avoid *ruidos*, to alarm no one.[23]

If this was a game, albeit in difficult conditions, there were no more important players than the commercial cities of Burgos and Bilbao, which critically needed each other and needed to be believed by the other. Both had brokers, agents, and traders stationed throughout the Iberian Peninsula and Europe. The Catholic Monarchs in the late fifteenth century had licensed the consulate of Burgos to, among other things, make decisions regarding fleets and merchant insurance for goods arriving in the port of Bilbao, which did not please the latter city. Queen Juana gave Bilbao its own trade guild in 1511. Throughout the sixteenth century the two interdependent cities, while continuing to squabble, together "represented one of the most important pillars of the Spanish economy, one of its great poles of growth."[24] Shipowners in Bilbao had close commercial and family links to merchants in Burgos, from whence most northern coastal production was distributed throughout the peninsula and which also channelled peninsular products north to the ports. Bilbao was a centre for fishing, timber, shipbuilding, and iron. It was an inexpensive port to operate out of, a storage depot, and a market in itself, and by the end of the sixteenth century it had emerged as the leading Cantabrian port. In 1568 when Laredo (less favourably situated) fell to epidemic, ships from the Low Countries had shifted their cargo to Bilbao, so everyone knew what was at stake.[25] Bilbao, despite having been infected earlier by the plague than inland cities, which put it at an immediate disadvantage, was on the rise, while Burgos was most certainly past its prime.[26] But the great Castilian city, which had the honour of being addressed above all other cities as "the very noble and very most loyal city of Burgos, seat of Castile," was not quite yet out of the picture, if for no other reason than geography.[27]

A letter from the Burgos *corregidor*, Diego de Vargas Manrique, to the Council of Castile in early 1598, as Burgos and Bilbao played their deadly game of deceit and false hope, shows he understood perfectly the pitfalls of relying on other people's word. "In Burgos," he wrote, "it is said, and it has been written, that Vitoria has *peste*, with five or six houses closed up. Many times I have determined that similar news turns out to be false, the result of various sorts of enmities and jealousies, which I would like to put a stop to with punishments." But, he told the council, public health was of such urgent importance that he had to proceed as if the news were true, given that Vitoria – midway between Bilbao and Burgos – "has so much business and commerce, as it is the place where all the merchandise and supplies coming from the Vizcayan ports and much of the Cuatro Villas pass through."[28] Vargas also wrote to Vitoria, stressing the need to "put the common good before the particular good." Judging from the Burgos end of the correspondence, Vitoria had complained that Bilbao was lying about Vitoria's state of health; Vargas seems to have heard that Bilbao was halting all messengers from Vitoria and refusing all contact with anyone coming from that city. "I do not know if this is the result of jealousy or greed or anything else," Vargas wrote, "but if it were discovered that there had been false testimony and the person or persons who were guilty were from my district, they would be punished such that you would be very satisfied, because such testimony can be very costly and harmful." Similar falsehoods born of enmity had been uttered in his jurisdiction and had been punished, he said. In any case, he assured Vitoria, his city had "never given credence to the news nor denied communication with anyone from Vitoria nor put the city's name on the list of sick places."[29]

In April 1598, Burgos officials took safety measures after hearing that Laredo and other nearby ports were pestilent. The city decided that only goods coming from Bilbao, a "healthy port" (*puerto sano*), would be allowed to enter, which one has to imagine gave rise to a stream of false certificates.[30] But a few months later, word reached Burgos that maybe Bilbao was not so healthy after all. "This city has received information about [Bilbao] regarding the *mal contagioso de la montaña*," the Burgos councilmen wrote Bilbao. "We have been told that coastal towns are guarding against [Bilbao] ... In order that business and commerce with [Bilbao] not stop, given the great harm that would ensue, we have not wished to put it on the list until hearing back from you." The city added ominously at the end: "[A] spark can set off a great fire, and we pray to Our Lord that that not happen."[31]

Four months later, Bilbao was still cheerfully telling Burgos, and presumably other places, that things were fine, and Burgos appears to have been willing to go along, though there must have been information to the contrary by then. "We will let other cities that had gloomy news [*información siniestra*] know," Burgos reassured Bilbao.[32] Bilbao was grateful for the courtesy, its city council wrote on 31 August, and returned the favour with the wise tactical move of finally admitting that in fact there was a little illness there after all but everything was under control. In the Ascao neighbourhood, "populated by many artisans and people with few possibilities, given the general dearth this year ... in the past twenty days some *vecinos* have fallen ill," Bilbao conceded. Security measures were being enforced; women and *vecinos* had been moved out, "more out of precaution and because of their weakness than out of necessity," the city hastened to add, which it was telling Burgos only "because a case like this calls for telling the truth in a straightforward manner." All the sick people were workers and/or poor people, who were receiving money, medicine, and medical care. Some twenty people had been moved into a house outside the city that had been turned into a hospital, and around thirty had died altogether during the distressing event (*sobresalto*). "Given the large number of people living in this city, that is not excessive," especially given that August and September were generally sickly months, "and at present thanks to the glory of God and His infinite goodness there is general health everywhere." Were anything to change, Burgos could rest assured Bilbao would let them know.[33]

In early September 1598, Burgos sent an emissary to Bilbao in the person of Francisco López, a city notary. He carried a letter from Burgos full of gracious sympathy and offers to help, meaning that by then the epidemic was assumed to have entered, but he also had instructions to ferret out the truth. The *corregidor* of Burgos was being cautious about actually putting Bilbao on the list of pestilent cities. A great deal was at stake. Burgos had heard, Vargas told his counterpart in Bilbao, Lic. Pardo, that Bilbao was sick, that houses were shut, streets blocked, people were leaving, and many other towns would not allow communication with Bilbao. His information came from witnesses and correspondence, he said. Nonetheless, and having sifted through the information he had, "with the esteem I have for that city [Bilbao] and my desire to preserve good relations and be a good neighbour, I have not permitted that Bilbao be added to the list, though it is true, as you know, that the slightest carelessness can allow the illness to enter."[34]

A few days later, the Bilbao city council, which by now was meeting in Portugalete (where López had arrived), quite obviously an indication that the city itself was pestilent, wrote again to Burgos. Some merchants and neighbours had moved to Portugalete, Bilbao explained, to better ensure that merchandise be safely unloaded from the ships and moved to Burgos and the rest of Castile. Now that Burgos knew of the "great health" reigning in the north thanks to the quarantine, Bilbao hoped Burgos would allow mule trains to enter from there, continuing the age-old custom of mutual recognition and respect of the two great cities. "In my land and jurisdiction thanks to God there is total health and so much security that I am shut off from all people from Bilbao and from all other suspicious parts, and thus Your Lordship may with all satisfaction and security admit and conduct business with me."[35]

The next day, 11 September, Bilbao wrote to say it had seen López's letter and thus knew of Burgos's willingness to help however it could. The city explained again that it had moved to Portugalete merely to better oversee the transfer of merchandise from the port to elsewhere in Spain. Cargo had been moved along the river to other towns, where it was being securely watched. As an example, a shipload of cod had just arrived on a boat from Newfoundland and the fish was being unloaded safely,

> and the same will be done with all the other cargo that arrives from there and from elsewhere, and many are expected both from there and from Flanders and Ireland and Andalucía and France and elsewhere. We beg Your Lordship, who has always supported us, that you do everything you can to ensure that merchandise from here be moved and admitted, with authenticated testimony, so that commerce and business not leave this coast, as those from San Juan de Luz and Bayonne [in France] and elsewhere wish it to, places that are spreading bad stories about Bilbao, with which for the moment, and until God says otherwise, they are not dealing, dealing rather only with this town [i.e., Portugalete] on which God in His mercy has bestowed great health.[36]

But the same day that Bilbao wrote this letter, Burgos decided not to take any chances, and Bilbao was declared off-limits. Two days later, Vargas issued his formal order to that effect, and Bilbao was added to the Burgos list.[37]

After that, the correspondence took on a more business-like tone. If Bilbao and the other Vizcayan towns wanted to continue doing business with Castile, they would have to abide by Burgos's conditions. First, given that Bilbao was so close to Portugalete, and given the large number of Bilbao *vecinos* who had moved to Portugalete, Burgos was severing ties with the latter town as well: "Communication is cut off, as well as with the people there, so that neither directly nor indirectly shall they do business or speak or receive any clothing or paper or anything else from the said town." Furthermore, given that Bilbao was such an important business centre and a depot for so many goods and that

> owners will want to remove [those] goods so as to be able to use them, and they have done so secretly and placed objects in houses outside the said city, you [the Bilbao city council] must order that under severe penalties no one must ship any items out of the city, either to Portugalete or to anywhere else, and that the things that have already been moved out must stay where they are and be guarded, and it does not matter if no one has gotten sick or died in these storage places because one cannot know if the workers who carried them there were sick, which would be the total perdition of this Kingdom.

Bilbao must keep perfect track of all goods, separating those already there from those yet to arrive at the docks. Someone must be appointed to oversee the packing of outgoing goods, which must all bear a certificate and must travel straight to Burgos. Burgos would send one of its own to Portugalete to oversee this work. That same day Burgos sent Francisco López to Vitoria. The capital of Álava, Vargas suggested, had spoken too highly of its own health; essentially, he said, he did not trust Vitoria anymore, a wise course of action.[38]

Two days later (18 September) the *corregidor* of Bilbao had to admit that people were now dying in Portugalete, prompting the exasperated Vargas to write to the Council of Castile: "The avarice of those in Bilbao who wanted to protect their goods in Portugalete has led the illness to spread." He had wanted to protect the fish and other goods coming from Newfoundland, but it was too late, and Portugalete had now joined Bilbao on the list, he said.[39] From Portugalete, matters shifted to Baracaldo, the next supposedly clean town the Vizcayan authorities chose as their headquarters. (It actually is closer to Bilbao than Portugalete, so the decision is hard to figure out.) Burgos now sent one Mateo Enríquez north to supervise the movement of merchandise from there at a daily salary of five hundred *maravedies*, to be paid by the sick towns. He carried a letter from Burgos to Baracaldo asking that the latter town "take great care that no merchandise that has been in Bilbao or in Portugalete directly or indirectly be allowed to enter, nor any merchandise that has been in contact with the said towns, and that sailors and masters from the ships there not be allowed to wander around and that they have no contact with people from those towns, nor should they go there."[40]

In mid-January Enríquez was still in Baracaldo, apparently still earning his five hundred *maravedies* per day, an arrangement that frankly puzzled Burgos: "We do not know why those who are paying your salary are keeping you there so long, but if they are paying you, we are very pleased, and let us know if anything changes."[41] Bilbao's health seemed to be improving already in December (though Portugalete was still sick), and Enríquez and Burgos both expressed concern that residents of Bilbao were returning too quickly to their city. But Enríquez's long and lucrative tenure as Burgos's eyes and ears came to an end on 19 January, when it emerged that he was at the centre of a fraudulent ring.

One Gaspar Duarte was immediately dispatched northward to bring the culprit back, along with the city's stamps and stamped paper, which he appeared to have been using freely and illicitly. Duarte received the usual instructions to avoid pestilent places at all cost. Once he located Enríquez he was to hand the city's letter to him, and if Enríquez refused to accompany him Duarte was authorized to call for the police.[42] While he was there, he was also supposed to carry out renewed investigations into the true state of health in Bilbao, which once again was assuring everyone that it was just fine. By February it appears Burgos was coming around to believing that Bilbao really was healthy once again.[43] Burgos – which itself would be ravaged in the coming months – may have taken Bilbao off its list, but Bilbao and its towns experienced the return of the disease (as did many other places) in the following months. They were anxious to save on guard money and desperate to go back to business.

It would be Burgos's turn during the spring, summer, and fall of 1599, by which time Vargas was dead, though not of plague. The first plague deaths to be acknowledged in the city council minutes occurred in March; however, the new *corregidor*, Francisco Valencia, admitted to the king that there had been earlier deaths in the San Esteban neighbourhood.[44] The city, which had been devastated by plague in 1565, continued in apparent denial, insisting to the crown, at the urging of its doctors, that the disease was not really *peste* at all. The city council's disingenuous indignation when other places refused its citizens entry coincided with the hospitalization of hundreds of people; by 15 May, a city councilman estimated that more than four hundred had died, and that was just the start.[45] But no matter how strained the city's credibility, it seemed safer to risk not being believed than to risk being put on the list.

The behaviour of town leaders reflected their individual character but also the degree to which they understood or believed in the tenets of good government that were part of every law, petition, charter, and mirror book since the Middle Ages. Those who resolved not to flee the disease had to consider not only economics and health, the well-being of some while not of others, but also their own conduct. They had to decide whom to listen to, how to placate, and whether to tell the truth.

Dissimulation or outright lies by *corregidores* who assured the outside world as well as their own residents that their city was just fine were clearly part of a strategy to ensure material survival. In the context of the plague, lies can be seen as a sort of additional fortification or wall protecting a town's interests, albeit temporarily. Whether or not the *corregidores* in the late sixteenth century were aware of it, there was a spirited debate among contemporary political theorists regarding the legitimacy of this particular construction and its furtherance or negation of good government.

Christian authorities were quite clear that there could be no excuse for lying. In St Augustine's eyes it was always wrong, and while Thomas Aquinas distinguished among several types of lies, they were all sins to varying degrees.[46] Juan Ginés de Sepúlveda, the great sixteenth-century theologian best known today for debating Bartolomé de las Casas on the justice of Spain's oppression of American natives, also took up the subject, inquiring into the legitimacy of withholding information in a judicial setting so as not to harm someone.[47] Machiavelli marked a shift, of course, in allowing the prince to engage in deceit and even evil if necessary: "In order to maintain his state [the prince] is often forced to act in defiance of good faith, of charity, of kindness, of religion ... He should not deviate from what is good, if that is possible, but he should know how to do evil, if that is necessary."[48] The degree to which plague-era *corregidores* knew or cared about Machiavelli and the subsequent debate, including in Spain, is unknown to me. But the behaviour of these busy crown-appointed officials, who were prominent, well-connected, and often rising servants of the monarchy, nonetheless bears looking at in the context of contemporary discussions regarding what they should and should not do. All Spanish political writers believed prudence and morality had to balance one another, and that politics and Christianity were not incompatible. But though the means for ensuring a sound reason of state must be Christian, the discussions of *simulación* and *disimulación* display a recognition that things had changed and that, loathsome as Machiavelli might be, adjustments had to be made in statecraft.

Quite nicely for our purposes, the great Jesuit writer Pedro Ribadeneira calls Machiavelli "pestilential" (*pestilencial*).[49] Yet he wanders dangerously close to the vile Italian as he admits that deceit can be justified:

> It is not a lie, if great necessity or utility so demand, to utter words that are truthful in one sense even though the speaker believes that the listener, given the equivocal meaning of the words, will interpret them in a different sense. And what I am saying about words can also be said of deeds; many

> times, especially during war, they are performed in order that the enemy understand them to be something else entirely, even the opposite of one's intentions. And that is not a lie but rather doing things prudently for the good of the republic. And as Doctor Navarro says, there are two arts of simulation and dissimulation, one performed by those who, with neither reason nor gain, lie and pretend that what was not, is, and the other performed by those who prudently let it be understood, when necessity or utility so require and with neither deceit nor falsehood, that one thing might be another.[50]

The difference between this and Machiavelli's lies is very slight indeed, a situation that other Spanish writers also found themselves in, and Ribadeneira's advice about venturing out on such thin ice was admittedly weak: "When walking among enemies, one must go armed, using dissimulation against dissimulation; but one must be careful to not go so far as to offend God."[51] Machiavelli was not the only point of reference in this debate. Just six years before Ribadeneira published *Tratado de la religión*, the Flemish humanist Justus Lipsius had published his *Politica* and, like Machiavelli, he allowed the prince to lie for the sake of the common good. Paraphrasing part four of the *Politica*, Fernández-Santamaría notes, "The prince, living among foxes, must on occasion resort to fox-like conduct, especially if the public good so requires it. In short, 'a little water does not alter the nature of the wine; and neither does prudence cease to be prudence because a few drops of *disimulación* or *fraude* have been added. It is understood, of course, that the amount shall be small and aimed at a good end.'"[52]

Although Diego Vargas Manrique and his colleagues throughout Castile may not have been cognizant of the political and philosophical writings floating through European capitals and universities at the time, they all likely practised this art of mental reservation – stating lies while recognizing that although one's words were not quite true and might well be misunderstood, a greater good outweighed their falsity. The method, championed especially but not only by Jesuits, "was concocted in order to reconcile the ban on lying with such duties as saving lives and preserving secrets."[53] That is exactly what *corregidores* of cities suffering from or fending off the plague were doing. They admittedly were endangering some lives but perhaps, they hoped, they were saving others as they allowed foodstuffs to enter, looked the other way while peasants tended their fields, and sent messengers and spies to inspect infected towns, all the while insisting that their own towns were healthy. It was a constant balancing act, deciding what to risk today so as to ensure survival tomorrow, weighing profits and lives. That assessment was what lay behind all the public testimony and questionnaires. *Corregidores* needed to know for sure what the appropriate balance was. They needed information that allowed them to make educated guesses, gamble correctly, know whom to save and whom to sacrifice, when to lie and when to tell the truth. They used the instruments of justice to govern, even during times of plague, so as to ensure the common good. I have run across just one acknowledgment, albeit tacit, that this strategy of well-meant dishonesty did not work in the long run, and it comes from a chronicle written in Pamplona, which states that the city resolved to "not dissimulate at all but rather admit the disease and make sure of it and *give it a name*, because [if we] hide it ... it is difficult to remedy later on, and it is better to lose communication [i.e., commerce] than to suffer the damages the disease causes, and in any case secrets can get out."[54] Few if any other city councils acted as wisely.

If city councils could and did dissimulate, so could diseases. False plague was there to deceive physicians, just as false news lulled *vecinos* and false doors and keys mocked the guards. Indeed, falseness made a mockery of a community and the rules that had guided its governance since time immemorial. Thus the emphasis on dissimulation and veracity in civic, legal, and medical documents and accounts throughout early modern Castile. I began this essay by noting that things did not fall apart even in the face of a monstrous epidemic. Efforts to ensure that end entailed marking off claims and behaviours that conformed to some generally accepted *verdad*, which was true only because it had been testified to more than the contrary. The common good relied upon truth, even though everyone knew, as they fought to prove their version, that truth was relative. At the same time, falseness was what would save them in the short run, allowing them to eat for a while longer, shelter their friends, and continue conducting business. Only lies could save the integrity of their community. As for how to tell the difference, that was a matter for witnesses, notaries, judges, and reams and reams of paper.

ACKNOWLEDGMENTS

This chapter includes material from the author's 2019 book, *Life in a Time of Pestilence* (Cambridge 2019).

NOTES

1 14 June 1599. The letter is widely reproduced, for example in Alfredo Alvar Ezquerra, "Madrid reflejo de los problemas sanitarios de la península: La peste de 1596 vista por un galeno de la corte," *Anales del Instituto de Estudios Madrileños* 20 (1983): 203–18, at 207: "por la necessidad precisa que se [entiende] ay en los mis reynos de Castilla, de ocurrir a esta manera de peste, tan general y perniciosa, pareció ser cosa necessaria se hiziesse dello un tratado para que en todas las provincias y ciudades, villas y lugares dellos se entienda y sepa con certidumbre qué enfermedad es y qué orden se deve tener en la guarda y providencia." Unless otherwise indicated, all translations are by the author.

2 For a concise demographic synthesis, see Vicente Pérez Moreda, "The Plague in Castile at the End of the Sixteenth Century and Its Consequences," in *The Castilian Crisis of the Seventeenth Century: New Perspectives on the Economic and Social History of Seventeenth-Century Spain* (Past and Present Publications), ed. I.A.A. Thompson and Bartolomé Yun Casalilla (Cambridge: Cambridge University Press, 1994), 32–59; this article is an abridged version of a chapter in his much broader *Las crisis de mortalidad en la Espana interior (Siglos XVI–XIX)* (Madrid: Siglo Veintiuno, 1980). See also the landmark Bartolomé Bennassar, *Recherches sur les grandes épidémies dans le nord de l'Espagne a la fin du XVIe siècle: Problèmes de documentation et de méthode* (Paris: SEVPEN, 1969). Both writers, along with Bernard Vincent, "La peste atlántica de 1596–1602," *Asclepio* 28 (1976): 5–25, at 11, and Antonio Domínguez Ortiz, *The Golden Age of Spain, 1516–1659*, trans. James Casey (New York: Basic Books, 1971), 174, accept the half-million figure.

3 I am indebted to Julio Escalona for this observation.

4 Safe-conducts were called "*testimonios*," evoking the act of one person speaking on behalf of another.

5 Archivo de Villa (AV) Secretaría 1–138–4. Thirty-four streets are listed, but some are repeated, meaning either that they were to be visited twice or possibly the notary made a mistake.

6 Archivo Municipal de Burgos (AMB) HI 3653, 18 January 1597: "En la ciudad de Burgos este dicho día mes y año susodicho por ante mí el presente escribano público estando en la plaza desta ciudad Francisco de la Cruz, pregonero publico della, a alta y inteligible voz apregona lo ordenado y acordado por los senores atrás escrito [y] volvióse a pregonar … estando presentes muchas personas vecinos en … San Esteban y en la Plazuela de San Esteban y otras muchas partes … adonde suelen y acostumbran dar semejantes pregones a lo cual se habían hallado presentes muchas personas."

7 AMB-HI 3650, auto, 11 April 1598: "de suerte que sin daño y peligro a la salud se podría dar trato y comunicación a tal lugar en esta ciudad de Burgos y en las demás ciudades villas y lugares de estos reinos apercibiéndoles que si por su causa y culpa de declarar cosas contrarias de la verdad resultare algún daño o perjuicio serán gravamente castigados ... En la misma forma le pedirá al cabildo de los clerigos del tal lugar hagan por la misma orden su declaración." Morales made this tour because the towns said they had recovered and should now be allowed to traffic with the outside; he was checking on their true status. The tone, precision, and insistence of the questions are reminiscent of Philip II's famous surveys of Castile, the *Relaciones topográficas.*

8 AMB-HI 3650, auto, 11 April 1598: "de suerte que sin daño y peligro a la salud se podría dar trato y comunicación a tal lugar en esta ciudad de Burgos y en las demás ciudades villas y lugares de estos reinos apercibiéndoles que si por su causa y culpa de declarar cosas contrarias de la verdad resultare algún daño o perjuicio serán gravamente castigados ... En la misma forma le pedirá al cabildo de los clerigos del tal lugar hagan por la misma orden su declaración." Morales made this tour because the towns said they had recovered and should now be allowed to traffic with the outside; he was checking on their true status. The tone, precision, and insistence of the questions are reminiscent of Philip II's famous surveys of Castile, the *Relaciones topográficas.*

9 AMB-HI 3653, 4 July 1597. As Cogollos is just south of the city of Burgos, it is likely that the infected travellers from the north also went through the larger town.

10 Archivo Municipal de Segovia (AMS) leg. 456/1.

11 *Vecino* is usually translated as "citizen," though in practice it was not so precise. It might mean "resident" or a voting member of a town, and it might entail privileges and obligations. It became especially relevant during the plague for poor people, who were (in theory) eligible for health services only if they were *vecinos.*

12 Contemporary political thinkers believed justice was the ultimate purpose of government. Two essential primary sources are Jerónimo Castillo de Bovadilla, *Política para corregidores y señores de vasallos,* 2 vols (Madrid: Instituto de Estudios de Administración Local, 1978), facs of Antwerp: Juan Bautista Verdussen, 1704 [1597]; and Juan de Mariana, *De rege et regis institutione,* in Spanish translation *La dignidad real y la educación del rey,* ed. Luis Sánchez Agesta (Madrid: Centro de Estudios Constitucionales, 1981 [1599]). On the institutions of the judiciary, see Richard L. Kagan, *Lawsuits*

and Litigants in Castille, 1500–1700 (Chapel Hill: University of North Carolina Press, 1981).

13 Miguel Martínez de Leyva, *Remedios preservativos y curativos para en tiempo de la peste; y otras curiosas experiencias* (Madrid 1597), 54v; "albeytares e idiotas."

14 Valentín de Andosilla Salazar, *Libro en que se prueba con claridad el mal que corre por España ser nuevo y nunca visto: Su naturaleza, causas, pronósticos, curacion, y la prouidencia que se deue tener con él …* (Pamplona: Mathías Mares, 1601), 109v: "pseudo médicos con tiránicos intereses y vil ganancia haciendo mil disparates y temerarios atrevimientos con los enfermos dando una en el clavo y ciento en la herradura."

15 Bartolomé Bennassar extrapolated from documents at the Archivo General de Simancas (AGS) and parish papers to conclude that Valladolid lost from 17 to 18 per cent of its population to the plague in 1599, or around 6,600 people. *Valladolid au siècle d'or: Une ville de Castille et sa campagne au XVI siècle* (Paris: Mouton, 1967), 202–5.

16 Antonio Ponce de Santa Cruz, *Tractado de las causas y curacion de las fiebres con secas pestilenciales que han oprimido a Valladolid y otras ciudades de España* (Valladolid: Pedro de Merchan Calderón, 1600), 20r–21r: "Pues hay algunos que piensan que nunca tiene razón de peste un mal hasta que acomete a muchos y mata a los mas. Triste caso que haya un médico y una república de esperar a ver acabada la mayor parte de la gente para conocer qué enemigo tiene en casa … Entiendan de aquí adelante que la peste tiene su ser en el primer doliente sin esperar a que se comunique a otros … Pregúntoles yo a los que están en este error, quando ven un fuego de lejos que no les calienta, ¿aquel es fuego? Están obligados a decir que no … quieren que no sea peste porque no mata a muchos … que confunden el acto segundo con el acto primero."

17 Dozens of plague treatises were written during these years in Spain. The historian Luis Granjel found seventy-three for the seventeenth century (he began counting in the 1590s, during this plague): Luis S. Granjel, "Las epidemias de peste en la España del siglo XVII," *Asclepio* 29 (1977): 17–36. For lists of treatises, see Antonio Carreras Panchón, *La peste y los médicos en la España del Renacimiento* (Salamanca: Universidad de Salamanca, 1976); Randal P. Garza, *Understanding Plague: The Medical and Imaginative Texts of Medieval Spain* (New York: Peter Lang, 2008); Juan Ballesteros Rodríguez, *La peste en Córdoba* (Córdoba: Diputación Provincial, 1982); and José María López Piñero, "Los orígenes de los estudios sobre la salud pública en la España renacentista," *Revista española de salud pública* 80, no. 5 (September–October 2006): 445–56.

18 The observation is based on remarks by Carolyn A. Nadeau at the 2017 Renaissance Society of America meetings in Chicago; however, her book *Food Matters: Alonso Quijano's Diet and the Discourse of Food in Early Modern Spain* (Toronto: University of Toronto Press, 2016) does not specifically mention plague.

19 From a talk that Mendelsohn, of Queen Mary University of London, delivered at Stanford University on 18 November 2016, called "Learning in Public: Physicians, Barber-Surgeons, Lawyers, Housewives, Councilors, Neighbors in Early Modern Germany Communities."

20 Andosilla, *Libro en que se prueba,* chap. 24, 111r: "En esta quietud y tiempo se dice vino una moza disimulada de un lugar de los enfermos de este veneno, la qual murió con fiebre ardiente y su seca en brevísimo tiempo ... Mas como venía el enemigo con pasos tan lentos, fácilmente pudo engañar."

21 The case appears in two places, both of which I quote: Archivo de la Real Chancillería de Valladolid (ARCV) Registro de Ejecutorías, Caja 1838,8, fols 1–67, where it is oddly captioned as concerning theft of a large cape; and AMB-HI 3653, 2 June 1597: "su total ruina y destrucción ... desfrazándoles en hábitos muy diferentes de las que habían llevado a su casa constándole como lo había constado de sus efectos que venían enfermos y apestados ... donde la tierra se había asolado de peste." The case was eventually thrown out on a technicality.

22 Mark Harrison, *Contagion: How Commerce Has Spread Disease* (New Haven: Yale University Press, 2012), xvi.

23 Such subterfuge is typical of any disaster with potential social manifestations, not just plague. Richard Cobb, writing about hunger in eighteenth-century France, notes "public authorities ... had to move carefully as soon as dearth, and its more dangerous outriders, rumour and credulity, were announced once again in a province. It would be unwise to take large-scale action immediately, for this might indicate alarm on the part of those who knew the true state of affairs and would confirm the people in their worst fears; a panic would ensue, and would make matters much worse"; Cobb, *The Police and the People: French Popular Protest, 1789–1820* (Oxford: Clarendon Press, 1970), 216. Likewise, in plague-infested Venice in 1575, officials did everything they could not to alert the republic's trading partners, who might declare Venice off-limits. Its ambassadors simply denied that the epidemic had crossed the waters and invaded the crowded city; see Paolo Preto, *Peste e società a Venezia nel 1576* (Vicenza: Neri Pozza Editore, 1978), 31–4.

24 Jean-Philippe Priotti, *Bilbao et ses marchands au XVI siecle: Genese d'une croissance* (Villeneuve d'Ascq: Presses Universitaires du Septentrion, 2004), 31; on the consulates see Paul Jacob Hiltpold, "Burgos in the Reign of

Philip II: The Ayuntamiento, Economic Crisis, and Social Control, 1550–1600," PhD diss., University of Texas at Austin, 1981, 44.

25 The Laredo item in Priotti, *Bilbao et ses marchands au XVI siecle*, 116, citing Simón Ruiz correspondence; see also William D. Phillips Jr, "Spain's Northern Shipping Industry in the Sixteenth Century," *Journal of European Economic History* 17, no. 2 (Fall 1988): 267–301; and Carla Rahn Phillips and William D. Phillips Jr, *Spain's Golden Fleece: Wool Production and the Wool Trade from the Middle Ages to the Nineteenth Century* (Baltimore: Johns Hopkins University Press, 1997), 218, which notes that relations between the two cities became strained as Bilbao merchants began acting on their own account. I do not know if European nations stayed away from Bilbao's port during this plague, but I have to assume that they did, meaning that the game of mutual deceit among Spanish cities was reproduced more widely; on this subject in general see Harrison, *Contagion*, chap. 2, and, concerning a later plague, Cindy Ermus, "The Spanish Plague That Never Was: Crisis and Exploitation in Cádiz during the *Peste* of Provence," *Eighteenth-Century Studies* 49, no. 2 (Winter 2016): 167–93.

26 Paul Hiltpold, "Política paternalista y orden social en la Castilla del Renacimiento," *Cuadernos de Investigación Histórica BROCAR* 13 (1987): 135–6, citing his own dissertation, at p. 51, says Burgos's population dropped from 4,000 *vecinos* in 1550 to 1,500 by 1600.

27 British Library (BL) Eg. 356, vol. 1, fol. 32: "Los títulos que Su Magestad pone a las ciudades y villas de estos reynos de Castilla de boto en Cortes quando las escribe." Burgos is "la muy noble y muy más leal ciudad de Burgos cabeza de Castilla nuestra cámara" while the rest are just "noble," "muy noble," "muy noble y leal," or "muy noble y muy leal."

28 AMB-HI 3651, fol. 196, January 1598: "Escribesse y corre fama en Burgos de que en la ciudad de Vitoria ha tocado peste y que de ella ay cinco u seis casas cerradas, muchas veces he averiguado ser falsas nuevas semejantes y nacidas de diversos respetos de enemistades y envidias en que deseo enmendar con castigos … Aquella ciudad es de mucho trato y comercio por ser escala por donde vienen todas las mercaderías y bastimentos que salen de los puertos de Vizcaya y gran parte de Quatro Villas." "Quatro Villas" was the collective name given to Santander, Laredo, Castro Urdiales, and San Vicente de la Barquera.

29 AMB-HI 3650, 23 January 1598: "anteponer el bien común al particular … Si esto procedió de envida o codicia o algún otro respecto no lo sé pero si aberiguase haber habido en ello testimonio falso y la persona o personas fueron culpados siendo del distrito de mi comisión con castigo y ejemplo las trataría de manera que VM quedase muy satisfecho porque semejantes

testimonios son muy costosos y perjudiciales … nunca se dio crédito ni negó platica ni se puso en lista Vitoria de lugar enfermo." *Enciclopedia General Ilustrada del País Vasco*, vol. 53 (San Sebastian: Editorial Auñamendi, 2001), 195, says (with no source) that Vitoria suffered greatly, with the first plague case inside the city being recorded in May 1599. A contemporary said two thousand people died in the city and its villages (Vitoria then had barely four thousand inhabitants).

30 AMB-HI 3653, 14 April 1598.

31 AMB-HI 3653, 9 August 1598: "Esta ciudad ha tenido información [sobre] esa villa tocante al mal contagioso de la montaña nos avisan que en los lugares de la costa se guardan [contra Bilbao] … [Para] que no cese el trato y comercio de esa villa por el gran daño que se le seguiría hemos querido esperar a no ponerlos en la lista hasta ser avisados de VS … una centella prende un gran fuego que plega a nuestro señor no sea."

32 AMB-HI 3653, 20 August 1598.

33 BL Eg. 356, vol. 2, fol. 354r–v, 31 August 1598, six signatures: "La villa de Bilbao por su orden su alcalde regidores diputados y secretario." "[En] Ascao que es arrabal desta villa donde hay muchos oficiales y gente de poca posibilidad con la carestía general del año … han enfermado de veinte días a esta parte algunos vecinos de manera que han puesto en cuidado el lugar y aun movido libremente a mujeres y vecinos a salirse fuera más por temor y flaqueza de ánimo que no de necesidad, porque diciendo verdad a VSa con la llaneza que en semejante caso de requiere … para el gran número de gente que hay en esta villa no se puede tener por exceso, pues Agosto y Setiembre hacen sus ordinarios efectos, y al presente gloria a Dios por su infinita bondad hay salud en general en todo el pueblo."

34 AMB-HI 3650, 4 September 1598: "con la estima que hago de esta villa y deseo que tengo de que se conserve con ella buena correspondencia y hacerle buena vecindad no he consentido poner a Bilbao en la lista … si bien es verdad que el mal como VM sabe entra por qualquier defeto."

35 BL Eg. 356, vol. 2, fol. 353r–v, 10 September 1598, nine signatures, though the letter is written in first person; Bilbao addressed Burgos as *Su Señorío*: "En mi tierra y comarca por la bondad de Dios hay entera salud y tanta guardia que ynviolablamente estoy cerrado de qualquier genero de gente ansi de Bilbao como de todas las demás partes sospechosas y que con mucha satisfacción y seguridad puede VSa mandar admitir y abrir el trato conmigo que a menos desto no fuera justo certificarlo yo ni intentar cosa que no fuera tan importante a todos."

36 BL Eg. 356, vol. 2, fol. 352r–v, 11 September 1598, five signatures: "y harán lo mismo todos los demás que llegaren de alla y de otras partes que se

esperan muchas así de alla como de Flandes y Irlanda y Andalucía Francia y otras partes, suplicamos a VSa sea servido pues siempre VS ha hecho merced a la villa de Bilbao y a esta universidad y ha sido amparo de ella que en esta ocasión nos la haga a todos que el comercio de las mercadurías corría y sean admitidos llevándolas de aquí con testimonios auténticos que se darán con ella a los que las llevaren para que el comercio y trato no se vaya de esta costa como lo pretenden los de San Juan de Luz, Bayona y otras partes, poniendo toda la mala voz que pueden a Bilbao de adonde por ahora no se trata hasta que Dios hordene otra cosa sino de esta villa que por la misericordia de Dios hay mucha salud en ella."

37 AMB-HI 3653, 11 September 1598; AMB-HI 3650, 13 September 1598, auto.

38 AMB-HI 3653, 16 September 1598: "se quite la comunicación con ella y con las personas que en ella han quedado para que directa ni indirectamente se contraten ni hablen ni se reciba ninguna ropa ni otro género de cosa de la dicha villa ni papel ... los dueños de ellos las querrán sacar para se proveer dellos y han sacado VM al secreto y puesto en algunas casas fuera de la dicha villa VM mande so graves penas que de Bilbao no salga ninguna mercaduría para alli ni otra parte ni tampoco los que han salido y puesto en las casas que VM ... se muden donde están si no que estén guardadas porque no importa no haber enfermado ninguna persona ni muerto de las casas donde salieron porque no se puede saber si los trabajadores que las sacaron estaban heridos que se iría perder todo este Reyno."

39 AMB-HI 3650, 18 September 1598: "Con la codicia que tuvieron los de Bilbao de asegurar sus mercadurias en Portugalete me parece que se [extendió] el mal en aquella villa"; also AMB-HI 3650, Vargas to council, September 1598.

40 AMB-HI 3653, between 11 and 17 October 1598: "que tengan gran cuidado que ninguna mercaduría que haya salido de Bilbao ni Portugalete directa ni indirectamente la dejan entrar allí ni que haya comunicación con las dichas villas y se ponga limite a los maestros y marineros de los navíos que allí están donde puedan andar para que no comuniquen con personas de dichas villas ni vayan a ellas."

41 AMB-HI 3653, 9 January 1599: "no sabemos porque los que le pagan su salario le entretienen pero si ellos lo hacen y lo pagan holgamos dello y nos avise si le han mudado."

42 AMB-HI 3653, 19 January 1599 (minutes and a letter).

43 AMB-HI 3653, 7 and 9 February 1599.

44 AGS Estado leg. 183, doc. 267. The January deaths appear in a report by the Burgos *regidor* Andrés de Cañas, in BL Eg. 356, vol. 2, fols. 329–37; published by Francis Brumont originally in *Boletín de la Institución Fernán González* 26 (1984–5): 167–82, and appeared subsequently as "La peste de

1599: Una relación del regidor Andrés de Cañas," *BROCAR: Cuadernos de Investigación Histórica* 13 (1987): 155–66.

45 Brumont, "La peste de 1599," 157–8. On p. 165 he publishes a draft of a letter from the city to the king, today in BL Eg. 356, vol. 2, scoffing at the towns' insistence that Burgos was sick; if it were sick, the city reasoned, then it would have told the king. Actually, the *corregidor* had had the opportunity to do just that, in a series of reports requested by the king, which today are in AGS-E leg. 183, but instead he maintained the city was healthy.

46 Augustine's essays are "De mendacio" and "Contra mendacium"; the Aquinas reference is to *Summa Theologiae* 2a2ae, q. 110, arts. 1–4.

47 Juan Ginés de Sepúlveda, *Teófilo,* in his *Obras completas,* vol. 15, ed. José María Núñez González and S. Rus Rufino (Pozoblanco: Ayuntamiento de Pozoblanco, 2010), clxv–cxcii, 193–245. The treatise, a nineteen-chapter dialogue first published in Valladolid in 1538, coincided with the Inquisition trial of the Spanish Erasmist Juan de Vergara, who was accused, among other things, of keeping secret his communication with his brother, who also faced charges. My thanks to Luna Nájera for this reference.

48 Niccolo Machiavelli, *The Prince,* trans. George Bull (New York: Penguin, 1961), 101.

49 Pedro Ribadeneira, *Tratado de la religión y virtudes que debe tener el príncipe christiano para gobernar y conservar sus estados. Contra lo que Nicolas Machiavello y los políticos deste tiempo enseñan …* (Madrid: P. Madrigal, 1595), 273. For an introduction to Ribadeneira's criticism of Machiavelli, see J.A. Fernández-Santamaría, *Reason of State and Statecraft in Spanish Political Thought, 1595–1640* (Lanham: University Press of America, 1983), 18–24. Ribadeneira (1526–1611) is also sometimes referred to as Ribadeneyra.

50 Ribadeneira, *Tratado de la religión,* 289–90: "asimismo no es mentira (quando la necesidad o utilidad grande lo pide) decir algunas palabras verdaderas en un sentido aunque crea el que las dice que el que las oye, por ser equívocas, las podría tomar en diferente sentido. Y lo que digo de las palabras se puede también decir de las obras, que muchas veces (especialmente en tiempo de guerra) hay necesidad que se hagan con tal maña y artificio que el enemigo pueda entender otra cosa diversa, y aun contraria de lo que se pretende hacer. Porque esto no es mentir sino hacer las cosas con prudencia para bien de la República. Y como dice el Doctor Navarro hay dos artes de simular y disimular, la una de los que sin causa ni provecho mienten y fingen que hay lo que no hay, y que no hay lo que hay. La otra de los que sin mal engaño y sin mentira dan a entender una cosa por otra con prudencia quando lo pide la necesidad o utilidad." Fernández-Santamaría, *Reason of State and Statecraft,* 92, has a slightly different translation, as he

used the 1605 version of the original. According to Ronald W. Truman, *Spanish Treatises on Government, Society and Religion in the Time of Philip II: The 'de regimine principum' and Associated Traditions* (Leiden: Brill, 1999), 297, the Doctor Navarro referred to is the theologian Martín de Azpilcueta, who in 1584 wrote an essay on dissimulation.

51 Ribadeneira, *Tratado de la religión,* 285: "Que andando entre enemigos, necesario es que vayan armados y que con los disimulados usen de alguna disimulación; pero miren bien hasta dónde ha de llegar sin que Dios se ofenda." On the approximation between Spanish writers and Machiavelli see Keith David Howard, "The Anti-Machiavellians of the Spanish Baroque: A Reassessment," *LATCH: A Journal for the Study of the Literary Artifact in Theory, Culture or History* 5 (2012): 106–19.

52 Fernández-Santamaría, *Reason of State and Statecraft,* 88. Lipsius's work, which was put on the Index, is known as *Six Books on Politics or Civil Doctrine.* For more on Lipsius and these questions see Christopher Brooke, *Philosophic Pride: Stoicism and Political Thought from Lipsius to Rousseau* (Princeton: Princeton University Press, 2012), 19–20; also the superb analysis in Noel Malcolm, *Reason of State, Propaganda and the Thirty Years' War* (Oxford: Clarendon, 2007), 92–123. Lipsius's translation of Tacitus inspired a broad reception of the latter's political writings in late sixteenth-century Spain, many of which concerned reason of state; for more, see the works of Truman and Fernández-Santamaría cited above as well as Charles Davis, "Baltasar Álamos de Barrientos and the Nature of Spanish Tacitism," in *Culture and Society in Habsburg Spain: Studies Presented to R. W. Truman by his Pupils and Colleagues on the Occasion of his Retirement,* ed. Nigel Griffin et al. (London: Tamesis, 2001), 57–78.

53 Johann P. Sommerville, "The 'New Art of Lying': Equivocation, Mental Reservation, and Casuistry," in *Conscience and Casuistry in Early Modern Europe,* ed. Edmund Leites (Cambridge: Cambridge University Press, 1988), 159–84, at 176.

54 Ignacio Baleztena, ed., "Relación de la peste desta ciudad de Pamplona del año 1599," *Príncipe de Viana* 23 (1946): 377–94, at 391 [chronicle by Martín de Senosiain], my emphasis: "no disimular cosa y en consintiendo esta enfermedad y asiguráddose della darle nombre porque de quererlo ocultar ... tiene después dificultoso remedio y vale más que se pierda la comunicación que no los daños que causa quanto y más que por secretoras que anden se sabe."

chapter five

Policing Talent in Early Modern Jesuit Rome: Difference, Self-Knowledge, and Career Specialization

JAVIER PATIÑO LOIRA

From early in the history of the order, Jesuit superiors catalogued each member of a house according to his bodily and temperamental qualities.[1] It was a practice that used categories of Galenic medicine to gauge talents and place each individual in the job for which he was best suited. As the Society of Jesus became invested in education, the assessment of student abilities so as to rationalize career choice became fundamental in school administration as well. It decisively informed Jesuit scholarly and pedagogical practice, given the conviction that student success and, with it, the order's reputation depended on the wise management of the diversity of natural inclinations and dispositions that learners brought to the classroom.[2]

While such concerns stemmed from the need for efficiency, Jesuits did not hesitate to justify them through loftier motivations. By analysing three orations delivered to open the school years of 1596, 1613, and 1617 at the order's Collegio Romano, I will show that Jesuit professors deliberately construed the need to police, classify, and direct student talent (as opposed to the encouragement of free and therefore "unnatural" career choice) as a first and crucial step in the quest for truth and learning, the fight against heresy, and the enforcement of socially and politically responsible behaviour. They argued that failure to take the examination of talents seriously compromised the possibility of attaining certainty in any discipline of knowledge. Such concern must have appeared particularly valid at the time. Scepticism occupied the front lines of European science, casting doubt on the ability of Aristotelian logic and categories to produce true knowledge, as exemplified by Francisco Suárez's *Quid nihil scitur* (1581) and Francis Bacon's *The Advancement of Learning* (1605). For the scholars under consideration, the source of uncertainty lay elsewhere. They argued that individuals who set out to practise a discipline for which they are not naturally disposed are unable to tell appearances from the truth, depicting a scenario in which nothing mattered more to educators than properly allocating talents to a field in which they would be able to weigh the truth of a statement with certainty. In their arguments, Jesuit professors adduced the religious and political upheavals that had plagued sixteenth-century Europe as evidence that allowing individuals to freely exercise sciences and arts for which they might be unfit condemns a community to destruction. The individual's blindness to his strengths and limitations, itself a product of self-love that was not any less natural to human beings, only made the problem worse. As a consequence, Jesuit professors resolved that only the external and heteronomous assessment of talents, either by investigating the nature of the students or by teaching them how to overcome self-blindness and know themselves better, prepared scholarly communities for the pursuit of certain and sure knowledge.

Policing Wit: Career Choice and the Common Good of the Republic

By 1596, Rome's Jesuit College was at the heart of "the first free public education system that Europe or the rest of world had seen," a worldwide network of schools held together by the order's highly developed procedures of information and power management.[3]

As every year in the fall, the students gathered in the great hall or "aula" to listen to the oration that would open a new academic year. However conventional in format, inaugural discourses offered professors a rare occasion to display talent and voice opinions before large audiences. Collegio Romano scholars such as Famiano Strada, Tarquinio Galluzzi, and Vincenzo Guinigi had them collected and printed in volumes that were often re-edited and became bestsellers. Speakers often referred to orations they had recited in previous years. They would poke fun at the grey hairs they had grown since then or, more seriously, show that past concerns remained relevant. Some topics recurred time and again in speeches by different, unrelated authors, pointing to a commonality of interests.

In 1596, a professor named Francesco Maria Fattori (d. 1603) was in charge. His oration *De moderandis ingeniis* (On the guidance of wits) was a plea for educators to be aware that the republic's well-being depended on assigning students to the discipline in which nature has meant them to thrive. His conclusion stemmed from a series of principles that deserve close attention.

Fattori's opening lines celebrate human wit or *ingenium* as the greatest spectacle on earth and a source of wonder.[4] The meaning of "wit" at the time is slippery. The dictionary of the Accademia della Crusca (1612) quoted a definition of "ingegno" understood as the ability to learn something without the help of others.[5] In 1613, a revised edition of Cesare Ripa's repertoire of icons (originally published in 1593) stated that "there is nothing in the world so covered and hidden which the acuity of human wit is unable to reveal and make known."[6] Intellectual independence and resourcefulness, as well as the ability to pierce through the most tortuous problem, characterized *ingenium* in the literature of the time and rendered it an object of fascination. As early as 1570, Lodovico Castelvetro's commentary on Aristotle's *Poetics* stated that it is precisely "contemplating" the playwright's wit that causes the pleasure in a tragedy's plot twists.[7]

Fattori's oration negotiated the ambiguity between the meaning of "wit" as intellectual ability expounded so far and as difference in intellectual ability, "the native quality [*indoles*] through which we learn some thing or art, either with ease or with effort," as *ingenium* is described in *Bibliotheca selecta* (1593), Antonio Possevino's exposition of Jesuit educational curriculum and philosophy.[8] As a synonym for talent, "wit" designated something inborn that made each individual different from the rest depending on that at which he happened to be naturally good.[9]

Shifting from the first to the second meaning of *ingenium*, Fattori abandons the praise of wit's ability to grasp the truth and strikes a note of caution, warning his audience that letting students freely choose a path of study is not without danger. Educators should acknowledge that ingenuity manifests itself differently depending on the individual. History is full of examples of how wit's fertility leads to sterile and even destructive outcomes whenever individuals stray from the path that nature has set for them. Fattori borrows from the list of *mataiotechniai* or "idle arts" in Quintilian's first-century treatise *The Orator's Education* (2.20) the case of the man who sought to impress Alexander the Great with his ability to pin chickpeas onto a needle when throwing them from a distance. He evokes the chariots that a certain Mermecides built out of ivory, miniatures so small that they could ostensibly be covered by the wing of a fly.[10] A list of curious yet purposeless inventions prepares the ground for others that are not only useless but also harmful. At times, individuals hurt the community through their desire to master a discipline for which nature never called them. Episodes of sedition and heresy are often the product of minds that were unfit for the objects they tried to grasp. "A man full of wit," the conspirator Lucius Catiline almost destroyed the Roman republic when he applied himself to politics. The apostasies of Porphyry and Julian and the deviations in dogma of Nestorius, Arius, and Pelagius appear to Fattori as cases of wit misguided to theology. Heretics are often students who might have excelled in the arts and the sciences for which they had talent. The present, Fattori avers, is still suffering the consequences of anti-natural career choices such as those of Martin Luther and Jean Calvin.[11]

The man who pinned chickpeas and those who rebel against the faith have in common a failure to identify a discipline in which they are naturally capable of either finding the truth or creating something useful, depending on whether their talents lie in the sciences or the arts. Considered in general, wit may probe the secrets of heaven and earth. However, in its particular instantiation in each of us, it is constrained by inclinations that the individual should not neglect. Human beings differ from one another, and each is capable of succeeding in *just* one art or science. Aligning with one's nature is a guarantee of success, and just as the farmer starts by assessing the quality of the soil in order to grow a suitable crop, a student's particular and specific talent must be established before any decision regarding career choice comes to pass.[12] Otherwise, the mind struggles towards the truth and gets frustrated by objects that are not congenial to it and that it finds impossible to understand. Incapable of separating the appearances from the truth, it abandons the search for a certainty that has become unattainable and seeks novelty instead.[13] It follows that, when the topic under investigation is religious truth, the inability to distinguish with clarity may result in novel and unorthodox beliefs.

Yet why would anyone choose a discipline against the dictates of nature, if this leads to uncertain and merely apparent results? Fattori replies that the mind is blind to self-knowledge (*cognitio sui*), that is, the awareness of one's nature. Hubris (*superbia*) persuades the mind into thinking that there are no limits to what it may attain, thus preventing it from performing proper and thorough self-assessment: "Wit can use subtlety to examine everything else ... yet it cannot see itself, nor can it set itself restrictions that it would be illicit not to observe – or, if it can, it plainly refuses to do so."[14] Fattori's position reflects early modern scepticism about self-knowledge. The injunction "Know thyself" (*Nosce te ipsum*) was central to early modern moral, political, and courtly literature, especially as many manuals argued for the strategic value of being aware of one's resources in a world marked by deceit and competition. "No one can be a master of himself if he does not understand himself first. There are mirrors of the body, but not of the soul: let a judicious self-reflection play that part," advised Jesuit professor Baltasar Gracián in Aphorism 89 of his *Oráculo manual* (1647).[15] However, the concern for self-examination coincided with increasing doubts about the transparency of the subject to him or herself. As in Fattori's oration, many claimed that the passion of self-love inherent to the individual makes self-deception likely in any attempt at investigating one's moral and intellectual capabilities.[16] Decades later, François de La Rochefoucauld would famously summarize this by claiming that the mind behaves like the eyes, who "discover everything and are blind only to themselves."[17]

If self-assessment is plagued with difficulties and, even worse, adolescents are prey to the tyranny of whims and desires, at least the student should profit from the judgment of "wise men" (*sapientes*) entrusted with examining his talent.[18] The ancient Greeks and Romans placed great weight in testing the abilities of children. Fattori evokes the magistrate who allegedly oriented Athenian children to a career, fostering social order and stability. He recalls having read that, for Aristotle, assigning citizens to the disciplines for which they were talented was the basis for a healthy republic.[19]

Fattori's reflection on student talent opens up a space of inquiry into the link between education and heresy, the foremost religious and political problem in early modern Catholic Europe. However, devising and enforcing a method of student advising and orientation became crucial not only to avoid repeating errors that wreaked havoc with sixteenth-century politics and religion. At stake was also scientific knowledge and certainty. If the practitioners of a science or art for which they naturally have talent are the only ones able to separate appearance from truth, it follows that, unless educators are in turn certain of each student's nature, scholarship will confront a dreadful impasse in which no one may be sure that those responsible for producing truths are actually able to distinguish them from appearances.

Fattori's concern with handling difference was aligned with a procedure central to Jesuit administration and management detailed in the so-called *Formula scribendi* (Way of writing), approved in 1573 at the order's Third General Congregation and first printed in the 1580 edition of *Rules of the Society of Jesus.* The *Formula* instructed the superiors of each house or college in charge of compiling the annual catalogues (submitted to the provincial, then to the superior general in Rome) to describe each member's and novice's "wit, judgment, prudence, experience of things, advancement in studies, [and] natural complexion," so as to determine the task for which they were best suited.[20] The method was less systematic for non-Jesuit individuals who were pupils at the schools, although the order's plan and curriculum (*Ratio atque institutio studiorum*), developed between 1584 and 1599, advised that experts play a role in deciding on each individual's career. For instance, it was commonly advised that students who showed aptitude for a discipline should stay in it longer so as to reach some degree of specialization.[21]

Scholars have long seen efficiency as the goal of Jesuit student advising and orientation, and schools certainly sought to impress the wealthy patrons who funded the Society of Jesus's enterprises with results worthy of their investment.[22] Fattori, who addressed students rather than administrators, justified the examination of wits as a procedure that aimed beyond efficacy and responded to a loftier and further-reaching concern: the advancement of learning and eradication of heresy.

In linking the examination of wits to the fight against heresy, Fattori was following in the footsteps of Juan Huarte de San Juan's *Examen de ingenios para las ciencias* (Examination of men's wits), first printed in Baeza, Spain, in 1575. A physician by trade, Huarte (1529–1588) built upon Hippocratic and Galenic medical theory a method capable of explaining someone's aptitude for a particular art or science based on the constitution of his or her body. Huarte argues that, since all souls are created equal in the hands of God, the body is the cause of any difference in talent.[23]

The importance of taking the student's dispositions into account was hardly new. Leaving ancient sources aside, educational treatises as early as Pier Paolo Vergerio's *De ingenuis moribus et liberalibus adulescentiae studiis* (The character and studies befitting a free-born youth; written before 1402) emphasized that individuals differed in talent and inclination.[24] Juan Luis Vives's *De tradendis disciplinis* (On education, 1531) advised keeping a boy "one or two months in the preparatory school that his disposition may be investigated. Four times a year let the masters meet in some place apart where they may discuss together the natures of their pupils and consult about them ... Let them apply each boy to that study for which he seems most fit."[25] However, Huarte would stand out from his predecessors for advancing a method based on medicine for unveiling a student's talent. Huarte claims that only natural philosophy, the science that accounts for God's management of creation through secondary, "natural" causes, can justify the variety of wits. In this he follows Galen, whose *Quod animi mores temperamenta sequantur* (That the habits of the soul follow the temperament; second-century CE, first printed in 1525) argues that from the moment the soul enters the body, it operates through the brain. Galen contended that the brain shares in the body's temperament: it may be hot or cold, with different degrees of humidity and dryness – variations that influence behaviour.[26] As Cristiano Casalini has noted, Huarte added to Galen's theory by extending the influence of temperament. The brain, Huarte claims, does more than condition habits: it determines cognitive skills as well.[27] In Huarte's account, each of the three faculties of the soul benefits from the primacy of a quality in the brain of the learner. Humidity favours excellence in memory: it renders the brain malleable, so that the images or *species* of things are impressed more easily upon it. Dryness avails for understanding, while heat fosters imagination. Cold, in turn, is entirely useless for the mind.[28]

Huarte claims to be the first to have discovered the specifics that connect each temperament with aptness for a discipline. A student learns Latin easily when he has a brain characterized by humidity, a quality associated with the excellence in memory required for languages. In contrast, to master dialectic he makes use of the understanding, a faculty that begs for dryness. If he is to shine in astrology, a discipline that uses imagination, he needs plenty of heat in his brain. Signs in a student's appearance, such as hair colour and consistency, skin tone, and even the way they laugh, offer educators clues as to the brain's temperament.[29] If they attend to them and orient advisees to the discipline for which they have talent, this will result in the common good through both the advancement of learning and the perfection of the arts, as Huarte eloquently claims in his dedication to King Philip II of Spain. When managed appropriately, the difference that is consubstantial to any group of individuals becomes a boon for the community.[30] Conversely, there is little that the individual can do to make his case for devoting his efforts to a science or art for which the examination has shown him to be unfit.

As noted by Casalini, the publication of Huarte's *Examen* in 1575 provided a terminology that enhanced the precision of the order's annual catalogues in recording the aptitude of members and novices.[31] This means that Huarte influenced the ways Jesuits thought about the connection between temperament and talent long before Fattori could read him, perhaps in Camillo Camilli's 1582 Italian translation.[32] It seems most likely that Fattori wrote his oration with Huarte's book open on his desk. The link between the examination of wits and the fight against heresy advanced by Fattori featured prominently in Huarte's dedication to Philip II, where he warned the king that "those who lacked a wit suitable to theology have destroyed Christian faith."[33] Of course, one might cite other precedents for this. In the aforementioned *De tradendis disciplinis*, Vives had already intimated that failure to orient students might lead them to gather "disgrace and a seed-plot of errors" from the school instead of tools to help them become better citizens. Educators might inadvertently "arouse the wild beast" in students who are wrongly advised, who would be "thus sent out as a source of injury to the state."[34] However, Huarte joined the debate in more specific terms. He explained that northern Europeans (a group that encompassed controversial figures, such as Erasmus, as well as others more explicitly condemned, such as Luther) excel in memory as much as they lack understanding, the faculty through which theologians speculate and make distinctions.[35] Huarte is also the source of Fattori when he quotes Cicero's analogy between doing something *inuita Minerua* (against what the goddess of wisdom commands) and the war of the giants against the gods. Defying nature (even one's nature) amounts to a form of sedition. Ignoring one's talent, Fattori adds, is similar to the torture of Sisyphus, who carries a rock uphill only to see it roll back from the top time and again – the emblem of self-defeating, hopeless rebellion that deserves to be punished accordingly.[36] Fattori's reliance on Huarte's *Examen* becomes especially clear from a minor reference included in the dedication of the latter to Philip II, which narrates that a demon warned Galen's father that his son should study medicine, for he was destined to excel as a physician and fail as a lawyer.[37]

The anecdote about Galen corroborates Fattori's familiarity with Huarte. Everything else that Fattori's oration shares with *Examen* was also present in Antonio Possevino's aforementioned *Bibliotheca selecta* (1593). This work, which became a text of reference in Jesuit schools, deserves some consideration here. Willingly or not, Possevino (1533–1611) disseminated Huarte's ideas among the contemporaries of Fattori. Possevino opened the first section of *Bibliotheca selecta*, entitled *Cultura ingeniorum* (The cultivation of wits; published separately in numerous editions and translated into Italian in 1598 as *Coltura degl'ingegni*) with an unacknowledged quote from Giovanni Pico della Mirandola's oration *De dignitate hominis* (On the dignity of man), first printed in 1496. Pico famously described man as lacking well-defined skills such as those with which other animals are born. In exchange, man was granted a protean and chameleon-like nature, which allows him to become whatever he or she wishes: "you, constrained by no limits, may determine your nature for yourself, according to your own free will ... [you are] the free and extraordinary shaper of yourself."[38] Possevino tempers Pico's enthusiasm with a note of caution. It was not enough to warn, as Pico had done, that liberty of study should not deliberately be used for anything harmful. Individuals should abide by stricter constraints to avert calamity, for Possevino, like Huarte, knew differing talents could lead to unintentional damage when we undertake a study for which nature has not granted us the disposition.

From 1604, re-editions of Possevino's *Cultura ingeniorum* often featured the subtitle "It passes a judgment on Juan Huarte's *Examen de ingenios.*"[39] Among early modern Jesuits, *Cultura ingeniorum* broadcast Huarte's ideas as much as it tried to counter them. Possevino accepted the connection between temperament and ability and supported the need for the examination of talents, but took issue with what he saw as Huarte's promotion of determinism of the body over the soul.[40] Possevino claimed that sin and faulty cultivation of one's wit (or "*cultura*") ought to be factored in as causes for the failure to master a discipline, so as to counterbalance the weight that *Examen* granted to temperament.[41] At a time when sharp lines were drawn between orthodox and heretical propositions, Possevino must have found the similarity between narrowing a student's freedom on the basis of his alleged nature and the doctrine of predestination deeply troublesome. For him, Huarte's book posed a threat to the dogma of free will, by suggesting that God had given each of us a nature that was good for exclusively one science or art. Even those who generally supported Huarte's theory saw that it enjoined the student to follow his nature "by love or by force," as aptly put by Franciscan friar Bartolomeo Meduna in his *Lo scolare* (The student, 1588), a work that Possevino probably knew and which shared his concern with avoiding any suspicion of determinism.[42] Possevino lamented that the "errors" of the 1574 edition of Huarte's *Examen* had passed on to Camilli's 1582 Italian translation, and advised his reader to stay away from the treatise until amended by Spanish inquisitorial authority.[43] The expurgated edition of Huarte's book appeared posthumously in 1594, the year following the first edition of Possevino's *Bibliotheca selecta.*

Possevino reassured his readers that choice was not negotiable, but he had his own way of reconciling Huarte's principles with free will. Since God operates through the laws of nature, whenever He wants any of us to contribute to the common good through the exercise of such and such science or art, He awards us the temperament best suited for it and gives us the freedom to choose it. Choosing a career in line with one's nature means freely choosing to conform to God's will.[44] In case this still suggested some degree of coercion, Possevino opened up the possibility that individuals contribute to society even in ways that contradict the nature assigned to them. At the same time, Possevino was highly sceptical that temperaments can be measured with any certainty, making it necessary to complement the examination of wits in some other way. He suggested investigating the child's familiar and social entourage for his inclinations rather than his body for traces of his temperament. Possevino's approach takes a step back from Huarte's optimistic but also deterministic stance, and strongly undermines it by asserting that through cultivation (*cultura*) individuals may get to places for which, in theory, they were not "naturally" suited. He thus reinstates some freedom of choice for learners, echoing Meduna's claim that effort and habit might become surrogates for nature.[45]

In light of such ongoing debates, it seems fair to argue that Fattori aimed to promote compliance among the younger students, the addressees of his oration. He sought to justify the need to follow the advice of Jesuit professors regarding career specialization. Instead of going to great lengths to articulate a position in moral and physiological terms, as did Huarte and Possevino, Fattori's discourse pursued the more immediate goal of fostering obedience. He argued that human beings are incapable of self-knowledge, thus paving the way for a paradigm in which only "the advice of the wise" can show a student his own nature. Fattori summarized this with a quote from book 22 of Titus Livy: "The best man is the one who can himself advise about a subject; then comes the one who is able to follow good advice; [but] the man who can neither advise nor receive advice, he is the least capable of all."[46] Since the first is not an option in the field of self-knowledge, Fattori explained that one should strive for second best. In fact, with the mind's hubris precluding the autonomy that self-knowledge could have granted the individual, obedience to school authorities remains the best alternative to stay away from intellectual wantonness (*cupiditas*), the sin that lures the mind into learning disciplines in which it cannot aspire to any certainty, thus undergoing the risk of frustration and, if things go wrong, potential outbursts of political and religious rebellion.

In the public and ceremonial context of the oration, Fattori depicts educators as those who know best what is good for the learner. He makes his point stronger by arguing that the good of the student coincides with that of the community, with heresy and sedition looming on the horizon as the consequences of failure to conform to one's talent. Two later orations delivered at Rome's Jesuit College by different professors in 1613 and 1617 resume and complicate the topic, showing that the choice between self-knowledge and compliance with authorities regarding one's career path occurs at the intersection of scholarly pursuits, ethics, and civic virtue. These texts locate intellectual and professional specialization at the core of the individual's identity within the community, transforming awareness of one's talent and submission to one's limitations into a virtue.

Specialization as Civic Virtue, or the Death of "Renaissance Man"

In a discourse delivered at Rome's Jesuit College in 1613 with the title *De multiplici doctrinarum studio contrahendo* (On undertaking the study of many disciplines), rhetoric professor Tarquinio Galluzzi (d. 1649) took issue with the claim that the appetite for knowledge is intrinsically noble. Thirteen years of instruction had shown him that the mind cannot grasp anything with certainty when it travels restlessly from discipline to discipline like a body dragged by the waves.[47]

In the tradition of following Pico without naming him, Galluzzi argues that when man sets out to shape himself through education, it would seem that his perfection lies in knowledge of the golden chain of all the disciplines of learning, which the ancients called "*encyclopedia.*" However, such promise is fraught with danger due to "the insatiable desire of learning" experienced by some, a temptation that drives individuals towards disciplines for which (as Fattori had argued) they are naturally unfit.[48] The wise have long agreed that not everything is for everyone. There was never anyone who mastered all the disciplines, not even Plato, who was flawed in natural philosophy, or Aristotle, who failed to understand theology. When even those considered most excellent undergo proper scrutiny, it turns out they can master one discipline and nothing more.[49]

If the totality of learning is so elusive, then choice becomes key. Galluzzi evokes Plato's idea of a magistrate to test the talents of children, yet unlike Huarte and Fattori, who saw career choice as a problem to be handled by state and school authorities, respectively, he depicts the examination of wits as an ethical rather than an administrative imperative. The individual ought to practise moderation in response to his desire to know everything. Galluzzi too quotes Cicero's analogy between ignoring one's nature and fighting the gods. As when he recalls a simile between wit and agriculture of which Huarte was fond, Galluzzi casts the conflict in terms of (in)justice: just as we must not require of the soil crops that it is not prepared to bear, we do affront (*iniuria*) to the decrees of nature whenever we are not satisfied with them.[50] The student should refrain from overstepping the boundaries that delimit his sphere within the community. That prudence and temperance are at the heart of the problem becomes obvious when Galluzzi conjures the sirens of Homer's *Odyssey*, who tried to lure the hero with the bait of knowledge. For the student, the sirens represent the danger of drowning in the *encyclopedia* when he wants to know too much. As in Pythagoras's comparison between knowledge and a market full of merchandise, measure is the remedy. Students cannot bring everything home because there is not enough room. Since they need to choose, they must first assess their needs by examining what they have or do not have.[51] In contrast with Pico's optimism more than a century earlier, Galluzzi reminds his audience that learning takes place with limited means (*angustiis*). Students should aim at a certain and delimited glory and renounce that for which they are not suited.

As Fattori before him, Galluzzi turns the injunction "Know thyself" into a prerequisite before undertaking the study of any discipline.[52] If Fattori had expressed his scepticism regarding the mind's ability to see itself without others showing the way, Galluzzi understands "*cognitio sui*" in terms that are inherently political and define the role of the individual in the community. For Galluzzi, the awareness of one's limits, understood broadly as the sphere in which one's action is licit, does not imply abandoning the potential of the collective. Instead, the individual's responsibility within the group becomes limited, although purportedly no less important. In Galluzzi's view, each student refrains from attempting the entirety of knowledge only to allow society as a whole to attain that which is denied to the individual, namely the *encyclopedia*. To illustrate this, he points out, somewhat disingenuously, that professors at his school teach only one discipline and do not claim to profess each and every subject. It is only as a gathering of people (*coetus*) that educational institutions such as Rome's Jesuit College aspire to the totality that single scholars cannot and indeed should not try to embrace. Moreover, what holds true for the microcosm of the college is also true for the republic: individual difference need not lead to fragmentation but, on the contrary, brings learners together through their need for one another. Galluzzi most likely found in Vives the idea that the division of the sciences and the arts depends on and at the same time fosters mutual need, much as the division of labour requires the community while simultaneously making it viable. He also transfers Aristotle's notion of man as "political animal" to scholarship: just as human beings cannot live alone, they cannot learn alone. The *encyclopedia* remains a valid and desirable ideal for the community, one that the collective may attain thanks to the moderation practised by the individuals who make up the body politic. Although Galluzzi never mentions Vives's *De tradendis disciplinis,* he might have found there the idea that prudence and temperance overcome hubris (*arrogantia, superbia*), the love of ourselves that Fattori saw as thwarting self-knowledge, and replace it with the love of others that encourages sociability.[53] Galluzzi's praise of specialization is ideologically loaded, in a dialectic in which focused and limited learning becomes synonymous with altruistic, socially responsible behaviour. In contrast, any attempt at overstepping and knowing "too much" represents selfishness. The corollary is clear: he who aims at the *encyclopedia* neglects his duty and risks harming the community by considering himself self-sufficient.

Galluzzi lends new meaning to the concerns shared by Huarte, Possevino, and Fattori regarding differences in talent. He shows that what historiography has branded as "Renaissance Man" is a siren, a snare that risks bringing about political and religious disruption. Galluzzi replaces such dreams with a call for specialization: citizens contribute to the common good when they use temperance to remain satisfied with the place allotted to them in society. He explains that the inscription "Dedicated to religion and the good arts," placed on the façade of Rome's Jesuit College in 1583, describes an institution with chairs for multiple disciplines. Multiplicity and difference are the basis of education, and knowledge is the fruit of a community learning together. He concludes by exhorting students to know themselves in order to judge the role, limited but sufficient, in which they are called to serve the community. As a reader of Possevino, Galluzzi turns the notion that believers freely serve God in the task given to them into a model that is essentially social, in which citizens contribute to the community while refusing to overstep the boundaries of their fellows and neighbours. Despite Galluzzi's promise of happiness, however, he does not explain how individuals are expected to identify the discipline for which God and nature has called them. This was a pressing matter, given that, as intimated by Meduna and Possevino, it is hardly possible to assert with any certainty *which* talent one possesses, let alone to discard the possibility that one might excel in other fields. Galluzzi mobilizes arguments from classical moral and political theory to lock individuals within limits that he defines as natural. For the sake of certainty and harmony, he discourages intellectual ambition and interdisciplinarity.

Even though it is likely that Galluzzi's oration is representative of widespread concerns among educators at the turn of the seventeenth century, it did not prevent Jesuit scholars from pursuing encyclopedic endeavours. Names such as Athanasius Kircher (1602–80) come to mind at once, but at an even more basic level, and despite Galluzzi's claims to the contrary, Jesuit professors used to teach more than one discipline throughout their career following more or less systematic patterns, and he was no exception to the rule.[54]

In 1617 Galluzzi became a professor of ethics at Rome's Jesuit College. At the same time, Vincenzo Guinigi (d. 1653) took over the chair of rhetoric. On that occasion, Guinigi delivered his speech *De habendo in litterarum aggressione delectu ex cuiusque naturae propensionibus* (On choosing according to each one's propensity at the beginning of studies). He picks up on the link between self-knowledge and career choice, lamenting that often students set out to learn a discipline without first taking into consideration "their nature's propensity and inclination," which is, "so to speak, of one sort, and prepared for a single kind of study." Due to self-ignorance (*ignoratio sui*), they fail to assess what they are good for, and at the first difficulty they conclude that they are unfit for learning of any kind.[55] Echoing Galluzzi, Guinigi claims that students are unfair to nature in so doing. However, the consequences are even worse when they do not give up studying: they proceed recklessly, laying the grounds, as Huarte and Fattori had feared, for political and religious harm.[56]

Yet what is the path towards self-knowledge, and what is "self-knowledge" exactly, according to Guinigi?

In contrast with the scepticism that characterized Fattori's stance, Guinigi holds that the individual may get to know who he is, and be certain about it. He asserts that God has placed "likenesses of the mind" (*simulachra animi*) in our bodies, "most certain and unerring signs of [one's] nature" (*notas … naturae certissimas*) that make it possible to deduce what the individual "has inside" much as the coat of arms on the façade of a palace reveals its inhabitants. To turn the student into "a sharp judge … [of] the force of his wit" and to encourage him to "consider himself honestly," Guinigi depicts the four temperaments and how one may detect them from outward appearances.[57] The dry and cold melancholic, always alone, pale-skinned, and slow-paced, has a talent for philosophy and everything that involves the understanding, but is incapable of a quick and ingenious reply. It is the hot and humid sanguine who excels in this, and who always seems to have a witty and facetious epigram sculpted on his forehead. For Guinigi, self-knowledge and the injunction "Recognize who you are" (*agnoscite quinam sitis*) translate into material and anatomic terms. The inside is read from the outside in search of qualities that are "intimately latent ... under the secrets and recesses of the human body" (*sub arcana reconditaque corporis humani*), as though behind a curtain. By paying careful attention one may determine the individual's "*constitutiones*," a term that closely echoes what the annual catalogues prepared by Jesuit superiors often categorized as "*complexio naturae.*"[58] The veins and the blood as channels for identity is more than simply a metaphor, and instead aligns with a contemporary trend of political discourse that identified the anatomy of the body with the exploration of the soul, as in Francisco de Quevedo's *Visit and anatomy of the head of the most eminent Cardinal Richelieu* (1635), which imagines anatomist Andrea Vesalius revealing Richelieu's machinations by exploring the cavities of the cardinal's brain.[59] The idea that knowing someone's temperament entailed knowledge of the individual and could provide a means for political and personal rivals to disclose and prevent that individual's plans was widely represented in the literature from Guinigi's time, from Baltasar Álamos de Barrientos's *Tácito español* (1611) to Eustache de Refuge's *Traité de la cour* (1616).

Guinigi innovates in that he approaches the investigation of the student's temperament, which for Huarte and Fattori entailed administrative perspectives and the involvement of state or school authorities, from the personal and reflexive stance that characterized Galluzzi's injunction to know oneself. As a consequence, students become capable of, but also responsible for, understanding *who they are*, based on temperamental criteria. Students need to "explore [themselves] carefully and diligently [to see] what they have" in terms of their body and brain.[60] Guinigi reminds his audience that, even recently and within the walls of Rome's Jesuit College, there have been examples of how the excellence of nature may degenerate into crime due to the lack of self-examination.[61] Discipline in the school is, above all, self-discipline.

Guinigi claims that his description of the four temperaments affords utmost certainty to anyone who makes use of it to understand who he is.[62] His method equates self-knowledge with identifying the group to which one belongs. In fact, as shown by Ursula Renz, seventeenth-century thinkers often understood the injunction "Know thyself" not as a search of one's uniqueness, but as awareness of what is common to human beings in general, manifested through differentiation into classes.[63]

The call for specialization launched by Galluzzi and Guinigi turned any attempt to overstep the limits of one's nature into a crime of usurpation. In their accounts, the language of citizenship, property rights, and spatiality intersected with that of virtue. Prudence and temperance appeared as antidotes to hubris and the temptation to pursue the totality of knowledge, letting the student know himself and his limits so as to avoid what, following the logic expounded so far, one might properly call theft. Galluzzi explored the topic in greater detail as he invoked the poet Battista Mantuano, who failed to excel in his art because he was not content "with the name he secured [as a poet], [nor was he] ... *prudent enough to refuse* a reputation that was more uncertain and borrowed from *sources that were foreign to him* [*ex alienis fontibus*]" (my italics).[64] If early modern usage made "natural" synonymous with "native," it follows that (as was claimed by Guinigi) the student "will pursue as something foreign all that which is not congenial (that is, natural) to [him]." He will feel he is not at home, in a conception that draws boundaries among objects of learning, codifies knowledge as property, and defines talent as ownership.[65] Fattori had characterized straying from one's nature as equivalent to wanton, unbridled desire, a simile that aligned with Meduna's assertion that by studying a discipline unnatural to us we risk becoming its "slaves" rather than its "masters."[66] While the fear that one might be owned rather than own might prove effective, the analogy between property rights and talent conjured by Galluzzi and Guinigi was no less operational. It created a fiction of civic virtue and altruism ideologically effective for educators to promote conformity among students.

Guinigi's oration ends with a facetious anecdote that further illuminates the equation between countering one's nature and theft. It is the story of fourteenth-century painter Bonamico di Buffalmaco, initially narrated by Bonamico's contemporary Franco Sacchetti, which Guinigi likely read in Giorgio Vasari's second edition of *Le vite de' più eccellenti pittori, scultori, e architettori* (1568). Hired to paint the walls of a church, Bonamico found out one day that someone had painted over his work. The criminal mimicked Bonamico's traits in a childish and unskilled fashion, seemingly aimed at destroying his reputation. To the amusement of all, it turned out that Bonamico's alleged enemy was in fact the bishop's ape, who observed the painter as he prepared his colours and drew his figures, and eventually undertook to imitate him. The counterfeiter destroyed the work of the true and legitimate artificer.[67] But how does the tale of Bonamico and the ape illustrate Guinigi's point?

Much like the parrot, in Vasari's day the ape exemplified the process of imitating someone else without fully understanding what he or she is doing.[68] Vasari's ape was probably meant as a mockery of those who imitate a painter's *maniera* by mimicking what is accidental and apparent in it rather than grasping what is "true" about it – his or her technique. Polemicists conjured those who believed they imitated Aristotle just because they stammered as the philosopher allegedly did. Abandoning one's nature in order to impersonate someone else implies entering a foreign space in which we lack any point of reference. Thus expelled from ourselves, we become unable to make distinctions with any certainty that they are correct.[69]

Guinigi re-signified Vasari's ape to target those who fail to conform to the role allotted to them by nature and study a discipline in which they are "foreign." Rejecting prudence and temperance, we let pleasure and debauchery take hold of us whenever we undertake a study in which we do not belong. Echoing Vives's warning that by advising a student into a career for which he is not adequate we risk having "the wild beast aroused in him" to his detriment and that of the state, Guinigi warns that we risk letting "the monster grow within our walls and our chest" as we feed and take care of it. In line with Fattori, Guinigi's ape is the emblem of a transgression that results in either sterility or harm: sterility because the tale is light and entertaining; harm because, when applied to other disciplines, it warns against "the largest disaster for mortals" that looms on the horizon, namely heresy.[70]

The values promoted by Guinigi come into focus when compared with a similar and related paradigm. In Aphorism 123 of the aforementioned *Oráculo manual*, Gracián reinterpreted a set of principles originating in a book by then more than a century old, Baldassare Castiglione's *Book of the Courtier* (first printed in 1528). Gracián advised the courtier to avoid affectation, for those who act in a way that appears unnatural to spectators are perceived as foreign (*extranjeros*) in what they do.[71] Even though Gracián and Galluzzi similarly categorize abilities in terms of nature and belonging, they seem to be worlds apart in the way they conceive of the individual's opportunity to learn and adapt himself to new environments – one might be tempted to say, following the metaphor, to "migrate." The courtier imagined by Castiglione is not exactly like the one that he inspires in Gracián, yet they share in the belief that learning of any kind is generally possible, even if the one who learns needs to dissimulate the effort invested in the process of acquisition. His goal is to seem to have been born with it. Castiglione's model and that of Gracián envision social mobility insofar as they conceive of a path for parvenus to approximate those who were born at court and are "naturally" graceful, that is, "native" to what they are expected to do. Rather than a paradox, "learning nature" is part of the challenge. Little of this seems to apply to Jesuit professors who, from Fattori to Galluzzi to Guinigi, discuss student advising and orientation with the school curriculum in mind. Unwilling to make concessions to liberty such as those found in Possevino (which stemmed, in part, from scepticism towards the certainty that obtains from the examination of wits), for them the student's nature represents a limit that he is strongly discouraged from transgressing. The three orations are notable for their attention to difference, yet they feature a pessimistic or at the least cautious approach to the individual's ability to overcome limitations. The benefit of bringing forth a Michelangelo or a Pico, they suggest, is not worth risking a Luther or a Calvin. As a project of social engineering, the death of "Renaissance Man" suggests notable gains in social stability and control. If one were to accept all of Fattori's premises, it would also mean that the pursuit of knowledge could occur within conditions that guarantee certainty and avoid the risk of sophistic and apparent reasoning incurred by those who are foreign to a discipline. As to the loss potentially involved in what they propose, none of the orators is able or willing to speculate.

Huarte's *Examen de ingenios* provided the three orations with a background of harmonious social order partially inspired in Plato's *Republic* and not entirely unrelated to works such as *Utopia*, published in 1516 by Vives's friend Thomas More. Yet the infallibility that Huarte claimed for the examination of wits, itself a product of the determinism that was inherent to temperament-based Galenic psychology, imposed restrictions on the liberty of the individual that compromised its assurance of personal and social prosperity. This makes Huarte's method and those derived from it appear rather dystopian to our eyes, and even to those of contemporaries such as Possevino, whose notion of "*cultura*" tried to promote a vision based on potentialities rather than limitations.[72] While by no means undisputed, the drive towards control and expediency that results from the advice of Fattori, Galluzzi, and Guinigi aligned with the climate of suspicion towards intellectual audacity and innovation in which their orations came into existence. Year after year, Jesuits depicted an environment fearful of religious dissidence and wary of the popularity of political ideas inspired by Machiavellianism and a reason of state that prioritized pragmatism over moral principles. This explains, at least in part, the student's absolute lack of freedom to question the path decreed for him – even in the case of Galluzzi and Guinigi, who promoted a fiction of socially aimed self-knowledge and specialization articulated around the belonging to a community, and which, by fostering the student's self-examination, attempted to restore some of the autonomy that Fattori had denied to learners. Some caveats are in place, however. As hinted earlier in the case of Fattori, the three orations need to be taken for what they actually are: not detailed argumentations in treatise form, but rather public discourses delivered in precise circumstances. They sought to instil in the students a social project and to define a role for the school within it. They aimed to persuade the audience that no decision made about a student was without a reason. One should exert caution, therefore, when drawing conclusions. It is important to keep in mind that some of the claims advanced by Fattori, Galluzzi, and Guinigi regarding intellectual, social, and educational perspectives might seem slightly disproportionate when taken outside the context of the situation in which they were delivered. The concerns they voiced about learning and pedagogy remain nonetheless significant, and so does the language they mobilized to formulate them.

On behalf of order, efficiency, and certainty in the acquisition of knowledge, Jesuit professors from the late sixteenth to the early seventeenth century built a model in which straying from one's "nature" necessarily entailed aping those who really had the talent to practise the discipline that interlopers were unlawfully trying to take from them. Scholars from Fattori to Galluzzi and Guinigi argued that self-ignorance (or, for Fattori, lack of obedience to those who are able to know a student's nature) brings ruin to the community, much like the ape did to Buffalmaco's painting. Practitioners of a discipline that is "foreign" to them paint over the truth with "their cosmetics and I know not what fake colours ... thereby extinguishing the living form of wisdom."[73] Galluzzi and Guinigi in other orations further developed the idea that "cosmetic" or unessential ingredients proliferate in the sciences and the arts whenever practitioners step beyond the field in which they are competent, with the result that, being "foreign," they confuse appearance and truth.[74] The possibility of attaining certain knowledge was the prerogative of those who respect the gifts that nature gave to them. The stakes of policing students' talents were enormous, for early modern Jesuits agreed that, while aping a painter might result in lines and colours that deface some figures, aping a statesman might easily lead to a new Catiline. Aping a theologian, in turn, would unleash upon the world nothing less than a new Luther, a new Calvin.

ACKNOWLEDGMENTS

I am greatly indebted to Barbara Fuchs for reading and providing invaluable feedback on this chapter. I would also like to thank Irene Pedretti, from the archive at Rome's Pontificia Università Gregoriana, for helping me with access to several of the sources I analyse.

NOTES

1 I use the pronouns "he," "him," and "his" for members of the Society of Jesus and for students at Jesuit schools, since these were invariably male. I reserve inclusive language for cases in which a statement might apply regardless of gender.

2 See especially Cristiano Casalini, "Discerning Skills: Psychological Insight at the Core of Jesuit Identity," in *Exploring Jesuit Distinctiveness: Interdisciplinary Perspectives on Ways of Proceeding within the Society of Jesus*, ed. Robert A. Maryks (Leiden: Brill, 2016), 189–211, DOI: 10.1163/9789004313354_012; for the debate on talent more generally, see Cristiano Casalini, "Disputa sugli ingegni: L'educazione dell'individuo in Huarte, Possevino, Persio e altri," *Educazione: Giornale di pedagogia critica* 1, no. 1 (2012): 29–51; also related is Marina Massimi, "Engenho e temperamentos nos catálogos e no pensamento da Companhia de Jesus nos séculos XVII e XVIII," *Revista latinoamericana de psicopatología fundamental* 11, no. 4 (2008): 675–87.

3 Paul Grendler, "Jesuit Schools in Europe: A Historiographical Essay," *Journal of Jesuit Studies* 1, no. 1 (2014): 7–25, at 7–8. See also, by the same author, *Jesuit Schools and Universities in Europe, 1548–1773* (Leiden: Brill, 2019), DOI: 10.1163/22141332-00101002; and, for the Italian case in particular, *The Jesuits and Italian Universities, 1548–1773* (Washington, DC: Catholic University of America Press, 2017). Regarding the role of Rome in Jesuit administrative and informational networks, see Markus Friedrich, "Governance in the Society of Jesus 1540–1773: Its Methods, Critics, and Legacy Today," *Studies in the Spirituality of Jesuits* 41, no. 1 (2009): 1–42; and Paul Nelles, "Chancillería en colegio: La producción y circulación de papeles jesuitas en el siglo XVI," *Cuadernos de Historia Moderna*, Anejo 13 (2014): 49–70, DOI: 10.5209/rev_CHMO.2014.46789. For the history of the order's Collegio Romano, see Ricardo García Villoslada, *Storia del Collegio Romano dal suo inizio (1551) alla soppressione della Compagnia di Gesù (1773)* (Rome: Pontificia Università Gregoriana, 1954).

4 Francesco Maria Fattori, *De moderandis ingeniis* ... Archivio della Pontificia Università Gregoriana (hereafter APUG), Ms. 117, fols 40r–45r, at fol. 40r.

Given that this is the only known manuscript preserving the oration, there is a margin of doubt concerning its attribution to Fattori.

5 "Ingegno … *But.* [Francesco da Buti] Una virtù interior d'animo, per la quale l'huomo da se truova quello, che da altri non ha imparato." *Vocabolario degli Academici della Crusca* (Venice: Giovanni Alberti, 1612), 444. For a thorough discussion of *ingenium* in early modern lexicography, see Alexander Marr, Raphaële Garrod, José Ramón Marcaida, and Richard J. Oosterhoff, *Logodaedalus: Word Histories of Ingenuity in Early Modern Europe* (Pittsburgh: University of Pittsburgh Press, 2018).

6 Cesare Ripa, *Iconologia … nella quale si descrivono diverse imagini* (Siena: Heirs of Matteo Florimi, 1613), 10. Unless otherwise indicated, all translations are mine.

7 Lodovico Castelvetro, *Poetica d'Aristotele vulgarizzata, et sposta* (Vienna: Gaspar Stainhofer, 1570), fols 40r, 106r.

8 Antonio Possevino, *Bibliotheca selecta qua agitur de ratione studiorum* (Rome: Typographia Apostolica Vaticana, 1993), 21C. In the dedication preceding the Italian translation of the first part of Possevino's *Bibliotheca selecta,* Mariano Lauretti makes "wit" synonymous with "intellect." Antonio Possevino, *Coltura degl'ingegni* (Vicenza: Giorgio Greco, 1598), 14.

9 With time, the term *genium* came to designate that which makes wits different from one another and implies individual difference. However, in the orations that I analyse here, "ingenium" refers alternatively to intellectual ability and to difference in intellectual ability. See Cristina Valini, "*Genius/ingenium:* Derive semantiche," in *Ingenium propria hominis natura,* ed. Stefano Gensini and Arturo Martone (Naples: Liguori, 2002), 3–26 passim; and Marr et al., *Logodaedalus,* passim.

10 Fattori, *De moderandis ingeniis,* fols 41r–42r. See Marcus F. Quintilian, *The Orator's Education,* trans. and ed. Donald Russell (Cambridge, MA: Harvard University Press, 2001), 403.

11 Fattori, *De moderandis ingeniis,* fol. 42r–v.

12 Ibid., fol. 42v.

13 Ibid., fol. 43r–v.

14 Ibid., fols 40v–41r.

15 Baltasar Gracián, *Oráculo manual y arte de prudencia,* ed. Emilio Blanco (Madrid: Cátedra, 1995), 151.

16 For the injunction to self-knowledge, see Jon R. Snyder, *Dissimulation and the Culture of Secrecy in Early Modern Europe* (Berkeley: University of California Press, 2009), 7. For early modern scepticism on the topic of self-knowledge, see Aaron Garrett, "Self-Knowledge and Self-Deception in Early Modern Moral Philosophy," in *Self-Knowledge: A History,* ed. Ursula Renz (Oxford: Oxford University Press, 2017), 164–82 passim.

17 François de La Rochefoucauld, *Collected Maxims and Other Reflections*, trans. and ed. E.H. Blackmore, A.M. Blackmore, and Francine Giguère (Oxford: Oxford University Press, 2007), 148–9.
18 Fattori, *De moderandis ingeniis*, fol. 43r.
19 Ibid., fols 42v–43v.
20 *Regulae Societatis Iesu* (Rome: Collegio Romano, 1580), 145; see Casalini, "Discerning Skills," 194–5; and Massimi, "Engenho," 676–7.
21 *Ratio studiorum*, sec. 458, numbered also as section 14 of the instructions "for those who for two years learn theology by themselves," is entitled *Naturae propensio attendenda* (That one should heed to the inclination of nature). It orders that students be oriented to the discipline towards which they feel inclination – always consulting the superior and making sure that this does not prevent them from learning the basics of the remaining disciplines in the curriculum. See Laszlo Lukács, *Monumenta Paedagogica Societatis Jesu* (Rome: Institutum Historicum Societatis Jesu, 1986), 5.445; in general, see Casalini, "Discerning Skills," 193–5, 204–5.
22 Casalini, "Discerning Skills," 189; also Grant Boswell, "Letter Writing among the Jesuits: Antonio Possevino's Advice in the 'Bibliotheca Selecta' (1593)," *Huntington Library Quarterly* 66, no. 3–4 (2003): 247–62, at 249, https://www.jstor.org/stable/3818082. For Jesuit administration and efficiency, see Friedrich, "Governance," 11 and passim.
23 Juan Huarte de San Juan, *Examen de ingenios para las ciencias*, ed. Guillermo Serés (Madrid: Cátedra, 1989), 223.
24 Craig W. Kallendorf, ed., *Humanist Educational Treatises* (Cambridge, MA: Harvard University Press, 2002), 56–9.
25 Juan Luis Vives, *On Education*, ed. and trans. Foster Watson (Cambridge: Cambridge University Press, 1913), 62.
26 Huarte de San Juan, *Examen*, 234–47.
27 For the role of Galen's *Quod animi mores* in Huarte's thought, see Casalini, "Discerning Skills," 195–8.
28 Huarte de San Juan, *Examen*, 395–6.
29 Ibid., 366–7.
30 Ibid., passim, and especially the dedication to Philip II, 149–56.
31 Casalini, "Discerning Skills," 190, 198.
32 For Huarte's fortunes in sixteenth- and seventeenth-century Italy, see Casalini, "Disputa," 29–51 passim.
33 Huarte de San Juan, *Examen*, 152–3, and see also Juan Huarte de San Juan, *Essame de gl'ingegni de gli huomini, per apprender le scienze ... di Gio. Huarte: Nuovamente Tradotto dalla lingua spagnuola da M. Camillo Camilli* (Venice: [Aldo Manuzio Jr], 1582), fol. *4v.

34 Vives, *On Education*, 63.

35 Huarte de San Juan, *Examen*, 414–17, and *Essame*, 126–8.

36 Huarte de San Juan, *Examen*, 233, and *Essame*, 14; Fattori, *De moderandis ingeniis*, fol. 43r–v.

37 Huarte de San Juan, *Examen*, 154, and *Essame*, fol. *4v; Fattori, *De moderandis ingeniis*, fols 43v–44r; Possevino, *Coltura*, 27.

38 Giovanni Pico della Mirandola, *Oration on the Dignity of Man: A New Translation and Commentary*, ed. Francesco Borghesi, Michael Papio, and Massimo Riva (New York: Cambridge University Press, 2012), 116–23. For Possevino's gloss on Pico, see Possevino, *Bibliotheca selecta*, 13E–14A.

39 Antonio Possevino, *Cultura ingeniorum … Examen ingeniorum Io. Huartis Expenditur* (Venice: Giovanni Battista Ciotti, 1604). On Possevino's psychological and educational theory, see Paul Richard Blum, "Psychology and Culture of the Intellect: Ignatius of Loyola and Antonio Possevino," in *Cognitive Psychology in Early Jesuit Scholasticism*, ed. Daniel Heider (Neunkirchen-Seelscheid: Editiones Scholasticae, 2016), 12–37, at 24–33.

40 Possevino, *Bibliotheca selecta*, 23D–24C; *Coltura*, 26. From here onwards, I provide page numbers both from the Latin original (*Bibliotheca selecta*, which includes a section called *Cultura ingeniorum*) and from the Italian translation (*Coltura*), except when a passage is present in one version only.

41 Possevino, *Bibliotheca selecta*, 19B–C; *Coltura*, 12.

42 Bartolomeo Meduna, *Lo scolare …* (Venice: Pietro Fachinetti, 1588), fol. 12r.

43 Possevino, *Coltura*, 21.

44 Possevino, *Bibliotheca selecta*, 23D–24B. This is developed at length in *Coltura*, 25–6.

45 Possevino, *Bibliotheca selecta*, 29D–30B; *Coltura*, 36–7; Meduna, *Lo scolare*, fol. 1v and also fol. 11v.

46 Fattori, *De moderandis ingeniis*, fol. 43r–v.

47 Tarquinio Galluzzi, *De multiplici doctrinarum studio contrahendo …* APUG, Ms. 1153, fols 38r–43v, at fol. 38r–v. The oration was printed as Galluzzi, "De encyclopaedia, siue de multiplici doctrinarum studio contrahendo …," in *Orationum Tomus I* (Rome: Bartolomeo Zanetti, 1617), 35–64.

48 Galluzzi, *De multiplici doctrinarum studio*, fols 38r, 42r–v.

49 Ibid., fols 42v–46v.

50 Ibid., fol. 47v.

51 Ibid., fols 40v–41r, 46v. The conceit of the world as a marketplace played a central role in writers such as Tommaso Garzoni and Baltasar Gracián, and crucially informed Pedro Calderón's *El gran mercado del mundo* (c. 1636). A former student of Madrid's Jesuit Colegio Imperial, Calderón introduces the allegory of two brothers who are given *one talent* each (here the name of

a coin) and need to exert extreme caution as they decide what to purchase. Pedro Calderón de la Barca, *El gran mercado del mundo*, ed. Ana Suárez (Pamplona: Universidad de Navarra, 2003). I am grateful to the anonymous reviewer who suggested this parallel.

52 Galluzzi, *De multiplici doctrinarum studio*, fol. 46v.

53 Ibid., fol. 46v. Vives, *On Education*, 38.

54 For the system of shifts in the allocation of disciplines to professors in Jesuit schools, see Paul Grendler, "The Culture of the Jesuit Teacher 1548–1773," *Journal of Jesuit Studies* 3, no. 1 (2016): 17–41, at 23–4, DOI: 10.1163/22141332-00301002.

55 Vincenzo Guinigi, *De habendo in litterarum aggressione delectu ex cuiusque naturae propensionibus*, APUG, Ms. 1153, fols 14r–23v, at fol. 14r. It was printed as Guinigi, "Habendum esse delectum in litterarum aggressione, ex ipsis ingeniorum procliuitatibus," in *Allocutiones gymnasticae* (Rome: Francesco Corbelletti, 1626), 69–98.

56 Guinigi, *De habendo*, fol. 16r–v.

57 Ibid., fol. 17r.

58 Ibid., fols 16v–17r. It is not impossible that Guinigi was evoking Pseudo-Boethius's thirteenth-century treatise *De disciplina scolarium* (On the discipline of students), a work that enjoyed numerous editions in the early modern period. There we find the injunction "Know thyself" following the mention of the four temperaments (introduced for different reasons than in Guinigi). Pseudo-Boethius, *De disciplina scolarium*, ed. Olga Weijers (Leiden: Brill, 1976), 109.

59 See Enrique Fernández, "La interioridad de Richelieu anatomizada por Quevedo," *Bulletin hispanique* 105 (2003): 215–29 passim, DOI: 10.3406 /hispa.2003.5156.

60 Guinigi, *De habendo*, fol. 21r.

61 Ibid., fols 21v–22r.

62 Ibid., fol. 20v.

63 Ursula Renz, "Socratic Self-Knowledge in Early Modern Philosophy," in Renz, *Self-Knowledge: A History*, 146–63, at 152.

64 Galluzzi, *De multiplici doctrinarum studio*, fol. 47v.

65 Guinigi, *De habendo*, fol. 21r.

66 Meduna, *Lo scolare*, fol. 11r.

67 Guinigi, *De habendo*, fols 22r–23r. The source is Giorgio Vasari, *Le Vite de' più eccellenti pittori, scultori, e architettori* (Florence: Giunti, 1568), 158–9.

68 The ape and the parrot signified slavish imitation, for instance, in the late fifteenth-century debate between Angelo Poliziano and Paolo Cortesi regarding the imitation of Cicero as a model to write Latin. Joan DellaNeva,

ed., *Ciceronian Controversies* (Cambridge, MA: Harvard University Press, 2007), 2, 8.

69 See Franziska Meier, "The Afterlives of Buffalmacco: The *Decameron*'s Impact on Giorgio Vasari's Two Editions of the *Vite*," *Modern Language Notes* 132, no. 1 (2017): 1–20, at 17–18, DOI: 10.1353/mln.2017.0000. For so-called "apish" forms of imitation, see DellaNeva, *Ciceronian Controversies*, 2–3.

70 Guinigi, *De habendo*, fol. 23r.

71 Gracián, *Oráculo manual*, 169–70.

72 Needless to say, few of Fattori's contemporaries would have agreed that the examination of talents provided entirely objective and secure results. In fact, it has been argued that the way Jesuit superiors used categories of temperament to describe members of the order in the annual catalogues included numerous cases of bias and even sheer corruption. See Casalini, "Discerning Skills," 201–4.

73 Guinigi, *De habendo*, fol. 23r–v.

74 Galluzzi delivered his oration *De doctrinae fuco depellendo* (On removing cosmetics from learning) in November 1615. It has been preserved in APUG, Ms. 1153, fols 25r–27r and 71r–73v and, in print, in Galluzzi, "De doctrinae fuco depellendo …," in *Orationum Tomus I*, 65–100. Guinigi's oration "That, as in every other thing, one should avoid excess in learning and superfluous knowledge," was printed in 1626. Guinigi, "Cauendum esse, ut in ceteris rebus, sic in disciplinis, luxum & superuacaneam scientiam …," in *Allocutiones gymnasticae*, 98–125.

PART 2

NEGOTIATING HISTORY AND THEOLOGY

chapter six

Stolen Saint: Relic Theft and Relic Identification in Seventeenth-Century Rome

A. KATIE STIRLING-HARRIS

Late in the evening of 18 March 1655, two Spanish friars, lay brothers of the traditional, or Calced, branch of the Order of the Most Holy Trinity and of the Redemption of Captives, left their monastery in Rome and hurried out into the night.[1] Slipping quietly through the darkened streets, they made their way from their monastery, located near the Piazza Barberini, to the church of San Tommaso in Formis, almost three kilometres away on the Caelian Hill.[2] The small church and its adjoining cloister had once belonged to their order, but by 1389 the Trinitarian order had lost control of the buildings and the rents associated with them to the canons of the chapter of St Peter at the Vatican, who in 1634 leased the church and its associated buildings to the ever-expanding urban villa of Girolamo Mattei, marquis of Giove.[3] Largely abandoned in a semi-rural sector of Rome, its hospital half in ruins and reduced to service as a granary, San Tommaso in Formis was a vulnerable target.[4]

Armed only with an iron pry bar, a flint and steel for striking a light, and a candle, Gonzalo de Medina and José Vidal scaled the garden walls that flanked the church but found the doors locked tight.[5] Nearby they found a stout wooden ladder and climbed it to reach the windows that provided light to the building's interior. They ripped away the linen curtain that substituted for window glass and clambered into the church, bringing the ladder with them. Once inside, they struck a light. The flickering candle would have revealed that the walls of the little church were decorated with frescos commemorating their order and its primary ministry, the redemption of Christian captives in Muslim lands.[6] Together, Vidal and Medina made their way towards a marble sarcophagus raised on pillars against one wall of the church and marked by an inscription that identified the tomb as that of St John of Matha (1150?–1213), the founder of the Trinitarian order. The two offered prayers and vows, and then set to work with the iron bar to dislodge the marble slab that closed the tomb. Inside, they discovered not one but three bodies. The bones of the saintly founder of the Trinitarians were in the middle, set apart from the others; above his skull was a handwritten prayer to the saint. On either side, pushed to the corners of the tomb and marked with identifying inscriptions, were the remains of two of the order's earliest generals.[7] The two thieves noted that while the two generals' bones were yellowed, those of St John of Matha were unusually white and quite long. The friars venerated the remains and then proceeded to remove the bones, placing them in a hastily improvised sack fashioned from Medina's woolen undershirt. They carefully replaced the pieces of the tomb so that it appeared intact, and exited the church by the same window they had entered, taking care to return the ladder to its original location. Medina and Vidal again traversed the city under cover of night. They returned, undetected, to their monastery, and hid their prize in a chest in Medina's cell.

The friars kept their secret for nearly three weeks, but eventually news of the theft reached the ears of their superior, Pedro Arias Portocarrero, the Trinitarians' solicitor general at the papal court, who took possession of the remains.[8] He ordered the two thieves to return to the church in order to retrieve the other two bodies and to leave in the tomb a note, written and signed by himself, that documented the removal of all three.[9] On the night of 6 April, Medina and Vidal braved a dangerous thunderstorm to return to the little church of San Tommaso in Formis. They accomplished the task but in the process they broke the lid of the tomb, a misfortune that ensured that the crime would eventually be discovered. By 11 April, the archpriest of the Vatican chapter, Cardinal Francesco Barberini (1597–1679), had opened an inquiry into the affair, and by mid-August Medina, Vidal, and Arias had been tried and convicted in absentia in the court of the cardinal vicar of Rome. On 30 August, a warning was posted on church doors throughout the city of Rome and its district. The *monitorio* ordered the thieves to present themselves before the court within eighteen days, and threatened penalties ranging from loss of status to prison, exile, and galley service for non-compliance.[10] The culprits, however, were long gone. Fearing punishment, Medina and Vidal had fled for Spanish-controlled Naples shortly after completing the second theft. Arias, too, was far from Rome. Having first entrusted the bodies of the two Trinitarian generals to the Spanish ambassador, he had disguised himself as an Augustinian friar and snuck out of the city to join his *confrères* in

Naples. Together, the three boarded a galley and escorted the stolen bones of St John of Matha to the safety of Spain.

Medina and Vidal's pious crime marked the beginning of a long and complicated controversy. *Furta sacra*, the theft of holy relics, had a long and distinguished history – medieval hagiography is littered with accounts of purloined bodies, some obscure, some belonging to Catholic Christianity's most famous and powerful saints. Cities and towns sometimes used theft as a tool to advance competing claims to a revered holy figure, and stolen saints often came to adorn the altars of monastic houses and civic communities seeking to enhance their worldly prominence and expand their spiritual resources. In some cases, the bodies of the saints served as war booty; in others, thieves justified their actions by pointing to personal devotion, an obligation to render cult to a neglected saint, or the wishes of the saint him- or herself, revealed in visions, dreams, or other inspirations.[11] Such was the logic cited by Friar Medina, who claimed that he and Vidal had been moved to commit the crime by the fact that Matha lay unvenerated in a semi-ruined church not controlled by the order that he founded, and by the rumour "that the Discalced religious of his order had tried to steal it, and it seemed to them more appropriate that his [Calced] religion have it than any other, since [Matha] had been [its] founder."[12]

For medieval Catholics, the act of theft did not necessarily imperil the authenticity of the remains; rather, acquisition by ruse or by violence (rather than by gift, sale, or discovery) guaranteed that a relic was indeed exactly what – or who – it was said to be.[13] By the mid-seventeenth century, however, *furta sacra* was neither common nor condoned, and while some other contemporary relic thefts do not seem to have occasioned questions about the authenticity of the stolen bodies, the two Trinitarians' action did not bring their founder's remains the honour and veneration they thought due, but instead exposed the bones of John of Matha to persistent doubts and debates about their identity.[14] How could one be sure that the relics in Madrid were the same as those that had lain in the tomb in Rome? How, indeed, could one be sure of the identity of any of the relics and remains held up to the faithful as those of saints?

These questions link the case of the stolen bones of St John of Matha to a broad and thoroughgoing crisis of certainty ongoing within early modern European culture.[15] As explorers expanded the limits of the known world and scholars engaged the classical past in new ways, long-established truths were increasingly cast into question. The encounter with the peoples of the Americas, for example, forced Europeans to reconsider traditional modes of explaining and engaging with alien cultures, while the revival of the ancient philosophical tradition of scepticism in both its Academic and Pyrrhonian veins fostered a re-evaluation of the sources and limits of human knowledge.[16] Developments in other fields of activity produced similar destabilizing effects. Rampant inflation, for example, and an expanding credit economy produced churning anxieties as budding economists struggled to comprehend the rapid fluctuations and devaluations of gold, a substance traditionally understood to be stable and unchanging in value.[17]

Most disorienting of all were the religious transformations of the sixteenth and seventeenth centuries, as Protestant and Catholic Reformations compelled Europeans to confront conflicting claims to theological truth and competing claims to the certainty of those truths. For early Protestants, for example, certainty of salvation and of scriptural interpretation was to be sought in the human experience of the Holy Spirit, while Catholic controversialists contended that certainty could only be found in the church, the true location of the Holy Spirit.[18] But could true knowledge of God be found in human experience? And how was one to know the true church from the false, the divine from the demonic, reality from appearance, being from seeming? The inquietudes spawned by these uncertainties were worked out in a host of arenas, from investigations of alleged mystics and would-be saints, to witchcraft trials and exorcisms of the demon-possessed, to concerns about counterfeit conversion and false identities, both religious and otherwise.[19] And while both sides came to embrace human knowledge as a means to faith, its limits and potential for error remained a site of much anxiety. So too was its potential to undermine the very theological truths that apologists sought to uphold – on both sides of the confessional divide, for example, the deep scholarship brought to bear in defence of religion threatened to undermine the foundational texts of Christianity.[20]

Among the many beliefs and practices rejected by Protestants, the worship of the saints and their remains frequently came in for special condemnation. While Catholic humanist critics like Alfonso de Valdés, John Colet, or Desiderius Erasmus sought to reform the veneration of the saints and to eliminate superstitious practices, many Protestant reformers aimed to do away with the cult entirely.[21] Jean Calvin's 1543 treatise against relics, for example, decried such "abuses" as John the Baptist's multiple heads and the veneration of animal bones as the remains of saints, and rejected the worship of "dead and insensible creatures" instead of "the onely livyng God."[22] Throughout Protestant Europe, reformers "cleansed" churches and chapels of their relics, which were often destroyed or consigned to anonymity in communal charnel houses.[23]

The Catholic Church responded vigorously to these criticisms.[24] As part of its larger push to clarify doctrine and to reassert the boundaries between the sacred and the profane, the Council of Trent (1545–63) reaffirmed the validity of the cult of the saints and their relics and tasked bishops with the eradication of superstitious or impious practices.[25] After a sixty-five-year "failure of papal nerve," by 1588 Rome resumed canonizations, but with reformed, more rigorous procedures under the administration of a new supervisory body, the Congregation of Sacred Rites.[26] Around the Catholic world, religious orders like the Jesuits encouraged relic piety among the laity, who responded eagerly.[27] Veneration of the saints and their remains continued to occupy as central a place in early modern Catholic devotional life as it had before Luther.

Yet relics continued to present challenges. If, as Cécile Vincent-Cassy has suggested, "after the Council of Trent, in the face of Protestant critics, the search for veracity led the Catholic Church to demonstrate the relics' historicity," holy bodies that lacked or possessed only faulty evidence of identity and/or provenance presented grave problems for officials charged with their authentication.[28] Even for the most convinced of devotees, relics that had been dislodged from their places of honour in churches and chapels, stripped from their reliquaries and from the *authentica*, the labels and tickets that fixed names to otherwise anonymous bones, or, as in the case of the remains of St John of Matha, stolen and spirited away, could give rise to disquieting doubts and upsetting uncertainties.[29] In this chapter, I explore some of the ways in which Catholic thinkers met the challenge of the uncertainty of relics. Through an examination of arguments brought to bear on the question of the identity of the body of St John of Matha, I consider how, by the second half of the seventeenth century, the theologians, canonists, casuists, and others who wrote about the remains of the saints sought certitude by defining the degree of certainty required to distinguish the true relics from the false. The form of certainty identified for relics, a lesser form known as moral certainty, accommodated their inherent ambivalence and the potential flaws in the documents and testimony that identified them. In effect, the application of the category of moral certainty accommodated doubt by defining relics as acceptably contingent and probable, subject to the limits of human testimony and human knowledge.

After Arias arrived in Madrid with the body, he took the question of how to proceed to Francisco de Arcos (?–1674), a fellow Trinitarian who was both a respected scholar and a royal preacher with excellent connections in the court of Philip IV.[30] The problem was a sensitive one, since the papal nuncio in Madrid had been ordered to apprehend the thieves.[31] However, while the Trinitarian order was international, its corporate identity was dominated by the Spanish membership and it enjoyed strong ties to the Spanish court.[32] Given these facts, Arcos opted to present the case directly to the king, who offered to write to Rome on the order's behalf and ordered the relics to be entrusted to the nuncio for safekeeping. On 24 November 1655, Arcos, Arias, and Gerónimo Vélez Matute, the order's *visitador*, handed over the bones of St John of Matha to Carlo Camillo Massimo (1620–1677), the papal envoy in Spain.[33] Nuncio Massimo inspected the remains, venerated them, and, when he had replaced them in the coffer in which they were stored, impressed his own seal on red wax in four places on the cords that bound the box. Carefully notarized records of the handover and recognition of the relics were stored in the nunciature's archive. These measures were not enough, however, to ensure the proper identification of the body, and in 1657 Medina, Vidal, and Arias gathered at the nuncio's tribunal in Madrid to testify about the events and the identity of the body that they had stolen. The witnesses recounted the crime for Giovanni Carlo di Camilis, auditor general of the nunciature, and his secretary Isidro Jacinto de Pau, describing in detail the location, disposition, appearance, and identifying inscriptions of the three bodies in the tomb. The matter went no further, however, since Arcos's contacts in Rome told him that the theft was too recent and feelings too raw for the authorities to countenance a petition to transfer Matha's bones to Madrid's Calced monastery.

While the Calced branch of the Trinitarian family might have been content to wait for a more propitious moment, the Discalced branch was not so disposed and, as one Calced critic commented, "impelled by their usual genius for sticking their noses into everything," began to gather information for a formal petition for identification of the relics to be considered by the Congregation of Sacred Rites.[34] Established in 1588 by Pope Sixtus V, the Congregatio Sacrorum Rituum is best known as the body that oversaw the formal processes of beatification and canonization of saints, but its purview also extended to larger issues of liturgy, ceremony, and cult. Relics, too, came under the congregation's authority – since the thirteenth century, authentication of the remains of candidates for beatification and canonization had been the exclusive province of the pope, while bishops held jurisdiction over newly discovered relics of known, approved saints.[35] In its twenty-fifth session, the Council of Trent affirmed this division of labour, but specified that particularly doubtful or questionable cases must be remanded to a provincial council and that the pope must also be consulted.[36] The relics of St John of Matha seem to have come under papal purview not because they had been stolen from the pope's own episcopal see and were now in the hands of the papal envoy, but because of the serious questions and doubts that surrounded them. For these reasons it was to the Congregation of Sacred Rites that the Discalced Trinitarians directed their petition in 1669.

By stealing the relics, Medina and Vidal had unwittingly opened a Pandora's box of problems, since in order for Matha's remains to be venerated by the public, their identity as the remains of the saint had to be firmly established. In Rome, testified Medina, the body of St John of Matha "did not receive the appropriate veneration, because the church [of San Tommaso in Formis] was half-ruined [and] in an unpopulated area within the city of Rome."[37] The Calced friars' theft of the bones was meant to ensure that the founder received proper honours (and to twit their Discalced confrères, who were said to have tried to steal the body for themselves).[38] Instead, the crime threw into question the identity of the relics and the licitness of their veneration. Rather than receiving the public cult that the thieves had sought, the body languished in obscurity in the oratory of the nuncio's residence in Madrid, and would now have to undergo a rigorous examination to establish its identity.

Pieces of the file on St John of Matha submitted in 1668 to the Congregation of Sacred Rites are found scattered in archives and libraries around the city of Rome. The most important are four anonymous briefs – three found among the papers of Cardinal Sigismondo Chigi (1649–78) held by the Vatican Library, one preserved in the Biblioteca Angelica – that laid out the arguments in favour of the identification of the bones in question as those of St John of Matha.[39] The three in the Vatican Library appear to be legal consultations on behalf of the Trinitarians and directed to the congregation's prefect, Cardinal Marzio Ginetti di Velletri (1585–1671). The longest of these spans some twenty-three folios, while the other two are quite succinct, only one to two folios long.[40] The document held by the Biblioteca Angelica is a short listing, only two folios long, of evidence in favour of the identity of the remains, directed to the congregation by the solicitor general of the Discalced Trinitarians. All four of these briefs laid out similar claims, but with differing degrees of detail and sophistication. Because there is a great deal of repetition among them, my discussion focuses primarily upon the arguments contained in the longest and richest of the four briefs. Together with related documents gathered from the Vatican Secret Archives, and other materials that can be partially reconstructed from the discussions of later commentators, these sources offer a rare view into the thorny questions that surrounded proof, certainty, and the identification of the holy.

The long brief opened by laying out five propositions that were then proved in the rest of the text. The first three framed the question of saintly relics in the terms and concepts of Aristotelian logic and, in so doing, established the terms and parameters of the debate over the relics of St John of Matha. Citing St Augustine together with Francisco Suárez, SJ (1548–1617), Gabriel Vázquez, SJ (1549?–1604), Pedro de Lorca (1561–1612), and other luminaries of early modern moral theology, the author of the brief contrasted metaphysical certainty with moral certainty. First, he argued:

> While metaphysical certainty is found only in situations or acts of supernatural faith, because they rely upon divine authority, with which falsity or the telling of falsehood is incompatible, moral and human certainty is not incompatible with [the possibility] that a matter or someone's assent to something that at present is judged to be sure is in fact false. On the contrary, [moral] certainty can be greater than the other [kind of certainty] because it is grounded upon better and more efficacious foundations.[41]

Moral, not metaphysical certainty, asserted the author in the second proposition, was the standard by which the bodies of the saints were judged, "but it is not impossible that the bodies that are venerated as holy are not of those saints."[42] Three examples illustrated the potential for error. In the catacombs underneath Rome, inscriptions and grave goods marked the tombs of martyrs, but because the graves of the saints lay right next to those of common Christians, confusion between the two might easily occur. Similarly, though historians disagreed about the fates of the bodies of St Peter and St Paul and the locations of the remains of St Benedict and St Scholastica, "these things notwithstanding, when other principles are considered, it is judged that the identity of such bodies is morally certain, and they are exposed for public veneration."[43]

The third proposition argued that moral certainty was not undermined by the possibility of contradiction, opposition, or the danger of falseness. The fact that moral certainty coexisted with the possibility of falseness did not abrogate it, since "as the axiom says, *ab actu ad potentiam bene valet consequentia*, but not from potential to actual."[44] The author of the brief illustrated with a commonplace example this traditional principle of scholastic logic, that while what really exists must also be judged to be possible, there is no valid inference from what is possible to what is actual. It was, he noted, certainly possible that he himself might have some defection of intention in his baptism and ordination, and thus might not truly be a priest, and that therefore the Host might not be consecrated. Refusal to adore the consecrated Host on that mere possibility, however, was neither pious nor prudent.[45]

The category here invoked, that of moral certainty, *certitudo moralis*, was no innovation. First articulated by Jean Gerson (1363–1429) in response to the theological confusion fostered by the Great Western Schism (1378–1417), moral certainty signified "a certainty that suffices for action," in which "moral risk avoidance becomes unnecessary and an agent is entitled to trust his beliefs without fear of error" because he has attained a level of certainty that is adequate to avoid sin.[46] Gerson grounded this principle from his reading of a well-known passage in Aristotle's *Nichomachean Ethics*, in which the Philosopher noted that "it is the mark of an educated man to look for precision in each class of things just so far as the nature of the subject admits: it is evidently equally foolish to accept probable reasoning from a mathematician and to demand from a rhetorician demonstrative proofs."[47] Both moral certainty and other varieties of uncertain certainty, such as probable certainty, which was an "opinion, an assent to one proposition, coupled with the acknowledgement that its opposite might be true," found new life in the wake of the Protestant Reformation, as competing claims to theological truth forced partisans on both sides of the confessional divide to articulate definitive positions.[48] In the face of Protestant arguments for the assurance of salvation granted to those to whom God had given the gift of faith, for example, the Council of Trent reiterated St Thomas Aquinas's rejection of absolute certainty, asserting that "no one can know, by that assurance of faith which excludes all falsehood, that he has obtained the grace of God."[49] Later Catholic apologists elaborated upon this. St Roberto Bellarmino, for example, contended that while one may have a "probable opinion" of one's own justification, absolute certainty is beyond human beings.[50]

By the latter decades of the sixteenth century, Gerson's concept of moral certainty became particularly important in casuistry, the early modern science of the conscience. Predominantly (though not exclusively) a Jesuit specialty, casuistry anatomized moral decision-making, especially in cases of uncertainty. Its enormous popularity in the early modern period suggests that casuists' moral systems hit a nerve in their response to the uncertainties of the age. Casuistry "sought to bolster confidence about certain values and principles; although ... it was the assurance of moral probability rather than certitude."[51] Probabilism, the dominant strain of casuistic reasoning until 1656, was pioneered in 1577 by the Dominican theologian Bartolomé de Medina (1527–1581). Medina's medieval predecessors had argued for a moral doctrine that demands that "in doubtful matters, the safer path is to be chosen."[52] That safer path, the option that will not lead to sin, was known at least in part by its probability – a concept understood by St Thomas Aquinas as "an opinion warranted by authority, and such probabilities vary in probative force according to the probity of the authority."[53] Medina elaborated on these older understandings by conflating doubt and opinion and suggesting instead that "if an opinion is probable [i.e., plausible] it is licit to follow it, though the opposite be more probable." This approach proved enormously successful among moral theologians and casuists alike. As Stefania Tutino's essay in this volume shows, it offered an acceptance of doubt and an acknowledgment of the limits – but not the impossibility – of human knowledge. Probabilist theologians elaborated a hierarchy of certainty that took into account these constraints. Juan Caramuel Lobkowitz (1606–1682), for example, described three types of certainty: metaphysical, physical, and moral. Metaphysical certainty was that "which necessarily is true, because from the absolute power of God it is not able to be otherwise." Physical certitude was a step down. It was known by the regular physical behaviour of things and the usual connections between cause and effect, but did not exclude the possibility of a miracle operating outside the natural order. By contrast, moral certainty, the weakest type, describes things that could possibly be other than what they usually are not only because of divine intervention but because of the actions of human beings.[54] Moral certainty "represented a certainty which was beyond reasonable doubt, but which did not entail logical necessity."[55]

Moral certainty's important role in casuistry was paralleled by its rise to prominence in other, related fields. By the second half of the seventeenth century, natural philosophers, both Protestant and Catholic, increasingly deployed the concept of moral certainty as a means of discussing scientific "facts" grounded in experiment and in human testimony.[56] In law, moral certainty came to occupy an important place in categories of proof and in criteria for judicial decision-making.[57] Canon lawyers, for example, expanded the role of moral certainty in the process of beatification, a status of sanctity that, by the 1630s, had come to be understood as a precursor to full canonization.[58] While theologians and jurists increasingly argued for the full certainty of papal inerrancy in canonization, most agreed that rulings on beatification should be understood as merely morally certain and potentially subject to error. The language of beatification and canonization decrees reflected the difference between the two, in that beatifications merely permitted veneration within a region or a particular religious order, but canonizations decreed and defined a holy person as a saint to be venerated by all of the faithful. In his 1622 bull beatifying Peter of Alcántara, OFM (1499–1562), for example, Pope Gregory XV "concede[d] and permit[ted]" the holy man's veneration by members of the Franciscan order, while in 1669, Pope Clement X's bull of canonization "decreed and defined Blessed Peter of Alcántara to be a saint and inscribed him in the catalogue of the saints."[59]

The extension of the category of moral certainty to relics appears to have emerged in the last decades of the sixteenth century. Leading moral theologians like Francisco Suárez (1548–1617) argued that relics could not be equal in their level of certainty (older relics, for example, were more uncertain), and that those publicly venerated by the universal church were subject to more stringent evidentiary demands than those given private cult. There was no risk of formal theological error, "since in human affairs no greater certainty [than moral certainty] is required."[60] By the second half of the seventeenth century, the application of moral certainty to relics was commonplace among moral theologians, casuists, and other writers who dealt with relics. The treatment of Francesco Bordoni (1594–1671) was typical.[61] Human knowledge was divided into three types – "scientific" (i.e., complete, perfect, true) knowledge, "opinion," and human testimony. The first two categories corresponded to two kinds of certainty. Scientific knowledge corresponded to a certainty that "touches on the truth of the principles of knowledge, in which nothing false can be concealed – this one pertains to natural wisdom and to divine faith, which is most reliable, in which it is impossible for anything false to be concealed," while opinion corresponded to moral certainty, at which the thinking intellect arrived when it judged a thing to be true, or close to true, on the basis of strong arguments. Unlike the first sort of certainty, moral certainty had to admit the possibility of doubt, error, or falseness, since it was grounded on opinion.[62] The third sort of knowledge, the knowledge of human testimony (*fides humana*), was grounded in the words or authority of others, "therefore, in this mode, we believe rather than know." This belief was particularly useful – even necessary – for the study of history, especially the ancient past.[63] Bordoni did not explain what kind of certainty could be ascribed to human testimony, but it seems likely that the corresponding category was also moral certainty, since both opinion and trust were necessary for the understanding of moral matters and thus for relics. Thus, "applying the adduced learning to our case [a contested relic, said to be a thorn from Christ's crown], scientific knowledge is not necessary for proving the truth of the fact, but opiniative knowledge suffices, and moral certainty, by which one thus reasonably and not rashly believes himself to regard the matter."[64]

Thus, while the validity and importance of the veneration of the remains of the saints was treated as a theological certainty, known through divine faith and through the tradition and consensus of the universal church, the teachings of the early church fathers, miracles and signs, and the decrees of popes and councils, individual or particular relics were understood to require a lesser degree of certainty.[65] Indeed, at least one author maintained that subjecting relics to more stringent standards of proof and a higher level of certainty would create grave problems. In his 1678 book on canonization and beatification, Carlo Felice de Matta (1622–1701) argued that

> it is very difficult, or rather impossible, to judge the identity of relics, because in order to have physical identity, two witnesses must depose that, for example, such and such a bone was removed from the body of such and such servant of God, known to them and that they themselves were present and watched it being stored in such a place from which, as they themselves knew, it was never removed, nor could it ever at any time or moment be taken away, without their having become aware of it themselves, giving compelling reasons.[66]

Given these limitations, de Matta urged that decrees approving relics for veneration be carefully phrased, using words like "held [to be authentic] or similar, by which will be excluded approbation of physical identity."[67] Were uncertain holy bones subjected to more demanding standards of proof, warned Pope Benedict XIV (1675–1758), "all holy relics would be exposed to the danger of uncertainty."[68]

In effect, just as probabilist casuists sought certainty by accommodating doubt and uncertainty in moral decision-making, writers on relics upheld the authenticity of holy remains while finding a place for ambiguity. In so doing, they responded both to the criticism of Protestants and to the devotional excesses of the faithful, as well as to the tension between the transcendent and the material that was inherent to relics. The Council of Trent had sought both to reaffirm the validity of the cult of the saints and their relics and to underscore the boundaries between sacred and profane people, places, and things. In the decades that followed the close of the council in 1563, theologians and confessors investigated the roots of the cult and systematized the disparate array of beliefs and practices that surrounded the bodies of the saints. However, their attempts to impose order had to take into account the ontologically blended quality of relics, in which were combined distinct or even opposed categories or qualities (e.g., the celestial and the earthly, the fragment and the whole, the absent and the present, the dead and the living). The extension of moral certainty to the identification and authentication of the physical remains of the saints enabled relic theorists to allow for their inherent ambivalence.

Perhaps the most comprehensive illustration of the tolerable uncertainty of relics is to be found in early modern treatises and manuals on the veneration of the bodies of the saints. These texts, which seem to have made their appearance in the first decade of the seventeenth century, gathered together the disparate discussions found in legal texts, apologetic treatises, *summas* of moral theology, confessors' manuals, the decrees of ecumenical and provincial councils, hagiographies, and histories to examine the divine and historical origins of the cult of relics, to explore the legal, moral, and liturgical issues they might present, and to codify the rules of evidence by which relics should be authenticated.[69] The most detailed of these manuals, the 1647 *Disquisitio: Sive de suspicienda, et suspecta earumdem numero reliquiarum, quae in diversis ecclesiis servantur, multitudine* of Jean Ferrand (1586–1672), a Jesuit rhetorician and theologian, explained the reasons for the repetition and multiplication of individual relics so mocked by Protestant critics, and outlined the forms of evidence by which one might recognize the real relics of the saints.[70] Ferrand identified three types of evidence for would-be relics: human, divine, and mixed human-divine. Among the varieties of human evidence, for example, he included the physical appearance of the remains, multiple forms of textual documentation, witness testimony, and local tradition. Divine evidence, by contrast, consisted of things like the miraculous qualities of the holy body (its incorruptibility, its emission of light, its capacity for movement, its subtlety), divine revelations, marvellous effluvia, and other miracles, while the mixed category included trial by fire, submersion of relics and other methods for achieving cures, and sermons, offerings, miracle books, pilgrimages, processions, and liturgical commemorations. For each form of evidence, Ferrand offered multiple examples and a careful analysis of its potential limitations.[71]

Near the end of his book, Ferrand directly addressed the problem of the uncertainty of relics. To counter the doubts and criticisms raised by Protestant critics like Calvin and Catholic sceptics like Heinrich Cornelius Agrippa, he argued that the intention of the worshipper outweighed the possibility of fraud or deception. The veneration of relics could not be idolatrous or superstitious,

> for in this veneration there is no falseness, neither on the part of the worshipper, nor on the part of the thing worshipped, unless wholly by accident, as the theologians say. The reason for it is that the religious honour bestowed upon such doubtful remains of the saints by every Catholic, venerating them not as false, suppositious, and utterly counterfeit, but rather as real, legitimate, and genuine … relics.[72]

In a like manner, he contended, though demons may imitate Christ, a deceived believer did not fall into idolatry or superstition, since the "target, chief end, and cause" of the worshiper's veneration was not Satan but Christ. In effect, Ferrand offered a workaround to the problem by shifting the terms of the question from certainty to intention and from the object to the subject. A quote from his confrère Gabriel Vázquez summed it up:

> But the fact that among some people there are sometimes unreliable relics does not prevent us from being obligated to worship reverently those that we consider reliable on the basis of human conjecture and reason. In conclusion, just as we say that it is not a sin of idolatry to adore a ray of light beneath which lurks a demon because someone thinks it to be Christ, in the same way, a person thinking that there is some particle of a saint when really there is not does not lose the benefit of his devotion.[73]

Ferrand's tripartite schema of evidence by which true relics could be distinguished from the false served also as indicators by which an investigator might recognize the moral certainty of the allegedly holy remains, since the type of certainty applicable to an object was inherent in the thing itself. Natural philosopher Rodrigo de Arriaga, SJ (1592–1662), for example, distinguished between moral, physical, and metaphysical certainty, each of which could be recognized by its distinct characteristics.[74] As Peter Dear has noted:

> It would be simple, and correct, to analyze "moral certainty," with its reliance on properly accredited testimony, as the social grounding of belief. It is guaranteed by "prudent and truthful men" rather than by the possibility of independent confirmation or some similar universal epistemic procedure. But it is crucial to note that Arriaga and the rest (including Descartes) do not themselves analyze it in that way. The assumption is always that moral certainty can be identified by its appeal to testimony, but that it is not in itself constituted by such testimony.[75]

Testimony did not create moral certainty, but instead served as a marker or indicator. In essence, the task of the investigator and authenticator of relics was one of discernment, of properly reading the evidence that pointed to the moral certainty of the remains.

To read the indicators that signalled the moral certainty of the body of St John of Matha and the licitness of public veneration of his remains, the two remaining propositions shifted in traditional form from universals to particulars. To frame the issue of the specific evidence for the identity of the bones, the author of the brief argued that "the intrinsic identity of any given thing cannot be known to us except through external signs (particularly speaking of the present case of holy bodies) or through tradition or through revelations."[76] Just as moral certainty was signalled by testimony, so too was an object's intrinsic or essential identity – that is, the indwelling essence that makes each thing itself – identified by similar means. As a comparison, the brief's author pointed again to the thousands of martyrs thought to lie buried within the Roman catacombs and noted that the moral certainty of the identification of their remains depended upon extrinsic indicators like inscribed epitaphs and palms, and the so-called vial of blood that signalled the presence of the holy. In the case of the relics of St John of Matha, the historical evidence (the epitaph upon the saint's tomb) and the physical proofs (the detailed account of the disposition of the bones provided by the two confessed thieves – their location, disposition, appearance, and identifying inscriptions) established the moral certainty of the remains. The brief's author waved away potential objections, such as the possibility that the two friars mixed up the bodies in the tomb and the impropriety of accepting evidence proffered by criminals, as both unlikely and irrelevant, and offered a handful of parallels drawn from Catholic hagiographic tradition, such as the Holy House of Mary at Loreto, the hand of St Gregory the Great at Cesena, and the bodies of St Peter and St Paul. Since in such cases one proceeded "from the definition to the thing defined, and the converse works as well," what was important was not the means by which the body was moved nor where it ended up, but rather that the indicators of identity and sanctity that were found in Rome were the same as those found in Madrid.[77] The two thieves' description of the bones matched that of the papal nuncio, and the evidence was enough to establish the moral certainty of the body's identity and the licitness of its public cult and veneration.

Grounded in scholastic argumentation and Aristotelian metaphysics, these arguments were complemented by the proofs offered by the second of the Vatican Library briefs, which drew on principles drawn from civil and criminal jurisprudence. Alluding briefly to the opinions of jurists Peter of Ancarano (c. 1333–1416), Giuseppe Mascardi (1540–1587), Prospero Farinacci (1544–1618), and the Jesuit relic theorist Jean Ferrand on the permissible presumption of the continuous identity of people, things, and actions over time, the anonymous author argued that together, the historical and physical evidence was enough to prove the moral certainty of the holy remains. Similarly, though the third Vatican brief and the document from the Biblioteca Angelica cited no metaphysical or legal supports, both offered comparable "signs" for the moral certainty of the bones drawn from the thieves' own deposition in 1657, from hagiographic precedent, and from the parallel case of the Roman catacombs. Such evidence, the authors argued, was appropriate, since "the body of the said holy founder is in the realm of material things."[78]

These inventive arguments cut no ice with the hard-nosed cardinals of the Congregation of Sacred Rites. The eight members who assembled on 12 January 1669 to consider the case ruled that "the identity of the body of St John of Matha is not established morally, since [the relics] have not been proven in proper form or legally. Let different proofs be brought forth and handed over to the congregation."[79] It appears that the cardinals did not contest the application of moral certainty; instead, they rejected the evidence adduced as proof. Though the assembled members of the congregation did not explain their opposition to the examples offered in the briefs, the comments of an anonymous official associated with the papal nunciature in Madrid around 1671 make it clear that the lack of proper documentation was the reason for the congregation's negative reply:

> The Trinitarian order, both Calced and Discalced, claimed that the holy body should be turned over to them, and to this end introduced their

> petition in the Congregation of Rites. But because it was removed from Rome without [proper] proceedings or any documentation, they could not prove the identity of the relic, [and] so not only could they not obtain its handover, but neither could it be exposed for public veneration.[80]

The anonymous commentator's emphasis on the lack of proper legal proceedings (*diligenza*) and formal documentation (*autentica*) suggests that the cardinals of the Congregation of Sacred Rites required better documentary evidence for the identity of the bones, such as a notarized attestation of the opening of the tomb and the transfer of the remains.

While the cardinals' insistence on this point may be in part an attempt to punish the Trinitarian order for the theft, it is also indicative of the degree to which the evidentiary norms for would-be relics had come to privilege legal instruments and written records.[81] In the century that followed the Council of Trent, procedures and evidentiary requirements for the identification and authentication of holy relics began to be codified and clarified. The council's decrees specified that bishops confronted with new miracle claims or new relics (i.e., newly discovered bodies of established saints, rather than remains of wholly unknown saints or candidates for canonization) were to consult with "theologians and other devout men and decide as truth and devotion suggest."[82] Two leading reformers, St Carlo Borromeo (1538–1584), cardinal archbishop of Milan, and Gabriele Paleotti (1522–1597), cardinal archbishop of Bologna, elaborated on Trent's bare-bones directions, drawing upon medieval precedents to establish modern procedural examples that shaped the responses of later prelates tasked with the investigation and authentication of relics.[83] Among the rules for proper treatment and veneration of relics elaborated by Borromeo's Fourth Council of Milan (1574) were a set of guidelines for the recognition of relics.[84] Presiding bishops were to examine first the "writings, records, documents, reliable annual accounts, or memorials of any sort" found in and around churches or attached to reliquaries, followed closely by witness testimony of "ancient and constant tradition."[85] The results of their investigations and transcriptions of the evidence were to be carefully recorded and placed in the episcopal archive for posterity. Four years later, similar criteria were brought to bear by Cardinal Paleotti upon the remains of St Agricola and St Vitalis. Before conducting a solemn translation, or movement, of the two early Christian martyrs, the cardinal himself examined books, authenticating writings, liturgical texts, and other written materials that documented the previous locations and translations of their remains, and subjected the relics to a careful physical inspection. Records of these investigations "made for the memory of future generations" were later placed in the episcopal archive.[86] The congregation's rejection of the supporting examples adduced in the case of St John of Matha suggests a similar preference for formal documentation.[87]

The congregation's increasing evidentiary demands paralleled ongoing developments in the process of saint-making, a process with which the identification of relics was intimately connected. Over the course of the sixteenth and seventeenth centuries, officials tightened procedures and requirements for beatification and canonization, with a notable emphasis on written evidence. While documentation of the heroic virtues, holy reputation, and miracles of the *beati moderni* (recently dead men and women with a reputation for holiness) might be relatively straightforward, promoters of canonization candidates who had died centuries before often faced major hurdles in the path towards sainthood. In 1645, for example, doubts about the authenticity of a key piece of documentary evidence – a thirteenth-century miracle register – halted the case of Pope Gregory X (r. 1272–6) for almost eighty years.[88] Long-venerated saints who lacked formal canonization faced similar difficulties. Rules promulgated in 1625 and 1634 prohibited the faithful from rendering cult to holy people without previous papal authorization and required proponents of would-be saints to demonstrate that their candidates had *not* received illicit veneration. The new regulations specified that exceptions would be made for cults at least a century old, but the implication was that such existing cults would have to pass through a process of examination and authentication, a process that, if successful, would result in an "equivalent" canonization.[89] While the evidence required for such processes included the words of living witnesses who could testify to the antiquity of a cult or the testimony of specialists about the age of votive tablets, paintings, lamps, altars, and other evidence of veneration, it also required a wide array of documentation, including ancient legal instruments, histories, and inscriptions.[90] In effect, would-be saints, both ancient and modern, faced new scrutiny of an "intensely legalistic rather than theological cast" and coloured by "a thirst for written evidence and a rigour in its examination without precedent in the history of canonization."[91]

This scrupulous care for documentation and the preservation of evidence was at least in part a response to both Protestant and Catholic reformers, whose devastating criticisms rendered uncertain both the saints and their bodies. Their mockery was not, however, the sole driver behind the increased attentiveness to evidence in the cult of the saints.

Writers of sacred history – a broad category that included a wide range of genres, from martyrologies and hagiography to ecclesiastical history – were not immune to trends at work in historical scholarship more generally. In the fifteenth and early sixteenth centuries, humanist scholars pioneered new philological and historical methods, eventually applying them to the lives of the saints.[92] This trend grew more pervasive after Trent, as scholars brought humanist historical criticism to bear on the liturgical and historical traditions of the church. The work of Cardinal Cesare Baronio (1538–1607), author of the *Annales ecclesiastici*, for example, submitted sacred history to new scrutiny. The cardinal ruffled the feathers of many local patriots when, following a careful re-examination of the hagiographic sources, he pruned many questionable saints from the *Roman Breviary* and the revised *Roman Martyrology* (1586).[93] In the early seventeenth century, Jesuit hagiographers known as the Bollandists undertook a similar project. Starting in 1643, Heribert Rosweyde (1569–1629), Jean Bolland (1596–1665), and their followers published the *Acta sanctorum*, a monumental project that sought to re-evaluate the earliest documentary sources for the lives of the saints and eliminate their more apocryphal elements.[94] In so doing, they sought to create a more solid, credible, and certain foundation for the cult of the saints and for the church's claims to unchanging historical continuity.

For some, historical criticism intersected with and was amplified by the expanding influence of ancient and modern scepticism and Cartesian doubt to create a crisis of historical credibility, of *fides historica*.[95] But while it is difficult to parse the congregation's laconic response, the wording of its ruling and its reported preference for documentation suggest that in this case, at least, the quest for certainty was less a philosophical problem than one of judicial procedure. Just as commentators on canonization procedure increasingly grounded their arguments for papal inerrancy in saint-making not in theology but in practical questions of legal procedure and proof, the cardinals cut the larger question of the identity of the remains of the saints down to size by confining uncertainty within the established, manageable category of moral certainty, a category known through proper proofs.[96] When the congregation ruled on the question of sainthood itself, "true *scientia* [was] only that which is juridically (even more than theologically) founded."[97] The same seems to be true of the bones of the saints. That the bones of St John of Matha were "not established morally, although formally" indicates that the problem lay in the specific proofs adduced by the briefs' authors – the issue was not so much *fides historica* in general, but the missing *fides* of notarized legal proceedings.

Part of the problem, too, may have been the faulty *fides* of the historical parallels brought to bear on the case, especially the briefs' frequent references to relics uncovered in the Roman catacombs. In the wake of the accidental discovery of a previously unknown tomb complex in 1578, the catacombs, major pilgrimage sites and sources of relics since the early Middle Ages, became the focus of renewed devotional enthusiasm.[98] Over the course of the succeeding centuries, Rome's underground tombs were ransacked for remains of martyrs that were then sent to churches and chapels around the Catholic globe.[99] Though most Catholics assumed that most if not all of the bodies in the catacombs were those of ancient martyrs for Christ, Protestant mockery and Catholic scepticism had called into question the criteria used in distinguishing the remains of the martyrs from those of the common dead.[100] A special committee convoked in the early 1630s to consider which inscriptions, grave goods, and other markers were to be considered sure indicators of sanctity failed to resolve the problem. By 1668, only one year before the case of St John of Matha came before the Congregation of Sacred Rites, questions surrounding the identification and treatment of catacomb relics had become so urgent that Pope Clement IX created a new oversight body, the Congregation of Indulgences and Relics, which quickly ruled that only two signs, the palm and the so-called vial of blood, could be considered certain indicators of the presence of martyrs' remains. In the light of this contemporaneous debate and at a time when the moral certainty of catacomb relics was itself the subject of considerable anxiety, comparisons between the identification of ancient martyrs' bones and the identification of the bones of St John of Matha may have been less than convincing.[101]

While the cardinals did not detail which points of evidence they rejected, perhaps the compromised *fides* of the only eyewitnesses, the thieves Medina and Vidal, was another factor that lay behind their demand for "*exempla … dissimilia.*" Their testimony was, as the author of the longest of the briefs acknowledged, the sole evidence for the prominent location of the saint's bones and the identifying texts. They were also the sole source for the only miracle alleged to have accompanied the theft events – a rather flabby and lackluster incident in which

> [while] passing by the monastery of the Spanish Discalced [friars] of their order at two o'clock at night, an hour when no bell should ring, they heard one sound in the aforementioned Discalced monastery, and they held it to be a miracle because they carried with them the said holy relics.[102]

Miracles had had probative force since the earliest origins of the cult of the saints, and while they remained obligatory proofs of sanctity for seventeenth-century candidates for beatification or canonization, in cases of relic identification they could stand as corroborative or even decisive evidence.[103] Miracles were not, however, unquestioningly accepted. In the tighter juridical structure of canonization and growing concerns about discerning true miracles from diabolical or human imposture, the credibility of miracles was tied ever more firmly to the trustworthiness and social standing of the witnesses who testified to them.[104] If, as we have seen, one recognized a morally certain thing by the testimony that signalled it, then the questionable credibility of the two thieves probably accounted for the congregation's distinction between the bones' "formal" but not "moral" identification.

If the application of moral certainty within the context of legal procedure was one means of addressing the problem of uncertain saintly relics, so too was its use in hagiography. Some, like Jean Bolland himself, accommodated doubt about events within the lives of the saints by devolving the task of discernment upon the reader.[105] Others adopted a different, complementary interpretive mode, one that approached the saints and their sources critically but gently, in a spirit of "pious affection." This hermeneutic, grounded in the traditional notion that history should serve higher ends, asked scholars to temper their criticism and their evidentiary demands and approach sacred history with at least one eye on its moral purpose – to approach the history of the saints and their remains with not just truth but Truth in mind.[106] A generous posture, and one that did not preclude critical inquiry but gave latitude for the imperfections of historical evidence, especially in matters of ancient history, pious affection intersected neatly with moral certainty. As the noted Spanish humanist Ambrosio de Morales (1513–1591) put it, questions of pagan antiquity did not require conclusive evidence or arguments, but instead "a good moral probability deduced from good principles and foundations, from which one forms reasons." If this was the case for the pagan past, it was even more so with matters of sacred history, which must be understood "morally" and with "pious affection," but also with critical judgment and attention to detail.[107] Indeed, even Daniel Papebroch (1628–1714), one of the most prominent of the Bollandists, acknowledged that when dealing with the relics of the saints, one must often proceed out of "a feeling of pious credulity" rather than "certain knowledge." Written or ocular evidence demonstrated relics' trustworthiness, but the evidence was often thin or imperfect, and could often be deceptive.[108] Lesser certainty required lesser proofs, so moral certainty required only moral evidence – that is, as the Jesuit canonist Antonio de Quintanadueñas (1599–1651) put it, it was sufficient that moral certainty be "deduced from probable arguments; moreover, it does not have to be necessary, clear, and unerringly conclusive."[109] In effect, the application of pious affection and moral certainty to relics – and to sacred history more generally – allowed scholars to rescue religious truth from the more destabilizing aspects of critical historical scholarship and to find a middle path between naive credulity and the extremes of historical Pyrrhonism.[110]

Though they rejected the evidence and the precedents adduced in the briefs, the assembled cardinals seem to have accepted that moral certainty was the appropriate form of certainty to apply to the identity of the remains of St John of Matha and to relics in general. In some ways, this is not surprising, as the tripartite epistemology laid out in the brief was a common feature on the scientific and philosophical landscape of the seventeenth century. The Catholic cult of the saints did not stand alone and isolated from the cultural and intellectual movements at work in other areas of inquiry. Officials investigating miracles and candidates for canonization, for example, increasingly employed techniques of observation and experimentation usually associated with early modern natural philosophy.[111] By the same token, the priests and prelates who engaged the thorny problems of relic identification and authentication participated with natural philosophers, historians, lawyers, and others in a wider culture of proof that answered the challenge of uncertainty by incorporating it into the epistemological foundations of their respective fields.[112] Both for relics in general and for the particular case of the stolen bones of the Trinitarians' founder, moral certainty offered a solution to the problem of uncertainty by accommodating doubt and imperfect knowledge. In so doing, it also reaffirmed the ambivalent character of the remains of the saints, in which were combined the mundane and the sacred, the fragment and the whole, the animate and the inanimate. Thus, the application of moral certainty to saintly relics may also be seen as a development within a larger, cross-confessional reaction to what Caroline Bynum has called the late medieval "crisis of confidence in Christian materiality," a crisis precipitated by the radically paradoxical nature of late medieval Catholicism.[113] Bynum posits that Protestant rejections and Tridentine reforms of the cult of the saints were engendered at least in part by fourteenth- and fifteenth-century Catholicism's simultaneous emphasis on inner focus and exterior action, mysticism and materiality. The moral certainty of holy remains, I suggest, expands upon Trent's reforming clarifications by responding both to the uncertainties raised by critics and to the ambiguities inherent in relics themselves.

Though the Congregation of Sacred Rites ruled against the identity of the bones of St John of Matha in 1669, the Trinitarians did not give up their quest. In 1671, the Secretariat of State ordered the current occupant of the Spanish nunciature, Cardinal Galeazzo Marescotti (1627–1726), to recognize (i.e., examine formally) the remains, which still languished in the nuncio's residence in Madrid.[114] Fifteen years later, though the body still lacked formal identification, Nuncio Cardinal Marcello Durazzo (1634–1710) handed over the bones of St John of Matha to the Discalced Trinitarians of Madrid, who placed them below the altar in a small chapel in the cell once occupied by Tomás de la Virgen (1587–1647), a Discalced Trinitarian friar famed for his sanctity.[115] The Trinitarians made another attempt to petition the congregation in 1715, but received the same negative response.[116] In 1721, the Trinitarians mounted a renewed effort, reinforced by letters of support from the Spanish monarchs, the archbishop of Toledo, and the city council of Madrid. This time, the case finally found favour with the congregation, which rescinded its previous decisions.[117] St John of Matha, once nearly forgotten, would now become the focus of elaborate festivities; the identity of his stolen bones, once doubtful, was officially morally certain.

ACKNOWLEDGMENTS

I have incurred many debts of gratitude in the course of preparing this article. The research and writing of this piece was supported by the Humanities Institute and the Academic Senate of the University of California, Davis. Many thanks to Pedro Aliaga Asensio, O.SS.T., who graciously granted me access to the rich materials held in the archive at San Carlino alle Quattro Fontane. I am very grateful to the many tolerant friends and colleagues who heard earlier versions of this essay and patiently offered corrections and suggestions for improvements. Special thanks to Daniel Stoltzenberg and to Emily Albu, and especially to John Rundin for their linguistic assistance. Needless to say, I bear full responsibility for all translations.

NOTES

1 My narrative follows the eyewitness account given by one of the culprits in 1657, published in Lucas de la Purificación, *Historia del sagrado cuerpo del glorioso patriarcha San Juan de Matha* [Madrid, 1723], 10–14.

2 Built in 1614, the Calced Trinitarian monastery of St Francesca Romana stood in via Sistina, across from the Augustinian church of St Ildefonso and St Tomás de Villanova. Prior to the construction of this house, the Trinitarians had been housed in Santo Stefano in Trullo, on the Piazza di Pietra. The church of St Francesca Romana was demolished in 1946 to make room for the Teatro Sistina, while Santo Stefano in Trullo was torn down in the mid-seventeenth century. See Mariano Armellini, *Le chiese di Roma dal secolo IV al XIX,* 1 (Rome: Edizioni R.O.R.E. de Nicolà Ruffolo, 1942), 370, 374.

3 Francisco de Vega y Toraya, *Crónica de la provincia de Castilla, León y Navarra, del Orden de la Santíssima Trinidad, Redención de Cautivos: Primera parte* (Madrid, 1720), 250, 271–7. For documents generated in the lengthy lawsuit between the Trinitarians and the Vatican chapter over possession of the church, see Biblioteca Apostolica Vaticana (BAV), Archivio del Capitolo di S. Pietro in Vaticano, Miscellanea I, XV. On the history of the church of S. Tommaso in Formis, see Alia Englen, ed., *Caelius I: Santa Maria in Domnica, San Tommaso in Formis e il Clivus Scauri* (Rome: L'Erma di Bretschneider, 2003), 393–438; Antonino dell'Assunta and A. Romano di S. Teresa, *S. Tommaso in Formis sul Celio: Notizie e documenti* (Isola del Liri: Soci Tipog. A. Macioce & Pisani, 1927).

4 Monica Morbidelli, "'*Ecclsiae sint plani operis*': Il primo insediamento trinitario a Roma: Storia e architettura," in *La liberazione dei "captivi" tra Cristianità e Islam: Oltre la crociata e il Gihād: Tolleranza e servizio umanitario: Atti del Congresso interdisciplinare di studi storici, Roma, 16–19 settembre 1998, organizzato per l'VIII centenario dell'approvazione della regola dei Trinitari da parte del Papa Innocenzo III il 17 dicembre 1198–15 safar, 595 H*, ed. Giulio Cipollone (Vatican City: Archivio Segreto Vaticano, 2000), 661–82.

5 According to Vega y Toraya, *Crónica,* 278, Medina was a Castilian whose home monastery was the Calced house in Madrid, while Vidal was Aragonese and based in Mallorca.

6 Englen, *Caelius I,* 407.

7 Antonino dell'Assunta, *Ministrorum Generalium Ordinis SS: Trinitatis Series* (Isola del Liri: Soc. Tip. A. Macioce & Pisani, 1936), 9–10, 14–18.

8 According to Arias's testimony in Archivio di San Carlino (ASC), legajo 16a, n. 6, unp., he occupied the position of *procurador general* between 1652 and 1655.

9 The text of the note is reprinted in Lucas de la Purificación, *Historia del sagrado cuerpo*, 16–17.

10 Selections from Cardinal Barberini's investigation into the theft are included in Biblioteca Nacional de España 4/42284 *Congregatione Sacrorum Rituum … Hispaniarum. Identitas corporis Sancti Ioannis de Matha Fundatoris Ordinis Sanctiss. Trinitatis Redemptionis Captivorum. Positio super identitate corporis* (Roma, 1669) and in *Hispaniarum identitatis corporis S. Ioannis de Matha, fundatoris ordinis Sanctissimae Trinitatis Redemptoris Captivorum. Positio super identitate dicti corporis* (Rome, 1714), 8–22. Portions of the *monitorio* are extracted in Francisco de Arcos, *Memorial que el … padre M. Fr. Francisco de Arcos … del Orden de la S.S. Trinidad de Redentores, remitiò al Padre Procurador General de Roma / Y vn devoto de nuestros Santos Patriarcas San Iuan, y San Felix dà a la estampa, por escusar el trabajo de copias, que piden de dentro, y fuera de la Religión* [Madrid, 1661], 17r.

11 Patrick J. Geary, *Furta Sacra: Thefts of Relics in the Central Middle Ages* (Princeton: Princeton University Press, 1990); Nicole Herrmann-Mascard, *Les reliques des saints: Formation coutumière d'un droit* (Paris: Éditions Klinksieck, 1975), 364–83.

12 "se avia dibulgado por la Ciudad, que los Religiosos Descalços de su Orden avían intentado robarlo, y les pareció más conveniente que los tuviesse su Religión, por aver sido Fundador, que no otros algunos." Lucas de la Purificación, *Historia del sagrado cuerpo*, 11.

13 Herrmann-Mascard, *Les reliques des saints*, 364–5.

14 María Tausiet, *El dedo robado: Reliquias imaginarias en la España moderna* (Madrid: Abada, 2013). See also the case of St John of the Cross, whose remains were stolen in the 1590s: Joseph de Santa Teresa, *Resunta de la vida de n. bienaventurado padre San Juan de la Cruz, doctor mystico, primer Carmelita Descalço, y fiel coadjutor de nuestra madre Santa Teresa en la fundación de su reforma* (Madrid, 1675), 123–5.

15 See especially Susan E. Schreiner, *Are You Alone Wise? The Search for Certainty in the Early Modern Era* (New York: Oxford University Press, 2011); Jeremy Robbins, *Arts of Perception: The Epistemological Mentality of the Spanish Baroque, 1580–1720* (London: Routledge, Taylor & Francis Group; [Glasgow]: University of Glasgow, 2014).

16 Anthony Pagden, *The Fall of Natural Man: The American Indian and the Origins of Comparative Ethnology* (New York: Cambridge University Press, 1982); Richard H. Popkin, *The History of Scepticism: From Savonarola to Bayle*, rev. and expanded ed. (New York: Oxford University Press, 2003).

17 Elvira Vilches, *New World Gold: Cultural Anxiety and Monetary Disorder in Early Modern Spain* (Chicago: University of Chicago Press, 2010).

18 Schreiner, *Are You Alone Wise?*

19 The literature in all of these areas is large and growing. For an entry point into pretense of sanctity, see Anne Jacobson Schutte, *Aspiring Saints: Pretense of Holiness, Inquisition, and Gender in the Republic of Venice, 1618–1750* (Baltimore: Johns Hopkins University Press, 2001). On witchcraft, demonic possession, and the discernment of spirits, two good starting places are Stuart Clark, *Thinking with Demons: The Idea of Witchcraft in Early Modern Europe* (Oxford: Oxford University Press, 1997); Moshe Sluhovsky, *Believe Not Every Spirit: Possession, Mysticism, and Discernment in Early Modern Catholicism* (Chicago: University of Chicago Press, 2007). On religious dissimulation, begin with Perez Zagorin, *Ways of Lying: Dissimulation, Persecution, and Conformity in Early Modern Europe* (Cambridge, MA: Harvard University Press, 1990); Miriam Eliav-Feldon, "Religious Dissimulation," in *Renaissance Impostors and Proofs of Identity* (New York: Palgrave Macmillan, 2012), 16–67. These issues resonated particularly strongly in the Iberian Peninsula, with its deep history of religious pluralism and mass conversions. See *After Conversion: Iberia and the Emergence of Modernity*, ed. Mercedes García-Arenal (Leiden: Brill, 2016).

20 See Sarah Mortimer and John Robertson, "Nature, Revelation, History: Intellectual Consequences of Religious Heterodoxy c. 1600–1750," in *The Intellectual Consequences of Religious Heterodoxy, 1600–1750*, ed. Sarah Mortimer and John Robertson (Leiden: Brill, 2014), 1–46; Dmitri Levitin, "From Sacred History to the History of Religion: Paganism, Judaism, and Christianity in European Historiography from Reformation to 'Enlightenment,'" *The Historical Journal* 55, no. 4 (2012): 1117–60.

21 Stéphan Boiron, *La controverse née de la querelle des reliques à l'époque du Concile de Trente (1500–1640)* (Paris: Presses universitaires de France, 1989); Alain Joblin, "L'attitude des protestants face aux reliques," in *Les reliques: Objets, cultes, symboles: Actes du colloque international de l'Université du Littorial-Côte d'Opale (Boulogne-sur-Mer) 4–6 septembre 1997*, ed. Edina Bozóky and Anne-Marie Helvétius (Turnhout: Brepols, 1999), 122–41.

22 Jean Calvin, *A very profitable treatise …* (London, 1561), unp. See Pierre Antoine Fabre and Mickaël Wilmart, "Le *Traité des reliques* de Jean Calvin (1543) : Texte et contextes," in *Reliques modernes: Cultes et usages chrétiens des corps saints des Réformes aux révolutions*, ed. Philipe Boutry, Pierre Antoine Fabre, and Dominique Julia (Paris: Éditions de l'École des hautes études en sciences sociales, 2009), 1.29–68.

23 E.g., an iconoclastic riot in Strasbourg on the eve of All Saints' Day, 1524, described in Lee Palmer Wandel, *Voracious Idols and Violent Hands: Iconoclasm in Reformation Zurich, Strasbourg, and Basel* (Cambridge: Cambridge University Press, 1994), 117–18.

24 Dominique Julia, "L'Église post-tridentine et les reliques : Tradition, controverse et critique (XVIe–XVIIe siècle)," in Boutry, Fabre, and Wilmart, *Reliques modernes*, 1.69–120.
25 *Decrees of the Ecumenical Councils*, ed. Norman P. Tanner (Washington, DC: Georgetown University Press, 1990), 2.775–6.
26 The expression is from Peter Burke, "How to Become a Counter-Reformation Saint," in *The Historical Anthropology of Early Modern Italy: Essays on Perception and Communication* (Cambridge: Cambridge University Press, 1987), 48–62. See also Simon Ditchfield, "Tridentine Worship and the Cult of Saints," in *The Cambridge History of Christianity*, vol. 6: *Reform and Expansion, 1500–1660*, ed. R. Po-Chia Hsia (Cambridge: Cambridge University Press, 2008), 201–24.
27 On relics in the Jesuits' global mission, see Luke Clossey, *Salvation and Globalization in the Early Jesuit Missions* (Cambridge: Cambridge University Press, 2008), 220–3.
28 Cécile Vincent-Cassy, "The Search for Evidence: The Relics of Martyred Saints and Their Worship in Cordoba after the Council of Trent," in García-Arenal, *After Conversion*, 143.
29 On *authentica*, see Paul Bertrand, "Authentiques de reliques: Authentiques ou reliques?," *Le Moyen Age* 112, no. 2 (2006): 363–74.
30 Arcos also served as a *calificador* for the Inquisition and held the *cátedra de escritura* at the University of Toledo. Antonino de la Assunción, *Diccionario de los escritores trinitarios de España y Portugal* (Rome: F. Kleinbub, 1898), 1.47–9.
31 Lucas de la Purificación, *Historia del sagrado cuerpo*, 18.
32 On the Trinitarians' presence at the royal court, see Ronald Cueto, "Some Observations on the Trinitarian Connections – Calced and Discalced – in the Court of Philip IV," *Bulletin of Spanish Studies: Hispanic Studies and Researches on Spain, Portugal and Latin America* 81, no. 3 (2004): 293–308.
33 Massimo, who became the patriarch of Jerusalem in 1653, was raised to the cardinalate in 1670.
34 "Tarde se les hazía ya a los muy reverendos padres Trinitarios Descalzos; impacientes, no podían esperar ya más tiempo para introducirse en esta causa, impelidos de su ordinario genio de quererse meter en todo." Vega y Toraya, *Crónica*, 285.
35 This division was first laid out by the Fourth Lateran Council (1215), and later reproduced in Gregory IX's decretals of 1234. See Stéphane Boiron, "Définition et statut juridique des reliques dans le droit canonique classique," in *Reliques et sainteté dans l'espace médiéval*, ed. Jean-Luc Deuffic and André Vauchez (Saint-Denis: Pecia, 2006): 19–31; Eugene A. Dooley, *Church Law on Sacred Relics* (Washington, DC: Catholic University of America, 1931).

36 Tanner, *Decrees of the Ecumenical Councils*, 2.776.

37 "que no tenía la veneración conveniente, por ser iglesia medio arruinada en despoblado, dentro de la ciudad de Roma." Lucas de la Purificación, *Historia del sagrado cuerpo*, 11.

38 Lucas de la Purificación, *Historia del sagrado cuerpo*, 11. During the latter decades of the sixteenth century, a reform movement within the Trinitarian order, led by Juan Bautista de la Concepción (1561–1613), led to a rancorous split between the Calced and Discalced branches. See Juan Pujana, *La reforma de los Trinitarios durante el reinado de Felipe II* (Salamanca: Secretariado trinitario, 2006).

39 BAV, Chig. E.II.47, fols 224r–247v, 248r–249v, 282r–282v; Biblioteca Angelica, ms. 1659, fols 272r–273r.

40 BAV, Chig. E.II.47, fols 244r–247v. Cardinal Ginetti was protector of the Trinitarian order in 1665, but I have not been able to ascertain whether he was still in this post as of 1669. See Antonino de la Assunción, *Diccionario de los escritores trinitarios*, 2.250. In 1665, in his capacity as prefect and deputized judge, Ginetti declared in favour of the *cultu ab immemorabili* of St John of Matha – an act equivalent to canonization. For testimony collected in connection with this case, see Archivio Segreto Vaticano (ASV), Congr. Riti, Processi 912, 913, and 3425; BAV, Chig. B.II.16.

41 "Certitudo enim metaphisica solum reperitur in rebus, seu actibus fidei supernaturalis, quia nituntur auctoritate diuina, cui repugnat falsitas, seu falsum dicere … Certitudo vero moralis, et humana est de his rebus, quae ut plurimum ita sunt, tamen possunt interdum deficere; sic que talis certitudo est omnino infallibilis, nec repugnat, quod de facto sit falsa res, seu assensus alicuius alicui, qui nunc iudicatur certus, ut ex infradicendis constabit. Rursus certitudo potest esse maior altera, quia maioribus, et efficatioribus fundamentis nixa est." BAV, Chig. E.II.47, fol. 244r.

42 "Sed non est impossibile quod corpora, quae coluntur ut sancta, non sint illorum sanctorum, ergo non datur certitudo metaphisica de identitate corporum, quae pro sanctis venerantur." BAV, Chig. E.II.47, fol. 244r–v.

43 "Et his non obstantibus, aliis fundamentis consideratis iudicatur certa moraliter identitas talium corporum, et publicae venerationi sunt exposita." BAV, Chig. E.II.47, fol. 245r.

44 "Nam argumentum à non repugnantia, seu posibilitate ad futuritionem, vel existentiam nullum, et inutile, imò absurdum est, ut enim axioma dicit ab actu ad potentiam bene valet consequentia, non vero à potentia ad actum." BAV, Chig. E.II.47, fol. 244v.

45 BAV, Chig. E.II.47, fol. 245v. The example recalls the ancient Donatist heresy.

46 Rudolph Schüssler, "Jean Gerson, Moral Certainty and the Renaissance of Ancient Scepticism," in *The Renaissance Conscience,* ed. Harald E. Braun and Edward Vallance (Malden: Wiley-Blackwell, 2011), 19.
47 Aristotle, *Nichomachean Ethics* I, 2, 1094b, in *The Complete Works of Aristotle: The Revised Oxford Translation,* ed. Jonathan Barnes (Princeton: Princeton University Press, 1984), 2.1730.
48 Albert R. Jonsen and Stephen Toulmin, *The Abuse of Casuistry: A History of Moral Reasoning* (Berkeley: University of California Press, 1988), 165–6.
49 Tanner, *Decrees of the Ecumenical Councils,* 2.674.
50 Stephen Strehle, *The Catholic Roots of the Protestant Gospel: Encounter Between the Middle Ages and the Reformation* (Leiden: Brill, 1995), 7. Bellarmino did not, however, entertain questions about the authenticity or identity of alleged relics. The cardinal flatly denied Calvin's contention that many of the saintly remains contained in churches were false, since "semper enim Ecclesia diligenter curavit, ne fraudes fierent, & praecipuè post decretum Concilii Lateranensis, ut nullae reliquiae publicè recipiantur sine auctoritate Romani Pontificis" (the church always took care to prevent deceits from happening, especially after the decree of the Lateran Council [1215] that no relics be publicly received without the authority of the Roman pontiff). Bellarmino, *Disputationum De Controversiis Christianae Fidei Tomus Primus* (Ingolstadt, 1588), 941–2.
51 Jonsen and Toulmin, *The Abuse of Casuistry,* 148. See also James Franklin, *The Science of Conjecture: Evidence and Probability before Pascal* (Baltimore: Johns Hopkins University Press, 2001).
52 On probabilism, see T. Deman, "Probabilisme," in *Dictionnaire de theólogie catholique,* 13.1 (Paris: Librairie Letouzey et Ané, 1936), cols 417–619; Ilkka Kantola, *Probability and Moral Uncertainty in Late Medieval and Early Modern Times* (Helskinki: Luther-Agricola-Seura, 1994); Rudolph Schüssler, "On the Anatomy of Probabilism," in *Moral Philosophy on the Threshold of Modernity,* ed. Jill Kraye and Risto Saarinen (Dordrecht: Springer, 2005), 91–113.
53 Lorraine Daston, "Probability and Evidence," in *The Cambridge History of Seventeenth-Century Philosophy,* ed. Daniel Garber and Michael Ayers (Cambridge: Cambridge University Press, 1998), 2.1112.
54 Julia E. Fleming, *Defending Probabilism: The Moral Theology of Juan Caramuel* (Washington, DC: Georgetown University Press, 2006), 123–4.
55 Schüssler, "On the Anatomy of Probabilism," 107.
56 R.W. Serjeantson, "Proof and Persuasion," in *The Cambridge History of Science,* vol. 3: *Early Modern Science,* ed. Roy Porter, Katharine Park, and Lorraine Daston (Cambridge: Cambridge University Press, 2003), 132–75, esp. 157–62; Lorraine Daston, "Probability and Evidence," in *The Cambridge History of Seventeenth-Century Philosophy,* 1108–44, esp. 1116–22.

57 For an introduction to the shift in Roman and canon law from a system of judicial decision-making based upon a fixed hierarchy of "full" and "partial" proofs to one grounded in degrees of certainty and probability, see Antonio Padoa-Schioppa, *Italia ed Europa nella storia del diritto* (Bologna: Il Mulino, 2003), 280–7; Isabella Rosoni, *Quae singula non prosunt collecta iuvant: La teoria della prova indiziaria nell'età medievale e moderna* (Milano: Dott. A. Giuffrè, 1995). On the role of moral certainty and the development of ideas of evidence in English law, see Barbara J. Shapiro, *Beyond Reasonable Doubt and Probable Cause: Historical Perspectives on the Anglo-American Law of Evidence* (Berkeley: University of California Press, 1991).

58 Giovanni Papa, *Le cause di canonizazzione nel primo periodo della Congregazione dei Riti (1588–1634)* (Rome: Urbaniana University Press, 2001), 170–214; Fabijan Veraja, *La beatificazione: Storia, problemi, prospettive* (Rome: S. Congregazione per le Cause dei Santi, 1983).

59 Marcos de Alcalá, *Chrónica de la Santa Provincia de San Joseph: Vida portentosa del penitente admirable San Pedro de Alcántara, fundador de toda la Descalzez Seráfica ... Primera Parte* (Madrid, 1736), 497–511. On moral certainty in canonization, see José Luis Gutiérrez, "La certezza morale nelle cause di canonizzazione, specialmente nella dichiarazione del martirio," *Ius Ecclesiae* 3 (1991): 645–70; Alberto Royo Mejía, "Algunas cuestiones sobre la heroicidad de las virtudes y la certeza moral jurídica en las causas de los santos," *Ius Canonicum* 34, no. 67 (1994): 189–226. On papal infallibility in canonization, see Pierluigi Giovannucci, *Canonizzazioni e infallibilità pontificia in età moderna* (Brescia: Morcelliana, 2008); Donald S. Prudlo, *Certain Sainthood: Canonization and the Origins of Papal Infallibility in the Medieval Church* (Ithaca: Cornell University Press, 2015).

60 "Aliud est enim loqui de publico et solemni ritu, seu honore reliquiarum, aliud de priuato ex singulari deuotione alicuius personae. Vt enim aliquae reliquiae publicè ab vniuersa Ecclesia colantur, primo necesse est, vt de sanctitate personae, vel per vniuersalem ecclesiae consensum, seu traditionem, vel per summi Pontificis canonizationem constet. Deinde oporteret, vt publica authoritate reliquiae proponantur vt verae, & ad talem personam pertinentes, haec autem autoritas est apud summum Pontificem, & episcopos, qui sufficientem diligentiam ante approbationem adhibere tenentur. Et quamuis harum reliquiarum non sit aequalis certitudo (aliae enim sunt antiquiores aliis) tamen supposita dicta approbatione, absolutè adorari posunt absque explicita conditione, tum quia in rebus humanis non est maior certitudo requirenda, & periculum formalis erroris, ut ita dicam, nullum est, cum in ratione formali adorandi non possit esse error, in qua ratione, virtute continetur conditio errorem excludens; tum etiam, quia si

interdum materialiter erretur, nulla erit culpa, cum bona fide, & prudenti modo procedatur." Francisco Suárez, *Commentariorum, ac disputationum in tertiam partem Divi Thomae* (Venice, 1598), 1.614–15 (Disp. 55, Sect. 1 and 2, on Aquinas, *ST* 3, q. 25, art. 6). Cf. Tomás Sánchez, *Opus morale in praecepta decalogi* (Antwerp, 1614) 346 (bk 2, ch. 43, nn. 13–14).

61 On Bordoni, see Massimiliano Zanot, *Francesco Bordoni (1594–1671): Teologo inquisitore storico*, 2nd ed. (Rome: Franciscanum, 1999).

62 "Duplex ergo est certitudo, una, quae immediatè attingit veritatem de ratione scientiae, cui no potest subesse falsum, & haec spectat ad scientiam naturalem, & ad fidem divinam, quae certissima est, cui impossibile est subesse falsum. Altera est certitudo moralis firma adhaesio Intellectus putantis, Rem iudicatam esse veram, in quantum credit saltem esse iudicium veritati proximum ex validis rationibus, & motivis, quibus nititur, tamen ignorat se veritatem attigisse, quia caret medio necessario." Franceso Bordoni, *Operum tomus quartus* … (Lyon, 1665), 165 (resol. 117, nn. 42–4).

63 "Tertium genus cognitionis affine opinioni est humana fides, quae est assensus unus determinatae partis ob auctoritatem, seu testimonium dicentia, ideo hoc modo magis credimus, quam scimus, nostra igitur credulitas firmatur ex alieno testimonio. Fides autem humana firmatur in Historia, quibus credere non solum aequum est, sed etiam valde utile, & quandoque necessarium … Utilitas ergo magna, immo quandoque necessitas credere Historiis &, illis esse credendum, & plene probare maxime in antiquis." Bordoni, *Operum tomus quartus* …, 165.

64 "Applicando doctrinam allatam casui nostro, ad probandam veritatem facti non est necessaria cognitio scientifica, sed sufficit cognitio opinatiua, et certitudo moralis, qua quis rationabiliter, & non temere credit rem ita se habere." Bordoni, *Operum tomus quartus* …, 165.

65 On evidence for the validity of relic veneration, see Suárez, *Commentariorum*, 612–13 (Disp. 55, sect. 1, on Aquinas, *ST* 3, q. 25, art. 6). Cf. Bellarmino, *Disputationum*, 927–36.

66 "Aduertendo tamen, dificillimum esse, vel potius impossibile, iudicare super identitate reliquiarum, quia ad habendum physicam identitatem, duo testes deponere deberent, tale os, ex. gr. desumptum fuisse ex corpore talis serui dei, ab ipsis cogniti, ipsis praesentibus, & videntibus, & ipsis pariter praesentibus, & videntibus fuisse repositum in tali loco, à quo nunquam fuit remotum, quod ipsi sciunt, nec potuisse vllo vnquam tempore, vel temporis momento remoueri, quin ipsi sciuissent, concludentissimas rationes reddendo." Carlo Felice de Matta, *Novissimus de sanctorum canonizatione tractatus: in quinque partes divisus* … (Rome, 1678), pt 4, ch. 29, §15, p. 437.

67 "Quod in causa recognitionis reliquiarum an vnquam obtineri possit, me remitto practicorum iudicio. Ac proinde cum de identitate reliquiarum haberi non possit nisi certitudo moralis, in decreto approbationis reliquiae addendum esset verbum, *habitae* vel aliud simile, per quod excluderetur approbatio physicae identitatis." de Matta, *Novissimus de sanctorum canonizatione tractatus*, p. 437.

68 "quae probatio quatenus reputaretur necessaria, omnes sacrae reliquiae incertitudinis periculo exponerentur." Benedict XIV [Prospero Lambertini], *De servorum Dei beatificatione et beatorum canonizatione*, 3rd ed. (Rome, 1749), 4.816 (part 2, ch. 25, n. 19).

69 Giovanni Battista Segni (1550–1610), *Reliquiarium, sive De reliquiis et venerat. sanctorum liber unus. In quo multa de necesssitate, praestantia, vsu, ac fructib. Reliquiarum pertractantur* (Bologna, 1600) and 2nd ed. (Bologna, 1610); Domenico Anfossi (c. 1640), *De sacrarum reliquiarum cultu, veneratione, translatione, atque identitate* (Brescia, 1610); Sancho Dávila y Toledo (1546–1625), *De la veneración que se deve a los cuerpos de los sanctos y a sus reliquias y de la singular con que se a de adorar el cuerpo de Iesu Christo ... en el Sanctíssimo Sacramento* (Madrid, 1611); Jean Ferrand, *Disquisitio: Sive De suspicienda, et suspecta earumdem numero reliquiarum, quae in diversis ecclesiis servantur, multitudine* (Lyon, 1647). See also Antonio Ricciulli (1582–1643), *Lucubrationum ecclesiasticarum libri sex* (Naples, 1643).

70 On Ferrand, see Carlos Sommervogel, *Bibliothèque de la Compagnie de Jésus, nouvelle édition*, vol. 3 (Louvain: Editions de la Bibliothèque S.J., Collège philosophique et théologique, 1960), col. 660–3.

71 Julia, "L'Église post-tridentine et les reliques."

72 "quia in ea veneratione nulla falsitas inest, neque ex parte adorantis, neque ex parte rei adoratae, nisi admodum per accidens, vt loquuntur Theologi: cuius rei ratio est, propterea quod quisquis Catholicorum huiusmodi dubias Diuorum exuuias religioso honore prosequitur; non eas veneratur, vt falsas, suppositias, & prorsus adulterinas, sed potius tanquam veras, legitimas, & germanas (vti quidem prudenter credit) Reliquias." Ferrand, *Disquisitio*, 519.

73 "Quod vero apud aliquos incertae aliquando Reliquiae sunt, non obest, quo minus eas, quas humanis coniecturis, ac rationibus certas habemus reverenter colere debeamus. Denique sicut dicimus non esse peccatum Idolatriae adorare radium luminis, sub quo Daemon delitescit, quando quis putat esse Christum; eodem modo, si quis putans aliquam esse particulam Sancti, quae revera non est, merito suae devotionis non caret." Ferrand, *Disquisitio*, 519.

74 Rodrigo de Arriaga, *Cursus philosophicus* (Antwerp, 1632), 224–6.

75 Peter Dear, "From Truth to Disinterestedness in the Seventeenth Century," *Social Studies of Science* 22, no. 4 (1992): 622–4.

76 "Identitas instrinseca alicuius rei non potest nobis innotescere nisi per signa exteriora praesertim loquendo in casu presenti de corporibus sanctis vel per traditionem, vel per revelationem." BAV, Chig. E.II.47, fol. 245v.

77 "Cum igitur in presenti casu constet de existentia corporis S. Joannis de Mata in suo proprio sepulcro, et de differentia ac distinctione à duobus aliis (quae postea accesserunt) per commemorationem propriam supra caput, et per maximum candorem ossium, et quod in termino ad quem, nempe in deposito habet cum et candorem , et commemorationem deducitur certitudo moralis humana, et prudens de identitate talis corporis a diffinitione ad diffinitum, et è converso valet consequentia. Est homo: ergo animal rationale, est animal rationale: ergo homo." BAV, Chig. E.II.47, fol. 246v.

78 "Certum est, quod corpus dicti sancti fundatoris est in rerum natura." BAV, Chig. E.II.47, fol. 282r.

79 "Non constat moraliter de identitate corporis Sancti Joannis de Matha, cum formiter, et legitimè non iustificantur. Deducta, et exempla assignata sint Congregationi dissimilia. Pro informatione." BAV, Chig. E.II.47, fol. 266r, underline in original. The attending cardinals were Carlo Gualterio (1613–1673), Flavio Chigi, *seniore* (1631–1693), Scipione Pannocchieschi d'Elci (1600–1670), Angelo Celsi (1600–1671), Sigismondo Chigi (1649–1678), Federico Sforza (1603–1676), Cesare Faccinetti (1608–1683), and Paolo Savelli (1622–1685). For some of the other decisions made that day, see *Decreta authentica Congregationis sacrorum rituum*, ed. Aloisii Gardellini, 3rd ed. (Rome: Congregatio de Propaganda Fide, 1856), 1.421–2. An annotation on the back of a draft copy of a petition to the congregation lists the dates on which the cardinals considered the matter. ASC, legajo 16a, unp.: "Las veces que se ha informado para tratar de este negocio en las congregaciones siguientes[:] Die 21. julii 1668. Die 15 septembris 1668. Die sabati 24. novembris 1668. Die 12 januarii 1669. Die sabati 16. februarii 1669. Y en esta última que se trató el punto salió, non constare de corporis identitate. Die 5 octobris 1669" (underline in original). The scrawled notes in BAV, Chig. E.II.47, fol. 266r make it clear, however, that the cardinals came to their decision in January.

80 "Pretesero le religione de Trinitarii cosi Calzati come Discalzati che gli dovesse consegnare il detto corpo santo, e per ciò introdussero la loro instanza nella Congregatione de Riti, mà come fù levato di Roma senza diligenza, et autentica alcuna non potendo constare de identitate della reliquia, non solo non poterono ottenere che le fosse consegnato, mà ne pure che fosse esposata di publica veneratione." ASV, Arch. Nunz. Madrid, 22.

81 E.g., Bordoni, *Operum tomus quartus* ..., 161 (resol. 117, nn. 14–18).

82 Tanner, *Decrees of the Ecumenical Councils,* 2.776.

83 On medieval procedures, see Herrmann-Mascard, *Les reliques des saints,* 106–42.

84 *Acta ecclesiae mediolanensis ab eius initiis usque ad nostram aetatem,* vol. 2, ed. Achille Ratti [Pius XI] (Milan: Pontificia Sancti Ioseph, 1890), cols 300–2.

85 "Primo ut scripta, tabulae, literae, certi annalium codices, aliave cujusvis generis monimenta, quae in iis ipsis ecclesiis, earumve atriis, atque aedibus, aut aliis locis extant, schedulaeque vasculis, arcisve sacrarum reliquiarum affixae inclusaeve recognoscantur accurate & diligenter, unde illarum vel translatio, vel collocatio ibi facta cognosci, aut alia ejusmodi notitia earumdem haberi queat. Testes praeterea conquirantur, si qui sunt, qui testimonium dent antiquae constantisque traditionis, ex qua certa earum cognitio constet: aut alia, sicut opus erit, id generis diligenter ad rei perspicientiam adhibeatur." *Acta ecclesiae mediolanensis,* col. 300.

86 "Quarum rerum omnium authentica documenta, ad posteritatis memoriam confecta, in archiuio Episcopali custodiuntur." Gabriele Paleotti, *Archiepiscopale bononiense sive De bononiensis ecclesiae administratione* (Rome, 1594), 279.

87 The weight of proof required at the apostolic level was substantially heavier than that required for authentication by a bishop. While I have not yet found a case in which episcopal approval of a relic was overturned by the congregation – such an action could potentially have been politically problematic – the 1643 case of the head of St Bruno, bishop of Segni, suggests that sometimes the cardinals used the differing burdens of proof in a strategic way. Asked to identify a skull fragment alleged to be that of the saint, the assembled cardinals could not come to a consensus because the available evidence was not strong enough to support approbation at the level of the congregation. The cardinals handed the case back to the town's bishop for judgment, perhaps in order to avoid depriving the local community of its beloved patron. Benedict XIV, *De servorum Dei beatificatione et beatorum canonizatione,* 801 (part 2, ch. 24, n. 9). On the relic of St Bruno of Segni, lost after profanation by Spanish troops in 1557 but rediscovered in 1626, see Bruno Navarra, *Filippo Michele Ellis: Segni e la sua diocesi nei primi decenni del '700* (Rome: Centro Studi del Lazio, 1973), 136–9.

88 Simon Ditchfield, *Liturgy, Sanctity and History in Tridentine Italy: Pietro Maria Campi and the Preservation of the Particular* (Cambridge: Cambridge University Press, 1995), 212–69.

89 Miguel Gotor, *I beati del papa: Santità, inquisizione e obbedienza in età moderna* (Florence: Olschki, 2001), 285–95, 308–31; Joseph Brosch, *Der Heiligsprechungsprozess per viam cultus* (Rome: Pontifical Gregorian University,

1938). On the evolution of the *casus exceptus* in the decades that followed Urban VIII's decrees, see Christian Renoux, "Canonizzazione e santità femminile in età moderna," in *Roma, la città del papa: Vita civile e religiosa dal giubileo di Bonifacio VIII al iubileo di papa Wojtyła*, ed. Luigi Fiorani and Adriano Prosperi (Turin: Einaudi, 2000), 735–6.

90 De Matta, *Novissimus de sanctorum canonizatione tractatus*, 412–13.

91 Ditchfield, *Liturgy, Sanctity and History*, 219. Cf. Lorraine Daston, *Classical Probability in the Enlightenment* (Princeton: Princeton University Press, 1988), 320–2.

92 David J. Collins, *Reforming Saints: Saints' Lives and Their Authors in Germany, 1470–1530* (Oxford: Oxford University Press, 2008); Alison Knowles Frazier, *Possible Lives: Authors and Saints in Renaissance Italy* (New York: Columbia University Press, 2005); Diana Webb, "Sanctity and History: Antonio degli Agli and Humanist Hagiography," in *Florence and Italy: Renaissance Studies in Honour of Nicolai Rubinstein*, ed. Peter Denley and Caroline Elam (London: Committee for Medieval Studies, Westfield College, 1988), 297–308.

93 For an entry point into the extensive scholarship on Baronio, see Giuseppe Antonio Guazzelli, "Cesare Baronio and the Roman Catholic Vision of the Early Church," in *Sacred History: Uses of the Christian Past in the Renaissance World*, ed. Katherine van Liere, Simon Ditchfield, and Howard Louthan (Oxford: Oxford University Press, 2012), 52–71.

94 For an introduction to the Bollandists, see David Knowles, *Great Historical Enterprises: Problems in Monastic History* (London: Nelson, 1963), 1–32; Flor Van Ommeslaeghe, "The 'Acta Sanctorum' and Bollandist Methodology," in *The Byzantine Saint: University of Birmingham Fourteenth Spring Symposium of Byzantine Studies*, ed. Sergei Hackel (London: Fellowship of Saint Alban and Saint Sergius, 1981), 155–63; Robert Godding, Bernard Joassart, Xavier Lequeux, François De Vriendt, and Joseph Van der Straeten, *Bollandistes: Saints et légendes: Quatre siècles de recherche* (Brussels: Société de Bollandistes, 2007).

95 Carlo Borghero, *La certezza e la storia: Cartesianesimo, pirronismo e conoscenza storica* (Milan: Franco Angeli Editore, 1983); Markus Völkel, *"Pyrrhonism historicus" und "fides historica": Die Entwicklung der deutschen historischen Methodologie unter dem Gesichtspunkt der historischen Skepsis* (Frankfurt: P. Lang, 1987).

96 Giovannucci, *Canonizzazioni e infallibilità pontificia*, 197–202.

97 "è veramente *scientia* solo ciò che è giurdicamente (prima ancora che teologicamente) fondato." Pierluigi Giovannucci, "Prospero Lambertini e la prova dei miracoli: Ulteriori riflessioni," *Ricerche di storia sociale e religiosa* 42, no. 84, n.s. (2013): 66.

98 On the catacombs in medieval Rome, see John Osborne, "The Roman Catacombs in the Middle Ages," *Papers of the British School at Rome* 52 (1985): 278–328; Irina Taïssa Oryshkevich, "The History of the Roman

Catacombs from the Age of Constantine to the Renaissance," PhD diss., Columbia University, 2003; Massimiliano Ghilardi, "Le catacombe di Roma nel Medioevo: Riflessioni recenti e prospettivi di ricerca," in *Subterranea civitas: Quattro studi sulle catacombe romane dal medioevo all'età moderna* (Rome: Edizioni dell'Ateneo, 2003), 17–41.

99 Stéphane Baciocchi and Christophe Duhamelle, eds, *Reliques romaines: Invention et circulation des corps saints des catacombes à l'époque moderne* (Rome: École française de Rome, 2016).

100 For one Protestant attack on catacomb relics, see Anthony Munday, *The English Romayne lyfe* (London, 1582), 42. For the opinions of an prominent Catholic critic, the Jesuit scholar Juan de Mariana (1536–1624), see George Cirot, *Mariana, historien: Études sur l'historiographie espagnole* (Bordeaux: Feret & fils, 1904), 418–23.

101 Giovanni Battista de Rossi and Antonio Ferrua, *Sulla questione del vaso di sangue: Memoria inedita con introduzione storica e appendici di documenti* (Vatican City: Pontificio Istituto di Archeologia Cristiana, 1944). See also Massimiliano Ghilardi, *Sanguine tumulus madet: Devozione al sangue dei martiri delle catacombe nella prima età moderna* (Rome: Aracne, 2008). The text of the 1668 papal brief on this is published in D. Bartolini, *Congregazione particolare dei Sagri Riti con segreto pontificio deputata da Sua Santitià per esaminare e difinire la questione se veramente i vasi de vetro, e di terra cotta posti fuori o dentro i loculi dei sepolti nei sagri suburbani cimiterj contenghino il sangue dei martiri; e perciò se debbano ritenersi come segno indubitato di martirio* (Rome: Tipografia della Rev. Camera Apostolica, 1863), 23.

102 "y passando por el Convento de los Descalços de su Orden de los Españoles, con ser las dos de la noche, ora, en que no se debia tocar campana alguna, oyeron tocar vna en el dicho Convento de Descalços, y lo tuvieron por Milagro, por llevar consigo las dichas Santas Reliquias." Lucas de la Purificación, *Historia del sagrado cuerpo*, 14. BAV, Chig. E.II.47, 246v–247r.

103 Benedict XIV, *De servorum Dei beatificatione et beatorum canonizatione*, 801–4 (part 2, ch. 24, nn. 10–13); Antonio Ricciullo, *Lucubrationum ecclesiasticarum libri sex* (Naples, 1643), 71.

104 Fernando Vidal, "Miracles, Science, and Testimony in Post-Tridentine Saint-Making," *Science in Context* 20, no. 3 (2007): 481–508; Simon Ditchfield, "Thinking with the Saints: Sanctity and Society in the Early Modern World," *Critical Inquiry* 35, no. 3 (2009): 552–84, at 567. That the issue of admitting the testimony of thieves was an important one is shown by the proofs presented in 1721, when the Congregation of Rites reconsidered the case. In his arguments, Prospero Lambertini, the

future Pope Benedict XIV, defused the problem by listing some twelve precedents, drawn from ecclesiastical history from the fourth through the sixteenth centuries, of stolen relics whose identity and authenticity was known primarily through the words of the thieves themselves. Lambertini also eliminated any reference to the relics of St Benedict and St Scholastica, the location of whose remains had been the subject of bitter controversy during the 1660s. Benedict XIV, *De servorum Dei beatificatione et beatorum canonizatione*, 827–8 (part 2, ch. 25, n. 53); Amalia Galdi, "S. Benedetto tra Montecassino e Fleury (VII-XII secolo)," *Mélanges de l'Ecole française de Rome: Moyen Âge* 126, no. 2 (2014): 2–20.

105 Jan Machielsen, "Heretical Saints and Textual Discernment: The Polemical Origins of the *Acta Sanctorum* (1643–1940)," in *Angels of Light? Sanctity and the Discernment of Spirits in the Early Modern Period*, ed. Clare Capelans and Jan Machielsen (Leiden: Brill, 2013), 103–41.

106 Katrina B. Olds, *Forging the Past: Invented Histories in Counter-Reformation Spain* (New Haven: Yale University Press, 2015), esp. 193–5. In its emphasis on combining critical scholarship with the needs of faith, pious affection shared a *semper eadem* orientation to the past found also in ecclesiastical historians like Baronio and writers on positive theology. See Jean-Louis Quantin, *Le catholicisme classique et les Pères de l'Église: Un retour aux sources (1669–1713)* (Paris: Institut d'Études Augustiniennes, 1999), 103–11; Henri Gouhier, "La crise de la théologie au temps de Descartes," *Revue de théologie et de philosophie*, 3rd series, 4, no. 1 (1954): 19–54.

107 "Para todo lo que desto se tratara, conuiene mucho aduertir, como en la materia deste santo negocio no puede auer euidencia, ni argumentos que del todo concluyan, sino vna buena probabilidad moral deduzida de buenos principios y fundamentos, de donde se forman razones, que tienen toda la fuerça de que es capaz la materia. Esto es lo que traté al principio de los discursos generales de las antigüedades, que puse en ésta mi corónica, por el autoridad de Aristóteles y Marco Tulio: y tiene mejor lugar aquí, por ser estas cosas de suyo difíciles de aueriguar, y que se deue tener en mucho qualquier aparencia de buena razón y conueniencia, que se pueda hallar. Quanto más que para procederse bien en este santo negocio, son menester tres cosas. Y la primera y muy principal es pía affeción, para no resistir con porfía a lo que moralmente se dexa entender, quando se deduze de buenos fundamentos. La segunda es zelo y recelo concertado y regido con cordura, para no dexarse persuadir sin buena razón. Lo tercero se requiere notar muchas particularidades, y con noticia y experiencia saberlas bien considerar, para deduzir dellas, lo mucho que se puede y deue inferir." Ambrosio de Morales, *Los cinco libros postreros de la Corónica*

general de España (Córdoba, 1586), 272. Morales made these observations in connection with his discussion of a series of relic finds in Córdoba in 1575.

108 "In hac autem materia potius quam alibi procedendum magis ex piae credulitatis affectu, quam ex notitia certa eorum, per quorum manus tranfierunt illae: & Episcopi, qui ex prudenti judicio procedere jubentur a Tridentino in illis recognoscendis & publico exponendis, acquiscere debent, cum scriptam vel oculatam fide eis probatur, Reliquiam aliquam bona fide acceptam a loco, ubi fuerat in honore; vel cum verosimilibus antiqui cultus indiciis repertam alicubi, velut talis, vel talis Sancti; licet ejusmodi probatio & fallere possit, & fallat saepe. Aequum enim est, ut ibi subsistat humana inquisitionis diligentia, ubi ulterior labor esset frustraneus; & a superstitionis periculo tuta sit Reliquias venerantium religio, quatenus ea tendit in primarium suum objectum, id est Sanctorum honorem, etsi fortassis eorum ipsae non essent, quae ut tales proponuntur." Daniel Papebroch, *Responsio Danielis Papebrochii ex Societate Jesu theologi ad Exhibitionem errorum per adm. r.p. Sebastianum a s. Paulo … evulgatam anno MDCXCIII Coloniæ … Pars secunda ad posteriores XII articulos: cum articulo XXV de post-notatis* (Antwerp, 1697), 365–6. Cf. Girolamo Imbruglia, "Dalle storie di santi alla storia naturale della religione: L'idea moderna di superstizione," *Rivista storica italiana* 101, no. 1 (1989): 35–84, at 56–62.

109 "Porro de certitudine requisita in approbandis his Reliquiis plura Doctores docuerunt; moralem vero sufficere deductam ex probabilibus argumentis, non autem esse necessariam evidentem, & infalibiliter concludentem communis est omnium consensus." Antonio de Quintanadueñas, *Singularia theologiae moralis: ad septem ecclesiae sacramenta* (Sevilla, 1645), 1.194. On Quintanadueñas, see José María Díaz Moreno, "Antonio de Quintanadueñas, S.J. (1599–1651): Apuntes para la semblanza de un canonista extremeño," *Cauriensa* 3 (2008): 319–33.

110 Jean-Louis Quantin, "Reason and Reasonableness in French Ecclesiastical Scholarship," *Huntington Library Quarterly* 74, no. 3 (2011): 401–36, esp. 418–26. The hermeneutic of pious affection seems to have been extended primarily to old or ancient relics, since the bodies of the recent holy dead were subject to the increasingly stringent evidentiary requirements and procedures of canonization, and were thus less likely to be called into question.

111 See, among others, Gianna Pomata, "Malpighi and the Holy Body: Medical Experts and Miraculous Evidence in Seventeenth-Century Italy," *Renaissance Studies* 21, no. 4 (2007): 568–86; Vidal, "Miracles, Science,

and Testimony"; Bradford A. Bouley, *Pious Postmortems: Anatomy, Sanctity, and the Catholic Church in Early Modern Europe* (Philadelphia: University of Pennsylvania Press, 2017).

112 Barbara J. Shapiro, *Probability and Certainty in Seventeenth-Century England: A Study of the Relationships between Natural Science, Religion, History, Law, and Literature* (Princeton: Princeton University Press, 1983); Peter Harrison, "Miracles, Early Modern Science, and Rational Religion," *Church History* 75, no. 3 (2006): 493–510. For some, doubt about relics and experimentation could lead to a deepened faith. See Jennifer Hillman, "Putting Faith to the Test: Anne de Gonzague and the Incombustible Relic," *Journal of Medieval and Early Modern Studies* 44, no. 1 (2014): 163–86.

113 Caroline Walker Bynum, *Christian Materiality: An Essay on Religion in Late Medieval Europe* (New York: Zone, 2011), 272–3.

114 For a description of the proceedings, see Benedict XIV, *De servorum Dei beatificatione et beatorum canonizatione*, 814 (part 2, ch. 25, n. 16). A notarized record of the solemn procedure and of his findings was sent to the congregation, while a second notarized copy was placed in the box that housed the bones. ASV, Arch. Nunz. Madrid, 22.

115 Benedict XIV, *De servorum Dei beatificatione et beatorum canonizatione*, 815 (part 2, ch. 25, n. 17). According to a margin note in ASV, Arch. Nunz. Madrid, 16, "Ne per parte della religione de Trinitarii calzati ni è stata fatta istanza alcuna per la consegna di detto corpo." For two very different views on the donation, see (Calced Trinitarian) Vega y Toraya, *Crónica*, 283–95, and (Discalced Trinitarian) Alexandro de la Concepción, *Historia del sagrado cuerpo*, 18–23.

116 It remains somewhat unclear whether the matter was brought before the congregation three or four times. There exist three formal responses from the congregation (1669, 1715, and 1721), but a draft opinion on the issue by Cardinal Francesco Maria Casini's (1648–1719) *auditor* notes that the 1715 petition marked the Trinitarians' "terza supplica" for the identity of the body of their founder. ASC, leg. 16a, unp.: "Votum eminentissimi Casini in congregatione ordinaria habita die 27 iulii 1715."

117 Benedict XIV, *De servorum Dei beatificatione et beatorum canonizatione*, 815–29 (part 2, ch. 25, nn. 18–54); ASC, legajo 16a, unp.: "Memoria sobre la identidad del cuerpo de N. P. S. Juan de Mata."

chapter seven

Baptizing "uncertain human beings"? Probabilist Theology and the Question of the Beginning of Human Life in Seventeenth-Century Catholicism

STEFANIA TUTINO

This essay uses a specific case study as a lens through which we can examine the intellectual, cultural, and epistemological implications of early modern Catholic moral theology. More specifically, it explores the role that the doctrine of probabilism played in allowing early modern Catholic theologians to grapple with and manage both moral and epistemological uncertainty.

Developed around the middle of the sixteenth century, probabilism represented a significant and controversial novelty in Catholic moral theology. Against a deep-seated theological tradition that defended the need for a rigid application of moral rules, early modern probabilists maintained that one could legitimately follow a course of action if, in the absence of absolutely certain norms governing the matter, such course of action was supported by a probable opinion, however tenuous and disputable that opinion might be. By the second half of the seventeenth century, probabilism had become intrinsically linked to the Jesuits, who were among its first theorists and most enthusiastic adopters, and to a system of morality that emphasized, and in some cases exploited, the elasticity of moral rules. As such, it became the subject of virulent anti-probabilist and anti-Jesuit propaganda (at times brilliant, as was the case with Pascal's *Provincial Letters*).

Historians of early modern Europe have traditionally ignored probabilism, and virtually all the existing studies of this doctrine tend to treat it almost exclusively as a branch of moral theology.[1] This situation is now changing, and many scholars – coming from different perspectives and pursuing different agendas – have started to recover the wider historical significance of early modern probabilism.[2] This newly found historical interest in the doctrine of probabilism is a welcome and important development: by engaging more deeply with probabilism and with moral theology, historians can gain valuable insight into the intellectual and cultural history of early modern Catholicism.[3] As I argue elsewhere, early modern probabilism was an important venue to examine fundamental epistemological questions, such as the nature of probability as opposed to certainty and the relationship between knowledge and moral responsibility. Seen in its proper historical context, I contend, probabilism was not simply a tool to justify morally lax behaviour, but a means to articulate a veritable epistemology of uncertainty.[4]

In the following pages I seek to demonstrate the epistemological value of probabilism by showing how some early modern Catholic moral theologians used this doctrine to argue for the legitimacy of baptizing severely premature fetuses. The question of baptizing fetuses is inextricably linked with the problem of establishing when human life begins, which over the course of the seventeenth century had become increasingly more dramatic and more uncertain.

The moment in which we are born, like the moment in which we die, is a crucial one in the life of any human being. Our biological birth, however, does not exactly coincide with the beginning of human life, and while identifying the former is easy, establishing the latter is one of the most complicated, delicate, and still mysterious aspects of the definition of humanity. Despite recent extraordinary advances in technology and medicine, we still argue fiercely about when exactly a fetus becomes a person, and the current debates over abortion are a symptom of how difficult it is for us as a society to find an answer that can accommodate all of our ideological tenets, existential anxieties, social obligations, biomedical knowledge, and religious beliefs. The same anxiety surfaces also at the opposite side of the spectrum of human life, as the recent debates concerning euthanasia and other approaches to end-of-life care show. Thanks to modern medicine, many of us who live in the Western world can count on a longer life expectancy than ever before in the history of the planet. Yet, despite such admittedly marvellous improvements in the duration and quality of life, all of us still die in the end. Just as in the case of birth, in the case of death theologians, medical doctors, and legislators do not always agree on the extent to which we have the right to control our own death. At stake in this conflict are the same fundamental questions regarding the definition of the nature of humanity, as well as the moral obligations we have towards human life, including our own.

Like many of us today, Catholic theologians in early modern Europe looked at the question of the beginning of life with fascination, but also with a growing anxiety, especially after the emergence of new medical and philosophical theories on the nature and development of fetuses. Traditional theologians based their views on the Aristotelian (and Thomist) theory of animation. Oversimplifying what in reality was a relatively varied spectrum of opinions, I will say that this traditional view postulated that at the moment of conception, the parents (especially the father) transmit to the fetus a series of biological functions. Nevertheless, before the fetus can become a proper human being, it must be fully "animated," that is, endowed by God with the *anima rationalis*, which by the early modern times had become a synonym of the Christian immortal soul. In order for the immortal soul to inhabit the fetus, the fetus must have acquired a basic human form. Unlike the moment of animation, which was conceived as a specific event, the formation of the fetus is a process that, in Aristotelian-Galenic terms, starts when the fetus begins to assume the human form and is thus suitable for animation, and ends when it is fully formed (i.e., equipped with the necessary organs and limbs to survive outside the mother's body). Medieval and early modern theologians, preachers, philosophers, and medical doctors offered slightly different estimates for how much time it takes for the fetus to become animated after being conceived, but in general terms this time interval was believed to amount to about forty days in the case of men, and much more (usually about eighty and up to ninety days) in the case of women.

Positing the existence of this time interval was not only consistent with the traditional philosophical view, but also seemed to provide an explanation for the controversial passage in Exodus 21:22–3, which appeared to distinguish between different kinds of abortions, worthy of different punishments:

> If men strive, and hurt a woman with child, so that her fruit depart from her, and yet no mischief follow: he shall be surely punished, according as the woman's husband will lay upon him; and he shall pay as the judges determine. And if any mischief follow, then thou shalt give life for life.[5]

Differentiating between animated and pre-animated fetuses could make sense of this biblical distinction. If we look at the Catholic legislation on abortion, with the exception of the intransigent and short-lived policy of Pope Sixtus V, canon law and papal decrees tended to put animated and pre-animated fetuses into two separate categories: while aborting an animated fetus was a mortally sinful action and indeed a homicide, aborting a pre-animated fetus, albeit still a grave sin, was nevertheless not a homicide, and in some exceptional circumstances it could even be excused in both the internal forum of the conscience and the external penal forum. This means that in some particular cases, the death of a fetus might be forgiven both as a sin and as a crime, such as, for example, when it occurred as an unintended and unprovoked effect of an action that was otherwise morally and legally legitimate.[6]

After the Reformation, questions concerning the beginning of life became distinctively important for the Catholic Church. In its effort to oppose Protestants, the Catholic Church reinforced the theological necessity of infant baptism, by which it could claim its authority over Catholics at the very moment of birth. At the same time, the controversial doctrines of "rogue" Aristotelian philosophers like Pietro Pomponazzi, Jacopo Zabarella, and Cesare Cremonini, who had begun to cast some doubt on the immortality of the soul, caused Catholic theologians to look at the relationship between soul and body with renewed intensity. The stakes could not have been higher: as the post-Tridentine church was fighting to remain, as Adriano Prosperi put it, the sole authority in charge of "opening the doors of the eternal life for the souls," it was more necessary than ever to understand how and when exactly these souls came to life.[7]

In the meantime, novel theories had started to challenge traditional ways of thinking about both the animation and the formation of a fetus. On the question of formation, early modern physicians and biologists could count on a rapidly expanding network of scientific communities, as well as a new instrument, the microscope, which adapted the same technological advancements used for Galileo's lenses, crafted to look at the infinitely large, to explore the infinitely small. A series of important theories and experiments drastically altered the fields of embryology and human reproduction in the seventeenth century. In particular, Theodore Kerckring, Regnier de Graaf, and Jan Swammerdam all made important discoveries about the female reproductive system. They began to dissect, examine, and describe ovarian follicles and eggs, which put a serious experimental and conceptual dent in the traditional view of the essentially passive role of the female reproductive system in the process of creating life, and which suggested that the formation of the individual life might actually start much earlier than at a relatively advanced stage of pregnancy. The male reproductive system was also the object of stunning new discoveries, which further complicated the traditional account of formation of the fetus in the womb. An important figure in the history of seventeenth-century experimental embryology was the microscope builder and experimental scientist Antonie Van Leeuwenhoek, who in 1677 identified spermatozoa as small living creatures swarming in the body of men.[8]

On the philosophical front, the seventeenth century saw the advancement of novel alternatives to the traditional understanding of the process of animation. The most controversial and influential of these alternative views was proposed by Thomas Fyens, a professor of medicine and philosophy at the University of Louvain. In 1620, Fyens published a short book with a bold thesis: fetuses are animated not after forty or eighty days, but by the third day after conception at the latest.[9] Fyens started from the assumption that humans were radically different from any other living creatures, such as animals and plants, and the essence of that difference was the immortal soul created and implanted by God. Now, since a human cannot be called such unless she is endowed with a soul, it follows that the soul must be implanted in the human embryo as early as possible, regardless of the stage of formation of the body of the fetus. Since the soul, not the body, makes the human being essentially human, it is possible and indeed correct to postulate the existence of an embryonic human being even though the body is still being formed, as long as there is a soul. By contrast, it is not possible to imagine a human whose body is growing without a soul, because a body growing without a soul cannot be a human body.[10]

Fyens's theory immediately became the centre of the philosophical and theological debate, acquiring influential endorsements, such as that of Pierre Gassendi, and provoking an aggressive reaction from those theologians and natural philosophers who believed that interposing a time interval between conception and animation was consonant not only with the philosophical tradition of Western Christendom but also with the traditional exegesis of Exodus 21.[11] Fyens's view was challenged not only on theological and legal grounds but also scientifically by physicians and students of biology such as Jan Marek (or, in his Latinized name, Johannes Marcus) Marci, a pupil of Athanasius Kircher who went on to become the rector of the University of Prague and the official physician to the Holy Roman Emperors Ferdinand III and Leopold I. In 1635, Marci published a text entitled *Idearum operatricium idea,* in which he advanced a number of different theories in the field of speculative embriology. When Marci discussed the problem of the animation of the fetus, he opposed both the traditional view and Fyens's new hypothesis, arguing instead that for as long as the fetus remains in the womb, it cannot, and in fact does not, receive the immortal soul. The fetus, for Marci, was like the seed of any other organism, planted by the man and nourished by the woman. While the male sperm provides the *virtus formatrix*, or the capacity for developing, the uterus of the mother provides the conditions for the development to take place. As long as it remains in the maternal womb, the fetus undergoes the process of growing into its fullest human form, yet it remains a part of the mother's body and therefore necessarily borrows, so to speak, the soul from her (as Marci put it, "the fetus in the uterus is a part of the mother, like one of her fingers"[12]). The fact that the fetus in the womb is essentially an appendage of the mother's body explained why a sudden alteration of the mother's imagination could produce serious and at times fatal consequences for the health of the fetus.[13] According to Marci, animation (i.e., the infusion of the fetus's own individual immortal soul) is completed only after the fetus is fully formed, when the now fully human baby is expelled from the mother's body and ready to live on its own. Thus, the fruits of miscarriages or severely premature births are not fully animated, and consequently not yet human.[14]

In the midst of this new and multidimensional debate, Catholic theologians, physicians, and natural philosophers could not reach a consensus, and instead were confronted with a growing sense of confusion and uncertainty. Even Paolo Zacchia, the official doctor to Pope Innocent X and probably the greatest seventeenth-century medical forensics expert, recognized that as time went by, uncertainty around these issues increased rather than decreased. In his influential manual of legal medicine entitled *Quaestiones medico-legales*, whose publication stretched over thirty years, Zacchia admitted that the topic of pregnancy was already distinctively obscure because of the intrinsically mysterious nature of the processes taking place inside a woman's body. In fact, Zacchia believed that when it comes to matters related to pregnancy, it is impossible to know anything "through certain, infallible, demonstrative and evident signs," and instead we can only rely on "conjectures and probable signs."[15] Concerning the question of establishing the exact moment at which the fetus receives the immortal soul, Zacchia believed that the recent debates further increased the connatural uncertainty and obscurity inherent in the hidden and, for the most part, unknown process of human gestation. He confessed to his readers that as he began to consider the issue, he had agreed with the traditional view on the forty-day period between conception and animation. The recent new theories, however, and especially

Thomas Fyens's, had forced him to re-evaluate his position, and now Zacchia had become convinced that the traditional view led to many "absurd" consequences, while the opinion that "the *anima rationalis* is created and infused by God immediately at the exact moment of conception," albeit "novel," was "much more consonant with the truth."[16]

While Zacchia and many of his colleagues might have found this uncertainty difficult to deal with, one subset of Catholic theologians actually thrived in uncertainty: whenever Catholic intellectuals left the comfortable boundaries of epistemological certainty and entered the tough world of probability, the tough probabilist theologians got going. Indeed, probabilist theologians immediately jumped at the opportunity to both take stock of the uncertainty surrounding the beginning of life and use the space created by uncertainty to advance the theological debate.

The uncertainty surrounding the beginning of life was not simply academic, so to speak, but had momentous implications for Catholic theology and the liturgical life of every Catholic man and woman, because it affected the traditional understanding and practise of infant baptism. As I noted, after the Reformation the Catholic Church reaffirmed its commitment to infant baptism, opening the doors of heaven (and firming up the new members' confessional allegiance) as early as possible. From a theological point of view, the necessity of baptism was especially crucial when a newborn was in danger of dying, because if the baby were to die without being baptized, through no fault of her own, her little soul would be prevented from ever being saved.

Given such high risk and such high stakes, the Catholic Church tried to both keep a firm stance on the necessity of infant baptism and assuage the dramatic concerns of parents by making sure that no baby was left behind on the road to salvation. Priests, and in some cases even physicians and midwives, were instructed in how to perform emergency baptisms in case the newborn appeared in danger of dying, and the Church reassured those first-line fighters in the war to keep newborns safe from eternal damnation that in order for baptism to be legitimate, it was not necessary for the entire body of the newborn to be out of the mother's body; as long as it was possible to touch with baptismal water the head of the baby outside or even, in some cases, inside the uterus, baptism would be valid.

Despite these measures, however, doubts and scruples multiplied. It is true that in many doubtful cases concerning the administration of baptism and indeed of all sacraments, the church allowed rituals to be performed *sub conditione* (i.e., on the condition that the faithful were able and legitimately entitled to receive the sacrament), but it is also true that administering a conditional sacrament was not a universal solution to all of the many novel dilemmas that continued to arise. For instance, what happened if a midwife who was trying to wet the head of the baby with baptismal water could not tell whether she was actually touching the body of the baby rather than simply the amniotic sac? What about the cases in which it was not possible to establish with absolute certainty whether a soon-to-die newborn baby had managed to stay alive long enough to receive baptism, or whether she was already dead as the sacrament was being administered (which would have made baptism not only invalid, but also sacrilegious, for baptizing dead flesh was prohibited)?[17]

Within this maze of doubts, however, one thing was certain: if the mother miscarried before forty days, there was no need to worry about baptism, because what the mother expelled was nothing but "*molae*" (i.e., a mass of flesh, blood, and other discharges that bore no resemblance to, and contained no trace of, human life). What happens, though, if we begin questioning the time interval between conception and animation? How can we be sure that the result of early miscarriages are *molae* and not an animated embryo? And if these early miscarriages are in fact animated, by deciding not to baptize them would we not be condemning these still unformed souls to hell? Was the church certain enough of its speculative knowledge and empirical evidence to justify what could in fact be the ultimate betrayal of its duty to bring to heaven as many innocent souls as possible?

The Tuscan clergyman Girolamo Fiorentini, a member of the Clerics Regular of the Mother of God, could not shake off these questions. In 1658, he published a short book entitled *Disputatio de ministrando baptismo humanis foetibus abortivorum* in which, after summarizing the main voices in the recent debates over animation and formation, he concluded that the question of when a fetus becomes a person was hopelessly uncertain, and in fact was becoming ever more uncertain as more opinions were proposed and more medical discoveries made. Given the current state of the debate, Fiorentini believed it was fully probable that animation could occur at any point during the pregnancy.[18] Once we assume that, then we must also assume that priests legitimately can, and indeed must, act on this probability and baptize any fetus regardless of how advanced the pregnancy might be. Since baptism is crucial for any Catholic man and woman, and since newborn babies are most vulnerable to the danger of dying without it, charity demands that priests attend to the needs of these most vulnerable souls and do what they can to bring them to heaven.

Moreover, Fiorentini reminded his readers that this dilemma was not the only doubtful case that the Catholic Church faced and not the only situation in which the church needed to reconcile its duty to provide the spiritual comfort of the sacraments to as many Catholics as possible with the obligation to avoid doctrinal missteps. For instance, priests might not know for sure whether the confession of a dying man was complete and performed properly, or whether a previously administered baptism was valid. In all of those cases, the church allowed the possibility of celebrating these sacraments *sub conditione*, which means that priests could administer the last rites on the condition that the dying man had in fact confessed all his sins with the heartfelt desire to repent, and that they could baptize children on the condition that they had never received a valid baptism before. Why couldn't the church allow the same provision in the case of extremely premature fetuses?[19]

Fiorentini cast his arguments in explicitly probabilist terms and justified his position by invoking the epistemological category of probability and by drawing the moral implications that any probabilist theologian would draw. In fact, before publishing his book, Fiorentini sent a copy of the manuscript to the famous and controversial probabilist theologian Juan Caramuel and asked for his opinion. Caramuel's response was so favourable that Fiorentini decided to print it in the paratext of his 1658 book. Caramuel agreed wholeheartedly with Fiorentini that the question of the beginning of life was inherently uncertain, and therefore priests can, and in fact must, baptize fetuses who might or might not be alive. If, in this situation of doubt, a priest decided not to administer baptism, he would risk condemning an innocent soul to hell. By contrast, if he decided to administer baptism *sub conditione*, he would be carrying out his duty while simultaneously avoiding potential sacrilege in case the fetus was either dead or inanimate.[20] In sum, Caramuel was very proud of Fiorentini's effort to snatch from limbo or from hell souls who would have ended up there not because of their sins, but rather because of the "excessive scruples, ignorance, and prejudice" of those who had refused to act on the probability of fetuses being alive. Fiorentini's novel, learned, and solid doctrine seemed to Caramuel an excellent example of the wider efforts carried out by "the most glorious minds of our time" to update theology, refresh it, and "bring it to great perfection."[21]

Fortified and reassured by Caramuel's approval, Fiorentini grew bold and started to defend his position in public debates. Members of his order also jumped on the wagon of their confrere's hot new theory, and began to attack its adversaries quite virulently as backward defenders of a doctrine that, after Fiorentini's book, had obviously become obsolete and incorrect. The debate between Fiorentini's friends and foes grew heated and aggressive, and in 1664 the Congregation of the Index of Prohibited Books received an official complaint. The author was Gregorio della Torre, a member of the Canons Regular of the Lateran, who had agreed to publicly debate the question of baptism of fetuses. Torre proudly supported the traditional view, founded "on the common and accepted distinction between animated and non-animated fetuses," but instead of receiving praise for his effort to "follow the common usage of the church" and oppose novelties, Torre was mercilessly attacked by Fiorentini and other members of his order. Thus, Torre wanted the Cardinals of the Index to take a look at Fiorentini's book, from which the controversy originated, and judge whether it was expedient to censure it.[22]

The censors of the Index did not question the fact that Fiorentini's opinion was based on reasonable, and therefore probable, arguments, and that it enjoyed the support of other famous theologians. In fact, the censors were not interested in attacking or even discussing in any detail the legitimacy of Fiorentini's probabilist method of arguing. After all, Augustine himself had recognized that the question of the beginning of life was intrinsically obscure and therefore implied a measure of uncertainty. What they could not condone, however, was that Fiorentini dared to present his new and untraditional opinion as the only sure way to deal with baptizing fetuses in a manner that was consonant with the Catholic doctrine, which implied that the usual practice of the church, developed over centuries and supported by so many authorities, was erroneous.[23] For this reason, the Index judged that Fiorentini's book, as it stood, could not be allowed, but if Fiorentini wanted to argue for his opinion, he should correct his book so as to avoid suggesting that he was right and the tradition of the church wrong.[24]

Fiorentini was not discouraged. First, he started to circulate his work widely and collected numerous endorsements from very different kinds of people, all with their own stakes in the debate. Among the many enthusiastic readers, we should mention the theologians of the Sorbonne, who took the opportunity to comment on the book to condemn abortion; the members of faculty of medicine of the universities of Prague and Vienna, who were pleased to see that even though Fiorentini did not exactly share Fyens's or Marci's positions, nevertheless he seemed to hold their and their fellow medical doctors' authority in high regard; and, once again, Juan Caramuel, who was happy to reiterate his fervent approval.[25]

In the meantime, Fiorentini worked with the Cardinals of the Index on correcting his book. He knew that the cardinals agreed with him that the question of the beginning of life was hopelessly uncertain, and consequently his solution of baptizing fetuses was probable. They only wanted to avoid having his probable solution presented as if it were certainly correct, which would have implied that the common way of dealing with this issue (i.e., not performing baptism), was erroneous. Thus, he told the Index that he was going to correct his book by adding a new preface, in which he specified that the book proposed to baptize fetuses "only by way of doubt" and as a possible solution to an open-ended discussion, without any pretence of "introducing a new ritual" and dictating "a grave obligation" for the priests to baptize all and every fetus.[26] The congregation, evidently pleased by Fiorentini's solution, approved the publication of the emended version, which appeared in Lucca in 1665 and which, aside from the new preface, was virtually identical to the first.[27]

Although the censors from the Index did not appreciate Fiorentini's attempt to use the epistemological probability of the opinion that life begins at conception to argue for the necessity of radically changing the doctrinal norms on infant baptism, they realized that the question of the beginning of life was indeed uncertain. Therefore, probability was a solid tool to advance the theological debate, provided that such advancements did not infringe on the normative authority of the pope and the Curia to establish how sacraments should be administered. Thus the Roman censors wanted to make sure that Fiorentini presented his opinion precisely as an opinion, which – no matter how probable – was still not certain enough for Fiorentini to dictate any rule on baptizing fetuses. To this effect, they had Fiorentini emphasize, not eliminate, the probabilist nature of his reflection. But asserting the epistemological probability of a specific course of action and thus legitimizing its use in practice could have momentous normative consequences. In fact, if and when the pope decided to issue a definitive and final judgment on the question of the beginning of life, he could pick any speculatively probable and morally legitimate alternative and transform it into the only certain and officially prescribed way of addressing this question; since Fiorentini's opinion had been approved as probable, it might very well become the one chosen by the pope.

Fiorentini realized that condoning, and in fact highlighting, the probability of his opinion could pave the way to having it fully accepted as the official answer to the problem of baptizing fetuses, and he was utterly convinced that as time went by, and as theologians, physicians, and natural philosophers examined in greater detail the question of the beginning of life, the traditional view would appear more and more flawed, while his opinion would gain more currency. Confident in his assessment, in 1671, six years after publishing his emended *Disputatio*, Fiorentini reached out to Pope Clement X. He told the pope that the first edition of his *Disputatio* had been approved by "many Catholic universities and by a great number of theologians," and that even though "an ill-disposed person" had denounced the book to the Index, nevertheless the congregation had realized that the doctrine contained therein was not contrary to the orthodoxy of the church, and in fact the Index had allowed Fiorentini to reprint his book with a short additional preface. This decision, he argued, was the ultimate admission of the legitimacy of Fiorentini's opinion, which in turn served as evidence that the question of establishing the beginning of life was "a serious and important matter." For this reason, Fiorentini asked the pope to form a special committee "of cardinals and priests" to examine the question and report their conclusions to the pope, so that the pope could issue a definitive judgment.[28]

In the spring of 1671, the pope granted Fiorentini's request and began assembling the committee, which was officially appointed on the 12th of August. The committee was relatively large, comprising theologians (including Juan Caramuel), cardinals, canonists, and the medical doctor Florido Salvatori, personal physician to the pope.[29] Unfortunately, we have no record of the final decisions taken by the papal committee on Fiorentini's opinion. Nevertheless, we know that it must not have been unfavourable to Fiorentini, partly because the papal committee included Caramuel, who was an outspoken supporter of both Fiorentini's theory and the probabilist doctrine on which it was based, and also because after 1671 Fiorentini continued to publish undisturbed, and in fact with the full approval of the Roman Curia.

In 1672 Fiorentini published, with the *imprimatur* of Giacinto Libelli (the Master of the Sacred Palace), a sequel of sorts to his previous *Disputatio*, in which he updated his readers on the most recent arguments and discoveries in support of his opinion, including Theodore Kerckring's 1671 experiment, which, Fiorentini claimed, allowed him to conclude that a fetus is equipped with a distinctive head "three or four days after conception at the latest."[30] In 1674, Fiorentini printed yet another enlarged version of his *Disputatio*, this time making his probabilist approach explicit even in the title of the book, in which the "*foetus abortivorum*" had become "*homines dubii*."[31]

The fact that the Catholic Church let Fiorentini continue defending his theory indicates that the church recognized the fundamental uncertainty of the question of the beginning of human life and allowed Fiorentini's probabilist approach as a useful and legitimate way of addressing this uncertainty. It did not mean, however, that the church had decided to adopt Fiorentini's certainly probable solution as the definitive answer to a question that remained (and, in some sense, still remains) uncertain.[32]

Two centuries later, and from the other side of the Atlantic Ocean, the question of baptizing fetuses returned to the Holy Office. In 1823, the diocesan synod of Bardstown, in Kentucky, issued a decree containing many recommendations concerning sacraments, on which "the instruction of the Christian people especially depends." Among the various recommendations, the synod established that Catholic priests should "insist with mothers and midwives to have all aborted fetuses baptized at any time." In the case that the miscarried babies looked more like "a formless mass" than human beings, priests should still baptize those formless (but possibly animated) masses, albeit *sub conditione*, provided that they were not "already putrefied."[33] In May of 1827, the congregation *De propaganda fide* transmitted the decrees of the Synod of Bardstown to the Holy Office and asked the congregation to judge whether those decrees were legitimate.[34] The Holy Office took the summer to examine the question, and in September made a final decision. Although the congregation praised the bishop of Bardstown, Benedict Joseph Flaget, for his commendable "zeal to save the souls" of his flock, nevertheless it wished that he had either avoided ratifying some of the decrees concerning the sacrament of baptism issued at his diocesan synod or "at least issued them in a manner that was more consonant with the Roman Ritual and with the prescription of the Holy Office," which is why Bishop Flaget should "emend or modify" the decrees of the synod so as to avoid departing from the Ritual.[35] One of those problematic decrees in need of modification was precisely the one concerning the baptism of fetuses. The Holy Office wanted the bishop of Bardstown to receive a copy of "the decree issued by the Sacred Congregation of the Index on this matter on 5 April 1666, concerning a short book published in Lyon in 1658," which was none other than Fiorentini's *Disputatio*. The Holy Office reminded the American prelate that Fiorentini had been forced to declare that the legitimacy of baptizing fetuses was only probable, and that such probability in no way changed the traditional approach of the church to infant baptism.[36] The congregation also implicitly suggested a way for the bishop to correct the decree by noting that Fiorentini had been allowed to reprint his work only after being reminded of the difference between fetuses who "showed human features" and fetuses who did not show any sign of life. While it was legitimate, and in fact necessary, to baptize the former, the latter were to be considered as a kind of "bodily excrement" rather than as human beings, and therefore they should not be baptized.[37]

At the beginning of 1828 Bishop Flaget received a copy of the Inquisition's decision, and responded by reassuring the Holy Office that the message from Rome had made it across the Atlantic loud and clear. He had already entrusted one of his theologians, Francis Kenrick, to make a summary of the cardinals' final judgment and to publicize it widely to all the priests in the Diocese of Kentucky, and he wanted the Roman cardinals to know that his disobedience came from ignorance, not from his will to oppose in any way the supreme theological authority of the Roman See.[38]

If we consider the firm position taken on this issue by the Catholic Church today, we might be somewhat surprised to find such a strong reluctance on the part of the nineteenth-century Curia to take a stand on the question of the beginning of life, and such a resolute opposition to any innovation in the traditional way of administering baptism that might suggest that fetuses must be considered human beings from the moment of conception. Obviously, from a purely theological point of view, when Pope Pius IX in 1854 proclaimed the dogma of the Immaculate Conception, he also necessarily established that Mary and, by extension, all human fetuses are endowed with a soul at the moment of conception (and in fact the same Pius IX officially removed from the teaching of the church the distinction between animated and pre-animated fetuses a few years later, in 1869). Nevertheless, such a drastic change of heart on a question that had remained uncertain for most of the history of the church might deserve a more thorough historical, cultural, and epistemological investigation. Furthermore, even though the church of today seems quite certain of the precise time at which fetuses become human beings, it might be worth remembering that even as late as 2006, Cardinal Carlo Maria Martini said that the new scientific and medical advancements have made the task of establishing when life begins and ends more complex, not easier, because of the proliferation of "border areas, or grey areas," in which "the true good of men and women is not evident."[39]

I am glad to leave to others the task of investigating what is evidently good for men and women today; I simply want to point out that the question of the beginning of life has been a grey and uncertain area throughout the history of post-Reformation Catholicism. Indeed, early modern Catholic culture was steeped in uncertainty. Catholic ecclesiastical and intellectual leaders were becoming acutely aware of the proliferation of different, and at times contradictory, sources of knowledge coming not only from within the Catholic ranks, but also from political authorities, as well as from the world of natural philosophy and the emerging experimental sciences. In addition, early modern Catholic theologians had started to develop a keen appreciation for historical change, realizing that doctrines over which there had been consensus had now come under dispute, and, conversely, opinions that used to be absurd had found new and at times stringent argumentative foundations as well as numerous supporting authorities. In this situation, probabilism represented a powerful, novel, and controversial tool not only to take stock of the growing moral and epistemological uncertainty that these changes provoked, but also to provide a solution to the proliferation of doubts and dilemmas by integrating novelties within the Catholic intellectual and theological system.

NOTES

1 See, e.g., Albert R. Jonsen and Stephen Toulmin, *The Abuse of Casuistry: A History of Moral Reasoning* (Berkeley: University of California Press, 1988); Julia A. Fleming, *Defending Probabilism: The Moral Theology of Juan Caramuel* (Washington, DC: Georgetown University Press, 2006); and Rudolf Schüssler, *Moral im Zweifel*, 2 vols (Paderborn: Mentis 2003–6). As evidence of the lack of attention to the historical dimensions of the doctrine of probabilism, in most existing studies on probabilism the classic reference work is still the intellectually narrow and theologically polemical entry of the Dominican theologian Thomas Deman in the *Dictionnaire de Théologie Catholique*, vol. 13, 1936 ("Probabilisme," cols 417–619).

2 On the importance of probabilism in the religious history of early modern Europe, see Jean-Pascal Gay, "*Doctrina Societatis?* Le rapport entre probabilisme et discernement des esprits dans la culture jésuite (XVIe–XVIIe siècles)," in *Le discernement spirituel au XVIIe siècle*, ed. Simon Icard (Paris: Nolin, 2011), 23–46. Both James Franklin and Barbara Shapiro note the role played by probabilism in the development of modern science and modern jurisprudence: see Franklin, *The Science on Conjecture: Evidence and Probability before Pascal* (Baltimore: Johns Hopkins University Press, 2001); Shapiro, *Probability and Certainty in Seventeenth-Century England* (Princeton: Princeton University Press, 1983) and *Beyond "Reasonable Doubt" and "Probable Cause": Historical Perspectives on the Anglo-American Law of Evidence* (Berkeley: University of California Press, 1991). On the more general

question of the historical significance of Catholic moral theology in early modern Europe, see Jean-Pascal Gay, *Morales en conflit: Théologie et polémique au Grand Siècle (1640–1700)* (Paris: Éd. du Cerf, 2011).

3 On this point, see the considerations advanced by Jean-Louis Quantin in "Le Saint-Office et le probabilisme (1677–1679): Contribution à l'histoire de la théologie morale à l'époque moderne," in *Mélanges de l'école française de Rome* 114, no. 2 (2002): 875–960, at 875.

4 Stefania Tutino, *Uncertainty in Post-Reformation Catholicism: A History of Probabilism* (Oxford: Oxford University Press, 2018).

5 The King James version of this passage from Exodus maintains a crucial and fundamental ambiguity concerning the exact nature of the "mischief" that would justify punishing abortion as a homicide. This same ambiguity has always characterized the interpretation of this passage throughout the textual history of the Sacred Scripture. In the Septuagint version of the Bible, the difference in punishment was based on the different stages of development of the fetus, whereas in the Vulgate (as well as in the Hebrew Bible) the different punishment depended on whether the mother died as a result of the violent act. On the exegetical problems with this passage, see Cornelius Houtman's commentary *Exodus* (Leuven: Peeters, 2000), 3.160–71.

6 On the legislative and theological complexity of abortion in post-Reformation Catholicism, see John Christopoulos, "Abortion and the Confessional in Counter-Reformation Italy," *Renaissance Quarterly* 65 (2002): 443–84; and P. Renée Baernstein and John Christopoulos, "Interpreting the Body in Early Modern Italy: Pregnancy, Abortion and Adulthood," *Past and Present* 223, no. 1 (May 2014): 41–75. For an overview of the place of abortion in moral theology and canon law, see Paolo Sardi, *L'aborto ieri e oggi* (Brescia: Paideia, 1975).

7 Adriano Prosperi, *Dare l'anima: Storia di un infanticidio* (Turin: Einaudi, 2005), quoted at 251 (but see Prosperi's entire chap. 6). For an overview of the question of birth and baptism in early modern Europe, see also Jacques Gélis, *L'arbre et le fruit: La naissance dans l'Occident moderne, XVIe–XIXe siècle* (Paris: Fayard, 1984), and, from a different perspective, John Bossy, *Christianity in the West: 1400–1700* (Oxford: Oxford University Press, 2010), chap. 2. The classic text on the history of the sacrament of baptism is Jules Corblet, *Histoire dogmatique, liturgique et archéologique du sacrement de baptême*, 2 vols. (Paris-Bruxelles-Geneva: Palmé-Albanel-Trembley, 1881–2).

8 For a synthetic and accessible scientific discussion of these seventeenth-century discoveries in the field of embryology and human reproduction, see Matthew Cobb, *Generation: The Seventeenth-Century Scientists Who Unraveled*

the Secrets of Sex, Life, and Growth (New York: Bloomsbury, 2006). On the historical and technological context, see Edward G. Ruestow, *Microscope in the Dutch Republic: The Shaping of Discovery* (Cambridge: Cambridge University Press, 1996), and Eric Jorink, *Reading the Book of Nature in the Dutch Golden Age, 1575–1715* (Leiden: Brill, 2006). For the philosophical implications of these discoveries, see Walter Bernardi, *Le metafisiche dell'embrione: Scienze della vita e filosofia da Malpighi a Spallanzani (1672–1793)* (Florence: Olschki, 1985).

9 Thomas Fyens, *De formatrice foetus liber in quo ostenditur animam rationalem infundi tertia die* (Antwerp, 1620).

10 See especially ibid., quaestio VIII, "Quae ergo & qualis sit illa anima qua semini post conceptionem primo advenit ac conformationem facit, vegetativane, sensitiva, an rationalis," 158–220.

11 On the reaction to Fyens's work see Prosperi, *Dare l'anima*, 261–7.

12 Marci, *Idearum operatricium idea* (Prague 1635), fol. 165v: "est autem faetus in utero, non minus quam sit digitus pars aliqua Matris." All translations, unless otherwise noted, are my own.

13 On this topic, see Herman W. Roodenburg, "The Maternal Imagination: The Fears of Pregnant Women in Seventeenth-Century Holland," *Journal of Social History* 21 (1988): 701–16, and Marie-Hélène Huet, *Monstrous Imagination* (Cambridge, MA: Harvard University Press, 1993).

14 Marci, *Idearum operatricium idea*, esp. chaps 2–4, fols 105v and ff. On Marci's and Fyens's theories in the context of the wider theological debate, see Vincenzo Lavenia, "'D'animal fante': Teologia, medicina legale e identità umana: Secoli XVI–XVII," in *Salvezza delle anime e disciplina dei corpi: Un seminario sulla storia del battesimo*, ed. Adriano Prosperi (Pisa: Edizioni della Normale, 2006), 483–526.

15 Zacchia, *Quaestiones medico-legales* (Lyon, 1661), vol. 1, book 1, title 3, q.I, 50: "Praegnantia in quocumque tempore sit nullatenus cognosci potest per signa quaedam certa, infallibilia, demonstrativa, ac evidentia … Praegnantia per aliquas coniecturas & signa quaedam probabilia aliquo modo cognosci potest."

16 Ibid., vol. 2, book 9, title 1, q.I, 1–2: "De Animatione foetus humani verba facere, cum mihi sese alias obtulisset occasio, coactus sum communissimae opinioni adherere, quae vult, Animam Rationalem post quadraginta dies foetum informare … Sed inter Recentiores, Thom. Fien … demonstrare conatus est, foetus humanum triduo perfici, ac tertia die ad summum, & ut serius Rationalem Animam recipere … Ego vero hanc communissimam opinionem … ad trutinam revocans … non posse ullo modo salvari, & magna, & innumera absurda, quae de necessitate ad eam consequi

animadverti, novae ac veritati multo magis consonae adhaerere coactus sum, nempe Animam Rationalem a Deo Optimo Maximo tum primum creatam, & infusam in ipso primo conceptionis momento praesentem esse." On Zacchia's considerations, see Lavenia, "'D'animal fante,'" 518–23; Prosperi, *Dare l'anima*, 266–7; and Baernstein and Christopoulos, "Interpreting the Body in Early Modern Italy."

17 These and other similar cases are discussed in Prosperi, *Dare l'anima*, 175 and ff.

18 Fiorentini, *Disputatio de ministrando baptismo* (Lyon, 1658), 169: "illa sententia [tempus primae animationis est valde dubium] dicitur tum speculative tum practice probabilis, quae non sola ratione sed etiam auctoritate fulcitur."

19 Ibid., s. 11, 170–85. On Fiorentini's text, see also Prosperi, *Dare l'anima*, 271–8, and "Scienza e immaginazione teologica nel Seicento: Il battesimo e le origini dell'individuo," *Quaderni Storici* 100 (1999): 173–98. An English version of this latter essay is available: "Science and the Theological Imagination in the Seventeenth Century: Baptism and the Origins of the Individual," chap. 13 in *Christianity and Community in the West: Essays for John Bossy*, ed. Simon Ditchfield (Farnham: Ashgate, 2001), 206–31.

20 Caramuel to Fiorentini, in *Disputatio de ministrando baptismo*, unfol.: "foetus habens dubiam vitam potest & debet baptizari ... At foetus animatus qui meo errore iudicatur aut nondum animatus, aut mortuus, & agere vivus, qui meo errore iam obiissse putatur, sunt in aeternae damnationis periculo, salvi erunt si congrua sacramenta recipiant, aut alias in aeternum peribunt. Ergo crudelis sum & sanguinis Divini reus, si nolim abluere alterum & alterum a peccatis absolvere. Quamobrem si in dubio sacramenta administro conditionate, infero nulli iniuriam, etiam in casu quo careant anima illa corpora de quorum vita dubitatur."

21 Ibid.: "Vale igitur Pater eruditissime, bellum infer Lymbo (aut etiam forte Inferno de statu enim infantum qui caruerunt aquae Sacramentalis beneficio nihil hucusque definivit Ecclesia) & quia eum non potes exspoliare animabus, quas eo invexere ignorantiae scrupulosae, praeiudicia, ob quae multis infantibus qui erant re vera vivi cum tamen viderentur mortui fuit Baptisma negatum, grandi ore potius concionare quam disputa, ne Obstetrices & qui Embryonibus aborientibus adsunt, pergant desipere, hoc est ne Christi meritis efficaciam invideant, infantibus dubia, aut probabili praeditis vita, viam ad gratiam & gloriam occupantes. Vale iterum ut doctissimis libris exornes Theologiam, nostro aevo sublimium ingeniorum concursu ad magnam perfectionem promotam." The questions of what happened to the souls of unbaptized babies and the exact nature

of limbo were hotly debated throughout the history of Catholic theology. For an analysis of the theological debates in the early Renaissance, see Chiara Franceschini, "Dibattiti sul peccato originale e sul Limbo a Firenze (1439–1450)," in Prosperi, *Salvezza delle anime,* 215–54. For a cultural history of limbo see Chiara Franceschini, *Storia del limbo* (Milan: Feltrinelli, 2017).

22 See Archivio della Congregazione per la Dottrina della Fede [hereafter ACDF], Index Diarii VI, 17 November 1664, fol. 139v: "Fuit lectum memoriale P.D. Gregorii della Torre Canonici Regularis Lateranensis sequentis tenoris: ... Gregorio della Torre canonico Regulare lateranense humilissimo oratore del EE VV Rev. riverentemente espone come in un publico congresso essendosi servito della commune et accertata distintione del feto humano in animato et non animato li fu da persona privata ivi presente riprovata e detto che non si dava feto humano inanimato come già havea publicato poco prima in una sua opera stampata et intitolata De Baptismo Abortivorum. Parve al oratore di ragione sostenere detta distintione come la sostenne in detto publico congresso dal quale sbrigato con ogni religiosa carità avvisò quel tale che non doveva reprovare una distintione tanto celebre e così necessria per risolvere molti dubii di coscienza, et anche l'aggiunse che in materia del battesimo degl'aborti era bene seguitare l'uso commune della Chiesa e non introdurre dottrine nove e li lasciò in scritto quelle ragioni che potevano persuadere l'uno e l'altro ... Pertanto restano l'EE loro humilmente supplicate a far matura consideratione ... per prenderne poi quella resolutione che stimeranno megliore." Another copy of Torre's petition can be found in ACDF, Index Protocolli PP, fol. 346r.

23 "Neque recens est in Ecclesia quaestio, ante an post formatum corpus animetur foetus, unius meminit Augus.in Enchiridio ad Laurentium cap. [23] 85 [86] his verbis: scrupulosissime quidem inter dictissimos quaeri ac disputari potest (quod utrum ab homine inveniri possit ignoro) quando incipiat homo in utero vivere, utrum sit quaedam vita occulta quae nondum motibus viventis appareat. Haec ille, satis innuens rem sibi obscuram, et plenam dubitationis videris ... Nemo tamen hucusque ausus est propter eam disputationem atque dubitationem, veterem attentare doctrinam et novam edere quam Florentinus proponit." The censures to Fiorentini's work can be found in ACDF, Index, Protocolli PP, fol. 342r and ff. (quoted at fol. 343r–v).

24 See ACDF, Diarii VII, 22 June 1665, fol. 4v: "E.mi decreverunt ... librum vero D.Florentinii suspendi donec corrigatur interea admonendum autorem ut corrigat."

25 Fiorentini published a vast sample of the numerous endorsements he received in the second, emended edition of his *Disputatio de ministrando*

baptismo (Lucca, 1665). On these endorsements, see also Prosperi, *Dare l'anima,* 276–7.

26 Girolamo Fiorentini, Lucca, 2 August 1665, in ACDF, Index Protocolli PP, fol. 350r–v at fol. 350r: "Riceverà V.P.Re.ma con questa mia la corretione del mio libbretto de baptismo Abortivorum, che da cotesti EE.mi SS.ri miei e da lei mi è stata comandata ... Ho fatta questa correttione come vede separata dal'opera sotto nome di Parergo da aggiungersi in fronte della nuova stampa ... Mi sono valso del'amorevole consiglio suggeritomi in nome di V.P.R.ma di trattare per modo di dubio e problematicamente la propositione, e mi sono dichiarato non havere mai preteso di indurne obligo grave e di peccato mortale, e tale veramente è stata sempre la mia intentione, si come la verità è che non ho mai preteso (Dio guardi) di indurre nella santa chiesa nuovo rito. Haverei però gran desiderio quando ella giudicasse essere conforme alla mente della Sacra Congregatione."

27 ACDF, Index, Diarii VII, 5 April 1666, fol. 8r: "Pater Secretarius certam reddidit Sac.Congregationem qualiter ... Hieronimus Florentini librum suum de ministrando baptismo foetibus humanis abortivis correxit et correctum iterum impresserit ... E.mi decreverunt ut sic correctus permittatur et non aliter et hoc in decreto librorum prohibendiorum imprimendo notificetur."

28 Fiorentini to the pope, 1671, ACDF Dubia Baptismi I, 1618–98, folder n. 15, fol. 378r–v: "Girolamo Fiorentini Chierico Regolare della Madre d'Iddio oratore humilissimo espone a V.S.tà che havendo di professo essaminata la materia dell'amministratione del battesimo alli feti humani che nascono immaturi mandò alle stampe la sua opinione l'anno 1658. Fu ricevuta da molte accademie cattoliche e da gran numero di Teologi, come appare dalle censure che sono poste avanti il libbro ristampato e che s'essibisce a V.S.tà. Doppo 6 anni in circa fu portato il libbro nella S.Congregatione dell'Indice per opra di persona all'Autor poco ben affetta con supposto che contenesse dottrina contraria alli S.Canoni. La S.Congregatione doppo di haverla dentro tali limiti essaminata permisse il detto libbro con ordinare all'Autore certa dichiaratione che in un foglio si da' impressa nel principio del libbro. Per tanto l'oratore prostrato a suoi SS.mi Piedi li rappresenta la gravità e la rilevanza della materia di che si tratta, e quando V.S.tà col suo sapientissimo giudizio illuminato dallo spirito divino ve la riconosca, la supplica a voler deputar una congregatione di SS.ti Cardinali e Prelati, che l'essaminino e ne faccino di poi a V.S.tà relazione."

29 The complete list of the members of the committee can be found in ibid., fol. 379r–v.

30 Fiorentini, *Disputatio II de baptismo humanis foetibus abortivis sub conditione ministrando* (Rome, 1672), 16–17: "Dicet hic aliquis, maximus recessus a 40 die est prima dies conceptionis sive congressus maris cum foemina, ergo pro isto tempore nullum fundamentum habemus opinionis probabilis. Respondeo si hoc tempore nulla vitae humanae filamenta sint effigiata, ita ut aperto per sectionem ovo, si tamen fieri potest, sive secundinarum involucro, iam concreto, appareant vitae humanae prima rudimenta, non adest prudens motivum ad coniectandum adesse in foetu animam rationalem, propterea dixi primis diebus, non prima die foetum abohortivum [*sic*] esse sub conditione baptizandum & nunc valde probabiliter existimo tertia vel quarta die esse animatum, quia ex recentissima experientia quam Theodorus Cherchringius medicus Amstelodamensis affert, factam anno superiore 1671 in foetu tertiae vel ad summum quartae diei, constat apparuisse 'caput clare a corporis mole distinctum & in capite inquit quasi per nebulam adnotata organorum puncta, corporis autem reliqui rudis adhuc indigestaque moles' videbatur."

31 Fiorentini, *De hominibus dubiis baptizandis pia prothesis* (Lyon, 1674).

32 For more details on this, see Tutino, *Uncertainty*, chap. 11.

33 ACDF, Dubia Baptismi XIII, 1828–30, folder n. 7, unfol.: "Cum aedificatio populi Christiani maxime ex administratione Sacramentorum dependeat, curabunt Missionarii, ut cum omni attentione, gravitate, & modestia hoc officio fungantur: Rituale Romanum soepius perlegant, & omnia quae ad hanc functionem pertinent in congruo ordine, nitore & decentia servent … Insistant Pastores apud Matres & Obstetrices, ut quocumque tempore baptizentur faetus [*sic*] qui in abortione emittitur, quamvis nulla humana forma appareat; in quo tamen casu baptizetur massa informis, nisi jam putrefacta appearat, sub conditione 'si capax es.'"

34 The secretary of *De propaganda fide* to Raffaele Mazio, Assessor of Holy Office, 22 May 1827, ibid., unfol.: "Essendo mente della Sagra Congregazione di Propaganda che il giudizio sopra i Decreti del Sinodo tenuto nel 1823 in Bardstown riguardanti l'amministrazione del Battesimo … venga rimesso al Sant'Offizio, l'Archivescovo d'Iconio Segretario della Sagra Congregazione suddetta trasmette a V.S.Ill.ma a Roma una copia delle due Ponenze in cui trattasi della menzionata materia e si contiene tutto ciò che concerne gl'indicati Decreti."

35 Ibid., unfol.: "12 Septem.1827. Transmissa a S.Congregatione de Propaganda Fide ad Supremam S.Congregationem S.Officii Synodo Ecclesiae Bardensis in America Septentrionali diebus 5 et 6 Augusti anni 1823 celebrata … Em.mi, auditis DD. Consultorum suffragiis, rem totam Baptismi in 2.a sessione expositam simul complectentes, censuerunt

dandas esse a S.Congregatione de Propaganda Fide litteras R.P.D.Episcopo Bardensi humanitatis officiique plenas, in quibus peculiaris erga ipsum existimationis studiique significationes ei praebeantur, nec non egregia ipsius voluntas ac religionis zelus S.Sedi luculenter perspectus, verbis amplissimis collaudentur. In iisdem autem litteris significetur, praedictam Sacram Congregationem valde optasse ut quaedam de quibus Episcopus in sua Diocesana Synodo egit, aut nullatenus attigisset aut exactius et conformius ad Ritualis Romani et Sacrarum Congregationum praescripta in Synodalibus Decretis suis prosecutus fuisset. Hinc non posse non vehementer Episcopum ipsum hortari, ut Decreta praedicta aliqua saltem in parte prudenter emendentur aut modificentur ... qua occasione rursus diligens studium Ritualis Romani, ad cuius leges quo magis possibile sit, sese conformare tenentur ipsis inculcet."

36 Ibid., unfol.: "Quod spectat ad Decretum de baptismo foetus, qui in abortione emittitur, incipiens 'Insistant Pastores,' S.Congregatio communicari mandavit Decretum S.Indicis Congregationis, hac de re latum die 5 Aprilis anni 1666, occasione cuiusdam Opusculi Lugdini editi anno 1658, 'De hominibus dubiis, seu de baptismo abortivorum' inscripti, in quo docebatur abortivos omnes quantumvis minimos esse baptizandos. Memorato autem in decreto S.Congregatio sequentem fieri iussit ab Auctore operis declarationem: 'Hanc ergo sententiam de baptismo abortivorum tota hac disputatione comprehensam, et praesertim sectione XI expressam, ab E.mis Patribus S.Congregationis iussus explicare libens volensque gravissimo prudentissimoque doctissimorum Principum iudicio et imperio pareo, et in primis assero, me nihil in praesenti materia definiendo dicere, sed uti rem probabilem, et per modum problematis proponere; deinde adverto, me neminem, quod ad praxim attinet, sub mortali obligare, sed tantum rationes speculativas id suadentes exponere, ac in suspenso relinquere, sicuti nec inducere novum aliquem ritum in Ecclesiam, cum id ad S.Rituum Congregationem Summumque Pontificem spectet.'"

37 Ibid., unfol.: "Praecepit insuper S.Congregatio praedicto operis Auctori ut explicaret se de iis loqui abortivis, qui omnino sensibiles essent, ac prima saltem ostenderent humani corporis lineamenta, qui enim baptismum suscipit, oportet, ut sit non minus ipse sensibilis quam sacra ipsa lotio suscipienda, praeterea foetus baptizandus est, non autem semen neque mola, aut caro excrementitia. Quae quidem omnia cum fideliter Auctor exequutus fuisset in nova operis editione Lucae impressa, S.Congregatio ita decrevit: 'Disputatio de hominibus dubiis non permittatur nisi correcta iuxta impressionem Lucae ex Typographia Hyacinthi Pacii.'"

38 The bishop of Bardstown to the congregation *De propaganda fide,* 4 February 1828, in ibid., unfol.: "Decisio Sanctae Romanae Inquisitionis circa quaedam Synodi Bardensis decreta Romae data 30 die Octobris 1827 ad me pervenit mense Januarii 1828, et cum illa reverentia et cordis submissione quae Episcopum Catholicum et filium Ecclesiae Romanae adddictissimum decent acceptata fuit. Illico R.D.Kenrick praecepi ut excerperet quae decreverunt E.mi Cardinales, eorumque resolutionem omnibus Dioecesis meae Sacerdotibus manifestam feci. Quoad eorum meamque adhaesionem Sanctae Romanae Inquisitionis decretis, nullum omnino dubium in mente Em.orum Cardinalium exoriri debet. Ex ignorantia enim peccare vel errare possumus, sed voluntarie et pertinaciter, Deo iuvante, nunquam delinquemus."

39 Cardinal Martini's phrases come from a conversation he had with the physician (and later mayor of the city of Rome) Ignazio Marino, which was published in the spring of 2006 by the Italian magazine *L'Espresso,* http://espresso.repubblica.it/palazzo/2006/04/27/news/dialogo-sulla-vita-1.623.

chapter eight

Truth and Human History in Melchor Cano's *De locis theologicis*

FERNANDO RODRÍGUEZ MEDIANO

(ENGLISH TRANSLATION BY JONATHAN NELSON AND NICHOLAS CALLAWAY)

The proper and true opposites of the Virtues are those things which bear a great similarity and kinship to Virtue itself, both of them belonging to the same kind: such as *liberalitas, fortitudo, audatia, parcitas, avaritia, cautus, timidus.* Thus the opposite of a religious person is a hypocrite, not a heretic.

Francisco Sánchez de las Brozas, "Doctrina del estoico filósopho Epicteto, que se llama comúnmente *Enchiridion*"

Melchor Cano (1509–1560) is one of the most important European theologians of the early modern era. He was a key representative of what is called the Salamanca School,[1] and a delegate to the Council of Trent. His work is essential for understanding the theological definition of Catholicism at one of its crucial junctures, the middle of the sixteenth century. *De locis theologicis* (1563), his *magnum opus,* was well known and widely read in Europe. In this work, Cano proposed "theological places" (*loci*) upon which one could establish theology's authority. These "places" were (1) Holy Scripture, (2) the traditions of Christ and the apostles, (3) the authority of the Catholic Church, (4) the councils, (5) the Roman Church, (6) the Holy Fathers, (7) scholastic theologians and canon law, (8) natural reason, (9) the authority of the philosophers, and (10) human history with its qualified witnesses.

Scholars have noted the theological importance of Melchor Cano's work and its concept of a new theological method,[2] capable of braving the new environment of humanist culture in the context of Tridentine reform. Cano incorporated many humanist tools into a "renewed understanding of Thomist scholastics."[3] The very concept of the "place" (*locus*) comes from rhetoric, as a tool for identifying the discursive topics from which to "extract all argumentation for every class of debate."[4] The polemical character of Melchor Cano's project is evident in his stated aim, which was to provide theology with instruments for argumentation based on authority (theology) and on reason (philosophy).[5] This operation, in which theology appeals to rhetoric, pits truth against the mere appearance of truth (or verisimilitude), and brings human history within theology's purview as part of the construction of a scientific "discourse."

The focus of the present article is this definition of human history as a "theological place." If one accepts this definition, then theology ceases to provide the grounds for truth in human history. Rather, it is just the opposite: here it is human history that serves to establish the truth of theology. Profane history therefore becomes the vehicle for a form of truth. Others have already pointed out the importance of this shift in Cano's work. For Paolo Prodi, the advent of human history being viewed as a "theological place" in Cano's thought makes his work central to understanding the rise of a profane historiography project within the Catholic world.[6] Some have gone so far as to define this project as a "daring Copernican revolution" in the historiography of Cano's time, lifting "the taboo protecting sacred and church history, to the benefit of profane history."[7]

This chapter studies the relationship between truth, theology, and human history in order to explain the context in which Cano's project emerged. To this end, my argument will be developed in three parts. First, I will explore what truth meant for Melchor Cano, using his *Calificación* (that is, a theological examination and qualification of a proposition) of Archbishop Bartolomé de Carranza's *Catecismo* during the Inquisition's trial against Carranza. The issue of hypocrisy comes up continually in these *Calificaciones*. This concept has a deeply theological component but also a logical one, thus providing key insight into the problem of determining a proposition's truthfulness, with a mind to the gap between what is said and what is meant. In the second part, I shall briefly set out Melchor Cano's reasons for presenting human history as an argument for theological truth. In parallel to this, I will explain his argumentation concerning the historical value of Holy Scripture. Both dimensions are, I believe, part of a single argument about the value of history. The final section will tackle the problem of the distance between the sacred and the profane, using another intellectual figure linked to the University of Salamanca, Pedro Malón de Chaide. There is in Malón's work an especially dramatic contrast between sacred and profane history, and it contains a statement of the formal problem of how to write true history, especially with reference to books of the Bible. The example of Malón illustrates the problematic character of Melchor Cano's project in Spain during the second half of the sixteenth century, a culturally and politically defining moment for the Spanish monarchy.

What Was Truth for Melchor Cano?

In the Bible, truth is characterized in several instances (e.g., Psalms 15:2, Proverbs 8:7) as involving both the heart and the mouth. The challenge of this distance between the two – to the extent that it raises the problem of truth as a product of the interior-exterior relationship – has a moral and a hermeneutical dimension. This has been suggested by Stefania Tutino in connection with the difficulty of "equivocations and mental reservations" in Spanish theology, between the moral realm and hermeneutics.[8] Not surprisingly, one of the authors that Tutino studies is Martín de Azpilcueta, who wrote an essential work on the topic, *Commentarius in cap. humanae aures.* In it, he deliberates on the problem of mental reservations and the disjuncture between what is said and what is thought, discussing it more as a hermeneutical issue than a moral one, analysing what it means to "speak."[9] Azpilcueta had been Archbishop Bartolomé de Carranza's lawyer during the latter's trial at the hands of the Inquisition – one of the highest-level inquisitorial cases in sixteenth-century Spain. One part of the trial had to do with the issue of *correctio fraterna*; that is, what the proper space for private correctness was, and when this should cease and give way to public correctness. Put a different way, it was an attempt to define the limits of the Inquisition's jurisdiction over the "forum of the conscience." Two Dominicans, Melchor Cano and Domingo de Cuevas, brought the suit against Carranza and acted as *calificadores* during the trial, defining the heretical propositions contained in the *Comentarios al catecismo cristiano.*[10] Although the *Calificación* was signed by both Dominicans, it was essentially Melchor Cano's work. It is an extremely significant document in sixteenth-century Spanish religious history, containing a carefully argued presentation of Carranza's erroneous propositions, several of which had to do precisely with this problem of the relationship between what is said and what is thought.

One of these erroneous propositions was related to forms of prayer, and stated, "The first consideration is of the words spoken in prayer. Hypocrites go no further than this consideration; and although this is good, one should not stop there."[11] For Cano and Cuevas, it was an error to equate imperfection with hypocrisy, for the latter was a sin. Children, when praying, speak the words without fully grasping their meaning because children are imperfect, but this does not mean they are hypocrites. In the same way, Cano and Cuevas condemned Carranza's proposition: "Concerning the hypocrites who carry these things in their mouths without them having originated in their mouths, St Paul says [1 Cor. 14:14]: 'For if I pray in a tongue, my spirit prays, but my mind is unfruitful.'" They condemned it because praying with the tongue was, according to the apostle himself, a work of the Holy Spirit, and therefore could not be considered hypocrisy.[12] Another condemned proposition said:

> when we are told to revere the name of God, it is not commanded because of the name spoken with the tongue or written with the pen, because this is a created thing of little value, which a person ought not to revere at all.[13]

For Cano and Cuevas this was a scandalous proposition, since by the same reasoning there would be no obligation to offer reverence to crucifixes and images; these too are human creations, yet they deserve reverence "for what they signify."[14] Another proposition, that "no one should be offended by words when these do not offend the faith, and the spirit of the person speaking is Catholic,"[15] had a double meaning for Cano and Cuevas, one good and one bad, though the latter was much more evident. While it was true that words spoken by Catholics did not offend, the same words were offensive when spoken by heretics. St Hilary had said, "Sensus, non sermo, facit crimen," but it was also true that in the Gospel of St Matthew (12:37) it was said: "by thy words thou shalt be justified, and by thy words thou shalt be condemned." Religious judges, being men, cannot access the inner thoughts of another person except by conjecture based on words and outward actions. Carranza's proposition was particularly dangerous at a time in which heretics cleverly hid their convictions behind ambiguous words, pretending to be wholesome Catholics.[16]

Through these propositions condemned by Cano and Cuevas we see clearly the moral, linguistic, and disciplinary dimensions of the confrontation with forms of illuminist spirituality, which purported to go beyond appearances and external devotion to make real contact with God. To confront this kind of spirituality meant arguing for the necessity of reaching the hearts of the faithful through conjectures based on external manifestations and spoken words. This whole process of reasoning in fact necessitates arguments that belong to the *fuero externo*, the "natural external right," in order to produce any definition of truth, whether on the moral plane or in hermeneutics; and makes it necessary to weigh the concrete circumstances in which a proposition is enunciated.

Melchor Cano: Holy Scripture as History

In the *calificación* that Cano and Cuevas wrote concerning Carranza's catechism, various condemned propositions were directly concerned with Holy Scripture and its interpretation. These included Carranza's interpretation of Psalm 71 as referring to Christ "in a mystical sense," when, according to the two Dominicans, the reference to Christ was "in a literal sense." This was a dangerous proposition, said Cano and Cuevas, because "one cannot extract an effective argument for our faith" from the mystical sense, and to interpret the scriptures in this way disarmed the church of its weapons against Jews and heretics.[17] Another condemned proposition said that "Jacob lied on the advice of his mother," passing himself off as Esau to receive Isaac's prophetic blessing. Jacob could not lie, countered Cano and Cuevas; rather, the reason for his actions had a foundation in the theology of prefiguration:

> Everything that he did and said was a figure of what was to come; and the Holy Spirit, who is the spirit of truth, does not choose words of falsehood and lies to create figures of the truths of the Gospel. And it is true that Jacob's words are saved by the manner of speaking, used even in divine scripture. And wherever we can safeguard holy men from falsehood, we ought to do it, especially if the falsehood is particular, and based on self-interest, and spoken deliberately, and directed at a man as honourable as Isaac.[18]

This problem also appears in an important passage of Cano's *De locis theologicis*,[19] which deals not with the authority of human history but with Holy Scripture. Cano recognizes that there is a long tradition of discussion around the figure of Jacob: though his words were a lie in the strict sense, in the context of prefiguration they in fact told a greater truth. What is more, in passing himself off as his brother Esau, he had fulfilled God's prophecy. How can this apparent contradiction be explained?

According to the "legitimate norms of allegory," says Cano, a righteous man is a figure of the righteous, and a sinful man is a figure of sinners. By the same token, it would be absurd to think that a lie is a figure of the truth. This is so, he adds, in spite of what St Gregory said in his *Moralia in Job*,[20] and in spite of St Jerome himself, who used tropology freely, and whose only rule was that piety should come "from understanding." Despite this, Cano thought that allegory had limits, and that a metaphor should always refer to something proximate or similar: "we ought to handle the Divine Scriptures according to a sure rule."[21] Therefore, in the case of Jacob, in addition to other arguments, his supposed lie is in fact a prophetic truth: in stealing Esau's birthright from him, Jacob prefigured the faith of the Gentiles, which they seized from the Jews. Thus a fundamental principle was safeguarded: God can never deceive, neither for his own sake nor for the sake of anyone else.

The problem of biblical exegesis and the uses of allegory appears in vibrant form in the notable polemical exchange between Melchor Cano and Juan Ginés de Sepúlveda.[22] In this dispute, the latter defended the legality of the war carried out by the *conquistadores* against the native peoples of the Americas. This position led to a confrontation with Bartolomé de las Casas that left its imprint on the history of law and the development of legal theories of just war. Melchor Cano participated in this polemical exchange, siding against Sepúlveda. The two men's dispute centred on the interpretation of a biblical passage from the Acts of the Apostles, in which St Paul reproved the priest Ananias: "Then said Paul unto him, God shall smite thee, *thou* whited wall: for sittest thou to judge me after the law, and commandest me to be smitten contrary to the law?"[23] For Sepúlveda, this passage demonstrated that violence could be used against the impious, for St Paul had here acted *iniquo animo*. But Cano thought that to apply this expression to St Paul's heart (*animus*) could be considered heresy. The arguments on both sides revolved at length around the philological interpretation of the phrase, the presence of anger in other biblical passages, and, in the end, the proper techniques for interpreting the Bible. Besides arguing about the literal sense of the phrase in question, Cano added his allegorical interpretation: it was "a prophecy of the transmission of the priesthood."[24]

In explaining the role of scriptural authority as a theological *locus*, Cano briefly wrestled with the problem of the relationship between the literal and the allegorical. Although the historical value of scripture for Cano meant that contradictions and inconsistencies became indications of a deeper meaning, he nonetheless resisted the liberal application of tropology (i.e., the figurative interpretation of scripture). Rather, he believed that it followed certain rules, and that it was

> [not] reasonable to use a metaphor, figure, or image of something else unless the two things are approximate and similar, because it is necessary that the thing that is a figure of another should bear a similarity to it.[25]

It is difficult to determine the degree of similarity of an image to the thing it represents, and, for this very reason, this issue is fundamental for establishing the truth of a proposition.

Melchor Cano speaks of Holy Scripture at great length, discussing ways of translating it as well as interpreting it. This relates to the inexhaustible issue of meaning and literalness; of other languages' ability to transmit polysemy, misleading expressions, double meanings, and other linguistic phenomena peculiar to the language of origin; and of the value of the Vulgate Latin as opposed to the Hebrew and Greek, a question for which – as with the truth of the sacred text – the final resolution is the inspiration of the Holy Spirit.[26]

Melchor Cano: Human History as a Theological Place

What sort of truth derives from casting human history as a "theological place"? Those who detract from the authority of history say that no one can put his or her confidence in the trustworthiness of human beings, for humans are as easily inclined to falsehood as to truth. Thus theology, "which is based on complete truth," cannot be aided by human credibility, for humans are falsifiers, and they all, without exception, can both deceive and be deceived. Cano's response to this criticism is the following principle: "humans need to believe humans if they do not want to spend their lives as beasts." As St Augustine said,

> if a friend did not trust his friend, or a husband his wife, children their parents, siblings their siblings, citizens their fellow-citizens, or business partners their partners, not only would friendship perish, but so would all human society.[27]

For a society to be properly human, human beings need to believe in the word of their fellow humans. What is more, the beginning of all knowledge is trust: children need to trust their teachers in order to learn from them. This affirmation extends to the value of experience and testimony:

> Can anything be more foolish and childish than to deny the existence of what others saw because we have not seen it ourselves with our own eyes? Without a doubt, we need to exercise faith if we do not want to be more ignorant than children.[28]

From this general principle Cano draws three main conclusions:

1. Except for the sacred authors, no historian is a sure source; that is, no historian is appropriate for producing solid arguments in theology.

2. Serious and credible historians – as are undoubtedly to be found among both ecclesiastical and profane writers – furnish the theologian with arguments whose probability serves to demonstrate his line of reasoning, and to refute the false opinions of his adversaries.
3. If several historians, all of whom are renowned and prestigious, agree on a particular event, then their authority furnishes a sure argument for establishing theological dogma, even by means of a sequence of solid reasoning.[29]

In this light, Cano's text becomes a long disquisition on the relationship between truth and human history, and about how the latter ought to be used by theologians.

Cano weighs what credibility to lend to popular traditions, and whether, as St Jerome affirmed, "it is a true rule of History ... to put down in writing what the common people think, even when it is actually false."[30] For Cano, some affirmations of the common people are clearly false, but others, even if in fact false, are nevertheless true in a certain sense. For example, when they affirm that St Joseph was the father of Christ, it is, in its proper sense, false, but in a certain sense it is authentic, given that Joseph was the father who nurtured him and was the husband of his mother. In the same way, wisdom sometimes uses words that are true "in a certain sense," as in the Gospel of Matthew (6:16: "Moreover when ye fast, be not, as the hypocrites, of a sad countenance: for they disfigure their faces, that they may appear unto men to fast"), where the Lord calls the hypocrites "sad" when they were merely simulating sadness. "In popular parlance," Cano concludes, "the names of things are used in place of the meaning of things."[31] Certain wise men, in order to separate themselves from what they considered the credulity of the common people, went to the opposite extreme and became unbelievers.[32]

Cano also sets down various rules for how to discern which historians ought to be believed. In the first place, one needs to consider the honour and integrity of the person. This quality can extend to profane historians like Julius Caesar, Suetonius, Diogenes Laertes, or Tacitus, from whom one can expect "a certain level of natural integrity" (*una cierta honradez natural*). What is more, some of these pagan writers showed more integrity than certain Christian writers and did not hide the vices of the philosophers and emperors about whom they wrote. In support of this, Melchor Cano cites Luis Vives and his criticism of certain histories concocted by church historians.[33] On the other hand, the truth of a history is to some extent independent of the historian's morality: it is one thing to say that honest men are truthful, but quite another to say that all evil men are liars.[34]

Cano's argument in this chapter ends with an affirmation that is central to the problem of reasoning and truth:

> It is not necessary for a theologian to always adopt sure principles. Arguments that are fit at least for persuading, if not for convincing, can be developed from principles that have a measure of dubiousness, so long as such principles are probable. A theologian would be foolish to try to add necessary things to necessary things in all his syllogisms. The fact is, many things are complex and somewhat obscure. Therefore, theological prudence will naturally desire to inculcate them, not demonstrate them; to explain them in some way, not to clear them up with weighty evidence. So, if anyone has perhaps used the probability of human reliability as grounds for developing arguments of this sort, he could certainly be wrong occasionally, but he cannot reasonably be reproached.[35]

Cano therefore upholds the value of probability as a fundamental instrument in rhetorical argumentation, thus establishing the role of human history as part of the field of truth.

Pedro Malón de Chaide: The Historian as Liar

The idea that human history carried a form of truth was by no means universally accepted. As already mentioned, the Bible describes truth as taking shape somewhere between the heart and the mouth; what happens on that journey from point A to point B is the object of a great deal of moral, political, and linguistic interpretation. This is the case, for example, in Psalm 11 in the Vulgate (given here in English as Psalm 12 of the King James Version):

> 1/ Help, Lord; for the godly man ceaseth; for the faithful fail from among
> the children of men. 2/ They speak vanity every one with his neighbour:
> with flattering lips and with a double heart do they speak. 3/ The Lord
> shall cut off all flattering lips, and the tongue that speaketh proud things:
> 4/ Who have said, With our tongue will we prevail; our lips are our own:
> who is lord over us? 5/ For the oppression of the poor, for the sighing of the
> needy, now will I arise, saith the Lord; I will set him in safety from him that
> puffeth at him. 6/ The words of the Lord are pure words: as silver tried in
> a furnace of earth, purified seven times. 7/ Thou shalt keep them, O Lord,

> thou shalt preserve them from this generation for ever. 8/ The wicked walk on every side, when the vilest men are exalted.

The identification of evil with falsehood, expressed so forcefully here, opens the door to a number of different interpretations. Who are those who lie to their neighbours, who flatter with their lips but harbour deception in their hearts? Who are those who prevail by their tongues, who are defended by their lips, who do not recognize any lord over them? Commentators identify these evil people differently. Importantly for this discussion, we will see how, in contrast to Cano's view of human history, Malón de Chaide would later associate the liars of Psalm 11 with historians. First, however, let us examine how two of his predecessors tackled Psalm 11 and interpreted the figures of evil and falsehood.

Before Malón de Chaide, Martin Luther explained the liars of the Psalm in the context of his own conflict with Rome, as we can see in his commentary on verse 4:

> As if they said, Let no one hear anyone besides us. We are the leaders and teachers of the people. They ought to listen to us, and (as the Bulls of our proud popes now swell in the church), we are the proper interpreters of the scriptures. It belongs to us to frame laws. It is our province to approve and to condemn every man's sayings and writings. The power of the Keys is with us alone ... These ungodly take away from all the power of teaching, judging, and speaking, and arrogate and keep it to themselves alone: though they are, in reality, themselves the most ignorant and wicked of all men upon the face of earth. And this description I would apply to the men of our age and time ... The state of the church in our day is not a little worse than even the description contained in this verse.[36]

Luther's commentary does more than simply show how the psalmist's words could be aligned to the various interests of the commentators: it also demonstrates the relationship of truth to problems of scriptural exegesis, and textual and political authority.

However, the connection of this problem to history becomes even clearer in another exegetical tradition that goes back at least to Jaime Pérez de Valencia, a Valencian Augustinian, bishop, and theologian of the fifteenth century (1408–1490), and a man very close to Rodrigo de Borja, the future pope Alexander VI. Pérez de Valencia was the author of an important book of polemics, the *Treatise against the Jews*,[37] written shortly before the expulsion of the Jews from Spain in 1492. He also wrote an important work of biblical exegesis, particularly of the Psalms, which was to have a significant influence upon sixteenth-century hermeneutics. Scholars have uncovered various issues that make Pérez de Valencia's biblical studies interesting. In the first place, his is an example of a distinctly Spanish exegetical style, connected to Hebrew exegesis and a specific idea of the relationship between the literal and mystical senses of scripture. At the same time, Pérez de Valencia shows a powerful desire for the reform of the church and a strong commitment to the Augustinian tradition – for example, in relation to the issue of grace. These characteristics have led many historians to consider Pérez de Valencia a fifteenth-century "Reformist," a sort of Luther *avant la lettre.*[38] In fact, Pérez de Valencia's influence on Luther is well known.

In his commentary on Psalm 11, Pérez de Valencia explains who the liars that speak vainly are: in the first place, Cain or those who built the Tower of Babel; then magicians, soothsayers, seers, and superstitious persons; in the next place, judges and lawyers who ruin the poor, widows, and children in order to fill their own pockets; and poets who, in order to weaken human beings, invent false words about false gods. Liars are also orators, poets, and writers who fill their books with falsehoods in order to please princes and obtain their favour, such as Homer writing about the Greeks, Livy on the Romans, Curtius Rufus on Alexander the Great, or Herodotus writing about the Persian kings.[39]

This brings us back to sixteenth-century Spain and the issue of scripture and history, as Pérez de Valencia's attack on some of the great classical historians was later reproduced by Pedro Malón de Chaide (1530–1589) in his *Discursos predicables literales y morales de la Sagrada Escriptura,* published in 1588 by Hyeronimo de Saona, "Augustinian monk."[40] Like Hyeronimo de Saona, Malón de Chaide was an Augustinian, and at the University of Salamanca had been a disciple of Fray Luis de León, in the intellectual milieu of the Biblicists there, with all that this implied: translation of the Bible into the vernacular, the defence of literal exegesis and, in general, a way of relating to Holy Scripture that would lead to the inquisitorial trials against the Hebraists of Salamanca.

The first part of the *Discursos predicables* is dedicated to St John, whose youth made him a model of innocence, tenderness, and intimacy in his love for Christ. Malón uses St John's youth to speak about the relationship between parents and children, and the education of the young. Thus, Discourse VI deals with truth and "with how important it is to teach them to love the truth";[41] it constitutes a short homily on truth and falsehood, based on a commentary on Psalm 11. Malón here recalls Pérez de

Valencia's deprecation of historians when he speaks about how truth has disappeared from the world, and discusses the topic of lascivious men who attempt to deceive "poor and easy little women" (*pobres y livianas mujercillas*) with empty words. Equally vain are "poets and flatterers ... Historiographers, knaves, minstrels, friends of ditties and bawdy songs."[42] These men's words are the words of flatterers who praise their lords "like Homer praised the Greeks; Livy, the Romans; Curtius Rufus, Alexander; Herodotus, the men of Persia."[43] When commenting on the verse "qui dixerunt, linguam nostram magnificamus," Malón criticizes the arrogance that makes men feel they are lords of their tongues and possessors of eloquence: "We can speak our minds without anyone hindering us, our tongue is our law ... praising and magnifying our property and persons ... Our tongue is our God, we have nothing to fear."[44] Boastful and proud, men dare to say to God: "Who shall be our lord? Who shall lay laws on those who do these things?" The poets and orators reached this level of arrogance – poets like "Quintilian, Cicero, Livy, Sallust, and others, who attempted to eternalize themselves in the world by the power of their arms; I mean to say, the eloquence of their rhetorical tongues and pretty poetry."[45] These men are like the Pharisees, and they use their fine rhetorical ways of talking without considering that their tongue does not belong to them, but is a gift of God.

As one can see, Malón de Chaide quotes Pérez de Valencia almost literally, citing the same list of lying historians to whom the latter referred. Still, the quotation may have had a different shade of meaning when Malón was writing. For example, Quintus Curtius Rufus was the author of *History of Alexander*, which enjoyed wide distribution in Spain, having been translated into Castilian in the fifteenth century. However, the first Latin edition printed in Spain did not appear until 1524, and was the work of Lorenzo Balbo at the University of Alcalá de Henares.[46] It was part of a Complutensian publishing initiative with a decidedly humanist character, within the reformist tradition of the university founded by Cardinal Cisneros, and which also included an edition of the *Argonautica* of Valerius Flaccus that same year.[47] Thus, for Malón de Chaide, the allusion to hypocritical historians could well have been a reference to a specific cultural project represented by the University of Alcalá.

Malón de Chaide's commentary is much longer, and ends with a translation in verse of that particular psalm, rendered into Castilian by Malón himself. The problem of translation is important, as we shall see, for understanding the way the conflict between the truths of human and sacred history took shape. The problems of translation and of hermeneutics are similar, since both use linguistic criteria to determine the certainty of a particular proposition.

Sacred vs Profane

The attack on profane rhetorical and literary forms, and the clear distinction between sacred and profane literature, constitutes a central point of Malón de Chaide's literary activity. Throughout his writings, Malón insists on how pernicious it is for someone to mix "the sacred with the profane, a very prejudicial and dangerous thing in our unhappy times,"[48] and he laments the fact that in his day the number of vain and corrupt books seemed to be multiplying. Certainly, Malón's position was more radical than that of many of his fellow scholars of sacred literature. For instance, Francisco Sánchez de la Brozas, "El Brocense," a leading professor of rhetoric at the University of Salamanca, voices a very different stance in a letter to the Castilian translator of *Os Lusíadas*, Luis Gómez de Tapia. There, he praises true poets like Camões, and speaks of the righteous indignation that some true scholars feel "toward those who, being less learned and enlightened [*alumbrados*] than the poets, wish to reprove them, sometimes for their doctrine and sometimes for their carelessness." He gives the example of Virgil, who was criticized by some of these less enlightened scholars for saying that there were deer in Africa when Pliny had written that there were none. El Brocense states that he is inclined to believe Virgil, a great poet, who was reproached only by those who did not understand him.[49]

Malón de Chaide's attack on the classical poets, or El Brocense's defence of them, are but two examples in a long and intense controversy concerning the tension between sacred and profane literature. What makes Malón's stance interesting for this essay is that he, and the tradition to which he explicitly adhered, includes historiography in this debate about rhetoric, which inevitably brings up the old problem of the historical truth of scripture.

Malón himself is even more explicit on this point in what is undoubtedly his most important work, *Libro de la conversión de la Magdalena.*[50] Here, along with insisting on the need to radically separate human and divine literature, he again voices his criticism of secular poetry, comparing it to biblical poetry and, in general, to sacred poetry. As all students of the Bible then would have known, several of its books were written in verse: the Psalms of David, the Lamentations of Jeremiah, and – quite significantly – the book of Job.[51] Therefore, was this a stylistic form that was suitable for expressing the divine message? Could this form be translated into other languages or carried over to other types of texts? Even someone as distrustful of the rhetorical dimensions of discourse as Malón de Chaide felt the weight of the formal problem of the sacred text's authority.

This touches on the crucial issue of the vernacular translation of the Bible, which Malón himself had undertaken in some of his texts (in a highly problematic context, from the viewpoint of inquisitorial persecution). He defended his translations because, in the end, the truth of the sacred text depended more on the sense of the sentences than the literal rendering of each word. One might recall that renowned Spanish humanist Furió Ceriol carried on a bitter quarrel with Giovanni de Bononia, defending the translation of the Bible into the vernacular on the grounds that ultimately Hebrew was nothing more than the common language of the Jews, which God chose to use in order to make himself understandable to them. Moreover, Malón de Chaide brings up the issue of the biblical texts' style and their interpretation, and whether they should be considered as historical texts, a position that was inevitably linked to literal interpretation.

In reality, Malón de Chaide did nothing more than revive an old debate about Hebrew poetry, its characteristics, and the issue of whether the sacred books of scripture could be rendered as poetry. In general terms, it was a debate as to whether anything written in verse could be considered as literally historical. The book of Job, which Malón cited as an example of Hebrew poetry, was a notable example of this relationship between narrative style, interpretation, and truth. As Malón himself pointed out, St Jerome had already indicated, in the prologue to his translation of Job, that the book's style was "indirect and slippery" like an eel, its meaning becoming more elusive the tighter one tries to grip it. In this prologue, St Jerome speaks of Hebrew poetry and its metres, and says that several biblical books ought to be understood in the same way as the Latin and Greek poets Alcaeus, Pindar, or Horace, no matter how surprising this fact might appear to some. For this reason, the exegetical tradition concerning the book of Job, including the Augustinian Diego de Zúñiga[52] or, notably, the Jesuit Juan de Pineda (1558–1637),[53] constantly debated whether Job was a real historical person or a mere parable. Luther himself, when he translated the book, explained that its high literary value had forced him to produce not a "literal" translation of the text ("as the Jews and foolish translators would have done"), but a translation *ad sensum* that would allow the German reader to appreciate the text.[54] Pineda, for one, argued that Job was a real historical figure, as opposed to the opinion of the rabbis in the Talmud, or of contemporary "heretics" like Luther and the Anabaptists, who held that the book was a parable. This argument would be repeated later by other Catholic exegetes of Job: the heretics believed the book had an allegorical sense.[55] There were various reasons for this. First of all, the personal names and place names that appear in the story seem not to allude to real people or places, but rather to have a figurative value. In the same way, those in favour of the "parable" interpretation argued that such literary style or versification was not appropriate for expressing historical truth. The debate surrounding the style of the book of Job would be important for the European study of Hebrew poetry and the delimitation of biblical literary genres, and of the use of allegory in sacred history.[56] This kind of reflection appears not only in Malón de Chaide but also in others of his generation, like Fray Luis de León – men who combined the task of translating the Bible into the vernacular with an interest in literal interpretation.[57] In fact, Fray Luis – who had been Melchor Cano's disciple in Salamanca – even wrote an *Exposición del libro de Job*. The work was a translation, a biblical commentary attending to different levels of literalness, and a reflection on the relationship between language, rhetoric, and metre, while also posing the problem of the book's historicity.[58]

To return now to Pineda, he and the other commentators who argued in favour of the book of Job's historicity faced the task of elucidating a singularly uncomfortable text, with difficult passages such as chapter 2, which tells of a conclave in God's presence that the devil attends and addresses. To imagine that the book related real events that occurred in history meant that one had to explain, in this particular case, how the devil could be present in heaven speaking to God. Various arguments were offered. Fray Luis, for example, said that one of two explanations was possible: either the author had depicted it as a consultation in a king's court so that readers could understand it – since scripture addresses them in terms that they can know and comprehend – or else the author wrote the scene according to the vision he had of it,

> using images and figures that presented themselves to his imagination or his eyes ... Such figures are seen by the prophets either in true reality, or in their fantasy, or with their eyes; and such images have their own reality, but it is not the same as the one they depict, nor are they the thing itself; but

> rather they are figures of it that God creates; and, with regard to what they signify, they conform to factual truth, but in the manner of their signification they are fitted and made proportionate to our understanding.[59]

The reception, commentary, and translation of the book of Job, and the arguments presented in defence of its historical veracity, pose a series of questions. What is the difference between allegorical and literal explanation, and how does one apply these to interpreting a biblical text? To what extent might a literal style of biblical interpretation be related to the rise of a form of profane history, a phenomenon that did indeed arise in the Reformed world, with its commitment to a literalist style of biblical interpretation? In the end, what is the relationship between truth and literality? Or, to phrase it differently: what is "literal truth"?

Mixing the Sacred with the Profane

The "Copernican revolution" embodied in Melchor Cano's contribution lies in his attempt to integrate human history with theological thought in a single dialectical construction. His project interconnects faith and reason, so that theological truths must be supported rationally, and also makes it possible for theology to assimilate humanist intellectual and rhetorical tools, so as "to illustrate the faith from the standpoint of human sciences."[60] In reality, Cano's work is most important as "method." As he himself wrote, many people had made innumerable contributions to theology, but had lacked method (*sin arte*); yet method was a surer guide than nature itself.[61] His work's methodical character was directed at defending theological truth. The very concept of *locus* in Cano's title is drawn, as we have seen, from rhetoric; indeed, his final chapter is a discussion of "the use of theological places in scholastic disputation." Within this general method, human history as an argument in favour of the truth of theology is intended to be used in conjunction with the other "places" (*loci*) that Cano considers in his work, such as natural reason or philosophy.[62]

However, if we focus specifically on history itself, we can see that Cano's reasoning develops on two planes: discussing the historical truth of Holy Scripture, and defending the value of human history as a form of theological truth. Based on this twofold argument, Cano establishes a set of hermeneutical rules related to the tension between allegorical and literal interpretation, and their respective limits. This is a radical move that brings theology closer to the dialectical methods of the human sciences, and affords the category of the "probable" a fundamental place in the realm of truth. One of the lasting and far-reaching elements of this method was precisely this category of the "probable," which was to play an essential role in the moral and epistemological universe of seventeenth-century Europe.

Melchor Cano's project was the product of the intellectual problems revolving around nation and scripture in Spain during the second half of the sixteenth century. These concerned how to write the sacred history of Spain as well as the related question of the translation and interpretation of scripture, both of which necessarily intersected and collided with the cultural and political project of the Spanish crown, crystallizing into a complex process with sometimes traumatic outcomes. One need only remember the Inquisition trial against Fray Luis de León (Malón de Chaide's teacher) and other Hebraists at the University of Salamanca, in which some of the matters touched on in this article were at issue. The horror of mixing the sacred with the profane (*miscere sacra prophanis*), as Malón de Chaide expresses it in his criticism of profane literature,[63] reflects the sense of crisis regarding how literary styles are defined, what the rules of use should be for tropology and rhetorical figures, the limits of representation, and ultimately how to determine whether or not a discourse is true. The portrayal of historians as liars and the condemnation of profane history appear to be a response to the challenge of granting hermeneutical value to human history. This came at a unique moment when it was possible to propose that a problem could be apprehended through reason by reducing it to history, and that human experience could become a form of universal knowledge.[64]

ACKNOWLEDGMENTS

This essay received the support of the European Research Council under the European Union's Seventh Framework Programme (FP7/2007–2013) / ERC grant agreement number 323316. PI: Mercedes García-Arenal.

NOTES

1 Juan Belda Plans, *La Escuela de Salamanca y la renovación de la teología en el siglo XVI* (Madrid: Biblioteca de Autores Cristianos, 2000), 501–750.

2 Juan Belda Plans, "Introducción general histórico-teológica," in Melchor Cano, *De locis theologicis*, ed. and Spanish trans. Juan Belda Plans (Madrid: Biblioteca de Autores Cristianos, 2006), XXXIII–CXLI.

3 Fabrizio Mandreoli, "Il De locis theologicis di Melchor Cano: Appunti su un metodo teologico interpretato sui 'tempi lunghi,'" *Rivista di Teologia dell'Evangelizzazione* 14, no. 28 (2010): 281–301.
4 Cano, *De locis theologicis*, 3.
5 Ibid., 10.
6 Paolo Prodi, "La storia umana come luogo teológico," in *Profezia vs Utopia* (Bologna: Il Mulino, 2013), 217–42.
7 Jacques Lafaye, *De la historia bíblica a la historia crítica: El tránsito de la conciencia occidental* (Mexico City: Fondo de Cultura Económica, 2003), 276–80.
8 Stefania Tutino, *Shadows of Doubt: Language and Truth in Post-Reformation Catholic Culture* (Oxford: Oxford University Press, 2014), 10–39.
9 Ibid., 20–4.
10 Melchor Cano and Domingo de Cuevas, "Qualificación hecha por los maestros Cano y Cuevas del Catechismo [y de otros escritos] 1558–9," in *Fray Bartolomé de Carranza. Documentos históricos. VI. Audiencias III (1563)*, ed. J. Ignacio Tellechea Idígoras (Madrid: Real Academia de la Historia, 1981), 225–384. This important document was first published by Fermín Caballero (Caballero, 1871: 536–615).
11 Cano and Cuevas, "Qualificación," 350–1: "la primera attençión es a las palabras que se dizen en la oraçión. En esta attención paran los hipócritas; e aunque es buena, no se ha de parar en ella."
12 Ibid., 349.
13 Ibid., 298: "quando se manda dar reverençia al nombre de Dios, no se dize por el nombre que se dize con la lengua o se escribe con la pluma, porque éste es una cosa criada de poco valor, a la qual el hombre no debe reverençia alguna."
14 Ibid., 299.
15 Ibid., 297: "a nadie han de offender los bocablos, quando no offenden a la ffe, e el ánimo del que habla es cathólico."
16 Ibid., 297–8.
17 Ibid., 295.
18 Ibid., 319–20: "todo aquello que hizo e dixo fue figura de lo porvenir; e no escoge el Espíritu Sancto, que es espíritu de verdad, palabras de falsedad e mentira para figurar las verdades de el Evangelio. Y es çierto que las palabras de Jacob se salvan en modo de hablar y usado aun en la divina Escriptura. E donde podemos excudar de mentira a los sanctos barones, hémoslo de hazer, mayormente si la mentira es çevil e fundada en interese e dicha de propósito, e a un hombre tan onrado como Issac."
19 Cano, *De locis theologicis*, 22–5.

20 The quotation from the *Moralia in Job* refers to the commentary on Job 18:3, in which St Gregory the Great said (according to the Castilian translation of Chancellor Pero López de Ayala), "many times in this life it happens that good things come to bad people, and bad things to good people." López de Ayala, *Las Flores de los "Morales de Job,"* ed. Francesco Branciforti (Florence: Felice le Monnier, 1963), 143. Obviously, here Cano is arguing in favour of his idea that the good is a figure of the good, and the bad is a figure of the bad – an argument with a clearly logical dimension.

21 Cano, *De locis theologicis,* 25.

22 Juan Jesús Valverde Abril, "Teología y humanismo: La correspondencia entre Juan Ginés de Sepúlveda y Melchor Cano," *Florentia Iliberritana* 17 (2006): 291–335.

23 Acts 23:2–3.

24 Valverde Abril, "Teología y humanismo," 291–335.

25 Cano, *De locis theologicis,* 24.

26 Ibid., 109ff.

27 Ibid., 567.

28 Ibid., 568.

29 Ibid., 568–9.

30 Ibid.

31 Ibid., 586–7.

32 Ibid., 587.

33 Ibid., 645–6.

34 Ibid., 650.

35 Ibid., 662.

36 Martin Luther, *Commentary on the First Twenty-Two Psalms,* trans. Henry Cole, (London: W. Simpkin and R. Marshall, 1826), 2.11–12.

37 Jaime Pérez de Valencia, *Tratado contra los judíos,* Spanish trans. Justo Formentín and María José Villegas (Madrid: Aben Ezra sEdiciones, 1998).

38 Agustín Cortés Soriano, "Claves para la comprensión de la figura y el pensamiento teológico de Jaime Pérez de Valencia," *Revista Agustiniana* 35: 961–88.

39 Jaime Pérez de Valencia, *Iacobi Perez de Valentia [...] in psalmos davidicos lucubratissima expositio* (Paris: apud Franciscum Regnault, 1533), fol. 21r.

40 Javier Clemente Hernández, *El legado oculto de Pedro Malón de Chaide* (Madrid: Editorial Revista Agustiniana, 1999).

41 Pedro Malón de Chaide [Hyerónimo de Saona], *Discursos predicables literales y morales de la Sagrada Escriptura* (Barcelona: Emprenta de Ioan Amello, 1588), 37ff: "de lo que importa enseñarles a que amen la verdad."

42 Ibid., 47: "poetas y aduladores … Historiógraphos, truhanes, guitarreros, amigos de cantilenas, de canciones deshonestas."

43 Ibid., 46–7.

44 Ibid., 49ff: "podemos dezir nuestro parecer sin que nadie nos impida, nuestra lengua es nuestra ley … magnifica y engrandece nuestras casas y personas … Nuestra lengua es nuestro Dios, no tenemos qué temer."

45 Ibid.: "Quintiliano, Tulio, Titolivio, Salustio y otros pretendiendo eternizarse en el mundo por la fuerça de sus braços, quiero dezir, eloquencia de sus rethóricas lenguas y hermosas poesías."

46 Jenaro Costas Rodríguez, "La primera edición del texto latino de Quinto Curcio en España," in *Munus quaesitum meritis: Homenaje a Carmen Codoñer*, ed. Gregorio Hinojo Andrés and José Carlos Fernández Conde (Salamanca: Ediciones de la Universidad de Salamanca, 2007), 193–203.

47 Marcel Bataillon, *Erasmo y España: Estudios sobre la historia espiritual del siglo XVI* (Mexico City: Fondo de Cultura Económica, 1998, 6th repr.), 159.

48 Malón de Chaide, *Discursos predicables*, "Prólogo," n.p.

49 Francisco Sánchez de las Brozas, *Opera omnia*, ed. Gregorio Mayáns (Geneva: Apud Fratres de Tounes, 1766), 3.491–2.

50 Pedro Malón de Chaide, *Libro de la conversión de la Magdalena, en que se ponen los tres estados que tuvo de pecadora, penitente y de gracia* (Alcalá de Henares: Justo Sánchez Crespo, 1603). On this point, I am expanding on the arguments in my essay "Biblical Translation and Literalness in Early Modern Spain," in *After Conversion: Iberia and the Emergence of Modernity*, ed. Mercedes García-Arenal (Leiden: Brill, 2016), 66–94.

51 Malón de Chaide, *Libro de la conversión de la Magdalena*, fols 6v–7r.

52 Diego de Zúñiga, *In Iob Commentaria* (Toledo: Ioannes Rodericus, 1584), 2ff.

53 Juan de Pineda, *Commentariorum in Iob libri tredecim* (Seville: in Collegio S. Hermenegildi, 1598), ii and ff.

54 Maurice J. O'Sullivan, *The Books of Job* (Newcastle: Cambridge Scholars, 2007), 22.

55 Esteban Aguilar y Zúñiga, *Combates de Iob con el demonio* (Madrid: Carlos Sánchez, 1641), fol. 1ff.

56 Robert Lowth, *De sacra poesi hebraeorum* (Oxford: Clarendon, 1753), 309ff.

57 Rodríguez Mediano, "Biblical Translation and Literalness."

58 Fray Luis León, *Exposición del libro de Job*, ed. Javier San José Lera (Salamanca: University of Salamanca, 1992), 1.151–2.

59 Ibid., 158–9: "por imágines y figuras que se la pusieron en la imaginación o en los ojos … Las quales figuras en realidad de verdad, o con la fantasía, o con los ojos las veen los prophetas, y son esas imágenes que tienen su ser, pero no el mismo que representan, ni son ello mismo, sino figuras suyas

hechas por Dios, y que en lo que significan son conformes al hecho de la verdad, y en la manera como lo significan se ajustan y proporcionan con nuestro entender."

60 Belda Plans, *La Escuela de Salamanca*, 671.

61 Ibid., 681.

62 Jacob Schmutz, "Melchor Cano: La philosophie comme lieu théologique," in *Philosophie et théologie à l'Époque Moderne: Anthologie*, ed. Christophe Bardout (Paris: Les Éditions du Cerf, 2010), 3.117–28.

63 Malón de Chaide, *Libro de la conversión de la Magdalena*, 336.

64 Furió Ceriol, *El Concejo i Consejeros del Príncipe* (Antwerp: Viuda de Martín Nucio 1559), fols 23–5.

chapter nine

Ambivalent Origins: Isaac La Peyrère and the Politics of Historical Certainty in Seventeenth-Century Europe

CARLOS CAÑETE

Over the last few decades scholars have increasingly turned to the many manifestations of the early modern epistemic crisis. Many contributions have explored how the discovery of other geographical and written worlds, as well as the conflicts between different forms of Christianity in the wake of the Protestant and Catholic Reformations and the subsequent rivalry between competing forms of authority, led to the proliferation of uncertainty. Multiple manifestations of this epistemic instability have been identified, ranging from religious doubt to anxieties over historical chronology and a renewed concern with philosophical scepticism. Those explorations have certainly offered a richer and more nuanced vision of the intellectual and cultural circumstances of the sixteenth and seventeenth centuries in Europe. However, we still need to reconsider the transition between this context of uncertainty and the mirage of certainties that we commonly attribute to the philosophical and social programs of European modernity that followed.

Some years ago, William Bouwsma offered a narrative of the transformation from Renaissance liberations and uncertainties towards a seventeenth-century "culture of order."[1] He proposed that, starting in the late sixteenth century, and as a reaction to previous uncertainties, a quest for certainty permeated all spheres of intellectual and cultural production, from philosophy and religion to governance and the arts. However, he added, this was not to be understood as a complete substitution of certainty for uncertainty but, rather, a shift in the continuous tension between those two attitudes. More recently, Stefania Tutino has gone beyond this somewhat linear interpretation to show how the affirmation of certainties in post-Reformation culture was not a reaction against uncertainty but instead went hand in hand with the exploration and recognition of the enigmatic and the uncertain.[2] Thus, the transition to modern convictions, to the construction of meaning according to new ways of defining universalism and truth, was not a univocal and predetermined process. Yet we are still attached to a linear and progressive narrative from uncertainty to certainty in part because modern ideals have been built on this sterilized genealogy.[3] In contrast to this linear narrative, it is increasingly evident that what is commonly interpreted as the rise of the "New Philosophy" in the seventeenth century was never a single and coherent doctrine but rather a field of problems or concerns that resulted in competing responses.[4] Hence the main characteristic of this period is not any particular solution to the problem of knowledge but rather the interrogation of the nature of truth itself. This period of interrogation inaugurates the modern obsession with the need to establish a robust system that can provide epistemological and social certainties.[5]

Moreover, these recent contributions have also shown that, contrary to traditional approaches that centred the epistemic transformations in the Protestant context, those changes were the product of cross-confessional and transnational processes. Yet we still do not have a good account of how these transnational, cross-confessional processes also led to the hardening of identities and differences that have marked history ever since. Many decades ago, Paul Hazard observed that the intellectual and cultural panorama that resulted from the early modern epistemic crisis was far from unproblematic: the universalism of social emancipation, the critical interpretation of tradition, and the systematic study of nature coexisted with the particularism of the construction of national identities and the hierarchies imposed by a progressive conception of human nature.[6] Hence, the process of epistemic reconstruction in early modern Europe was driven by universalistic intentions with a transnational scope that paradoxically and simultaneously affirmed particular identities and interpretations.

This essay explores one of the ways this preoccupation with the status of truth and the goal of reconstructing historical certainty could lead to ambivalent results, even as it aimed for universalism and integration. In the first half of the seventeenth century, new theories of human origins and progressive views of human nature posed significant challenges to the traditional views of history. My starting point will be the work of Isaac la Peyrère, a French Calvinist lawyer who during the first half of the seventeenth century offered a millenarian reinterpretation of the sacred scriptures that suggested, among other things, that there had been humanity before Adam. La Peyrère's work is regarded as key to the epistemic transformations leading to modern ideals, including modern biblical criticism and the secular vision of human history. It is also interpreted as a major source for other central concepts in intellectual history since the seventeenth century, such as polygenism, modern racism, and philosophical scepticism. Finally, his ideas have been considered as the most prominent challenge to traditional worldviews, "more than the Copernican theory or the mechanistic view of nature,"[7] with a decisive impact on seventeenth-century transformations and epistemic reconstructions. Even though his name barely appears in the genealogies of modernity, "no one did more to make this revolution happen than the little-remembered French Calvinist Isaac La Peyrère."[8] Thus, scholars today note La Peyrère as central to intellectual history, although we still remain mostly ignorant of the particularities of his work – a situation that has made of La Peyrère's figure a kind of intellectual ghost, constantly lurking but invisible. This contradiction – a prominent intellectual impact with a minimal concrete presence in the history of thought – is probably what Richard Popkin had in mind when he stated that La Peyrère was "the real spectre haunting Western Thought."[9] As this essay will show, the most productive way to contextualize the implications of La Peyrère's ideas is to break the spell of that spectral presence by fully exploring his work rather than continuing to portray him as a sort of intellectual exception. To dispel the supposed exceptionality of his ideas, we need only situate his writings in relation to coetaneous productions, thus ensuring a fuller understanding of both La Peyrère and the broad intellectual context in which he worked.

That Little-Remembered French Calvinist

Isaac La Peyrère – also written Lapeyrère and De La Peyrère – (1596?–1676), was the first-born child of a Calvinist family from Bordeaux with prominent positions in the provincial and royal administrations. La Peyrère studied law and worked as a lawyer at the Parliament of Bordeaux. In 1624 he married Suzanne de Petit, and through this marriage obtained the fiefdom of Clayrac. The couple established their residence in Montauban, where La Peyrère was frequently involved in the violent confrontations between Calvinists and Catholics.[10] Little more is known about his early years, except an obscure episode in 1626 in which he was accused of atheism and impiety at the Calvinist provincial synod but soon acquitted with the support of an important number of pastors who interceded on his behalf at the Reformed National Synod.[11]

A few years later, in the late 1630s, we find him in Paris as a secretary to the prince of Condé. This position allowed him to travel extensively throughout Europe as a diplomatic emissary and to make the acquaintance of some of the most important contributors to the politics and letters of his time, including Mersenne, Pascal, Gassendi, and Campanella and, later on, Ole Worm, Menasseh Ben Israel, and Christine of Sweden. La Peyrère became a frequent participant in the collaborations and conflicts of the Republic of Letters. Years later he recalled this period in the apologetic work he wrote after the storm caused by his pre-Adamites:

> As soon as I had the liberty to see the world, and to make the acquaintance of all the spirits that exist, Paris, which is a compendium of the world, enriched me in every way. I have found prominent spirits in all of the sciences. Some devoted themselves to piety. Others were indifferent to it. And many others extravagantly wandered in impiety. They surprised me at first by the false brilliance of their reasons, and yet they did not impress me.[12]

Although he apparently conceived his idea of the pre-Adamites very early in his life[13] and discussed it with Protestant ministers during his years in Aquitaine,[14] he did not write it down until much later, in the early 1640s, when he was already in Paris. He composed a manuscript[15] that enjoyed some circulation[16] and even inspired an early refutation by Hugo Grotius.[17] This first version of his theory was mostly based on a reinterpretation of certain verses of Paul's Epistle to the Romans:

> Wherefore, as by one man sin entered into the world, and death by sin; and so death passed upon all men, for that all have sinned / For until the law sin was in the world; but sin is not imputed when there is no law / Nevertheless death reigned from Adam to Moses, even over them that had not sinned after the similitude of Adam's transgression, who is the figure of him that was to come.[18]

In his reinterpretation, La Peyrère suggested that the introduction of law to the world dated to Adam and not to Moses, as it was commonly understood. Hence, the time before the law when sin was not imputed should be understood as the time before Adam. According to La Peyrère, therefore, Paul was declaring that there was humanity before Adam, living in an unlawful world.

This preoccupation over the status of law and civility would be a constant for La Peyrère, the lawyer. In 1643, he published a book anonymously – as happened with most of his works, regardless of their topic – *Du Rappel des Iuifs*, which also discussed the nature of the relationship between God and humanity. He stated that, as humanity does not fully share the nature of God, the relationship between humanity and God could be understood as an "adoption," an "imitation of nature," as adoption was understood in civil law.[19] Then he described how this adoption had taken place: God first adopted the Jews as his sons, then the Gentiles, to become sons of God, had to be adopted by the adopted Jews.[20] La Peyrère evidently assumed a difference of nature not only between God and humanity, but also between the Jews and the Gentiles; his statement of this difference suggests his belief that Jews and Gentiles had different origins. The Gentiles were the pre-Adamites. Despite these differences, La Peyrère makes a strong case for the historical interdependence between these two peoples: the Gentiles/pre-Adamites were brought closer to God through the Jewish people and the latter were specifically made the chosen people to bring the former closer to God. The Gentiles/Christians had to understand that their salvation depended on the fortune of the Jewish people.[21] The only way to ensure salvation, La Peyrère continued, was to practise Christian charity by seeking the conversion of the Jewish people, integrating them into the Christian community and resituating them in the promised land. All this, he claimed, would be achieved under the rule of a temporal king who would be none other than a French king, who would also be the universal king announced in the scriptures. Only that would ensure the Second Coming and the beginning of the Kingdom of God. As we shall see, this work not only establishes his preoccupation with the pre-Adamites and his hypothesis of the different origins of humanity but inaugurates a whole conception of those ideas in relation to a millenarian view based on the integration of the Jewish community, both of which will become essential traits of his theory.

Until the early 1650s, La Peyrère continued accumulating material to defend his position regarding the pre-Adamites, expanding his inquiry to discussions about chronology, ancient sources, and ethnographic accounts. With this material in hand he elaborated a more detailed version of his theory. In 1655, apparently with the help of Christine of Sweden, he published the resulting work in Amsterdam. That edition was actually composed of two different works, the *Prae-Adamitae* and the *Systema Theologicum*.[22] Although published separately, the two anonymous publications have usually been bound together ever since. In fact, the English translation published the year after included the two works as a whole, adding a new preface dedicated "To all the Synagogues, to the

Jews dispersed over the face of the Earth."[23] Although the two works share the same argument – the existence of humanity before Adam – each work defends it differently. The *Prae-Adamitae*, a shorter work, is basically a revised version of his previous manuscript in which he argues his pre-Adamite theory through the reinterpretation of the verses in Paul's Epistle to the Romans. The *Systema Theologicum* is a longer and richer text, in which the author expands his argumentation with a commentary on the Old Testament and integrates ethnographical descriptions and alternative sources. The basic argument is that the two accounts of the origin of humanity narrated in the book of Genesis actually refer to two different creations of humans. The first describes the origin of the pre-Adamites, who were created as a part of the whole Creation, and therefore without special ties to God:

> Those Gentiles which were called Atheists and without a God, were called wicked, foolish, corrupt, abominable in their iniquities ... This was a lively portraiture of the Gentiles, because they are, and are simply called, the sons of men, and have nothing in their Nature to seek or reach God.[24]

The second account describes a later creation of humans, Adam and Eve, specially made by God to introduce law and religion in the world. They were the forefathers of the Jewish people, and only of them; therefore, the narrations contained in the Old Testament should be understood as exclusively the histories of the Jewish people. The accounts in the Bible did not possess a universal scope but were circumscribed to the region of Palestine and the vicissitudes of the Jews – for example, the Flood was not universal but occurred only in Palestine and did not kill people outside this territory. To support his arguments, La Peyrère entered into the contemporary debate about biblical chronology, presenting the problems posed to the traditional interpretation of the Bible by the Chaldean, Egyptian, and Classical accounts. He concluded that the whole problem rested on the belief that Moses was the sole author of the Pentateuch. He argued that Moses could have been the author of "some" of the Pentateuch, but that later copyists and transmitters altered and added to it. Hence, the Bible should not be understood as a fixed universal text, but rather a product of human action referring to particular events and peoples.

Obviously, to suggest that Moses was not the definitive author of the Pentateuch and that the Bible was a particular and altered narration was quite a blow to the notion of revelation. Immediately after the publication of the two works, La Peyrère was detained. His ideas were condemned by the Catholic, Protestant, and Jewish communities alike, and he was taken to Rome where he recanted his views and converted to Catholicism in a hearing with Pope Alexander VII. Afterwards he published two apologetic works[25] and continued working for the prince of Condé until 1665, when he retired and lived with the Oratorians in Aubervilliers, near Paris.[26] Despite his fate and although it is nowadays increasingly evident that La Peyrère was not the first one to criticize the Mosaic authorship of the Pentateuch,[27] nor to defend the existence of the pre-Adamites,[28] this has not impeded scholars from situating him as a cornerstone of the intellectual transformations of the seventeenth century. The French author is still considered a founder of modern biblical criticism, and as such critics situate his work in relation to the works of Thomas Hobbes, Spinoza, and Richard Simon.[29] Likewise, scholars portray his pre-Adamite theory as an abortive precursor of prehistory.[30] Because his work is situated as central to intellectual history, scholars have been interested in establishing the motivations for his ideas. During the last century, interpreters of his works have fallen into two groups: those who consider it as an example of atheist and libertine attitudes and those who regard it as a manifestation of some kind of religiosity.

Early examples of the libertine interpretation originated in France with René Pintard, who situated La Peyrère's ideas as a product of the milieu of free-thinkers in mid-seventeenth-century Paris, and in Germany with Adalbert Klempt and Otto Zöckler, who described La Peyrère's ideas as a decisive step for the progressive unfolding of secularism, natural science, and modernity.[31] The characterization of La Peyrère as a libertine or atheist has continued steadily over the years, and is a frequent feature of contributions from history of science and intellectual history, particularly those that take a positivist approach.[32]

In contrast to this view, we find those who characterize La Peyrère's ideas as the product of some sort of religiosity. Some of these contributions, from early on through the present day, have focused on the philo-Semitism of La Peyrère's works, interpreting his ideas as a manifestation of his supposed *converso* character, as did Leo Strauss and Hans-Joachim Schoeps. But the work of Richard Popkin is probably the main example of this trend. Popkin defined La Peyrère's system as a "Marrano theology."[33] This interpretation, however, has been increasingly challenged. Jean-Paul Oddos, in his biographical study of La Peyrère, provided evidence that questioned the idea of a *converso* origin to La Peyrère's family,[34] while Ira Robinson convincingly argued that La Peyrère's ideas were "entirely consonant with the normative view of the Jews by contemporary Christianity" and characterized his vision as "a combination of medieval apocalyptic thought, mystical symbolism and prophecy mixed with the new textual criticism and modern discoveries."[35] More recently, Andreas Pietsch has suggested that La Peyrère's thought could be easily ascribed to common forms of Christian spirituality in the seventeenth-century Republic of Letters.[36] Indeed, philo-Semitism was nothing strange in the context of Christian Hebraism and its repercussions for exegesis and political thought, whether monarchical or republican.[37] Also, millenarian positions had emerged in the Calvinist context since the beginning of the seventeenth century. These were characterized by an almost exclusive dedication to biblical exegesis and a penchant for more sober and less erudite argumentations.[38] This trend in Calvinist writing perfectly coincides with the millenarian biblism of La Peyrère, as well as the poorly learned character of his argumentation.[39] In fact, La Peyrère himself systematically attributes his reasoning to his Calvinist upbringing: "having been born into Calvin's sect, which in France is called Reformed; and having drunk it with [my mother's] milk."[40]

But those explanations also indicate, as Paolo Rossi pointed out,[41] that La Peyrère understood his own ideas as being in accordance with the general trends of his times and as unthreatening to Christian religiosity.[42] In fact, his concern over chronology and interpretation was consonant with a kind of religious controversy that was regarded as legitimate before the publication of his work on the pre-Adamites[43] and only afterwards became an extremely problematic matter that was identified with libertinism.[44] These considerations suggest that, contrary to traditional interpretations, La Peyrère's intention was not to undermine the foundations of sacred history, as was imputed to him after the publication of his works:

> and shall deliver me from the persecution of a phantom, who still wanders around the world; and who imputes to me that I only had the idea of the pre-Adamites to destroy the sacred history, and to knock down all the mysteries of the Christian religion.[45]

In this regard, it is revealing to observe how La Peyrère himself described the motivations that led him to compose his two essays on the pre-Adamites, which were included as a proem to his *Systema Theologicum.*[46] In the proem, he claims:

> For although I am my own greatest friend, yet truth's more dear to me, which I only professe.[47]

Previous interpretations of La Peyrère's thought have tended to focus on the critical and sceptical manifestations of his ideas. This approach seems legitimate enough considering that La Peyrère's own system rested on a sceptical view of the Mosaic authorship of the Pentateuch and of the integrity of the sacred scriptures. However, far less has been said about the affirmative, assertive dimension of La Peyrère's work. His sceptical approach was not a final objective per se but the means to establish truth, to restore certainty. La Peyrère's exegesis is not an exercise of irreligious scepticism but an attempt to offer an interpretation that could restore the integrity of the scriptures.[48] In this sense, La Peyrère is in line with the multitude of authors who since the sixteenth century had been offering reinterpretations that could reconcile the biblical narration with the profound shock of the discovery of new worlds and ancient sources.[49] These reinterpretations sought to re-establish sacred authority by integrating profane history and its methods.[50] In so doing, however, La Peyrère further degraded the impermeability of the intellectual boundaries between revealed and worldly truths, *malgré lui.*[51]

Transforming Histories

To better understand the affirmative dimension of La Peyrère's ideas it is essential to get a closer look at his view of history, a part of his work that has been largely neglected. As we saw above, La Peyrère argued that law was introduced in the world with Adam, not Moses. If sin existed before the law but it was not imputed, it follows that there should have been humanity before Adam. But precisely because there was no law, humanity before Adam was unruly and primitive: they were "wicked, foolish, corrupt, abominable," and lived in a "State of Nature," without a god. Adam was then created to introduce law in the world, inaugurating the "State of Law." He was created as an imitation of divine nature, as the adopted son of God, a status inherited by his progeny, the Jewish people. The pre-Adamites/Gentiles could improve their wicked condition by imitating the nature of the Jewish people – in other words, by being adopted by the adopted sons of God. That allowed the development of civility and the rule of law in the world. Jesus then came to the world to inaugurate the "State of Grace" and to announce the future "State of Glory."[52] The only way to finally reach the state of glory would be through the Gentiles' acknowledgment that their improvement depends on the Jewish people.

Contrary to the view, common in that period, that Adam was created perfect and wise and all of humanity's development after the Fall was a "recovery" of that wisdom,[53] La Peyrère's model suggests a different view of history. The pre-Adamites were first created as part of the general creation of the world and were brutal and ignorant. Even Adam had to acquire knowledge through hard work and dedication:

> Truly, in the beginning the prime causes and means of all sciences were in God, but the seeds of them were only sowed in Adam, which could not arise, but by meditation, reasoning with himself, by cultivating, and time. Adam might attain all arts and sciences; but not for that cause he attained to them that minute he was born.[54]

La Peyrère's vision of history is marked not by the perfect origin and later decay of humanity, but by its perfectibility. The brutal origins of humanity had to be corrected by a second creation, which he calls a "regeneration" or "renaissance."[55] This regeneration made possible the "transformation" of humanity:

> It is therefore by virtue, and through the effectiveness of an intellectual and divine mystery, that man's second creation, which is his transformation, had to be achieved, from a brutal man into a reasonable man, from a sinful man into a holy man, and from a mortal man into an immortal man.[56]

Key to this transformation was the introduction of law into the world with Adam, by which humanity could get rid of its "brutal affections."[57] The purpose of this "divine law" was to civilize humanity, a purpose that could only be understood through "civil Law," its offspring.[58] Law was transmitted by the adoption of the pre-Adamites by the adopted sons of God, also known as the descendants of Adam or the Jewish people. This transmission permitted the transformation of humanity, the development of polities, and the increase of knowledge. The final goal would be salvation, which would only come with the conversion of the Jewish people and their restitution in the promised land. This new time would come under the guidance of a French king who would be the universal king announced by the sacred scriptures.

If we consider these elements of his thought, it seems quite evident that La Peyrère held a progressive view of history. Decades ago, Ernest

Lee Tuveson showed how early modern millenarianism led to a progressive view of human history.[59] However, in La Peyrère's writings we find more than a linear exposition of history as a soteriological expectation.[60] He views humans as perfectible beings, both individually and collectively. Individual humans can improve with effort and time, growing and transforming themselves "by degrees" (*gradibus*) as Adam and even Christ did.[61] Collectively, human societies can also transform themselves to become well-ordered and peaceful polities, moving from the state of nature to the state of law.

Hence, La Peyrère's mode of restoring certainty offers a particular vision of history that goes beyond the mere defence of pre-Adamite origins or the critique of the Mosaic authorship of the Pentateuch. It affirms a progressive vision of history based on the idea of the transformability of humans, which establishes a model for the transformation of society. The centrality of law for this transformation and the prominence of the French monarchy in the ultimate salvation reinforce the idea of the state as guarantor of the improvement of society.[62] The fact that this improvement depends on the assimilation of religious minorities and the integration of individuals in a collective body establishes a model that, despite its universalist intentions, is determined by particular standards and interests. Assessing the import of La Peyrère's vision requires comparing it to other conceptions from the period.

As we have seen above, the work of La Peyrère is frequently compared to that of Thomas Hobbes (1588–1679). Historians of biblical criticism have long observed that there are coincidences in how both authors criticize the Mosaic authorship of the Pentateuch. The two authors argue that the Pentateuch itself narrates the death of Moses and that although the prophet could have written part of the text, it was later rewritten and expanded upon.[63] The observation of these coincidences opened the debate about the possible influence between La Peyrère and Hobbes. The fact that the *Leviathan* was published a few years before La Peyrère's works on the pre-Adamites led some scholars to conclude that it was Hobbes who inspired La Peyrère. However, the fact that Hobbes was exiled in Paris (1640–51) when La Peyrère had already written his manuscript and that they frequented the same intellectual circle led Popkin to suggest that Hobbes could have consulted and been inspired by La Peyrère in writing his own work.[64]

The comparison between the two authors generally ends here. However, there is room for a more profound consideration of the similarities in their vision of history and its relation to a political program. As in the case of La Peyrère, Hobbes's scepticism towards the traditional interpretation of scripture is only a first step towards the elaboration of an affirmative perspective on how it should be interpreted and, in turn, a model for how society should be governed. At the beginning of the *Leviathan*, in the dedicatory letter to Francis Godolphin written in Paris in 1651, Hobbes claimed that his critique of the Pentateuch was not only legitimate but also necessary for a greater (political) objective:

> That which perhaps may most offend, are certain Texts of Holy Scripture, alleged by me to other purpose than ordinarily they use to be by others. But I have done it with due submission, and also (in order to my subject) necessarily; for they are Outworks of the Enemy, from whence they impugne the Civill Power.[65]

Contrary to the claims that defined Hobbes's political philosophy as unhistorical, Pocock pointed out the pre-eminence of history in the work of the English philosopher.[66] Hobbes's reinterpretation of the scriptures, like La Peyrère's criticism and reinterpretation, defines a vision of history that is essential for his political project. Surely some readers will have noticed by now that the state of nature defined by La Peyrère as the time without law before Adam is very similar to the Hobbesian state of nature. For both authors, the original state of humanity was not the primordial perfection attributed to the times in the Garden of Eden but, rather, a brutal, ignorant, and violent existence, subjected to unruliness due to the lack of law. This reinterpretation serves to defend an alternative origin of humanity, which constitutes the starting point for a progressive vision of history based on the idea of the capacity for transformation, the perfectibility, of humans.

In 1650, when La Peyrère and Hobbes were both in Paris, a fascinating and strange book was published in England. Its author, the British physician John Bulwer (1606–56), is better known for his pioneering work on the human body and communication, and especially for his efforts to establish a system of communication for deaf people. In that book, titled *Anthropometamorphosis*, Bulwer followed his interests in the human body to survey how many different populations across the globe artificially modified their bodies. In the introductory section, Bulwer declares:

> I have heard to fall, somewhat in earnest, from the mouth of a Philosopher (one in points of common beliefe (indeed) too scepticall) that man was a meer Artificiall creature, and was at first but a kind of Ape or Baboon, who through his industry (by degrees) in time had improved his Figure & his Reason up to the perfection of man.[67]

Who was that philosopher who defended the idea that humans could artificially modify themselves "by degrees," to the point that one might argue that humans were originally apes or baboons? Apparently none other than Thomas Hobbes.[68] It is difficult now to know if Hobbes actually held the idea of the simian ancestry of humans, and it may well be just Bulwer's exaggeration, since he wrote his book as a reaction to Hobbes's ideas.[69] In any case, it seems clear that Hobbes defended a primitive origin of humankind, which is precisely what his state of nature was.[70] What is more relevant, however, is that this primitive state of humanity was for Hobbes the beginning of a progressive vision of history. The philosopher defended the premise that humans had the potential to artificially transform themselves. That capacity had determined the improvement of societies by the transformation of individuals for their integration in the collective body. This idea reinforces the image of the state as a body artificially constructed by the transformation of the individual bodies that compose it.[71] There is no better illustration of this than the famous frontispiece of the *Leviathan* depicting the incarnation of sovereignty as a giant human body composed of a myriad of individual human bodies. The figure reigns over a vast landscape with a city in the foreground, wears a crown, and holds the symbols of both temporal (sword) and ecclesiastical (crosier) powers. The scene is completed with a quote from the book of Job: "Non est potestas Super Terram quae Comparetur ei. Iob 41.24."[72]

Hobbes's political model derives from considering chaos and violence as the original state of humanity, a condition that could, however, be improved by the transformative capability of humans under the power of authority and law. Chaos and rebellion could be avoided by the artificial transformation of the collective body from harmful and damned to well-ordered and harmonious, while a strong authority could curb Job's "children of pride." One of the ways to craft this harmonious collective body was to ensure an undivided form of government. The sovereign should hold universal power, both temporal and ecclesiastical, and religious differences, although tolerated, should be solved by political design, accommodating individuals and minorities into a single public religion.[73]

Thus, the similarities between La Peyrère and Hobbes go beyond a sceptical perspective towards the traditional interpretation of the scriptures, as is commonly argued. For both authors, criticism serves to propose a reinterpretation of the scriptures. This reinterpretation offers an alternative vision of the origins of humanity in a brutal and primitive period. Those origins affirm a progressive view of history that supports a political program for the reinforcement of the authority of law and the state based on the transformation and assimilation of individuals and minorities into the collective body. As Noel Malcolm has signaled,[74] the fact that La Peyrère and Hobbes (and Spinoza[75]) arrived at similar conclusions – regardless of their acquaintance with each other's work – should lead us to consider a common ground of ideas emerging during that time that resulted in the affirmation of modern philosophical and political programs.

In this sense, the two authors could also be compared to Tommaso Campanella, who probably had made the acquaintance of La Peyrère in Paris right before his death.[76] Years before, Campanella had written a political treatise in which he presented a program for the reinforcement of the Spanish monarchy, which would implement the millenarian mission of the Spanish king as the universal monarch. Different peoples should be integrated under the sovereignty of the Spanish king, he argued, instilling mutual affection instead of hatred and promoting the unity of religion.[77] The objective should be to make all communities as similar as possible, attaining the unity of men as God ("the author of politics") has taught them. Integration could be achieved by gradually transforming the nature of the different communities through intermarriages and developing a common cultural and religious context. This transformation should not be restricted to the Iberian Peninsula but also applied to overseas territories and even to the enemies of the Spanish empire.[78] Years later, as an exile in Paris in La Peyrère's intellectual circle, Campanella reworked these ideas to offer a new interpretation that situated the French king as the universal monarch who would fulfil the millenarian mission by integrating all communities.[79] As the vicissitudes of Campanella's political program show, the call for a universalizing and transformative dimension of monarchy had a transnational and cross-confessional appeal even as it urged the consolidation of particular, proto-national identities.[80]

In the Spanish context, mass conversions of Jewish and Muslim communities and the subsequent need to integrate those converted minorities posed a tremendous challenge to traditional sociocultural categories. Suspicions about the sincerity of the converts – whether founded or unfounded – and the indeterminacy brought about by the dissolution of religious differences resulted in the emergence of a general atmosphere of anxiety over individual and collective identity. This climate was a fertile ground for the proliferation of sceptical attitudes and doubt, which permeated all aspects of life from everyday relationships to intellectual elaborations. New institutionalized narratives and devices to define individual and collective identity were developed in an effort to control these indeterminacies.[81] It is well known that this was the context for the proliferation of the policies of exclusion, such as "limpieza de sangre," and the development of antagonist historical narratives. However, it was also the context for the emergence of assimilationist attitudes, in which Spanish identities assumed oriental components.[82] This situation permitted the proliferation of reinterpretations of sacred history that offered alternative narratives of the origins of the Iberian communities by which those oriental components were integrated in the history of Spain.[83] There were also alternative narratives of origins that took this assimilationist trend to a universalist scale, seeking the integration of the population in overseas territories, including North Africa.[84] Those writings affirmed an assimilationist tendency that sought to integrate the different cultural identities of those territories by reinforcing and centralizing the state.[85]

One of the best examples of this assimilationist attitude in the seventeenth century is the work of Pedro de Valencia (1555–1620).[86] Valencia, an erudite chronicler of King Phillip III, addressed the problem of the authority and interpretation of the scriptures – as did his master, Benito Arias Montano, a major figure for the integration of oriental origins in the history of Spain.[87] Valencia has been considered a fundamental contributor to the development of philosophical scepticism in Spain, especially for his dissemination of the ideas of Sextus Empiricus.[88] However, even if Valencia held that every piece of evidence should be subjected to close scrutiny – including the sacred scriptures – his attitude implied confidence in the affirmative outcomes of the inquiry. As was the case for the authors discussed above, Valencia expected that interpretation would lead to the affirmation of the veracity of the scriptures and the certainty of divine providence as the guide for good government. This government would lead to the unification of all individuals under the Christian faith, eliding all differences in a universalistic, Pauline view of humanity.[89] Especially relevant was Valencia's push to integrate *converso* and Morisco communities in Iberia, which contrasted with the sceptical stance towards assimilation of many of his contemporaries.[90] In 1606, Valencia wrote a treatise addressed to the Spanish king Philip III in which he dealt with the problematic issue of what to do with the Morisco communities in Spain. In this treatise, he argued that, contrary to what other authors proposed, the Iberian converted communities had to be treated with Christian charity. This was not only for the benefit of those communities but, in the long term, was the best way to maintain the vitality of monarchical authority. He proposed eliminating the differences between old and new Christians, and seeking their transformation into a single unity through "permistión" or hybridization, the intermarriage between old and new Christians that, according to him, had been proven by history to be the best form of government and the best way to ensure peace and the improvement of societies:

> The force of reason, and of things themselves, urges us to seek the means of the *permistión*, which is the oldest and most praised means approved by reason and experience and with the best effects in the world for public peace and harmony, and for the security, growth, and perpetuation of kingdoms and empires.[91]

God had shown through history that this was the right way to govern. The transformation of differences into a single collective body had been His way to overcome the shortcomings of "gentilidad" (paganism), and so it should be with the Jews and the Moriscos:

> So God ended his own making *nomen eorum non nominetur amplius* and so ended paganism and so he wants to end the Jews and the Moors, assembling them into a new body and name of a republic.[92]

Once again, what may seem a sceptical position becomes an affirmative reinterpretation of the scriptures, based on alternative origins, that sustains a progressive view of history. In its turn, this understanding of history supports a political program for strengthening the authority of the monarchy based on the transformation and assimilation of individuals and minorities into the collective body. In the context of the intense debate that preceded the expulsion of the Moriscos (1609–13), Pedro de Valencia's treatise has been considered an example of religious tolerance. However, Seth Kimmel has shown that although it took an integrative position in comparison to others defending expulsion, Valencia's proposal falls short of being fully tolerant.[93] Although he defends the integration of the Morisco communities, he does so by proposing their assimilation into the collective body, dissolving their difference by their hybridization with old Christians:[94]

> It is convenient, therefore, not that the Moors should be equal to the old Christians in offices and honours of the kingdom, but that the Moors should be finished and that there should only remain and be old Christians

in the kingdom; all the people shall have one name and one spirit, without division, so that there should be no dissension.[95]

The Particularities of Universalism

As is the case for Pedro de Valencia, the work of Thomas Hobbes has usually been regarded as an appeal for religious tolerance. However, in Hobbes tolerance is restricted to the private sphere, whereas the final goal should be to accommodate all individual beliefs into a single public religion.[96] Something similar occurs with La Peyrère, whose writings have been interpreted as an example of conciliatory philo-Semitism,[97] but also a foundation for the affirmation of differences, polygenism, and modern racism.[98] The problem lies in the tension between our current understanding of tolerance and the practice of tolerance in seventeenth-century Europe. Toleration then did not always follow a principle of parity and frequently resulted in a practice of exclusion.[99] The practice of tolerance in early modern Europe was never absolute, but rather embedded in conflicts and the affirmation of identities.[100]

In his recent book *The Invention of Humanity: Equality and Cultural Difference in World History*, Siep Stuurman has shown that antagonism and the affirmation of alterity are hardly the only outcomes of cultural contact: instead, throughout history assimilationist narratives and the idea of equality have also been a recurrent result of those encounters.[101] Thus, we should not expect a simple, univocal structure in discourses describing other communities, but rather complex and ambivalent narratives constantly swinging between assimilation and rejection – as is the case with the pre-Adamite theory.[102]

The authors discussed all posit that the assimilation of religious or cultural minorities was possible, even desirable, which assumes a common basis between the different communities. This does not mean, however, that those authors did not conceive of those communities as different. Instead, even if humans had a different origin, they shared the capacity of perfectibility, which allowed them to transform themselves to become a single unity.[103] The problem, however, lay in how the authors thought this unity should be achieved: by the transformation of all individuals according to the particular standards set by the cultural and religious elites in which those authors operated (following the law, integrating into a single public religion, marrying to make a society of old Christians). This is how the universalism and the conception of equality of these proposals could nonetheless lead to the affirmation of nationalism, imperialism, and racism.[104]

Elsewhere we have argued that scepticism does not equal political neutrality.[105] Neither does the quest for certainty. During the first half of the seventeenth century, and contrary to the notion of a profound uninterest in history during that time,[106] the indeterminacy and scepticism produced by religious conflicts and cultural heterogeneity led to reinterpretations of the sacred scriptures that sought to re-establish certainty. They did so by affirming alternative origins, which offered the starting point for a progressive view of history based on the capacity of transformation of humans. They understood this capacity as a means to integrate different communities into a single unity for the improvement of societies. Thus, the quest for historical certainty went hand in hand with the construction of political certainty, based on a conception of the providential role of the state in the cohesion and development of society. The ultimate consequence of that vision was to be the reinforcement of the authority of the state, and it was to be accomplished according to the interests and the cultural and religious standards of the particular elites promoting those transformations in each state. Hence, a cross-confessional historiographical trend based on a universalist view of humans could paradoxically contribute to the affirmation of national identities and imperialistic attitudes. In this sense, these examples prefigure the ambivalent attitudes in the anthropological classification of humanity during the Enlightenment.[107] They might also help us to understand how, as Paul Hazard suggested, the intellectual and cultural panorama of the early modern epistemic crisis resulted in the simultaneous development of universalist, emancipatory aspirations and the affirmation of national particularism, hatred, and massacre.

ACKNOWLEDGMENTS

This essay received the support of the European Research Council under the European Union's Seventh Framework Programme (FP7/2007–2013) / ERC grant agreement number 323316. PI: Mercedes García-Arenal.

NOTES

1 William J. Bouwsma, *El otoño del Renacimiento (1550–1640)* (Barcelona: Crítica, 2001), originally *The Waning of the Renaissance, 1550–1640* (New Haven: Yale University Press, 2000).

2 Stefania Tutino, *Shadows of Doubt: Language and Truth in Post-Reformation Catholic Culture* (Oxford: Oxford University Press, 2014).

3 Bruno Latour, *Nous n'avons jamais été modernes: Essai d'anthropologie symétrique* (Paris: La Découverte, 1991); Dan Edelstein, *The Enlightenment: A Genealogy* (Chicago: Chicago University Press, 2010), 2.

4 Stephen Menn, "The Intellectual Setting," in *The Cambridge History of Seventeenth-Century Philosophy*, ed. D. Garber and M. Ayers (Cambridge: Cambridge University Press, 1998), 73–4.

5 Richard H. Popkin, "Theories of Knowledge," in *The Cambridge History of Renaissance Philosophy*, ed. Q. Skinner and E. Kessler (Cambridge: Cambridge University Press, 1988), 668–84.

6 Paul Hazard, *La crise de la conscience européenne, 1680–1715* (Paris: Boivin et Cie, 1935).

7 Richard H. Popkin, "Pre-Adamism in 19th Century American Thought: 'Speculative Biology' and Racism," *Philosophia* 8, no. 2–3 (1978): 206.

8 Anthony Grafton, *Defenders of the Text: The Traditions of Scholarship in an Age of Science, 1450–1800* (Cambridge, MA: Harvard University Press, 1991), 205.

9 Popkin, "Pre-Adamism in 19th Century American Thought," 206.

10 Jean-Paul Oddos, "Recherches sur la vie et l'oeuvre d'Isaac de Lapeyrère (1596?–1676)," PhD diss., Université des Sciences Sociales Grenoble II, 1974, 19–39.

11 Oddos, "Recherches," 41–2; Richard H. Popkin, *The History of Scepticism from Savonarola to Bayle* (Oxford: Oxford University Press, 2003), 221.

12 Isaac La Peyrère, *Apologie de La Peyrère* (Paris: Thomas Ioly, 1663), 66–7: "Dés que i'eus la liberté de voir le monde, et de connoître les Esprits qui y sont; Paris qui est un abregé du monde, m'enfournit de toutes sortes. I'y trouvay des Esprits transçandans en toutes les sciances. Les uns adonnez à la piété. D'autres indiferans pour elle. Et plusieurs qui extravaguoient dans l'impieté. Ceux-cy me surprirent d'abord par le faux brillant de leurs raisons, et ne m'esbloüirent pourtant pas." All translations mine unless otherwise noted.

13 La Peyrère, *Systema theologicum ex prae-adamitarum hypothesi. Pars prima* (Amsterdam: [Elzevier], 1655), ii: "Illa eadem et mihi olim inciderat suspicio; cum puer adhuc vel audirem, vel legerem historiam Geneseos"; La Peyrère, *Men before Adam* (n.p., 1656), i: "I had this suspicion also being a Child, when I heard or read the History of Genesis." Elsewhere he declares that he first came across the idea years later, while reading Paul's Epistle to the Romans (La Peyrère, *Apologie*, 8).

14 La Peyrère, *Apologie*, 11.

15 La Peyrère, *Exercitatio super vers. 12, 13 et 14 cap. V Epistolae S. Pauli ad*

Romanos, quibus inducitur primos homines fuisse creatos longe ante Adamum (Paris-A.N. M 799, n. 2; Paris-B.N. Moreau 845). For more details about the copies of the manuscript, see Miguel Benitez's catalogue of early modern clandestine manuscripts: *La cara oculta de las Luces: Investigaciones sobre los manuscritos filosóficos clandestinos de los siglos XVII y XVIII* (Valencia: Biblioteca Valenciana, 2003), 51.

16 Dirk Van Miert and Henk Nellen, "Media en tolerantie in de Republiek der Letteren: De discussie over Isaac de La Peyrère (ca. 1596–1676) en zijn Prae-Adamitae," *De Zeventiende Eeuw* 30, no. 1 (2014): 19.

17 Hugo Grotius, *De origine gentium americanarum dissertatio altera, adversus obtretactorem* (Paris: S. Cramoisy, 1643), 15: "Cui consequens est, ut credantur aut ab aeterno fuisse cum Aristotele, aut ex terris orti, ut de Spartis fabula est, aut ex Oceano, ut voluit Homerus, aut aliquos ante Adamum fuisse conditos homines, ut nuper aliquis in Gallia somniavit." It seems clear that Grotius knew about La Peyrère's theory during that year of 1643 since in the previous edition of his *Dissertatio* (Paris: S. Cramoisy, 1642) nothing is said about the "French dreamer." In fact, the 1643 edition seems a version intended to fight the ideas that opposed his own interpretation of the origins of the Amerindians. La Peyrère would have a few years later the opportunity to respond to Grotius's puns in his work about Greenland, criticizing the ideas of the Dutch scholar – who died a couple of years before – regarding the Scandinavian origin of the (northern) Amerindians: "I'aurois en cét endroit une belle occasion d'insister sur les autres mescontes du Dissertateur, de luy rendre ses paroles, et de le renuoyer au pays des Visions, et des Songes. Mais puis qu'il dort son dernier sommeil, laissons-le dormir en repos, et finissons ce discours pour nostre commune satisfaction." La Peyrère, *Relation du Groenland* (Paris: Agustin Courbe, 1647), 276–7.

18 Rom. 5:12–14, King James Version.

19 La Peyrère, *Du Rappel des Iuifs* (n.p., 1643), 9: "Adoption! qui n'est pas de Nature; mais que les Iurisconsultes ont definie une imitation de Nature."

20 Ibid., 17: "Disons! Que les Iuifs ont esté les Premiers hommes Adoptez Enfans de Dieu en Iesus-Christ. Disons en suitte; Que les Gentils pour estre Adoptez Enfans de Dieu en Iesus-Christ, qu'ils ont esté Adoptez en la Famille des Iuifs Adoptez."

21 Ibid., 19: "Les Gentils neantmoins sont obligez de croire et de reconnoistre que ce mesme Salut ne leur est venu que des Iuifs."

22 La Peyrère, *Prae-Adamitae. Sive Exercitatio Super Versibus Duodecimo, Decimotertio, & Decimoquarto, Capitis Quinti Epistolae D. Pauli ad Romanos. Quibus Inducuntur Primi Homines ante Adamun Conditi* (Amsterdam:

[Elzevier], 1655); La Peyrère, *Systema Theologicum, ex prae-Adamitarum hypothesi. Pars prima* (Amsterdam: [Elzevier], 1655).

23 La Peyrère, *Men before Adam.*

24 Ibid., 92; La Peyrère, *Systema Theologicum,* 78: "Qui dicti sunt gentiles athei, et sine Deo; vocati sunt impii, insipientes, corrupti, et abominabiles in iniquitatibus … Pictura haec fuit graphica gentilium, qua sunt et dicuntur simpliciter homines, et filii hominum: quaque natura sua nihil sunt ad Deum intelligendum et assequendum."

25 La Peyrère, *Lettre de la Peyrere, a Philotime. Dans laquelle il expose les raisons qui l'ont obligé à abjurer la secte de Calvin qu'il professoit, & le livre des Preadamites qu'il avoit mis au jour* (Paris: Agustin Courbe, 1658); and La Peyrère, *Apologie.*

26 During this time, he continued writing about Scandinavia, his other main topic: *Relation de l'Islande* (Paris: Louis Billaine, 1663); a previous work was *Relation du Groenland* (1647). He published a proselytizing work: *Suite des letres escrites a monsieur le Comte de la Suze, pour l'obliger par raison à se faire Catolique* (Paris: Simeon Piget, 1662). He also continued working on his political-millenarian system for the reunification of all confessions, but this time without making any references to the pre-Adamites. He produced a manuscript, *Des Iuifs, Elus, Reietés, et Rapelés,* which was never published. Richard H. Popkin, *Isaac La Peyrère (1596–1676): His Life, Work and Influence* (Leiden: Brill, 1987), 19. There is speculation about whether he actually maintained his views on the pre-Adamites. It is only clear that during this time he kept making references to the matter in his correspondence, e.g., see Letter from La Peyrère to Ismael Bouilliau, 18 February 1661, BNF-Collection Bouillau, vol. 22, Fr. 13040.

27 Paul Sonnino, "Torah, Torah, Torah: The Authorship of the Pentateuch in Ancient and Early Modern Times," in *The Rhetoric of Power in Late Antiquity: Religion and Politics in Byzantium, Europe and the Early Islamic World,* ed. R.M. Frakes, E. DePalma Digester, and J. Stephens (London: Tauris, 2010), 241–75.

28 David N. Livingstone, *Adam's Ancestors: Race, Religion, and the Politics of Human Origins* (Baltimore: Johns Hopkins University Press, 2008), 1–25.

29 Popkin, *The History of Scepticism,* 219–38; Jeffrey L. Morrow, *Three Skeptics and the Bible: La Peyrère, Hobbes, Spinoza, and the Reception of Modern Biblical Criticism* (New York: Pickwick, 2016).

30 Don Cameron Allen, *The Legend of Noah: Renaissance Rationalism in Art, Science and Letters* (Urbana: University of Illinois Press, 1949), 133; Alain Schnapp, "The Pre-Adamites: An Abortive Attempt to Invent Pre-history in the Seventeenth Century?" in *History of Scholarship: A Selection of Papers from the Seminar on the History of Scholarship Held Annually at the Warburg Institute,*

ed. C.R. Ligota and J.-L. Quantin (Oxford: Oxford University Press, 2006), 399–412.

31 For a more detailed survey of this current of interpretation, see Andreas N. Pietsch, *Isaac La Peyrère: Bibelkritik, Philosemitismus und Patronage in der Gelehrtenrepublik des 17. Jahrhunderts* (Berlin: Walter de Gruyter, 2012).

32 Fritz Mauthner, *Der Atheismus und seine Geschichte im Abendlande* (Heppenheim: m-presse, 2010), 23.

33 Richard H. Popkin, "The Marrano Theology of Isaac La Peyrère," *Studi Internazionali di filosofia* 5 (1973): 97–126.

34 Oddos, "Recherches," 16.

35 Ira Robinson, "Isaac de la Peyrère and the Recall of the Jews," *Jewish Social Studies* 40, no. 2 (1978): 126–7.

36 Pietsch, *Isaac La Peyrère.*

37 Abraham Melamed, "The Revival of Christian Hebraism in Early Modern Europe," in *Philosemitism in History*, ed. J. Karp and A. Sutcliffe (Cambridge: Cambridge University Press, 2011), 63.

38 Howard Hotson, *Paradise Postponed: Johann Heinrich Alsted and the Birth of Calvinist Millenarianism* (London: Springer, 2000), 7–9.

39 Grafton, *Defenders of the Text*, 211.

40 La Peyrère, *Lettre de la Peyrère, a Philotime*, 132–3: "que'estant né dans la secte de Caluin, qu'on appelle en France, Reformée; et que l'ayant imbibée auec la lait."

41 Paolo Rossi, *I segni del tempo: Storia della Terra e storia delle nazioni da Hooke a Vico* (Rome: Feltrinelli, 2003), 162.

42 La Peyrère, *Men before Adam*, 20: "Likewise whether we think that Adam was created alone, and that he was first of all men, or believe that other were begotten before Adam, all Christian Religion shall stil keep its own place and its own mysteries"; La Peyrère, *Prae-Adamitae*, 23: "Pari eventu, sive credimus Adamum fuisse creatum solum, et primum omnium hominum; sive ponimus alios homines ante Adamum fuisse genitos: stabit semper suo loco, et suis mysteriis religio omnis Christiana."

43 To illustrate this atmosphere of widespread concern over chronologies and the peopling of the world in the early seventeenth century, Don Cameron Allen (*The Legend of Noah*, 128–9) recalled the curious episode, commented on by Georgius Hornius, of the exorcism of a young girl in France conducted in 1604 by the Jesuit Pierre Cotton, during which allegedly a demon speaking through the girl even asked: "Quomodo insulae animalia acceperint, et eo homines post Adamum pervenerint?" Hornius, *De originibus americanis libri quatuor* (n.p.: Adrian Vlacq., 1652), 19. It should be said, however, that according to the first transmitter of the

story, Jacques-Auguste De Thou, it was the Jesuit father who asked the girl, Adrianne du Fresne, such a question (and many others) with the intention of finally obtaining answers to the most pressing controversies of the time from what he believed was a very learned demon. De Thou, *Historiarum sui temporis* (Geneva: Pierre de la Rovière, 1620), 5.1135–6. On the other hand, the biographer of Father Cotton argued that the story was a fabrication to undermine the reputation of the Jesuit order. Pierre-Joseph D'Orleans, *La vie du pere Pierre Coton* (Paris: Etienne Michallet, 1688), 87.

44 Rossi, *I segni del tempo,* 167.

45 La Peyrère, *Apologie,* ii: "et me deliuerera de la persecutión d'un Fantôme, qui erre encore dans le monde; Et qui m'impute, que ie n'ay eu la pansée des Preadamites, que pour destruire L'Histoire Sainte, et ranuerser tous les mysteres de la Religion Chrestiene."

46 La Peyrère, *Men before Adam,* iii: "A tryal of which I put forth in that Essay, which for that purpose I did compose, for the clearing of those verses of the Apostle; Nor considering the bulk of the work could I then make an end; Now I intend still by way of Essay to open the body of Divinity it self, by which the Doctrine of the Gospel, upon presupposition of men before Adam, may be laid open more at large, and that it may appear that this Tenet is no ways disadvantagious to our faith, which is in Christ"; La Peyrère, *Systema Theologicum,* iii–iv: "Cujus rei experimenta quaedam edidi in Exercitatione illa, quam ad elucidationem Versuum illorum Apostoli speciatim institui. Neque enim pro ratione opellulae omnia potui. Exponere nunc in animo est, continua Exercitationis causa et gratia, Systema ipsum Theologicum, quo doctrina omnis Evangelii, ex Prae-Adamitarum hypothesi, fusius explicetur: et appareat, Positionem hanc, ne dicam Fidei quae in Christo est, quoquo pacto officere."

47 La Peyrère, *Men before Adam,* v; La Peyrère, *Systema Theologicum,* v: "Quamvis enim mihi ipsi sim amicissimus; magis tamen mihi est amica Veritas. Quod unice profiteor." This phrase is a variation of the famous dictum "Amicus Plato sed magis amica veritas," which had a long history of transmission from antiquity to early modern times. Léonardo Tarán, "Amicus Plato sed magis amica veritas: From Plato and Aristotle to Cervantes," *Antike und Abendland* 30, no. 2 (1984): 93–124.

48 Amos Funkenstein, *Theology and the Scientific Imagination from the Middle Ages to the Seventeenth Century* (Princeton: Princeton University Press, 1986), 278.

49 Anthony Grafton, *New Worlds, Ancient Texts: The Power of Tradition and the Shock of Discovery* (Cambridge, MA: Harvard University Press, 1992).

50 Allen, *The Legend of Noah*; see also Fernando Rodríguez Mediano's contribution to this volume.

51 Sarah Mortimer and John Robertson, "Nature, Revelation, History: Intellectual Consequences of Religious Heterodoxy c. 1600–1750," in *The Intellectual Consequences of Religious Heterodoxy 1600–1750,* ed. S. Mortimer and J. Robertson (Leiden: Brill, 2012), 19.

52 La Peyrère, *Prae-Adamitae,* 10–12; La Peyrère, *Men before Adam,* 6–9.

53 Peter Harrison, *The Fall of Man and the Foundations of Science* (Cambridge: Cambridge University Press, 2007).

54 La Peyrère, *Men before Adam,* 201; La Peyrère, *Systema Theologicum,* 170: "Erant quidem in principio, et ante rerum principium, summae scientiarum omnium rationes et causae in Deo: sed illarum semina tantum jacta fuere in Adamo, quo tempore formatus est: quae non nisi cogitatione et ratiocinio, cultura et tempore, ex Adami potenita educi potuerunt. Potuit Adamus scientias, artes, et disciplinas omnes assequi; sed non eas idcirco assecutus est, momento illo quo formatus est."

55 La Peyrère, *Apologie,* 97.

56 Ibid., 104–5: "C'estoit donc par la vertu, et par l'éficace d'un Mystere intellectuel, et diuin, que se deuoit faire la seconde creation de l'homme, qui est sa transformation, d'homme brutal en homme raisonnable, d'homme pecheur en homme saint, et d'homme mortel en homme immortel."

57 Ibid., 103.

58 Ibid., 105: "Et que nous ne saurions par consequant auoir une plus claire intelligence des Mysteres de la Iustice Divine, que par les raports qu'ils ont auec les Mysteres de la Iustice ciuile."

59 Ernest Lee Tuveson, *Millennium and Utopia: A Study in the Background of the Idea of Progress (*Berkeley: University of California Press, 1949).

60 For more insight on the development of the progressive view of human history in the early modern period, see Margaret Hodgen, *Early Anthropology in the Sixteenth and Seventeenth Centuries* (Philadelphia: University of Pennsylvania Press, 1964), 433–77.

61 La Peyrère, *Systema Theologicum,* 119; La Peyrère, *Men before Adam,* 141–2.

62 This position fits well with his integration in an intellectual context that defined politics as the means to conform a society without trouble or particularism. See Jean-Paul Oddos, *Isaac de Lapeyrère (1596–1676): Un intellectuel sur les routes du monde* (Paris: Honoré Champion, 2012).

63 Thomas Hobbes, *Leviathan, or the Matter, Forme and Power of a Common Wealth Ecclesiasticall and Civil* (London: Andrew Crooke, 1651), 199–200; La Peyrère, *Systema Theologicum,* 172–4; La Peyrère, *Men before Adam,* 204–5.

64 Popkin, *Isaac La Peyrère: Life, Work, Influence,* 72.

65 Hobbes, *Leviathan,* ii.

66 J.G.A. Pocock, "Time, History and Eschatology in the Thought of Thomas Hobbes," in *Politics, Language and Time: Essays on Political Thought and History* (New York: Atheneum, 1971), 149.

67 John Bulwer, *Anthropometamorphosis: Man Transform'd: or, the artificial changling historically presented, In the mad and cruell Galantry, foolish Bravey, ridiculous Beauty, filthy finenesse, and loathsome loveliness of most nations, fashioning and altering their bodies from the mould intended by Nature* (London: William Hunt, 1653 [1650]).

68 Susan Wiseman, "Monstrous Perfectibility: Ape-Human Transformation in Hobbes, Bulwer, Tyson," in *At the Borders of the Human: Beasts, Bodies and Natural Philosophy in the Early Modern Period*, ed. E. Fudge, R. Gilbert, and S. Wiseman (New York: Palgrave, 1999), 227.

69 William E. Burns, "The King's Two Monstrous Bodies: John Bulwer and the English Revolution," in *Wonders, Marvels and Monsters in Early Modern Culture*, ed. P.G. Platt (Newark: University of Delaware Press, 1999), 187–202.

70 It should be mentioned that Hobbes himself, in a famous passage of the *Leviathan*, declares that this state of nature might not correspond to a particular historical moment but rather to a possible condition of humans: "It may per adventure be thought, there was never such a time, nor condition of warre as this, and I believe it was never generally so, over all the world: but there are many places, where they live so now. For the savage people in many places of America, except the government of small Families, the concord whereof dependeth on naturall lust, have no government at all; and live at this day in that brutish manner, as I said before" (63). However, in the Latin translation of the *Leviathan* (1668), Hobbes changed this claim with a mention of the Genesis, thus associating the state of nature with an original historical moment of humanity. Helen Thornton, *State of Nature or Eden? Thomas Hobbes and his Contemporaries on the Natural Condition of Human Beings* (Rochester: Rochester University Press, 2005). Thus, despite the apparently contradictory character of his claims, it has been argued that Hobbes's ideas were compatible with the pre-Adamite views shared by a group of British authors even before the publication of La Peyrère's work. William Poole, "Seventeenth-Century Preadamism, and an Anonymous English Preadamist," *The Seventeenth Century* 19, no. 1 (2004): 8. According to Margaret Hodgen, "[For Hobbes] humanity had started at the bottom, and the bottom was a brutish condition of *bellum omnium contra omnes*, like that reportedly existing in savage America." *Early Anthropology*, 490.

71 In this regard, it is worth considering the equivalences between Hobbes's political writings and his more philosophical works, in which he tries

to overcome the shortcomings posed by sceptical perspectives with the suggestion that knowledge is built by the transformation through reason of the "world of bodies." Gianni Paganini, "Hobbes among Ancient and Modern Sceptics: Phenomena and Bodies," in *The Return of Scepticism: from Hobbes and Descartes to Bayle*, ed. G. Paganini (New York: Springer, 2003), 3–35.

72 "There is no power on earth to be compared to him"; "Upon earth there is not his like" (Job 41:33, King James Version).

73 Brockliss, "La era de la curiosidad," in *El siglo XVII*, ed. J. Bergin (Barcelona: Crítica, 2002), 192; Glen Newey, *The Routledge Guidebook to Hobbes' Leviathan* (London: Routledge, 2014), 47, 253.

74 Noel Malcolm, *Aspects of Hobbes* (Oxford: Oxford University Press, 2002), 398.

75 Spinoza has also been placed in the group of authors who outlined a critique of the Pentateuch that served as the basis for the development of modern biblical criticism. Jean Bernier, *La critique du Pentateuque de Hobbes à Calmet* (Paris: Honoré Champion, 2010), 27. Yet the similarities between Spinoza, La Peyrère, and Hobbes go beyond the mere critique of the Mosaic authorship of the Pentateuch. For example, in his *Tractatus*, Spinoza does not conceive the critique of the scriptures as an end in itself but, rather, as a first step to ensure the validity of the sacred text for developing a particular political program. Michael A. Rosenthal, "Spinoza's Dogmas of the Universal Faith and the Problem of Religion," *Philosophy & Theology* 13, no. 1 (2001): 56–7. He does so by suggesting that the original state of humanity was that of primitiveness and brutality. He considered that this state of nature corresponded to a period before the introduction of the law in the world and defended this by alluding to the words of Paul in the Epistle to the Romans: "Atque hoc idem est, quod Paulus docet, qui ante legem, hoc est, quamdiu homines ex naturae imperio vivere considerantur, nullum peccatum agnoscit." Baruch Spinoza, *Tractatus theologico-politicus* (Hamburg: Heinrich Kunraht, 1670), 176. This state of nature thus inaugurates a progressive view of history based on the idea that humans can transform themselves with effort and dedication:

> Non enim omnes naturaliter determinati sunt ad operandum secundum regulas et leges rationis; sed contra, omnes ignari omnium rerum nascuntur, et antequam veram vivendi rationem noscere possunt et virtutis habitum acquirere, magna aetatis pars, etsi bene educati fuerint, transit, et nihilominus interim vivere tenentur, seque, quantum in se est, conservare, nempe ex solo appetitus inpulsu. (ibid.)

The use of reason had permitted humans to assume that they lived better (and more freely) together and under the law, which ultimately led to the development of the state as the best means to provide for the security and development of humankind (ibid., 177). For more details on Spinoza's "selective and appropriative way," see Anthony Grafton, "Spinoza's Hermeneutics: Some Heretical Thoughts," in *Scriptural Authority and Biblical Criticism in the Dutch Golden Age: God's Word Questioned*, ed. D. Van Miert, H. Nellen, P. Steenbakkers, and J. Touber (Oxford: Oxford University Press, 2017), 177–96.

76 Popkin, *Isaac La Peyrère*, 39.

77 Tommaso Campanella, *La monarquía hispánica* (Madrid: Centro de estudios constitucionales, 1982 [1601]), 117.

78 Campanella, *La monarquía hispánica*, 143–56.

79 Tommaso Campanella, "La monarquía de las naciones," in *La monarquía del Mesías: Las monarquías de las naciones*, ed. P. Mariño Gómez (Madrid: Centro de estudios constitucionales, 1989 [1635]), 171–264.

80 John M. Headley, *Tommaso Campanella and the Transformation of the World* (Princeton: Princeton University Press, 1997), 198.

81 Mercedes García-Arenal, "Introduction," in *After Conversion: Iberia and the Emergence of Modernity*, ed. Mercedes García-Arenal (Leiden: Brill, 2016), 1–18.

82 Barbara Fuchs, *Exotic Nation: Maurophilia and the Construction of Early Modern Spain* (Philadelphia: University of Pennsylvania Press, 2009).

83 Mercedes García-Arenal and Fernando Rodríguez Mediano, *The Orient in Spain: Converted Muslims, the Forged Lead Books of Granada, and the Rise of Orientalism* (Leiden: Brill, 2013); Katrina B. Olds, *Forging the Past: Invented Histories in Counter-Reformation Spain* (New Haven: Yale University Press, 2015), 126–39.

84 Pedro Sarmiento de Gamboa, *History of the Incas* (Cambridge: Hakluyt Society, 1907 [1572]), 22: "We have indicated the situation of the Atlantic Island and those who, in conformity with the general peopling of the world, were probably its first inhabitants, namely the early Spaniards and the first Mauritanian vassals of the King Atlas." See also Bernardo de Aldrete, *Varias antigüedades de España, África y otras provincias* (Antwerp: Juan Hafrey, 1614).

85 Antonio Feros, *Speaking of Spain: The Evolution of Race and Nation in the Hispanic World* (Cambridge, MA: Harvard University Press, 2017), 82–3.

86 Valencia was among a group of authors who defended the claim that Moriscos and old Christians shared a common ancestry. Antonio Feros, "Retóricas de la expulsión," in *Los moriscos: Expulsión y diáspora: Una perspectiva internacional*, ed. M. García-Arenal and G. Wiegers (Valencia: Universidad de Valencia, 2013), 72–3.

87 It should be mentioned that Arias Montano, in his study regarding the origins of human populations contained in his polyglot edition of the Bible – the *Antwerp Polygot* – already suggested that although different peoples had different institutions, languages, and religions, they could be made into one spirit and one single body: "Etsi vero singularum nationum diversa fuerunt instituta, diversa linguarum genera, diversi antea religionis cultus; attamen uno omnes animo esse debere, atque adeo in unum corpus coire posse videntur." *Phaleg: Sive de gentium sedibus primis, orbisque terrae situ, liber* (Antwerp: Christophe Plantin, 1572), iii. This statement follows his view that human nature is characterized by life among others and that this social condition is the context for the development and perfectibility of humans. Juan José Jorge López, *El pensamiento filosófico de Benito Arias Montano: Una reflexión sobre su Opus Magnum* (Merida: Editora regional de Extremadura, 2002), 272.

88 John Christian Laursen, "Pedro de Valencia's Academica and Scepticism in Late Renaissance Spain," in *Renaissance Skepticisms,* ed. G. Paganini and J.R. Maia Neto (Dordrecht: Springer, 2009), 111–23; and Laursen, "Skepticism and Cynicism in the Work of Pedro de Valencia," in *Skepticism in the Modern Age: Building on the Work of Richard Popkin,* ed. J.R. Maia Neto, G. Paganini, and J.C. Laursen (Leiden: Brill, 2009), 139–58.

89 Grace Magnier, *Pedro de Valencia and the Catholic Apologists of the Expulsion of the Moriscos: Visions of Christianity and Kingship* (Leiden: Brill, 2010), 23, 199, 365, and 398.

90 Mercedes García-Arenal, "Mi padre moro, yo moro: The Inheritance of Belief in Early Modern Iberia," in García-Arenal, *After Conversion,* 327–9.

91 Pedro de Valencia, *Tratado acerca de los moriscos de España* (Badajoz: Unión de bibliófilos extremeños, 2005), 147: "La fuerza de la razón y de las mismas cosas nos aprieta y apremia a que busquemos el medio de la permistión, que es el medio más antiguo, más loado y aprobado con razones y experiencia y el de mejores efectos que se ha hallado en el mundo para la pública paz y concordia, para la seguridad y acrecentamiento y para la perpetuidad de los reinos e imperios."

92 Valencia, *Tratado,* 156: "Así acabó Dios a los suyos haciendo que *nomen eorum non nominetur amplius* y así acabó la gentilidad y así quiere ha de acabar a los judíos, a los moros, juntándolos en un nuevo cuerpo y nombre de república." The Latin phrase, meaning "their name not to be named again," seems to be alluding to a particular verse in the Song of Moses (Deuteronomy 32): "Dixi: Ubinam sunt? cessare faciam ex hominibus memoriam eorum" (Deut. 32:26, Vulgate); "I said, I would scatter them

into corners, I would make the remembrance of them to cease from among men" (Deut. 32:26, King James Version). Here Valencia seems to follow the commentary by Cornelius Jansen, the Elder, bishop of Ghent: "perdam eos penitus de terra sicque cessare faciam memoriam eorum inter hominess, ut amplius non nominetur inter varios populous unus populus." *Paraphrasis in psalmos omnes davidicos* (Lyon: Pierre Landry, 1586), 333.

93 Seth Kimmel, *Parables of Coercion: Conversion and Knowledge at the End of Islamic Spain* (Chicago: University of Chicago Press, 2015).

94 Political programs to assimilate minorities did not stop after Valencia's work, nor even after the expulsion of the Moriscos. In his 1624 *Memorial* addressed to King Philip IV, the count-duke of Olivares offered a diagnosis of the Spanish empire and recommended a policy of unification for the strengthening of the monarchy that included measures of legal and ethnic homogenization across the various kingdoms:

> Tenga V. Majd. por el negocio más importante de su Monarquía el hacerse rey de España; quiero decir, señor, que no se contente V. Majd. con ser rey de Portugal, de Aragón, de Valencia, conde de Barcelona, sino que trabaje y piense con consejo maduro y secreto por reducir estos reinos de que se compone España al estilo de Castilla, sin ninguna diferencia … que si V. Majd. lo alcanza será el príncipe más poderoso del mundo … procure poner la mira en reducir sus reinos al estado más seguro, deseando este poder para el mayor bien y dilación de la religión católica, conociendo que la división presente de leyes y fueros enflaquece su poder y le estorba el conseguir fin tan justo y glorioso y tan al servicio de Nuestro Señor … que V. Majd. favoreciese los de aquellos reinos introduciéndoselos en Castilla, casándolos en ella y los de acá allá, y con beneficios y blandura los viniese a facilitar de manera que viéndose casi naturalizados acá con esta mezcla, por la admisión a los oficios y dignidades de Castilla se olvidasen los corazones de manera de aquellos privilegios, que por entrar a gozar de los de este reino igualmente, se pudiese disponer con negociación esta unión tan conveniente y necesaria.

John H. Elliot, José F. de la Peña, and Fernando Negredo, ed., *Memoriales y cartas del Conde-Duque de Olivares* (Madrid: Marcial Pons, 2013), 120–1.

95 Valencia, *Tratado,* 156: "Conviene, pues, no que los moriscos sean iguales en oficios y honras del Reino con los cristianos viejos, sino que los moriscos se acaben y que solamente quede y haya en el Reino cristianos viejos; que sea toda la pública gente de un nombre y de un ánimo, sin división, para que no haya disensión."

96 Newey, *The Routledge Guidebook,* 253.

97 H.J. Schoeps, *Philosemitismus im Barock: Religions- und geistesgeschichtliche Untersuchungen* (Tubingen: Mohr Siebeck, 1952).

98 Popkin, "Pre-Adamism in 19th Century American Thought"; Justin E.H. Smith, *Nature, Human Nature, & Human Difference: Race in Early Modern Philosophy* (Princeton: Princeton University Press, 2015), 102–4. It is worth noting, however, that Smith seems to suggest that in La Peyrère the pre-Adamite humanity referred exclusively to the people outside Europe and especially their supposed descendants in the newly discovered territories (103), whereas, as we have seen, the French author held that the descendants of the pre-Adamites were all those without Jewish ancestry, including Europeans.

99 Mortimer and Robertson, "Nature, Revelation, History," 12.

100 Benjamin J. Kaplan, *Divided by Faith: Religious Conflict and the Practice of Toleration in Early Modern Europe* (Cambridge, MA: Harvard University Press, 2010).

101 Siep Stuurman, *The Invention of Humanity: Equality and Cultural Difference in World History* (Cambridge, MA: Harvard University Press, 2017).

102 Carlos Cañete, "Serendipity at the Clark (Once Again): On Africanism, Preadamite Theory, and the Richard Popkin Papers," *The Center & Clark Newsletter* 61 (2015): 8–10.

103 Elisabeth Quennehen, "Le problème de l'unité du genre humaine au XVIIe siècle: Contribution à l'histoire de l'idée polygéniste," PhD diss., Université Paris I, 1993, 313: "Ce qui fonde l'unité du genre humain, ce ne sont pas les liens du sang, mais sa vocation universelle au salut, voilà le message de La Peyrère."

104 Giuliano Gliozzi, *Adamo e il Nuovo Mondo: La nascita dell'antropologia come ideología coloniale: dalle genealogie bibliche alle teorie razziali (1500–1700)* (Florence: La nuova Italia editrice, 1977); Richard H. Popkin, "Millenarianism and Nationalism – A Case Study: Isaac La Peyrère," in *Millenarianism and Messianism in Early Modern European Culture,* vol. 4: *Continental Millenarians: Protestants, Catholics, Heretics,* ed. J.C. Laursen and R.H. Popkin (Boston: Kluwer, 2001), 77–84.

105 Fernando Rodríguez Mediano and Carlos Cañete, "When Hell Is Other People: Interiority and Skepticism in António Lopes da Veiga," *Culture & History* 6, no. 2 (2017): e012, http://dx.doi.org/10.3989/chdj.2017.012.

106 Bouwsma, *El otoño del Renacimiento,* 282; Jacques Lafaye, *De la historia bíblica a la historia crítica: El tránsito de la conciencia occidental* (Mexico: Fondo de Cultura Económica, 2013), 358.

107 See Claude Blanckaert, "Contre la méthode: Unité de l'homme et classification dans l'anthropologie des Lumières," *Etudes de lettres* 3–4

(1998): 111–26. One very telling example of the resonance of these ideas during the Enlightenment lies in the closing remarks that Jean-Jacques Rousseau made in his (sort of) reversal of Hobbes's ideas, the *Discours sur l'origine et les fondements de l'inégalité parmi les hommes* (Amsterdam: Marc Michel Rey, 1755): "pourquoi l'homme originel s'évanouissant par degrés, la Société n'offre plus aux yeux du sage qu'un assemblage d'hommes artificiels et de passions factices qui sont l'ouvrage de toutes ces nouvelles rélations, et n'ont aucun vrai fondement dans la Nature" (179).

Contributors

Carlos Cañete is currently a lecturer at the Autonomous University of Madrid (Spain). Previously, he was a researcher at the Institute of Mediterranean Languages and Cultures (CSIC, Spain, 2011–18) and has also been a fellow of the Center for Seventeenth- and Eighteenth-Century Studies (UCLA, 2014) and Fulbright Visiting Scholar at Princeton University (2017). He specializes in the history of Spanish Orientalism and Africanism, and the intellectual history of narratives regarding the origins of human populations. He is the author of the forthcoming *A History of the Spanish Africanist Paradigm (15th–20th Centuries)* (Marcial Pons, 2019) and co-author of *The Archaeology of the Jesuit Missions in Ethiopia (1557–1632)* (Brill, 2017).

Barbara Fuchs is a professor of Spanish and English at the University of California, Los Angeles, where she directs the Working Group on the *Comedia* in Translation and Performance and its "Diversifying the Classics" initiative. Recent projects include *The Poetics of Piracy: Emulating Spain in English Literature* (Penn, 2013); *Representing Imperial Rivalry in the Early Modern Mediterranean* (Toronto, 2015), co-edited with Emily Weissbourd; a translation of Lope de Vega's rediscovered *Women and Servants* (Juan de la Cuesta, 2016); *The Golden Age of Spanish Drama,* with Gregary Racz (Norton Critical Editions, 2018); and *90 Monologues from Classical Spanish Theater,* translated and edited with Laura Muñoz and Jennifer Monti (Juan de la Cuesta, 2018). Fuchs is also an editor of the *Norton Anthology of World Literature* (2012, 2018).

Mercedes García-Arenal is a research professor at the Instituto de Lenguas y Culturas del Mediterráneo, CSIC, Madrid. She is currently PI of ERC Synergy Grant 2018 (2019–25): "The European Qur'an: Islamic

Scripture in European Culture and Religion 1150–1850" (ERC-2018-SyG / 810141 – EuQu). Her research focuses on the religious and cultural history of Iberia and the Muslim West, mainly on religious minorities and relations between Christian, Jews, and Muslims: conversion, polemics, messianism, religious dissidence, and dissimulation. She was the PI until 2018 of the ERC Advanced Grant "Conversion, Overlapping Religiosities, Polemics and Interaction: Early Modern Iberia and Beyond" (project CORPI, 323316). The results of the collective efforts of this project are the books edited by her, *After Conversion: Iberia and the Emergence of Modernity* (Brill, 2016); with Stefania Pastore, *Doubt to Unbelief: Forms of Skepticism in the Iberian World* (Legenda, 2019); also with Stefania Pastore, *Visiones imperiales y profecía. Roma, España, Nuevo Mundo* (Abada, 2018); with Giovanna Fiume, *Parole Prigionere. I graffiti delle carceri del Santo Uffizio di Palermo* (Istituto poligrafico europeo, 2018); with Gerard Wiegers, *The Expulsion of the Moriscos from Spain: A Mediterranean Diaspora* (Brill, 2014) and *Polemical Encounters: Jews, Christian and Muslims in Iberia and Beyond* (Pennsylvania State University Press, 2019); and as author with Fernando Rodríguez Mediano, *The Orient in Spain: Converted Muslims, the Forged Lead Books of Granada, and the Rise of Orientalism* (Brill, 2013).

Paul Michael Johnson is an assistant professor of Hispanic studies at DePauw University, where he specializes in early modern Spanish literature, cultural studies, and the history of emotion. Since 2013, he has been a member of the international research group *History and Philosophy of Experience* (FFI2016–78285-R). His first book, forthcoming from University of Toronto Press, is entitled *Affective Geographies: Cervantes, Emotion, and the Literary Mediterranean.* Among other venues, his work has appeared in *Modern Language Notes, eHumanista, Cervantes,* and the *Norton Critical Edition of* Don Quijote. Most recently, he authored the critical introduction to the first modern edition of Luis Vélez de Guevara's *Celos, amor y venganza, o No hay mal que por bien no venga* (Juan de la Cuesta, 2018). He is currently writing a book on the cultural history of shame in early modern Spain.

María Luz López-Terrada is a senior researcher (*investigadora científica*) at INGENIO (CSIC-UPV). She has spent the last thirty years researching and writing about the social history of medicine in Spain. In particular, her research focuses on the history of sanitary assistance and the practice of medicine in the sixteenth and seventeenth centuries, particularly in the sphere of the Spanish monarchy. She has published various scholarly works on the history of hospitals; the control of medical practice, especially in Valencia and including the presence of extra-academic forms of medicine in the sixteenth and seventeenth centuries; and the representation of medicine in literature, particularly Golden Age Spanish theatre. The result of this later project is the edited book *Medical Cultures of the Early Modern Spanish Empire* (Ashgate, 2014). She is currently researching the construction of the identities of women who practised medicine in seventeenth-century Spain, situating these identities within widely held cultural beliefs from the period as well as professional knowledge concerning medicine, health, and illness. The second research focus is the natural history of the same period, especially the introduction of American plants into Europe.

Ruth MacKay has worked as a university lecturer, newspaper editor, writer, translator, and interpreter, having been awarded fellowships from the American Council of Learned Societies, the National Endowment for the Humanities, and the Fulbright Commission, amongst others. She is the author of four books: *The Limits of Royal Authority: Resistance and Obedience in Seventeenth-Century Castile* (Cambridge, 1999); *"Lazy Improvident People": Myth and Reality in the Writing of Spanish History* (Cornell, 2006); *The Baker Who Pretended to Be King of Portugal* (Chicago, 2012); and *Life in a Time of Pestilence: The Great Castilian Plague of 1596–1601* (Cambridge, 2019). She lives in San Francisco.

Javier Patiño Loira is an assistant professor at the University of California, Los Angeles. He earned his PhD from Princeton University in 2016. At present, he is writing a book on the development by seventeenth-century Jesuit scholars, both in Spain and in its overseas territories, of a psychological and aesthetic theory that could account for the pleasure that contemporary audiences took in far-fetched metaphors, paradoxical statements, and smart sayings. Javier has published articles and chapters on early modern book-collecting practices, the reception of Aristotle's *Poetics*, seventeenth-century ideas on royal favoritism or *privanza*, and early modern debates on education, especially in connection with Jesuit theory and practice.

Fernando Rodríguez Mediano is a research scientist (*investigador científico*) at the CSIC (Spanish National Research Council). His areas of expertise are sociology of religious elites in Morocco (fifteenth to seventeenth centuries); Moroccan hagiographical and biographical literature;

relations between Spain and Morocco (sixteenth to seventeenth centuries); Spanish Protectorate over northern Morocco (1912–56); and the origins of Spanish modern Orientalism (seventeenth century). Among his publications are *Familias de Fez (ss. XV–XVII)* (CSIC, 1995); *The Orient in Spain: Converted Muslims, the Forged Lead Books of Granada, and the Rise of Orientalism* (Brill, 2013) with Mercedes García-Arenal; "Justice, amour et crainte dans les recits hagiographiques marocains," *Studia Islamica* 90 (2000), 85–104; "Justice, crime et châtiment au Maroc au XVIe siècle," *Annales: Histoire, Sciences Sociales* (May–June 1996), 611–27; and "Fragmentos de orientalismo español del s. XVII," *Hispania* 66, no. 222 (Jan.–Apr. 2006), 243–76.

A. Katie Stirling-Harris is an associate professor of history at the University of California, Davis. Her current book project examines the case of the stolen bones of St John of Matha as a case study in the development of concepts of proof and evidence in the early modern cult of relics. She is the author of *From Muslim to Christian Granada: Inventing a City's Past in Early Modern Spain* (Johns Hopkins University Press, 2007).

Stefania Tutino is a professor of early modern history at the University of California, Los Angeles. Her research focuses on the intellectual and cultural history of post-Reformation Catholicism, with a special interest in the relationship between conscience and law in Catholic political thought, the historical role played by the Society of Jesus in early modern Europe, the history of Catholic censorship, and the intellectual and cultural implications of Catholic moral theology.

Index

THE UCLA CLARK MEMORIAL LIBRARY SERIES

1. *Wilde Writings: Contextual Conditions*, edited by Joseph Bristow
2. *Enchanted Ground: Reimagining John Dryden*, edited by Jayne Lewis and Maximillian E. Novak
3. *Culture and Authority in the Baroque*, edited by Massimo Ciavolella and Patrick Coleman
4. *Ritual, Routine, and Regime: Repetition in Early Modern British and European Cultures*, edited by Lorna Clymer
5. *Momigliano and Antiquarianism: Foundations of the Modern Cultural Sciences*, edited by Peter N. Miller
6. *Monarchisms in the Age of Enlightenment: Liberty, Patriotism, and the Common Good*, edited by Hans Blom, John Christian Laursen, and Luisa Simonetti
7. *Thinking Impossibilities: The Intellectual Legacy of Amos Funkenstein*, edited by Robert S. Westman and David Biale
8. *Discourses of Tolerance and Intolerance in the European Enlightenment*, edited by Hans Erich Bödeker, Clorinda Donato, and Peter Hanns Reill
9. *The Age of Projects*, edited by Maximillian E. Novak
10. *Acculturation and Its Discontents: The Italian Jewish Experience between Exclusion and Inclusion*, edited by David N. Myers, Massimo Ciavolella, Peter H. Reill, and Geoffrey Symcox
11. *Defoe's Footprints: Essays in Honour of Maximillian E. Novak*, edited by Robert M. Maniquis and Carl Fisher
12. *Women, Religion, and the Atlantic World (1600–1800)*, edited by Daniella Kostroun and Lisa Vollendorf
13. *Braudel Revisited: The Mediterranean World, 1600–1800*, edited by Gabriel Piterberg, Teofilo F. Ruiz, and Geoffrey Symcox
14. *Structures of Feeling in Seventeenth-Century Cultural Expression*, edited by Susan McClary
15. *Godwinian Moments*, edited by Robert M. Maniquis and Victoria Myers
16. *Vital Matters: Eighteenth-Century Views of Conception, Life, and Death*, edited by Helen Deutsch and Mary Terrall
17. *Redrawing the Map of Early Modern English Catholicism*, edited by Lowell Gallagher
18. *Space and Self in Early Modern European Cultures*, edited by David Warren Sabean and Malina Stefanovska
19. *Wilde Discoveries: Traditions, Histories, Archives*, edited by Joseph Bristow

20. *Jesuit Accounts of the Colonial Americas: Intercultural Transfers, Intellectual Disputes, and Textualities,* edited by Marc André Bernier, Clorinda Donato, and Hans-Jürgen Lüsebrink
21. *Skepticism and Political Thought in the Seventeenth and Eighteenth Centuries,* edited by John Christian Laursen and Gianni Paganini
22. *Representing Imperial Rivalry in the Early Modern Mediterranean,* edited by Barbara Fuchs and Emily Weissbourd
23. *Imagining the British Atlantic after the American Revolution,* edited by Michael Meranze and Saree Makdisi
24. *Life Forms in the Thinking of the Long Eighteenth Century,* edited by Keith Michael Baker and Jenna M. Gibbs
25. *Cultures of Communication: Theologies of Media in Early Modern Europe and Beyond,* edited by Helmut Puff, Ulrike Strasser, and Christopher Wild
26. *Curious Encounters: Voyaging, Collecting, and Making Knowledge in the Long Eighteenth Century,* edited by Adriana Craciun and Mary Terrall
27. *Clandestine Philosophy: New Studies on Subversive Manuscripts in Early Modern Europe, 1620–1823,* edited by Gianni Paganini, Margaret C. Jacob, and John Christian Laursen
28. *The Quest for Certainty in Early Modern Europe: From Inquisition to Inquiry, 1550–1700,* edited by Barbara Fuchs and Mercedes García-Arenal